Empirical Approaches to Social Representations

Empirical Approaches to Social Representations

Edited by

Glynis M. Breakwell and David V. Canter

Department of Psychology
University of Surrey, UK

CLARENDON PRESS • OXFORD
1993

Oxford University Press, Walton Street, Oxford OX2 6DP
Oxford   New York   Toronto
Delhi   Bombay   Calcutta   Madras   Karachi
Kuala Lumpur   Singapore   Hong Kong   Tokyo
Nairobi   Dar es Salaam   Cape Town
Melbourne   Auckland   Madrid
and associated companies in
Berlin   Ibadan

Oxford is a trade mark of Oxford University Press

Published in the United States
by Oxford University Press Inc., New York

A catalogue record for this book is available from the British Library

Library of Congress Cataloging in Publication Data
Empirical approaches to social representations/edited by Glynis M.
Breakwell and David V. Canter.
Includes bibliographical references.
1. Social perception.   2. Social psychology   3. Social groups.
I. Breakwell, Glynis M. (Glynis Marie)   II. Canter, David V.
III. Title: Social representations.
HM131.E535   1993   302'.12 − dc20   92-28703
ISBN 0-19-852181-2

Typeset by Colset Pte Ltd, Singapore
Printed in Great Britain by
Bookcraft (Bath) Ltd
Midsomer Norton, Avon

Acknowledgement

The authors would like to thank the Economic and Social Research Council for supporting the original workshop.

Contents

Part II

Contributors

Michael Billig
Department of Social Sciences, Loughborough University of Technology, Loughborough, Leicestershire LE11 3TU, UK.

Linda Blud
Senior Psychologist, Home Office Prison Department, London, UK.

Glynis M. Breakwell
Department of Psychology, University of Surrey, Guildford, Surrey GU2 5XH, UK.

David V. Canter
Department of Psychology, University of Surrey, Guildford, Surrey GU2 5XH, UK.

Willem Doise
Faculté de Psychologie, Université II, Rue General Dufour 24, CH-1211-Genève 4, Switzerland.

Gerard Duveen
Department of Education, University of Cambridge, 17 Trumpington Street, Cambridge CB2 1QA, UK.

Nicholas Emler
Department of Psychology, University of Dundee, Dundee DD1 4HN, UK.

Rob Farr
Department of Social Psychology, The London School of Economics and Political Science, Houghton Street, London WC2A 2AE, UK.

Christopher R. Fife-Schaw
Department of Psychology, University of Surrey, Guildford, Surrey GU2 5XH, UK.

David Good
Department of Social and Political Sciences, University of Cambridge, Free School Lane, Cambridge CB2 3RQ, UK.

Sean Hammond
Department of Psychology, University of Surrey, Guildford, Surrey GU2 5XH, UK.

Barbara Lloyd
University of Sussex, Psychology Arts, Falmer, Brighton, BN1 9QN, UK.

Andy McKinlay
Department of Mathematics and Computing, University of Dundee, Dundee, DDI 4HN, UK.

Lucia Mannetti
Dipartimento di Psicologia dei Processi di Sviluppo e Socializzazione, Università di Roma — La Sapienza, Via degli Apuli 10, 1-00185 Roma, Italy.

Circe Monteiro
Mestrado em Desenvolvimento Urbano, Universidade Federal de Pernambuco, Recife-Pernambuco, Brazil.

Jocelyne Ohana
Laboratoire de Psychologie Sociale, Ecole des Hautes Etudes en Sciences Sociales, 105 Blvd. Raspail, 75006 Paris, France.

Jonathan Potter
Department of Social Sciences, Loughborough University of Technology, Loughborough, Leicestershire LE11 3TU, UK.

S. Caroline Purkhardt
Department of Psychology, University of Surrey, Guildford, Surrey GU2 5XH, UK.

Janet E. Stockdale
Department of Psychology, The London School of Economics and Political Science, Houghton Street, London WC2A 2AE, UK.

Giancarlo Tanucci
Dipartimento di Psicologia dei Processi di Sviluppo e Socializzazione, Università di Roma — La Sapienza, Via degli Apuli 10, 1-00185 Roma, Italy.

David Uzzell
Department of Psychology, University of Surrey, Guildford, Surrey GU2 5XH, UK.

Margaret Wetherell
Faculty of Social Sciences, The Open University, Walton Hall, Milton Keynes MK7 6AA, UK.

Bruna Zani
Università degli Studi di Bologna, Dipartimento di Scienze dell'Educazione, Via Zamboni 34, 40126 Bologna, Italy.

Aspects of methodology and their implications for the study of social representations

Glynis M. Breakwell and David V. Canter

The range of empirical approaches in social representation research

This book focuses upon the methods by which social representations can be studied. It has been often argued that specifying the methods appropriate for the examination of social representations is difficult because there are complexities and ambiguities in their theoretical formulation. By exploring how a number of researchers from very different perspectives have examined social representations, greater conceptual clarity and consensus does begin to emerge. This book, therefore, deliberately sets out to define and elaborate upon the nature of social representations by close examination of the methods used for studying them.

However, by focusing upon research methods, another conceptual ambiguity emerges which is apparent in all discussions of social science research. This centres on the meaning of the term 'methods'. Different meanings are assigned to the notion of research methods and each of them carries quite distinct implications for the conduct of research and the exploration of social representations. Even more importantly, each aspect of research method also carries, usually implicitly, assumptions about the nature of the topic being studied – a theme to which we will return in more detail in the final chapter. The first meaning of 'method' concerns the process of data collection. At one level this involves the strategy or design of the study. At another level, it involves the tactics used to elicit data.

Perhaps the most critical distinction within the realm of research strategy is that between experimental and non-experimental designs. In experimental studies there is the fundamental assumption that a temporally linear process of causes and effects can be identified. The change or variation in treatment introduced by the experimenter, or selected in quasi-experimental or field studies, is thought to be a distinct causal agent whose effects can be isolated to some reasonable degree. No such assumption is inevitable in non-experimental studies. Researchers engaged in non-experimental designs may have the objective of uncovering a system of interrelated causes and effects that do not allow any linear sequence of influences to be identified. In understanding this dimension on which design types can be ranged, it is best to think in terms of control. Experimental designs offer the researcher the prospect of control and manipulation of the occurrence of the targeted phenomena. Quasi-experimental designs offer some control through the selection of time, place, and sample. Non-experimental designs offer no control other than that derived from choosing the sample and the type of data to be collected.

Research design needs to be distinguished from the techniques by which the data are collected, such as questionnaires, open interviews, card sorts, and so on. These may be fruitfully thought of as the tactics of research in distinction to the strategies. Here the major distinction is between tactics that depend upon the production of data specifically for the research, as when people have to fill in questionnaires or draw maps, and those tactics that work with material that has been generated independently of the research process, such as content analysis of newspaper reports or children's play.

Theoretically, the distinction between naturally-occurring and elicited data is that the former are assumed to have a role in the world of daily actions when they are explored within material existing outside the research context, while specially-elicited material may be seen as revealing phenomena that are available only, if at all, in a very complex way in daily life. The need for specially-elicited forms of data comes about when it is seen that more simplified measures of the issues being examined are needed, in order to test theories, than would be generally available. The researcher structures the elicited data in order to address the theory directly in a way that will rarely occur naturally. It would, however, be an error to assume that naturally-occurring data remain particularly free of influence from the researcher's design preoccupation; such data are shaped, or even distorted, by the very processes of selection and recording.

Strategies and tactics interact to generate a complex array of empirical approaches to social representations. Inevitably experimental procedures, because of the manipulations involved, are more likely to use elicited material than are non-experimental studies, but there is no simple relationship between choices of research strategies and tactics. Moreover, the research possibilities are expanded much further by other equally important aspects of the meaning of research methodology.

The next aspect of research method that needs to be considered is the source of the data that is being used. What people say or write, the tasks they perform, and the records or traces they leave are all different sources of data which may be explored in a structured or open-ended way, using a variety of different data-collection instruments. A questionnaire as a tactic for research may centre on what a person does or thinks, just as behaviour as a data source may be studied using open-ended video recording or on-the-spot assignment to categories.

Psychologically, though, there are profound differences between two broad classes of data sources; those that are derived from what people say and those that emerge from what people do. In studies of behaviour, the person can be regarded as an object whose understanding of their own situation may or may not be considered. Once speech is involved, cognitive processing has to be taken into account and the meaning of the utterance to the person speaking is paramount. It is therefore not surprising that studies of social representations are almost entirely concerned with material that has its roots in the written and spoken word.

As with strategies and tactics, there is no simple relationship between the source of data and the mode of data collection. In the study of social representations a very rich mixture has been used. Similarly there is no simple relationship between strategy, tactic, source of data, and the final aspect of research method, the form of data analysis. Experimental designs will tend to use classical inferential statistics but, as a number of chapters in this book show, advanced statistical analysis procedures no longer make that essential. Similarly, open-ended verbal material collected in a non-experimental research design which in the past might have been subjected to elementary descriptive analysis may now be squeezed by various analytic frameworks to reveal its innermost depths. In general, the study of social representations, like many areas of behavioural and social science, has been overtaken by the gentle but powerful revolution in the use of multivariate statistics made possible by near-universal access to vast computing power.

Yet the complexity of multivariate analysis, which features in many chapters of the present volume, should not hide the substantive change in psychological theory-building that the use of these procedures implies. Rather than seeing the social and psychological processes under examination as made up of a few variables which can be measured by unidimensional instruments and which have their effect in simple and direct ways, the use of multivariate statistics takes as its starting-point the assumption that important psychological processes will be revealed only through the interplay of many variables in a reasonably complex system.

The many methods used to study social representations actually indicate something of the stand that the researchers themselves are taking on the nature of social representations and the processes inherent in those representations. The great variety and mixture of strategies, tactics, sources of data, and modes of analysis serves to demonstrate that social representations are treated as rich and complex phenomena. The way they are conceptualized covers a large proportion of the spectrum of conceptualizations open to researchers.

In contrast to the view that social representations are essentially part of an anthropological perspective not open to the precise analysis of experimental studies, it is interesting to recognize that seminal social representation research was conducted within the experimental tradition (Codol 1974, 1984; Abric 1982, 1984; Abric and Kahan 1972). In such work, artificial and controlled environments have been created to allow researchers to manipulate both the cues eliciting a representation and the form in which the representation can be expressed. Subsequently, the research has used quasi-experimental designs taking advantage of naturally-occurring situations which were likely to initiate change in the form or content of a representation (Di Giacomo 1980; Galli and Nigro 1987; Mahjoub *et al.* 1989; Sotirakopoulou 1991).

The studies of the underlying causal mechanisms within social representations have nonetheless been fewer than those studies that seek to explore an existing system of relationships that are present in a natural context. The majority of studies have relied upon non-experimental designs where the researcher systematically samples existing representations (Hewstone 1986; De Rosa 1987; Milgram 1984; Pailhous 1984; Chombart de Lauwe 1984).

The type of research design used has not overly constrained the form of data collection employed. Researchers have been eclectic when assaying representations: experimentalists have used observation and interviews, ethnographers have used questionnaires. However, as already noted, in keeping with the central role of meaning and signification in the theory of social representations, it is not surprising to find that the majority of studies have used procedures that involve direct interactions with respondents, requiring them to reveal something of their cognitive and emotional processes, through interviews, questionnaires, and the elicitation of drawings. Other studies have worked with naturally-occurring accounts by collating textual or media productions.

Interviews with individuals (Herzlich 1973; Campbell 1984; Jodelet 1984; Emler and Dickinson 1985; Emler *et al.* 1987; Molinari and Emiliani 1990) or with a group (Emiliani *et al.* 1981; Campbell and Muncer 1987; Zani 1987) have been used most often. The nature of the interview format has differed widely from the intensive unstructured approach to the extensive totally-structured type. Free-association techniques have been used to great effect (Verges 1987) within interviews; so have tasks involving matching and estimation of similarities (Semin and Chassein 1985; Stockdale *et al.* 1989). As a method of data elicitation, interviewing has been accompanied by both qualitative and quantitative methods of data analysis. In recognition of the inherently complex nature of social representations, multivariate analyses have often been used to explore the structure of the social representations revealed in an interview.

Questionnaires have been used within the social representational framework to explore a variety of targets. These range from the concept of intelligence (Mugny and Carugati 1989; Carugati 1990) to AIDS (Echebarria and

Paez 1989) and from behaviour in experimental games (Abric and Kahan 1972) to patterns of causal attribution (Augustinos 1990). It is rare, however, for questionnaires, whether unstructured or highly structured, to be used in a study as the sole means of accessing a social representation. Usually they are accompanied by observation, interviews, or other means of self-expression. Questionnaires tend to generate data that can be subjected to quantitative analyses but open-ended questions have often been included and have resulted in qualitative descriptive analyses.

In recognition of the place in the general theory of the significance of social representations for day-to-day social processes, it is as expected that many studies have taken naturally-occurring communications as central. Observation, sometimes participant and often non-interactive, has therefore been frequently used to monitor social representations. It is a particularly appropriate method, since it can be used to lay bare the patterns of communication which are hypothesized to be central to the development of a social representation. It can also expose social practices in which social representations are embedded (Jodelet 1991). It has been found to have a particularly valuable place in the battery of methods open to those who study the representations held by children (Lloyd and Smith 1985; Lloyd 1987; Lloyd *et al.* 1988; Lloyd and Duveen 1990; Corsaro 1990). Observation has sometimes been tied to sophisticated forms of content analysis reliant upon real-time video or audio recording. More often, observation has been followed by partial recording, dependent upon the memory of the observer and selective reporting of significant events or themes.

Observation is sometimes used to overcome the limitations imposed by dependency upon verbal or literary reports of social representations; drawings are used to the same end. Drawings were first used to access representations of particular places (Milgram 1984; Pailhous 1984) but have subsequently been used to tap representations of targets which are less spatially defined, such as mental illness (De Rosa 1987) and radioactivity (Galli and Nigro 1987). Content analysis of drawings — examining for communalities of components or structure — is rarely tied to a subsequent statistical analysis.

Secondary sources, including film, TV and radio, publications, and archival material, have been used extensively to examine the structure and longevity of social representations. For instance, Chombart de Lauwe (1984) explored changes in the representation of childhood by analysing children's literature, films, and advertisements. Kruse *et al.* (1988) investigated social representations of gender roles by textual analysis of magazines. McGurk (1991) chose to treat fairy tales as a source of information about the social representations of economics which are presented to children. This approach to data collection focuses upon representations as cultural products reified in social artefacts. Statistical treatment of the findings from content analyses is usual, but mostly descriptive rather than analytical.

Even this cursory review of the empirical approaches used to study social representations illustrates that virtually every method known to social science has been used at some point. There has been no restriction on the empirical imagination imposed either explicity or implicitly by the research community. This serves to demonstrate that the theory is not restrictive in the form or structure that social representations are assumed to take. A variety of models of the nature of representations is feasible within the broad framework sketched by Moscovici and his associates.

Moscovici has encouraged methodological eclecticism. His own work ranges from laboratory experimentation to textual analysis. However, the absence of any methodological orthodoxy which can be followed has caused considerable confusion and some conflict. Acolytes of one methodological approach have castigated and scorned disciplines of another. The prime accusation is that any method of data collection or analysis other than one's own cannot really capture the essence of a social representation. Since Moscovici has been determined not to tie the social representation concept to any narrow operational definition, these accusations are difficult to refute but they are also impossible to substantiate. The problems lie in achieving agreement that the method used has actually accessed and recorded accurately and completely the target social representation. No ultimate arbiter of methodological taste or probity is available. There are no clear criteria which, once satisfied, ensure that the social representation has been catalogued. This has left researchers feeling continually at risk of rebuttal.

One of the aims of this book is to show that a number of different empirical approaches to the study of social representations are viable and can be complementary. Indeed, some of the finest research in this area has relied upon a multi-method approach (Jodelet 1991). There is therefore an attempt here to shift the focus of the methodological debate. The main question should not be which method to use but how to integrate findings drawn from different methods. When methods reveal somewhat different elements of a social representation, there are very real problems facing the researcher who tries to incorporate them into a single picture. The epistemological status of information gathered by each method may differ. Where methods generate contradictory images of the representation, there is the question of how to prioritize disparate information. There are no agreed procedures for integrating data derived from different approaches, but the issues which must be considered are addressed throughout the book.

In determining the viability of a method, it is important to bear in mind the particular theory it examines and the precise reason for its use. A method must be evaluated in terms of its capacity to achieve specified objectives within a particular scientific epistemology.

In the main, researchers studying social representations have sought to describe the content and structure of specific representations as naturally-occurring aspects of social systems. The methods chosen have been designed to satisfy that end. The operation of the systemic processes which the theory suggests underlie social representation (such as anchoring or objectification at the individual level, or propaganda at the level of the social system) has rarely been the specific object of study. Sometimes their operation is inferred, but mainly it is simply asserted.

Methods designed to explore these natural phenomena have to be capable of monitoring change in a representation over time. This means that research design should give more emphasis to longitudinal or cross-sectional time-sampling approaches than to the niceties of experimental rigour. Treating process as the object of study affects research design perhaps more than choice of method of data collection or analysis.

The structure of this book

There are two parts to this book. Part I includes chapters that discuss what theoretical issues should be researched within the social representations model. The chapters in this part examine how theory and methods relate. In Chapter 1, Farr emphasizes that social representations theory is in the tradition of grand theory in the social sciences and, as such, does not need to delineate methods which are appropriate to it. In Chapter 2, Billig examines the importance of rhetorical features in social representations and focuses specifically upon the operation of anchoring and objectification suggesting that these need to be explored empirically. Billig's arguments suggest that whatever methods are used to study social representations, they should not obscure the individual variations in levels of acceptance of the collective view.

In Chapter 3 Emler and Ohana, in arguing that individuals do not construct knowledge independently of their social context, suggest that methods which sample only individual understanding are pointless. They argue that developmental differences in representations can be explained by reference to comparisons across different social communities. In Chapter 4, Duveen and Lloyd illustrate the usefulness of ethnography as a method in exploring representations of gender. Uzzell and Blud, in Chapter 5, consider the available methodologies for examining representations of the past. Using analyses of museum displays, they show both how the display reveals representations and how it is assimilated by visitors into their own pre-existing representations. Chapter 6, by McKinlay, Potter, and Wetherell, suggests that discourse should be the focus for efforts in understanding representational processes.

Part I includes three other chapters. Chapters 7 and 8, by Doise and by Good respectively, are commentaries invited by the editors on chapters in the book. Doise takes this opportunity to emphasize that often, only parts of the grand theory of social representations are considered. He asks that we also consider Moscovici's arguments concerning the metasystem of inter-group relations which structure the form and delivery of social represen-tations. Good in turn suggests that the role of individual differences in the production and acceptance of social representations should be examined. In Chapter 9, Breakwell examines the methodological implications for any research which takes seriously both Doise's request that the metasystem is analysed and Good's argument that the individual's use of a representation should be a significant concern.

Part II of the book focuses upon methods of data analysis as they relate to substantive theoretical issues. In doing so, attention is drawn to the differ-ent forms of theoretical structure that are assumed by differing multivariate statistical analyses. Although the basic matrix algebra is similar for most forms of multidimensional analysis, the algorithms used to reduce the com-plexity of the data and to reveal the underlying structure of social representa-tions assume very different types of social phenomena.

For example, Hammond in Chapter 10, using correspondence analysis, and Purkhardt and Stockdale in Chapter 13, using more generic multidimen-sional scaling analyses, suppose that social representations vary along ortho-gonal dimensions. A number of statistically-independent axes are identified by their analyses on which the characteristics of any social representa-tion may lie. Here the characteristics are independent but the representa-tions themselves have no distinct boundaries being derived from continuous dimensions.

In contrast, Fife-Schaw in Chapter 12, using cluster analysis, argues that representations can be best modelled by algorithms that determine distinct statistical boundaries between one entity and another. So, although the dimensional analyses can be mathematically translated into cluster inter-pretations, for instance by assigning cut-off values to weightings on dimen-sions, the two approaches actually posit quite different structures for the phenomena under investigation; this has implications for the development of theory, especially for any model of change in representations. A clustering framework would suggest that changes would be discrete, or step-wise, whereas a dimensional model would predict smoother, more continuous changes.

The facet approach used by Canter and Monteiro in Chapter 11 sits between the dimensional and clustering frameworks. It presents a number of aspects of representations that are essentially categorical and shows how they can combine in use to generate continuous, overlapping variations in the social representations held by different groups sharing a common culture. The rather unusual form of analysis they use, partial order scalogram anal-ysis, while having a number of distinct qualities, is none the less a member of the family of multidimensional scaling techniques used in all the chapters in this section. In Chapter 14, Mannetti and Tanucci explore further the applications of these techniques, and in Chapter 15 Zani examines them in relation to other multivariate approaches.

The predominance of multidimensional scaling approaches over classical factor analysis in this domain is worthy of note. Three different forces seem to be at work in producing what amounts to a general consensus about the relevance of this form of statistics, although a lively debate is developing on the strengths and weaknesses of each particular approach. The first is the agreement that the raw material available for the study of social representations does not lend itself to sophisticated measurement — it is at best weakly ordered data, and more typically qualitative. Statistical procedures that respect the level of measurement of the data are preferred. The second influence is probably more profound. This is the acceptance that social representations can be accurately described as they occur naturally only if the statistical techniques used do not force the data to fit some strong mathematical model. The third influence follows from the first two. It is the desire to see representations for what they are. Analysis procedures that generate graphical and multidimensional output have the immediacy of visual illustration, which can be very useful in understanding a representation.

It follows that research using multivariate statistics has had to grapple more overtly with the key question of under what circumstances and with which statistical procedures are social representations most validly described. Thus the most methodologically complex studies may be seen to connect most closely with the theoretical questions at the heart of the study of social representations. The final chapter discusses the way in which the various methods used in the book have helped to clarify and develop our understanding of the nature of social representations and of the appropriate ways in which they may be studied empirically.

References

Abric, J.C. (1982). Cognitive processes underlying co-operation: the theory of social representations. In *Co-operation and helping behaviour*, (ed. V.J. Derlega and J. Crzelak). Academic Press, London.

Abric, J.C. (1984). A theoretical and experimental approach to the study of social representations in a situation of interaction. In *Social representations*, (ed. R.M. Farr and S. Moscovici), pp. 169–83. Cambridge University Press, Cambridge.

Abric, J.C. and Kahan, J.P. (1972). The effects of representations and behaviour in experimental games. *European Journal of Social Psychology*, **2 (2)**, 129–44.

Augustinos, M. (1990). The mediating role of representations on causal attributions in the social world. *Social Behaviour*, **5**, 49–62.

Campbell, A. (1984). Girls' talk: the social representation of aggression by female gang members. *Criminal Justice and Behaviour*, **11 (2)**, 139–56.

Campbell, A. and Muncer, S. (1987). Models of anger and aggression in the social talk of men and women. *Journal for the Theory of Social Behaviour*, **17 (4)**, 489–511.

Carugati, F. (1990). Everyday ideas, theoretical models and social representations. In *Everyday understanding: social and scientific explanations*, (ed. G.R. Semin and R.J. Gergen). Sage, London.

Chombart de Lauwe, M.-J. (1984). Changes in the representation of the child in the course of social transmission. In *Social representations* (ed. R.M. Farr and S. Moscovici), pp. 185–209. Cambridge University Press, Cambridge.

Codol, J.P. (1974). On the system of representations in a group situation. *European Journal of Social Psychology*, **4 (3)**, 343–65.

Codol, J.P. (1984). On the system of social representations in an artificial social situation. In *Social representations*, (ed. R.M. Farr and S. Moscovici), pp. 239–53. Cambridge University Press, Cambridge.

Corsaro, W.A. (1990). The underlife of the nursery school: young children's social representations of adult rules. In *Social representations and the development of knowledge*, (eds. G. Duveen and B. Lloyd), pp. 11–26. Cambridge University Press, Cambridge.

De Rosa, A.S. (1987). The social representations of mental illness in children and adults. In *Current issues in European social psychology* Volume 2, (ed. W. Doise and S. Moscovici), pp. 47–138. Cambridge University Press, Cambridge.

Di Giacomo, J.P. (1980). Intergroup alliances and rejections within a protest movement (Analysis of the social representations). *European Journal of Social Psychology*, **10**, 329–44.

Echebarria, A. and Paez, D. (1989). Social representations and memory: The case of AIDS. *European Journal of Social Psychology*, **19**, 543–51.

Emiliani, F., Zani, B., and Carugati, F. (1981). From interaction strategies to social representation of adults in a day nursery. In *Communication in development*, (ed. W.P. Robinson), pp. 89–107. Academic Press, London.

Emler, N. and Dickinson, J. (1985). Children's representations of economic inequalities: the effects of social class. *British Journal of Developmental Psychology*, **3**, 191–8.

Emler, N., Ohana, J., and Moscovici, S. (1987). Children's beliefs about institutional roles: a cross-national study of representations of the teacher's role. *British Journal of Educational Psychology*, **57**, 26–37.

Galli, I. and Nigro, G. (1987). The social representation of radioactivity among Italian children. *Social Science Information*, **26 (3)**, 535–49.

Herzlich, C. (1973). *Health and illness: a social psychological analysis*. Academic Press, London.

Hewstone, M. (1986). *Understanding attitudes to the European community: a social-psychological study in four member states*. Cambridge University Press, Cambridge.

Jodelet, D. (1984). The representation of the body and its transformations. In *Social Representations*, (ed. R.M. Farr and S. Moscovici), pp. 211–38. Cambridge University Press, Cambridge.

Jodelet, D. (1991). *Madness and social representations*. Harvester Wheatsheaf, Sussex.

Kruse, L., Weimer, E., and Wagner, F. (1988). What men and women are said to be: social representations and language. *Journal of Language and Psychology*, **7**, 243–62.

Lloyd, B. (1987) Social representations of gender. In *Making sense: the child's construction of the world*, (ed. J. Bruner and H. Haste), pp. 147-62. Methuen, London.

Lloyd, B. and Duveen, G. (1990). A semiotic analysis of the development of social representations of gender. In *Social representations and the development of knowledge*, (ed. G. Duveen and B. Lloyd), pp. 27-46. Cambridge University Press, Cambridge.

Lloyd, B. and Smith, C. (1985). The social representation of gender and young children's play. *British Journal of Developmental Psychology*, **3**, 65-73.

Lloyd, B., Duveen, G., and Smith, C. (1987). Social representations of gender and young children's play: a replication. *British Journal of Developmental Psychology*, **6**, 83-8.

Mahjoub, A., Leyens, J.P., Yzerbut, V., and Di Giacomo, J.P. (1989). War stress and coping models: representations of self-identity and time perspective among Palestinian children. *International Journal of Mental Health*, **18** (2), 44-62.

McGurk, H. (1991). The development of economic understanding: fairy tales and other literature as instruments in young children's economic socialisation. In *Social psychology of political and economic cognition*, (ed. G.M. Breakwell), pp. 143-59. Academic Press/Surrey University Press, London.

Milgram, S. (1984). Cities as social representations. In *Social representations*, (ed. R.M. Farr and S. Moscovici), pp. 289-309. Cambridge University Press, Cambridge.

Molinari, L. and Emiliani, F. (1990). What is an image? The structure of mothers' images of the child and their influence on conversational styles. In *Social representations and the development of knowledge*, (ed. G. Duveen and B. Lloyd), pp. 91-106. Cambridge University Press, Cambridge.

Mugny, G. and Carugati, F. (1989). *Social representations of intelligence*. Cambridge University Press, Cambridge.

Pailhous, J. (1984). The represention of urban space: its development and its role in the organisation of journeys. In *Social representations*, (ed. R.M. Farr and S. Moscovici), pp. 311-27. Cambridge University Press, Cambridge.

Semin, G. R. and Chassein, J. (1985). The relationship between higher order models and everyday conceptions of personality. *European Journal of Social Psychology*, **15**, 1-15.

Sotirakopoulou, P. K. (1991). Processes of social representation: a multi-methodological and longitudinal approach. Unpublished PhD thesis. Department of Psychology, University of Surrey.

Stockdale, J., Dockrell, J.E., and Wells, A. J. (1989). The self in relation to mass media representations of HIV and AIDS — match or mismatch? *Health Education Journal*, **48** (3), 121-30.

Verges, P. (1987). A social cognitive approach to economic representations. In *Current issues in European social psychology*, Vol. 2, (ed. W. Doise and S. Moscovici), pp. 271-305. Cambridge University Press, Cambridge.

Zani, B. (1987). The psychiatric nurse: a social psychological study of a profession facing institutional changes. *Social Behaviour*, **2**, 87-98.

Part I

1 Theory and method in the study of social representations

Rob Farr

Science as culture and the culture of science

It would be truly surprising, especially to a community of social scientists, if culture were not to emerge as an important variable in scientific research. There are many important components of culture, of which science is only one. I believe it is a singular achievement, on the part of Moscovici, that he has identified 'science' as a worthy object of research in social psychology (Moscovici 1987). The sciences that he has studied, to date, include psychoanalysis (Moscovici 1961, 1976), mass psychology (Moscovici 1985) and sociology (Moscovici 1988). Not only has Moscovici placed culture (including science) back on the agenda of social psychology, but his theory of social representations enables us to see the culture of science in a new light. The techniques of research that have been devised by the practitioners of any particular science constitute important elements within the culture of that science. I shall focus on this aspect of the theory in the present chapter.

Wundt, earlier, had identified language, religion, customs, myth, magic, and related phenomena as the objects of study in his *Völkerpsychologie* (1900–20). This was still a viable framework for social psychology when Murchison published, in 1935, his two volume *Handbook of social psychology* (Murchison 1935). This can be established, quite readily, by a quick scanning of its table of contents. Moscovici has modernized this particular conception of social psychology, and significantly enlarged its scope, by his inclusion of science. His theory of social representations takes us back to this earlier epoch in the evolution of social psychology in America. In some respects it is a 'retro-revolution' (Moscovici 1981). Unfortunately the current 'establishment' in social psychology in America measure the progress of their science in terms of how many light years away it is, now, from the conception of social psychology enshrined in the Murchison *Handbook*. This is one of the reasons why it is difficult for mainstream social psychologists, in America, to accept the theory of social representations. Elsewhere (Farr 1991*b*), I have established that the view of the establishment on the progress of social psychology is a *direct* consequence of their subscribing to a positivist philosophy of science when they write history. It is naive to assume that positivism is dead: it lingers on in the histories of the discipline that are now being written and in handbooks of research methods. It is its survival in the latter context that is germane to the theme of this chapter.

When the means to the achievement of some end becomes an end in itself we have an instance of what Merton called ritualism. It is a process that is ubiquitous in the evolution of organizations. Whilst Merton was writing about the sociology of organizations, the processes he describes apply equally to the conduct of research. Researchers are at least as meticulous as priests when it comes to the celebration of ritual. The research orthodoxies of today often enshrine the obsolete theories of yesteryear. While behaviourism is no longer the dominant paradigm it once was in the history of psychology, it is by no means dead today and lives on in research practice. I hope to show that an incompatibility between two theories (behaviourism and social representations) appears, today, in the highly disguised form of a methodological critique of the notion of social representations. It has to appear in this form because behaviourism is no longer a salient force in modern psychology. It is not a theory that, today, is taken seriously.

Not only is science part of culture, as Moscovici has demonstrated, but also culture is part of science. The most obvious cultural components of scientific research are its methodologies, its laboratories, and its research journals. Ritualism occurs because methodology easily becomes methodolatry. Wundt, Durkheim, and Freud all wrote about the nature of ritualism. They were concerned, however, with culture in the widest sense of the term — equivalent, in the social sciences, to the principle of inertia in the natural sciences. Culture, in the much narrower sense of the culture *of* science, is also an inertial force in the evolution of all sciences, including the natural sciences. This helps to explain the perpetuation, in research practice, of obsolete theories.

Whilst Moscovici in developing the theory chose Durkheim as a suitable ancestor he never accepted as appropriate to the study of modern societies, the purely static nature of Durkheim's collective representations. Hence, Moscovici expresses a preference for the study of social representations over the study of collective representations. Modern societies are much more dynamic and fluid than were the societies that Durkheim had studied. In developing what he terms an anthropology of the modern world, Moscovici (1981) could scarcely ignore science as an important element in the culture of most modern societies. He contrasts science with common sense and notes changes, over time, in the relationship between the two (Moscovici 1984). In Durkheim's day, science was often a consequence of the progressive refinement of common sense. Knowledge, in the process of becoming refined, becomes, of course, less and less common and, hence, more and more esoteric. In the modern world, Moscovici believes the direction of causality is often reversed, i.e. science is, quite commonly, the basis, rather than the outcome, of common sense.

In his initial investigation, Moscovici had studied the social representations of psychoanalysis and not the theory itself (Moscovici 1961, 1976). He is more interested in what is happening in society than in what is happening within a particular clinic or research laboratory. Social representations flourish wherever and whenever common sense prevails. Moscovici contrasts the consensual universe of the discourse of common sense with the reified universe of the discourse of the research scientist. It is the latter, rather than the former, universe of discourse that constitutes the focus of my attention in the present chapter. Whilst Moscovici believes that social representations are intimately related to a common sense understanding of events, I believe that they also play an important role in scientific research.

An important test of any new theory is whether it enlarges or restricts the scope of a discipline. In regard to psychology, Marie Jahoda (1972) thought that, on this criterion alone, behaviourism compared unfavourably with psychoanalysis. I concur with her judgement in regard to these two rival theories (Farr 1981): behaviourism has impoverished, rather than enriched, the discipline of psychology. I would prefer to compare behaviourism with social representations than with psychoanalysis. I believe that the theory of social representations is more likely to enlarge than to impoverish the scope of social psychology. One respect in which it does this is by reinstating the notion of culture, as I have outlined in the previous paragraphs.

In an article in the companion volume to this one I have described collective representations as widespread beliefs (Farr 1990). There, I was concerned with culture in the broad sense of the term. Here I am concerned, more narrowly, with the culture of science and, yet more narrowly still, with the culture of one particular science. The theory of social representations, as this is developed by Moscovici, confers significance on the information that circulates in society concerning the object of study. This refers to culture in general — whether the culture of the masses or the more restricted culture of such elite groups as research scientists. The implications of this new theory for methods of research in social psychology are discussed, more fully, at a later point in the present chapter, such as the importance of including, in each study of a social representation, an analysis of the contents of the mass media of communication that relate to the object of study.

A theory often enables us to see familiar phenomena in a new light. As Moscovici once observed, there were trees before there were ecologists. Ecology, however, enables us to view trees differently to how we normally see them. In the same way, the theory of social representations confers a new significance on many old methods of research. It is the theory that is new, not the methods of research. One cannot, of course, consider methods of research in isolation from theory. I have just argued above, for example, that certain methods of research might serve, merely, to perpetuate obsolete theories. It is a myth of positivism, as a philosophy of science, that methods of research are neutral with respect to theory; it is crucial that there should be a suitable match between theory and method. Theory is also important in helping one to locate phenomena that, otherwise, would be extremely difficult to pin down. Right from the outset I was convinced that, in the French corpus of research on social representations, an error of translation had occurred when the theory was transposed from the field to the laboratory (Farr 1984*a*). I felt it was wrong to be looking for social representations *in* the minds of individual subjects participating in experiments. The theory, however, led me to locate the social representations in the *culture* of the laboratory rather than in the minds of individuals. Without the theory I would not have known where to look for the phenomenon.

Psychology as a human science and the birth of behaviourism

The idea of psychology as a human science, which is strong in France but not in the UK or the USA, is a compound of two separate representations — that of the human species and that of science. Two very different forms of psychological science emerge depending upon whether one privileges either the representation of man or the representation of science. Psychoanalysis is a particularly fine example of the former type of science and behaviourism of the latter. Even within forms of behaviourism there is a dramatic difference (see Farr 1980*a*,*b*, 1987*a*) between the social behaviourism of G. H. Mead, in which the uniqueness of the human species is the predominant representation, and Watsonian behaviourism, in which the predominant representation is that of psychology as a branch of natural science. If psychoanalysis and behaviourism (of either the Watsonian or Skinnerian varieties) were accepted as prototypical forms of psychological science, then the study of social representations is much closer to the former, than to the latter, type of science.

Elsewhere (Farr 1981) I have noted how behaviourism is, itself, a particularly fine example of what Moscovici means by a social representation. It was born when Watson applied a *particular* representation of science to the subject matter of psychology. He made psychology a branch of natural science by declaring it to be the science of behaviour. His particular representation of science was an out-of-date version of physics. We are still living with the consequences of this particular representation of psychological science. It directly affects the layout of psychological laboratories and the sequence of events that occurs within their walls (Farr 1984*a*). The layout of a laboratory certainly reflects one's representation of the sort of science that one is practising. Too often, on the basis of a false analogy with the natural sciences, the laboratory has been thought, by those who work within it, to exist in a void that is both timeless and devoid of culture (Tajfel 1972). The walls of Freud's consulting room were much more permeable to the surrounding culture than are the walls of the typical psychological laboratory. In the heyday of behaviourism there was a marked discontinuity between the culture *of* the psychological laboratory and the culture *within* which it was located. In modern cognitive science there is no longer a discontinuity between the culture of the laboratory and the culture within which the laboratory is located, because we no longer have a behavioural conception of what a laboratory is.

Marie Jahoda (1977) portrays psychoanalytic theory as a psychological representation of the human body. She sees Freud's major achievement to have been the development of a psychological language for talking about the human body. If we now add to Jahoda's characterisations of psychoanalysis Moscovici's classic study of its diffusion within French culture, we come full circle (Farr 1981, p. 310):

Not only does a person's representations of his own body influence his clinical symptoms, but the science which is then fashioned to 'interpret' these symptoms itself constitutes a psychological representation of the human body which, once it is published, diffuses within a culture and becomes the basis of still further changes in the social representations of the human body.

Behaviourism, as a social representation, has not diffused widely into popular culture to anything like the same extent as psychoanalysis. Moscovici was able to pick up the reverberations of psychoanalysis as a social representation within various strata of French society in the late 1950s. Behaviourism is not as rich, in its pattern of diffusion, as psychoanalysis. It is strongest *within* the culture of scientific psychology. It is not a significant element within popular culture apart from when it appears in the occasional film such as *Clockwork Orange*. When a person found guilty of a criminal offence is handed over to a psychologist rather than being sent to prison this must engender, in the minds of the public, a certain image of psychology. Even within the profession of psychology itself, purely behavioural methods of treatment are considered to be peculiarly appropriate only for certain categories of subject such as animals, young children, the mentally ill, and those with a mental handicap.

A tale of two cultures

The link between theory and method is an important topic of debate in most scientific circles. The issue, even at the best of times, is a highly complex one. Complications set in, as in the case of research on social representations, when the theory is French and the methods of empirical investigation being proposed are those of American or British positivism. The contrast between rationalists and empiricists is a well-established theme in the history of Western philosophy. There could scarcely be two more contrasting figures, in terms of their respective philosophies of science, than Descartes and Bacon. One important difference concerns the value of theory in relation to research. Descartes valued it highly; Bacon distrusted it. These contrasting attitudes to the value of theory still survive on either side of the English Channel. The French continue to value theory, while British and American social scientists hold *purely* empirical research in high regard. It is part of the ethos of behaviourism that theory is held in such low esteem. It is easy to equate theory with metaphysics and the latter is a pejorative term in the vocabulary of behaviourism.

Misunderstandings arising from the contrast between the richness of theoretical ideas in French social science and the rigours of British experimental psychology are not of purely recent origin. Mary Douglas notes the contrast in her portrayal of the work of Evans-Pritchard for the Fontana Modern Masters series (Douglas 1980, p. 28):[1]

The failure of British psychologists to develop a sociological dimension to their experimental thinking, and the failure of the French to benefit from the British methodological advances, are themselves problems for the sociology of knowledge that are not explained by their not knowing of each other's work. They read, but they misunderstood.

These misunderstandings still persist. The canons of research orthodoxy that prevail in America and Britain are positivist ones, and are part of the legacy of behaviourism. Behaviourism, however, was never the significant cultural force in the development of psychological science in France that it has been in both America and Britain. It *may*, then, be inappropriate to use these criteria in one's critique of the theory of social representations. I shall put it no more strongly than that: I wish, merely, to raise it as a *possibility* that deserves to be considered.

The canons of orthodoxy in research are one source of the emands that Moscovici ought to have defined his terms, operationally, *in advance* of conducting his investigations. Yet one cannot know, in advance, either the form or the content of the social representations that will emerge from one's investigation (Moscovici 1987). Could Herzlich (1973), for example, reasonably have anticipated the key role that the notion of toxicity would play in shaping the social representations of health and illness held by her informants? Or could Jodelet (1991), to choose another example, reasonably have anticipated that she would evoke, in a rural setting in modern France, theories concerning the contagious nature of mental illness that are centuries old?

---

[1] I am grateful to Ms Diana Adlam for drawing my attention to this passage in Mary Douglas's book.

Behaviourism, as a theory, is antithetical to the theory of social representations. The opposition between the two theories appears, now, in the highly disguised form of a methodological critique of the theory of social representations.

The cultural differences to which Mary Douglas alludes in the above quotation are evident, today, in the responses of British and American psychologists to the nature and format of French research on social representations. Most social psychologists, who are trained professionally in the English-speaking world, find the French to be singularly uninformative when it comes to describing, precisely, how they carried out their research. Quite basic information is often either missing or difficult to locate, such as the size of the sample and how it was selected; when the study was carried out and the sequencing of its various phases; precisely how the data were analysed; the coding manual used for the various content analyses; and so on. Clearly there are important differences, of a cultural nature, in scientific protocol and in the format of research reports on either side of the English Channel. They constitute an impediment to Anglo–French collaboration in joint research.

In the English-speaking world, researchers are required (and perhaps trained) to be much more *explicit* about the methods they have used in carrying out a particular investigation, which is part of the positivist inheritance that was discussed in the preceding paragraphs. These conventions are necessary in the interests of maintaining international standards for the communication of scientific information. Those who reject the philosophy of science on which these claims are based would assert that the conventions are an example of what Manicas (1987) described as 'the Americanisation of the social sciences'. The requirement to be *explicit* about one's methods of research is closely linked to the notion of the *replication* of research: it should be possible for others, who may be critical of your findings, to replicate your study in their own laboratories. Orne (1962), too, stresses the importance of replication in regard to experimental research. As social representations are specific to a particular culture and to a particular point in time within the evolution of that culture, it would be inappropriate to think in terms of the *replication* of any particular study. Gergen (1973) was right to describe social psychology as history. History does not repeat itself.

Often the detailed information concerning the methods of research which the English-speaking social psychologist seeks is available in the form of a research report of only limited print-run that was distributed privately. Much of this technical detail is omitted from those studies that are published as books. The books have to be of interest to a wide readership with only a rather generalist knowledge of the human and social sciences. They would not sell if they contained too much technical detail. While there is a potentially viable market for technical reports in social psychology in the

English-speaking world, there is no such market in the French-speaking world. One just has to accept some of these cultural differences.

Moscovici's *primary* objective has been to establish social representations as phenomena that are worthy of study in their own right. The methods of investigation that he and others within this French tradition of research have adopted have always been *secondary* to the primary task of isolating and describing social representations. In the study of social representations, meaning is always problematic — as it is in psychoanalysis — hence the importance of interpretation. In behaviourism, meaning has never been a central problem *per se* because the terms (that is, the independent and the dependent variables) have been defined, operationally, in advance. They acquire their meaning, however, only in relation to a particular perspective, which is that of the researcher as an observer and recorder of the behaviour of others. Meaning, even in experiments, is, however, problematic as more than one perspective is involved (Farr 1978). I have also shown that this is so in the social psychology of the inter-view (Farr 1984b). Interviews are quite widely used in studies of social representations. The multiplicity of perspectives is inherent in the nature of life in society. Some of the research that has helped to establish this alternative perspective on experimenting has been carried out, at Aix-en-Provence, by Codol (1984) and Abric (1984, 1986) within the French tradition of research on social representations (Farr 1984a, 1987b). It constitutes an important contribution to the methodology of research in the social sciences.

The diversity of approaches to the study of a single phenomenon

It is important to relate the theory to research practice. It is a singular feature of the theory that it does not privilege any particular method of research. In this respect the theory is quite different from the dominant tradition of social psychology in America and Britain. This latter tradition privileges, wherever possible, the use of the experimental method. It is probably true to say that the theory of social representations is incompatible with this latter tradition. Indeed, it constitutes an important critique of that particular tradition.

The reason for this incompatibility, however, is *not* that it would be inappropriate to study *some* aspects of social representations experimentally. I have already referred, above, to the important experimental studies carried out at Aix-en-Provence. I shall refer, below, to yet another aspect of the theory that has been investigated in the laboratory, using experimental methods. Clearly, then, the French social psychologists who investigate social representations are not hostile to the use of experimental methods *per se*. It is, however, the case that social representations cannot be studied *exclusively* in the laboratory using experimental methods. This is primarily because they operate in society, rather than in the laboratory. They are historical phenomena; while most of the phenomena investigated, experimentally, in the laboratory are ahistorical. Many researchers represent the laboratory as being some sort of cultural vacuum (Tajfel 1972). Social representations are an integral part of culture. Elsewhere (Farr 1984a) I have spelled out, in some detail, why I believe that social representations cannot be studied, exclusively, in the laboratory and I shall not repeat myself here.

There is, then, no single royal road, in terms of the methods of research, to the study of social representations. This, in many ways, is a healthy state of affairs. Sometimes a method of research that previously was important and then went out of fashion is re-instated. This has happened, for example, with participant observation. This was the technique that Jodelet (1991) used in her study of the social representations of mental illness. It has also been used in applied research in the USA, for example Edgerton's study, in California, of mental handicap, Cicourel's studies of juvenile justice, and so on. Most of these American studies have been carried out by social psychologists within sociological traditions of social psychology like Cicourel, Goffman, and so on. The theory of social representations has reactivated the whole interface between anthropology and psychology. As a result of this rapprochement between the two disciplines, methods of research that are of central importance in anthropology or sociology are beginning, now, to be used in psychology, such as participant observation.

It might be more accurate to say, however, that this particular methodology (i.e. participant observation) always has been used by psychologists but without its use ever being consciously recognized. The experimenter, for example, always has been a participant as well as being an observer within the laboratory, though it is the latter, rather than the former, aspect of his or her role that is highlighted in the research report. This is because, historically, behaviourism represented the perspective of the investigator as an observer of others. Social psychologists such as Orne, in his research on 'demand characteristics' (Orne 1962) and Rosenthal, in his research on 'experimenter effects' (Rosenthal 1966), have forced experimenters to become more self-conscious about their own participation in the research process for example to consider the possibility that *they*, themselves, might be the source of some of the effects they otherwise observe and record (see Farr 1976, 1978). In the light of the experimental evidence it is difficult, now, for experimenters to ignore the fact that they are participating in research as well as observing phenomena.

The laboratory, as I noted in the previous section of this paper, is a highly artificial, and a rather peculiar, type of culture. In my own contribution to the Farr and Moscovici (1984a) volume on *Social Representations*, I demonstrated how the laboratory itself, together with the whole protocol of experimenting, were, themselves, a direct consequence of representing psychology as a branch of natural science (Farr 1984*a*). In other words, behaviourism is a social representation that psychologists have themselves created. It was a theory in its own right (and, hence, qualifies as a social representation) that has had a dramatic effect on what we consider to be proper methods of research in our discipline. It is the source of some of those striking differences between the two cultures which I outlined in a previous section (pp. 19–22).

Behaviourism is a social representation that has been of considerable historic importance in the evolution of psychological science in America and in Britain; it has been a much less important social representation in the evolution of psychological science in France. Once it is recognized for being what it is — just one social representation amongst others — then it loses much of its power to coerce and to constrain the research activities of the psychological community. There was a time in the USA, until about the mid-1950s, when behaviourism was a 'social fact' in the full Durkheimian sense of the term. Once, however, it ceased to be *the* social representation of psychological science and became, instead, merely *a* social representation, it lost most of its coercive force. Such changes in the culture of research are equivalent to a shift in the predominant paradigm for research as described by Kuhn (1962), that is behaviourism, after the late 1950s, was no longer paradigmatic for the development of psychology. I have developed the idea of behaviourism as a social representation in two separate, earlier, articles (Farr 1981, 1984*a*).

Since the theory of social representations is a realist model of social science (see Farr 1990), 'culture' has come, once again, within the purview of psychological research. It is fairly routine in French research on social representations to sample culture as well as cognition; to sample the contents of the mass media of communication as well as the contents of people's minds; and to sample objects as well as subjects. This results in an ecologically-valid form of social psychology. It is reminiscent of Brunswik's much earlier plea concerning the importance of sampling the environment as well as people's perceptions of it in studying visual perception (Brunswik 1956). Brunswik's plea was the initial stimulus that led Donald Campbell to devote a great deal of time, in the course of a long and a highly productive professional life, to improving the ecological validity of research in psychology (i) by separating the logic of experimenting from its locus in either a laboratory or a field setting (Campbell and Stanley 1966); (ii) by distinguishing between the internal and the external validity of experiments (Campbell 1957); (iii) by his promotion of experimental and quasi-experimental designs for research in societal settings (Cook and Campbell 1979); and (iv) by his advocacy of the use of non-reactive techniques of investigation in the social sciences (Webb *et al.* 1966).

French research on social representations has led, similarly, to a progressive reduction in the isolation of the laboratory from its surrounding culture and society. Elsewhere I have argued (Farr 1981) that the walls of Freud's consulting room were far more permeable to the surrounding culture than were the walls of the laboratories within which behaviourism was incubating. French researchers have used a wide variety of different techniques in order to study a single phenomenon, that is the phenomenon of social representations (Moscovici 1984). This is very much in the spirit of Campbell's advice concerning the importance of establishing psychological research on a sound ecological footing. The scientific rationale for this use of multiple methods in the investigation of a single phenomenon is that they incorporate different sources of error. This is preferable, in Campbell's view, to all of the data in the social sciences being contaminated by a single source of error, for example if all such data were highly 'reactive'.

A significant fraction of the data collected in research on social representations is of a non-reactive nature, quite often based on archival research, – it may include an analysis of the contents of books, magazines, films, comics, radio broadcasts, posters, television programmes, advertisements, and so on. Moscovici, for example, in his original study *La psychanalyse: son image and son public* (Moscovici 1961, 1976), included various analyses of the contents of some 253 different journals, magazines, and newspapers that were published in France over a 15-month period between January 1952 and March 1953. M.-J. Chombart de Lauwe's study *Un monde autre* (1971) is based almost exclusively on analyses of the content of the mass media of communication. She was concerned with tracing the social representations of childhood as these appeared in autobiography, biography, films in which a child featured as a central character, the literature that adults write for children to read, and so on. The non-reactive nature of these data helps to ensure that the social representations which emerge from the analysis do not change by virtue of being investigated. People, on the other hand, often behave differently when they become aware that they are the objects of interest to the investigator. Data collected under those conditions are likely to be highly reactive both in form and content. Most of the data of the social sciences are of this latter variety, hence Campbell's plea for the importance of using non-reactive methods, as the French do routinely.

There is much to be said, in my opinion, in support of a theory that introduces (or rather reintroduces) a different type of data into the domain of psychological research. In accepting the theory of social representations, researchers are committed to treating seriously the information that circulates in society concerning the object of their study. Often this involves an analysis of the contents of the mass media of communication. Stereotypes are to be found in the media as well as in people's minds (Farr 1990). Milgram found, for example, that even life-long residents within the different quarters of Paris, when they constructed mental maps of their native city, were influenced by the cultural artefacts that were created for the benefit of tourists such as maps of the Metro system, street plans, and so on. (Milgram 1984). In many ways, by accepting the theory of social representations, one is putting back the clock and accepting techniques of research that were fashionable some time ago.

Jaspars and Fraser (1984), for example, have shown how, in the Chicago of the 1920s, social attitudes and social representations were different aspects of one and the same phenomenon. This was before G. W. Allport, in his classic chapter on attitudes for the Murchison *Handbook* of 1935, 'individualized' the concept and thus transformed it from a social representation into a merely individual one (Allport 1935). It has remained an individual representation ever since. In the Chicago of the 1920s, a quite sharp distinction was drawn between values, which were a type of collective representation (and hence a cultural phenomenon), and social attitudes, which could sometimes be conceived of as the reflection in the individual of these cultural values, that is the subjective side of culture. Social attitudes were equivalent to what we would now call social representations, because the link with the cultural values was retained, at least in the 1920s in Chicago, both in theory and in research practice. It was not long, however, before these links were severed and the study of values became part of the provinces of sociology, philosophy, and anthropology while the study of attitudes became the central topic of research in psychological traditions of social psychology. By accepting the theory of social representations one can, once again, interrelate these two separate fields of research.

Jaspars and Fraser (1984) show how the techniques for the scaling of attitudes, which were devised by Guttman and by Thurstone, logically implied the notion of a collective representation of the object of the attitude. Thurstone trawled the mass media of communication of his own day in order to compile a large initial pool of opinion items with which to begin the construction of any of his now classic scales, for example attitudes to divorce, to the Church, to issues of war and peace, and so on. This betokens a concern, on his part, for the ecological validity of his scales in terms of the values that were current at the time (Farr 1989). If one accepts the Jaspars and Fraser (1984) argument, which I believe is a cogent one, then it should be possible to study social representations by looking, once again, at the methodology for constructing Thurstone and Guttman scales and so on. It was expensive to construct such scales in terms of both time and money. It was much more efficient to construct Likert scales, and so they rapidly became the norm once they were introduced in the aftermath of the Second World War. If G. W. Allport individualized the concept of attitude by the way in which he defined the term, then Rensis Likert individualized the technology of its measurement by requiring that the individual respond to each item in the scale and by his analysis of the scale in terms of its internal consistency. It is of historic interest to note that Moscovici first began to develop the notion of a social representation as a consequence of a correspondence in which he was engaged with Louis Guttman concerning the nature of scaling (personal communication). It was Moscovici's contention that there is a theory lurking within the methodology.

There is an area of research in psychology where the analysis of cultural values continues to be of some importance. It concerns the ideology of success and failure in certain Western cultures. It is only Ichheiser (1949), as far as I know, who has described the research in terms of an ideology but, in my opinion, this is a highly accurate description. There is an interesting link between this particular area of research and contemporary research on social representations (Farr and Moscovici 1984b). At one point in his monograph, Ichheiser describes himself as a Durkheimian who is studying the collective representation of the individual. The individual is represented as someone who is responsible for his or her own actions. It is this representation of the individual that becomes incorporated in the legal codes of many, mainly Western, countries. We unwittingly subscribe to this collective representation when we praise people for their successes and blame them for their failures. We are victims of it when others hold us to be responsible for our shortcomings in life. Ichheiser showed how the unemployed are often made to feel guilty about being out of work (Ichheiser 1943). We are powerfully influenced by this particular representation in the ways in which we explain successes and failures, both our own and those of others.

Heider (1958), in his analysis of the notion of responsibility, and in his theory of social attributions, made creative use of the way in which his fellow Austrian, Ichheiser (1949) had analysed the workings of the ideology of success and failure within certain Western cultures. As I have shown elsewhere (Farr, 1991a), there is a quite dramatic difference between individualism as a collective representation and the collective distribution of individual representations (as revealed, for example, by an opinion poll). The former is a cultural (and hence a collective) phenomenon whilst the latter is an individual phenomenon (and hence not really social). Individualism is a cultural value. It is more fully developed in Protestant cultures than it is in Catholic ones; it is more clearly articulated in capitalist economies than it is in socialist ones. In the context of the collective representations that were important to Durkheim (such as religion, myths, and so on), individualism was a negative cultural value. It appeared, in his sociology, in the guise of egoism and of anomie — it is associated with the disintegration of commonly-held social values (that is collective representations). It is scarcely surprising, then, if it took a theorist working within a different cultural context (Ichheiser, working in the context of German Kultur) to identify individualism as a coherent ideology in its own right. Ichheiser derived some of his ideas from the sociologist, Weber (1904/1905).

The work of Ichheiser and of Heider converge in what, today, is loosely called the field of social cognition. Ichheiser's monograph is a plea, from the perspective of a sociology of knowledge, for the importance of studying the impression we form of other people. Heider, at the same time, helped to initiate research in the field of 'person perception'. Ichheiser wrote a sociology of interpersonal relations, while Heider wrote about the psychology of such relations. The cultural dimension is explicit in Ichheiser, but remains implicit in Heider. The ideology of success and failure, in Ichheiser, becomes the psychology of praise and blame, in Heider. The two are, of course, closely interrelated. The cultural dimension appears in Heider but in a highly attenuated form. It is there, for example, in his notion of responsibility but appears as a form of linguistic analysis. By accepting the theory of social representations it becomes possible to explicate the cultural dimension in the whole field of social cognition — it becomes possible, once again, to highlight the key role of values. The explication of common sense was an important part of Helder's project. Moscovici also accords common sense an important status in his social psychology.

Another pair of researchers, in the same broad area of research, are McClelland and Atkinson. McClelland (1961) is concerned with *The achieving society* and so with analyses of cultural values, while Atkinson (Atkinson and Feather 1966) is more narrowly concerned with the psychology of the achievement motive. The work of McClelland complements that of Atkinson in much the same way as the work of Ichheiser complemented that of Heider (see, for example, McClelland *et al.* 1953). Like the latter duo they, too, work at two different levels, that is the level of culture and the level of the individual. We need a theory of the middle range, however, such as that of social representations, in order to precisely demonstrate how the two levels of culture and of cognition can be interrelated. By accepting the theory of social representations, one legitimizes the sort of data that McClelland works with, the analysis of such collective representations as myths and religions. It is comparatively rare, nowadays, for psychologists to operate at this particular level, that of cultural values. The research is important for another reason. Research on the achievement motive is one of the few areas of empirical research in modern psychology where researchers have contributed at all significantly to the literature on the methodology of content analysis (Atkinson 1958). It was not uncommon, as I noted above, for social scientists at Chicago in the 1920s to operate at the level of cultural values. Current acceptance of Moscovici's theory would encourage a renaissance of such research, together with a renewal of interest in the technology of analysing the contents of communications.

McClelland aimed to interrelate, in some sort of causal sequence, measures of achievement imagery, which he had obtained from his analysis of cultural myths, with various indices of economic growth. French social scientists, in some of their research on social representations, have been concerned, similarly, with an analysis of myths and so on, such as the voluminous work of M. J. Chombart de Lauwe (1971) on the myth of the child in contemporary society; the analysis by Jodelet (1985) of myths concerning the contagious nature of mental illness; and the analysis by Morin (1969) of the anti-semitic rumours that circulated in Orleans in 1969. The research of McClelland harks back to a venerable tradition of research of a more historical nature, that established a link between the Protestant Ethic and the spirit of capitalism (Weber 1904/1905) and between 'religion and the rise of capitalism' (Tawney 1926). These links are also likely to have been of critical importance in establishing the ideology of success and failure as outlined by Ichheiser. This tradition of research is kept alive, today, by Morishima (1982) who has shown how the variant of the philosophy of Confucius that developed in Japan is related to the process of industrialization whereas the form of the same philosophy in China is not so related.

It would be ideal if one could derive one's methodology from one's theory. Harré and Secord (1972) attempted to do just this when they launched their critique of the behaviourist methodology of experimental psychology. They derived their methodology from the criteria that Strawson, the philosopher, adduced for characterizing an individual. For Strawson, an individual was someone who could monitor his or her own behaviour and give an account of it. Research, therefore, ought to be based on the elicitation of accounts. This is a method of research that is popular amongst those investigating social representations. They could claim, quite plausibly, that it is consistent with Ichheiser's portrayal of the individual as someone who is responsible for his or her own actions. One need only argue that Ichheiser and Strawson were roughly comparable in the ways in which they characterized the individual. In other words there is a close link between moral autonomy, as portrayed by Ichheiser, and the ability to monitor one's own behaviour, as portrayed by Strawson. These two characteristics of the individual are certainly linked in the social psychology of the American philosopher, G. H. Mead.

The elicitation of accounts, then, is an attractive way of collecting data. It is not, however, such a revolutionary technique as Harré and Secord seemed to suggest. It has been used quite often by social psychologists, especially by those studying social representations. In the study of social representations it is important that researchers do not impose their own representations on those of their informants, which is why there is a general preference, among such researchers, for the use of unstructured techniques of investigation over the use of more highly structured techniques. Many studies are of a highly qualitative nature. I have treated Herzlich's study of the social representations of health and illness (Herzlich 1973) as an example of the methodology advocated by Harré (see Farr 1977a).

Moscovici (1973, pp. xiii and xiv), in his preface to the English edition of Herzlich's monograph on the social representations of health and illness, promised that the reader '. . . will find no questionnaires, scales or statistical tests . . . In my view, the contribution of the present study is much greater than that of many other studies which, although they use more sophisticated methods and may be, in a technical sense, more professionally "respectable", have been less well adapted to the object of their inquiry and therefore make a less genuine contribution to the progress of science'. While the French edition was similarly free of tests of statistical significance, it did neverthe less contain tables of data that were omitted from the English version of the text. Herzlich's research strategy involved eliciting accounts from her infor- mants concerning their representations of both health and illness. She then accepted these accounts at their face value and her various analyses of the contents of these interviews (which each lasted between one and a half and two hours) comprise the body of the text. Herzlich justifies '. . . the choice of the open interview as the *only* technique suitable for the collection of data' (Herzlich 1973, p. 13; my italics). This openness and flexibility was impor- tant, from the point of view of the theory, for the reasons outlined in the previous paragraph. She did invite her informants, however, to explain the origins of *both* health *and* illness.

In my re-analysis of the Herzlich data, I suggested that this particular set of circumstances for the interview was peculiarly conducive to eliciting the specific type of narrative she obtained (Farr 1977*a*). It was necessary only to assume one further circumstance, that all of her informants had positive conceptions of themselves. This is an extremely reasonable assumption. When they were invited to make attributional statements about the causes of two oppositely valued states such as health and illness then it was only natural, given the positive self-concepts of her informants, that they attri- buted the positive pole to the self and the negative pole to the non-self, or the environment. This is what she found. It is highly compatible with Heider's account of the social psychology of praise and blame (Heider 1958). Herzlich's use of the open-ended interview helped to ensure that her own representations of health and illness in no way constrained those of her infor- mants. Instead, the accounts that she elicited were structured by what her informants thought of themselves. It would be naive to assume that the social psychology of the research interview had no influence on the structure of the data obtained.

I argued that, in the course of her monograph, Herzlich had failed to demonstrate that the social representations of health and illness, which she had described so graphically, existed, in accordance with Durkheim's original conception, at a collective level. This was because she sampled indi- viduals, rather than communities of individuals and/or issues. I did suggest, however, that if she had sampled the debates concerning the appropriate levels of fluoride in community water supplies she might have found the evidence she sought. Indeed, her study does shed a fascinating light on why so many campaigns to increase fluoride levels in local water supplies have failed when this particular issue has been put to the vote at a community level. Why should one add something that, in greater concentrations, is a poison to something that is as 'natural' and as 'pure' as water — and all of this in the interests of health? She could also have sampled other health-related issues such as the progressive banning of smoking in public places. Health professionals ought to take into account people's conceptions of health and illness *before* devising their campaigns. Frequently the appeal is to the self-interest of the individual rather than to the welfare of the community. An analysis of letters to newspapers on a variety of health-related issues might have been a better sampling frame for Herzlich's study than eliciting accounts from individual residents of Paris or of a village in Normandy. Studies of both types are obviously needed. The question, here, is one of levels. Are the accounts elicited at the level of the individual or the community? It is a question of one's choice of research method in relation to one's theory. The content analyses in the Herzlich monograph were of the interview protocols. She did not include in her study any analyses of the content of the mass media of communication concerning health-related issues.

Herzlich was not alone in obtaining the sorts of accounts that she did in response to her particular line of questioning. Herzberg, under comparable conditions, invited accountants and engineers in Pittsburg in the 1950s to recount a time when they felt satisfied with their work and a time when they felt dissatisfied with their work (Herzberg *et al*. 1959). He also invited them to explain these two contrasting sets of feelings about their work. Like Herzlich, he, too, accepted their accounts at face value. This was the basis of his famous two-factor theory of work motivation. The factors relating to satisfaction with work were *different in kind* to those relating to dissatisfaction with work. The former factors were related to the ego needs of Maslow's hierarchy of needs, such as the need for autonomy, responsibility, and so on (Maslow 1954). Herzberg called the latter factors, those associated with dissatisfactions, 'hygiene' factors. Their removal did not lead to increased job satisfaction, though their absence did reduce dissatisfaction. Hence, Herzberg concluded, the two sets of factors are independent of each other.

This is, essentially, the same structure that Herzlich found in her analysis of the social representations of health and illness. If naive informants are invited, in the course of a single interview, to make attributional statements about two oppositely valued states such as health and illness, or satisfaction and dissatisfaction with work, then they will tend, as Heider (1958) pointed out, to attribute the positive pole to the self and the negative pole to the non-self (or the environment). This is what Herzberg found. The structure of the accounts he obtained was a direct consequence of the social psychology of his research interview and of the positive self-concepts of his informants. The same structure, then, holds across three very different domains of empirical research: the absence of illness is not the same thing as health (Herzlich 1973); the absence of dissatisfaction with work is not the same thing as satisfaction with work (Herzberg *et al.* 1959); and the absence of failure is not the same thing as success (Heider 1958). Thus we have Herzlich, Herzberg, and Heider collecting Harré-type accounts of health, of happiness, and of hope. The strong positive self-concepts of informants also helped to ensure that Herzlich was unable to distinguish between the accounts of Parisians and those of Normandy villagers, and Herzberg, similarly, was unable to distinguish between the accounts of accountants and those of engineers. It had been known for some time that Herzberg's theory was false and that his findings were method-specific. In my article (Farr 1977*b*) I was able to precisely demonstrate why Herzberg's findings were method-specific.

In the course of my two articles on Herzlich (Farr 1977*a*) and on Herzberg (Farr 1977*b*) I drew a distinction, in re-analysing their data, between bias and error. Bias could be reflected in the characteristic structure of the original accounts — as set out in the previous paragraph. This was a function, jointly, of the positive self-concepts of the informants and of the social psychology of the research interview. I reserved the term 'error' for mistakes in the interpretation of the accounts by the investigator. In the case of Herzlich the error was not a serious one — it was a question of mistaking the *level* of the phenomenon she was describing. She assumed that she had obtained evidence concerning collective representations, though she had only ever interviewed individuals. She was clear, however, that she was investigating their representations of health and illness. Herzberg's error was a much more serious one. He believed that he had established, on the basis of qualitative accounts elicited at a single point in time, evidence of a causal nature concerning the sources of satisfaction and dissatisfaction with work in the real world. The comparable error of Herzlich would have been if she had gone to the Secretary of State for Health and claimed that she had discovered the causes of health and illness! She knew she was only exploring people's representations of health and illness. Herzberg failed to appreciate that he was only investigating people's representations of satisfaction and dissatisfaction with work. Instead, he thought he was investigating causal structures in the real world.

This way of re-analysing other people's data is rather like an archeological dig. It is important to appreciate that more than one level of analysis is involved. There may be bias at the level of the informant (of the raw data). Superimposed on this there may be error on the part of the investigator in the interpretation of the data. Errors can, of course, also occur at the level of the person carrying out the re-analysis. Harré and Secord (1972), when they advocated the elicitation of accounts as the basic methodology of the social sciences, allowed for the possibility that the investigator need not accept accounts at their face value. It is usually possible to negotiate accounts, which is what good therapists do with the accounts they elicit from their clients. Negotiation becomes possible because more than one perspective is involved – the perspective of the therapist is different from that of the client. This is one of the advantages of participant observation over the interview as a method of research (Becker and Geer 1957). It retains, within the one methodology, the differing perspectives both of the actor and of the observer. It is an important method of research in the study of social representations (see above). It is also the preferred method of research in the symbolic interactionist tradition of social psychology (Blumer 1969; Rock 1979).

In my own approach to what I call the social psychology of the inter-view I stress the fact that more than one perspective is involved (Farr 1984*b*). Indeed I define an inter-view as a technique of research in which the investigator sets out to elicit perspectives, other than his or her own, on events. Investigators need not abandon their own perspectives – investigators are observers as well as being participants. By the simple expedient of inserting a hyphen I have tried to equate the social psychology of the interview with the more inclusive methodology of participant observation. It is a peculiarly appropriate approach to the study of social representations. It is the technique Freud used in devising psychoanalysis and that Piaget used when he explored the child's representation of the world.

When behaviourism was the dominant paradigm for research in psychology, the role of the observer was of paramount importance – but observers never considered themselves to be participants. That would have constituted a serious breach of the observer's neutrality. As Morin (1977) observed, in regard to biology, with the advent of positivism a separation developed between the world of the observer and the world 'as observed'. In psychology, behaviourism developed as a completely consistent psychology of 'the Other One' (Meyer 1921). It was only social theorists, like Heider (1958), who retained the perspective of Self (i.e. of P, the Perceiver) on O (i.e. the Other One). The theory of social representations makes salient, once again, the role of the actor in the social scene. It is, therefore, a constructivist form of social psychology. As Berlin (1976) observed in his study of Vico, 'In history we are the actors; in the natural sciences mere spectators'. It would be impossible to study social representations exclusively from the perspective of the natural sciences. They constitute a sociological tradition of social psychology. They are a good example of Gergen's thesis that social psychology is more history than science (Gergen 1973). The two roles – those of observer and of actor – are not necessarily incompatible, as I tried to show above. They can be combined in the role of the participant observer. This method of investigation is central to the social sciences. Once psychologists concede that the perspective of the observer is not the *only* perspective on human affairs, then a much wider range of research methods becomes available. Accepting the theory of social representations can be the first step in this liberating process.

Some critics have complained that the theory of social representations is far too imprecise for it to be of any practical value. I have not found this to be so, in my own experience. The theory itself enabled me to see, for example, that the phenomena described by Herzlich were not at an appropriate Durkheimian level (Farr 1977*a*). To choose another example, the theory was sufficiently precise for me to be confident that there had been an error of translation from the studies conducted in the field to the studies carried out in the laboratory (Farr 1984*a*). The laboratory studies were primarily concerned with the manipulation of representations in the minds of *individual* subjects. The theory ought, however, to apply at the level of the research community itself. I showed how behaviourism, when considered as a social representation, affects one's conception of what a laboratory is for, and of the research that is carried out within it. It was in terms of the theory of social representations itself that I knew where to look for the operation of a social representation and what to look for, that is to look for some sort of theory that guides experimental practice.

I hope I have said enough, in the course of this chapter, to show that the theory is compatible with the use of a wide variety of different research methods. It is not hostile, for example, to laboratory experimentation. The theory even sheds an interesting new light on the social psychology of the experiment. Another aspect of the theory that has been tested experimentally in the laboratory is the work on minority influence (Moscovici 1987). Many highly creative individuals like Darwin, Freud, Marx, Einstein, and so on were, at one time, in a minority of one in terms of their ideas and theories. Over time, however, they have come to change the collective representations of the eras in which they have lived and worked and of subsequent eras. Just how an individual could come to exert this sort of influence has been hinted at in the experimental studies of minority influence. These studies are a healthy corrective to the undue emphasis, in a great deal of American experimental research, on conformity pressures and on the maintenance of the status quo. It would not be possible to study social representations by conducting *all* one's research within the laboratory, but some aspects of the theory can be explored within such a context.

Moscovici (1963) was highly critical of an exclusive dependence on the public opinion poll as a way of assessing, for example, the impact of science on culture. This, however, has not prevented him from using public opinion polls himself (Moscovici 1961, 1976). The theory of social representations is highly relevant to the study of social change (including changes in public opinion). It does not, however, privilege a particular method of research, which is one of its great virtues. While the techniques of the opinion poll can identify just how widespread a particular belief might be within a given population, we need the theory of social representations to account for the dynamics of the change in public opinion and why the distribution of opinion takes the particular form it does (Farr 1990). Caroline Purkhardt is currently carrying out research on the transformative role of social representations in scientific research. What one needs is an appropriate theory and a diversity of different methods of research. This is what the theory of social representations provides.

References

Abric. J.-C. (1984). A theoretical and experimental approach to the study of social representations in a situation of interaction. In *Social representations*, (ed. R. M. Farr and S. Moscovici), pp. 169–83. Cambridge University Press, Cambridge.

Abric, J.-C. (1986). *Coopération, compétition et représentations sociales*. Cousset (Fribourg) Suisse, Delval.

Allport, G. W. (1935). Attitudes. In *Handbook of social psychology*, Vol. 2, (ed. C. A. Murchison), pp. 798–844. Clark University Press, Worcester, Mass.

Atkinson, J. W. (ed.) (1958). *Motives in fantasy, action and society: a method of assessment and study*. Van Nostrand, Princeton, N.J.

Atkinson, J. W. and Feather, N. T. (ed.) (1966). *A theory of achievement motivation*. Wiley, New York.

Becker, H. and Geer, B. (1957). Participant observation and interviewing: a comparison. *Human Organisation*, **16**, 28–32.

Berlin, I. (1976). *Vico and Herder*. Chatto and Windus, London.

Blumer, H. (1969). The methodological position of symbolic interactionism. In *Symbolic interactionism: perspective and method*, (ed. H. Blumer), Prentice Hall, Englewood Cliffs, N.J.

Brunswik, E. (1956). *Perception and the representative design of psychological experiments*. University of California Press, Berkeley.

Campbell, D. T. (1957). Factors relevant to the validity of experiments in social settings. *Psychological Bulletin*, **54**, 297–312.

Campbell, D. T. and Stanley, J. C. (1966). *Experimental and quasi-experimental designs for research*. Rand McNally, Chicago.

Chombart de Lauwe, M.-J. (1971). *Un monde autre: l'enfance: de ses représentations à son mythe*. Payot, Paris.

Codol, J. P. (1984). On the system of representations in an artificial social situation. In *Social representations*, (ed. R. M. Farr and S. Moscovici) pp. 239–53, Cambridge University Press.

Cook, T. D. and Campbell, D. T. (1979). *Quasi-experimentation: design and analysis for field settings*. Rand McNally, Chicago.

Douglas, M. (1980). *Evans-Pritchard*. Fontana Modern Masters series. Fontana, London.

Farr, R. M. (1976). Experimentation: a social psychological perspective. *British Journal of Social and Clinical Psychology*, **15**, 225–38.

Farr, R.M. (1977a). Heider, Harré and Herzlich on health and illness: Some observations on the structure of 'représentations collectives'. *European Journal of Social Psychology*, **7(4)**, 491–504.

Farr, R.M. (1977b). On the nature of attributional artefacts in qualitative research: Herzberg's two-factor theory of work motivation. *Journal of Occupational Psychology*, **50**, 3–14.

Farr, R.M. (1978). On the social significance of artefacts in experimenting. *British Journal of Social and Clinical Psychology*, **17(4)**, 299–306.

Farr, R.M. (1980a). Homo socio-psychologicus. In *Models of man*, (ed. A.J. Chapman and D.M. Jones), pp. 183–9. British Psychological Society, Leicester.

Farr, R.M. (1980b). Homo loquens in social psychological perspective. In *Language: social psychological perspectives*, (ed. H. Giles, W.P. Robinson, and P.M. Smith), pp. 409–13. Pergamon Press, Oxford.

Farr, R.M. (1981). On the nature of human nature and the science of behaviour. In *Indigenous psychologies: the anthropology of the self*, (ed. P. Heelas and A. Lock), pp. 303–17. Academic Press, London.

Farr, R.M. (1984a). Social representations: their role in the design and execution of laboratory experiments. In *Social representations*, (ed. R.M. Farr and S. Moscovici), pp. 125–47. Cambridge University Press.

Farr, R.M. (1984b). Interviewing: an introduction to the social psychology of the inter-view. In *Psychology for managers*, (2nd edn), (ed. C.L. Cooper and P. Makin), pp. 182–200. Macmillan, London.

Farr, R.M. (1987a). The science of mental life: a social psychological perspective. *Bulletin of the British Psychological Society*, **40**, 2–17.

Farr, R.M. (1987b). Social representations: a French tradition of research. *Journal for the Theory of Social Behaviour*, **17(4)**, 343–69.

Farr, R.M. (1990). Social representations as widespread beliefs. In *Psychological Studies of widespread beliefs*, (ed. C. Fraser and G. Gaskell), pp. 47–64. Oxford University Press.

Farr, R.M. (1989). The social and collective nature of representations. In *Recent advances in social psychology: an international perspective* (ed. J. Forgas and J.M. Innes) pp. 157–66. North Holland, Amsterdam.

Farr, R.M. (1991a). Individualism as a collective representation. In *Idéologies et representations sociales* (ed. V. Aebischer, J.P. Deconchy, and E.M. Lipianshy), pp. 129–43. Delval, Cousset (Suisse).

Farr, R.M. (1991b). The long past and the short history of social psychology. *European Journal of Social Psychology*, **21(5)** 371–80.

Farr, R.M. and Moscovici, S. (ed.) (1984a). *Social representations*. Cambridge University Press.

Farr, R.M. and Moscovici, S. (1984b). On the nature and role of representations in self's understanding of others and of self. In *Issues in person perception*, (ed. M. Cook), pp. 1–27. Methuen, London.

Gergen, K.J. (1973). Social psychology as history. *Journal of Personality and Social Psychology*, **26(2)**, 309–20.

Harré, R. and Secord, P.F. (1972). *The explanation of social behaviour*. Blackwell, Oxford.

Heider, F. (1958). *The psychology of inter-personal relations*. Wiley, New York.

Herzberg, F., Mausner, B., and Snyderman, B.B. (1959). *The motivation to work*, (2nd edn). Wiley, New York.

Herzlich, C. (1973). *Health and illness: a social psychological analysis*. Academic Press, London.
Ichheiser, G. (1943). Misinterpretations of personality in everyday life and the psychologists' frame of reference. *Character and Personality*, 12, 145-60.
Ichheiser, G. (1949). Misunderstanding in human relations: a study in false social perception. *American Sociological Review*, LV, monograph supplement, 1-72.
Jahoda, M. (1972). Social psychology and psychoanalysis: A mutual challenge. *Bulletin of the British Psychological Society*, 25, 269-74.
Jahoda, M. (1977). *Freud and the dilemmas of psychology*. Hogarth Press, London.
Jaspars, J.M.F. and Fraser, C. (1984). Attitudes and social representations. In *Social representations*, (ed. R.M. Farr and S. Moscovici), pp. 101-23. Cambridge University Press.
Jodelet, D. (1991). *Madness and social representations*. Harvester/Wheatsheaf, London.
Kuhn, T.S. (1962). *The structure of scientific revolutions*. University of Chicago Press.
McClelland, D.C. (1961). *The achieving society*. Van Nostrand, Princeton, New Jersey.
McClelland, D.C., Atkinson, J.W., Clark, R.A., and Lowell, E.L. (1953). *The achievement motive*. Appleton-Century-Crofts, New York.
Manicas, P.T. (1987). *A history and philosophy of the social sciences*. Blackwell, Oxford.
Maslow, A.H. (1954). *Motivation and personality* Harper, New York.
Meyer, M.F. (1921). *The psychology of the other one: an introductory textbook*. Missouri Book Company, Columbia, Missouri.
Milgram, S. (1984). Cities as social representations. In *Social representations*, (ed. R.M. Farr and S. Moscovici), pp. 289-309. Cambridge University Press.
Morin, E. (1969). *La Rumeur d'Orleans*. Edition du Seuil, Paris.
Morin, E. (1977). *La méthode, Vol. I: la nature de la nature*. Seuil, Paris.
Morishima, M. (1982). *Why has Japan 'succeeded'?* Cambridge University Press.
Moscovici, S. (1961). *La psychanalyse: son image et son public*. Presses Universitaires de France, Paris.
Moscovici, S. (1963). Attitudes and opinions. *Annual Review of Psychology*, pp. 231-60.
Moscovici, S. (1973). Preface to C. Herzlich, *Health and Illness: a social psychological analysis*. Academic Press, London.
Moscovici, S. (1976). *La psychanalyse: son image et son public*, (2nd edn). Presses Universitaires de France, Paris.
Moscovici, S. (1981). Foreword to P. Heelas and A. Lock, *Indigenous psychologies: the anthropology of the self*, pp. vii-xi. Academic Press, London.
Moscovici, S. (1984). The phenomenon of social representations. In *Social representations*, (ed. R.M. Moscovici), pp. 3-69. Cambridge University Press.
Moscovici, S. (1985). *The age of the crowd: a historical treatise on mass psychology*. Cambridge University Press.
Moscovici, S. (1987). Answers and questions. *Journal for the Theory of Social Behaviour*, 17(4), 513-29.
Moscovici, S. (1988). *La machine à faire des dieux: sociologie et psychologie*. Fayard, Paris.

Murchison, C. (ed.) (1935). *Handbook of social psychology*, 2 volumes. Clark University Press, Worcester, Mass.

Orne, M. T. (1962). On the social psychology of the psychological experiment: with particular reference to demand characteristics and their implications. *American Psychologist*, **17**, 776-83.

Rock, P. (1979). *The making of symbolic interactionism*, chapter 6, pp. 178-216. Macmillan, London.

Rosenthal, R. (1966). *Experimenter effects in behavioural research*. Appleton-Century-Crofts, New York.

Tajfel, H. (1972). Experiments in a vacuum. In *The context of social psychology: a critical assessment*, (ed. J. Israel and H. Tajfel), pp. 69-119. Academic Press, London.

Tawney, R. H. (1926). *Religion and the rise of capitalism*. Penguin Books, London.

Webb, E. J., Campbell, D. T., Schwartz, R. D., and Sechrest, L. B. (1966). *Unobtrusive measures: nonreactive research in the social sciences*. Rand McNally, Chicago.

Weber, M. (1904/1905). Die protestantische Ethik und der Geist des Kapitalismus. *Archiv fur Sozialwissenschaft und Sozialpolitik*, Volumes XX and XXI.

2 Studying the thinking society: social representations, rhetoric, and attitudes

Michael Billig

The notion of 'social representation' has been one of the most controversial concepts to have been formulated in social psychology in recent years. Large claims have been made for Serge Moscovici's vision of a social psychology based around the study of social representations. According to one supporter, this vision offers the chance of creating 'a unified approach for a whole series of problems situated at the crossing point between psychology and the other social sciences' (Jodelet 1984, p. 378). Inevitably, such an ambitious perspective has provoked strong criticism. There are those who claim that there is little novel about the concept of social representations (Eiser 1986; McGuire 1986) or that the novelty is spoilt by hopeless obscurity (McKinlay and Potter 1987; Potter and Litton 1985), or that the whole project is theoretically misconceived (Parker 1987). Some critics have sought to rescue the novelty from the obscurity by recommending that the concept of social representations should be replaced by other concepts such as that of 'linguistic repertoires' (Potter and Litton 1985; Potter and Wetherell 1987).

At first sight, the present analysis might seem to be providing yet another attack on the new conceptual revolution proposed by Moscovici. Certainly, it will be suggested that the central concept of social representations has been used in inconsistent ways, and some of the criticisms outlined in Billig (1988b) will be developed. It might appear that a rival approach, based on the study of rhetoric, is being advocated (Billig 1985, 1986, 1987; Billig *et al*. 1988). Nevertheless, one point must be emphasized strongly at the outset. The present criticisms are not motivated by a spirit of counter-revolution, which seeks to crush the new revolutionaries. Nor is the rhetorical position being promoted as if by a rival revolutionary sect, claiming the right to succeed social psychology's *ancien régime* once the ruling experimentalists have been driven from their palaces. Instead, the criticisms are intended to draw attention to the rhetorical features of social life. It will be suggested that social representation theorists will need to give due attention to these features if they are to fulfil their ambitious intellectual aims.

Moscovici (1984b) has claimed that the social representation approach aims to study 'the thinking society' and, in this respect, he emphasizes both the social nature of thinking and the importance of thinking in social life. The rhetorical approach does not dispute either of these two assumptions. What it claims is that the thinking, which is to be found in the thinking society, has a particular characteristic: such thinking is essentially rhetorical. The word 'rhetorical' here is not being used in any denigratory sense. 'Mere' or 'empty' rhetoric is not being contrasted with substantial thinking, with the implication that the 'thinking society' needs to divest itself of rhetorical thinking and replace it by 'proper' or 'logical' thought. On the contrary: rhetoric is being used in a positive sense, which draws attention to the argumentative dimensions of thinking. In classical times, the arts of rhetoric were the arts of argumentation, as rhetoricians used their skills to argue for their own cases and against those of their rivals. Today, the rhetorical approach suggests that such rhetorical, or argumentative, skills are integral to thought, for when people think they are explicitly or implicitly arguing, whether with others or with themselves. However, the argumentative dimensions of thought have not been duly recognized by social scientists. They are frequently overlooked by cognitive psychologists who have a narrow view of thinking, as well as by social theorists, who stress the cohesive role of ideology or societal rules (Billig 1987; Billig *et al.* 1988).

The early formulations of social representation theory did not explicitly recognize the social and psychological importance of argumentation. Yet there is no theoretical opposition between the assumptions of social representation theory and the rhetorical approach. In fact, if the thinking society is to be studied, then social representation theorists will need to treat the study of argumentation seriously. There are indications that this point is recognized by Moscovici (1987) and Emler (1987), so that the study of rhetoric might eventually provide an essential, and far from negligible, component of the study of social representations. However, the incorporation of rhetorical ideas into a social representational perspective cannot itself be achieved unthinkingly. If the rhetorical aspects of social representations are to be recognized, then some key concepts will need to be re-evaluated or re-adjusted, because the social representation approach was not initially formulated to deal specifically with rhetorical issues. Therefore, the present paper will examine some of the central concepts of social representation theory, in order that they can be extended to deal with the essentially argumentative aspects of thinking. The notions of anchoring and objectification will be rhetorically examined. It will also be suggested that social representation theorists, in their desire to overturn the theoretical orthodoxies of contemporary social psychology, should not turn their back on the concept of 'attitudes': instead, they should look directly at the rhetorical, or argumentative, nature of attitudes. In short, by studying argumentation, social representation theorists will be studying the thinking society.

Social representation approach and its opponents

One of the central themes of the rhetorical approach proposed by Billig (1987 and 1988*a*) is that the argumentative meaning of discourse should not be ignored. Unless one understands what counter-discourse is being attacked, either implicitly or explicitly, one cannot properly understand a piece of argumentative discourse. This applies equally to social scientific and psychological discourse. Social psychological theories, when considered on their own and in isolation from wider intellectual debate, can appear rather bizarre. Outsiders might find it difficult to appreciate why anyone should bother to formulate such theories. However, theories typically gain meaning from being criticisms of alternative theories. This is true of the theory of social representations. Taken on its own, it might be rather hard to understand why the approach should have attracted such fervent supporters and fierce critics. A re-working of some ideas from Durkheim, many years after the great sociologist's death, would hardly seem to warrant empassioned feelings, especially since the re-working has not always been effected in the most accessible of language.

The significance of the social representation approach does not derive from the fact that an old concept has been revived. It might be pleasant for modern theorists to possess a revived term, which can be used to decorate their articles rather like some *fin de siècle* hat ribbons. However, the significance of the approach is not confined to the formulation of a term, but the term itself has a wider, argumentative significance, for the approach constitutes a direct challenge to prevailing trends in social psychology. The social representation theorists are not confining their attacks to one particular theoretical development, for example lining up with the attribution theorists against the supporters of dissonance motivation. Their attack is much broader. If asked what types of social psychological investigation they are opposing, the social representation theorists could legitimately point to any recent issue of the *Journal of Personality and Social Psychology* and declare 'All this, we are arguing against.' The social representation theorists would sweep away the social psychological hegemony represented by such a journal and, to be quite candid and to show that intellectual revolution need not be bounded by geography, by most of the *European Journal of Social Psychology*. After the social representation theorists have successfully hoisted their revolutionary flag over the printing press of these journals, the contents would be substantially altered. Out would go the technical phrases of the old theories and in would come new words. Old ANOVAS and MANOVAS might have difficulty in convincing the new rulers of their reformed intentions. Not least of the changes would be the lists of cited material that follow academic articles in social psychology and which, sometimes (and most inappropriately), are referred to as the cited 'literature'. The post-revolutionary citations would be very different, as the revolutionaries exchange one intellectual heritage for another.

It is not sufficient, nor is it accurate, to say that the coming revolution will change everything. Instead, it is necessary to specify some of the main themes of the new movement, for the social representation theorists do not wish to overturn conventional social psychology simply because it exists, or worse still, simply because it is predominantly American. There are a number of specific features, which characterize the predominant trend of social psychological work, and against which social representation theorists have strongly argued. Three themes, in particular, can be mentioned: (i) conventional social psychology's individualism; (ii) its static nature; and (iii) its unthinking image of the thinker.

Individualism

The social representation approach constitutes a criticism upon the individualism of much social psychology. Intellectually, social psychology has tended to draw its ideas from individual, or biological, psychology, rather than from the social sciences. For example, balance theories were motivational theories, which concentrated upon the drive states of the individual. Festinger (1957) specifically drew a parallel between the hypothesized motivation to avoid dissonance and biologically-produced motivations to avoid hunger and thirst. Similarly, the current trend for cognitive social psychology has its intellectual roots in theories of individual information-processing. Moscovici (1982) has criticized in detail the individualistic notions of cognitive social psychology: the thinker is examined in social isolation, as if cognitive calculations are computed in a social void, and the content of the thoughts were produced by a cognitive Robinson Crusoe.

In *The open society*, Karl Popper (1960) discusses the relations between psychology and sociology, in terms of a debate between J. S. Mill and Marx. The case for psychology is argued by Mill, who suggests that social arrangements are to be reduced to the psychological states of individuals. Marx, by contrast, argues that psychological states, whether cognitive or motivational, are not theoretically anterior to social conditions, but must be understood in terms of social contexts: in Marx's terms, history creates consciousness. Although Popper's book was a fierce attack on Marxism, in this matter he sided most definitely with Marx. Similarly, the social representation theorists are continuing the argument against Mill, thereby siding with Marx, and indeed Popper, over Mill. It is a central theme of the social representationists that psychological states are socially produced, for 'it is as though our psychology contained our sociology in a condensed form' (Moscovici, 1984b, p. 65). Therefore, any psychology, whether Mill's sensationalist psychology or modern information processing theory, which takes the individual as its basic unit, is misconceived. It is for this reason that

Moscovici's term 'the thinking society' is not a solecism, committing the 'group mind fallacy'. It is a deliberately argumentative phrase, to be directed against those psychologies, which only take notice of 'the thinking individual', or rather, as will be seen, of 'the unthinking individual'. Therefore, Moscovici argues that an analysis of psychological matters should reveal social phenomena.

According to Moscovici, social representations are the crucial factor in the social determination of psychological states: 'rather than motivations, aspirations, cognitive principles and other factors that are usually put forward, it is our representations which, in the last resort, determine our reactions, and their significance is, thus, that of an actual cause.' (Moscovici 1984b, p. 65). The representations are not individually produced replicas of perceptual data, but are themselves social creations and, as such, part of social reality. According to Abric (1984, p. 179), 'all representations must surely be called "social representations".' The discipline of social psychology should turn from being an individualist or biological science to become 'an anthropological and a historical science' (Moscovici 1984a, p. 948).

The static nature of social psychology

In one of his early papers on the topic of social representations, Moscovici (1963) contrasts the static approach of conventional attitude research with the more fluid approach of social representations. Public opinion research was, by and large, 'static and descriptive' (1963, p. 252), as researchers contented themselves with gathering information about the percentage of people favouring this or that position. No serious theoretical breakthrough could be expected from such an approach, in which the same methodology, that of the formal questionnaire, was applied time and time again, in order to acquire increasing mountains of data. The dislike of methodology dominating intellectual inquiry has led Moscovici (1985) to claim, in answer to critics, that it is a strength of the concept of social representation that it lacks a definition. However, his argument cannot be directed against definitions as such, for the 1963 article contained a definition: 'Social representation is defined as the elaborating of a social object by the community for the purpose of behaving and communicating' (Moscovici 1963, p. 251). The opposition is to the power of the operational definition, whose general acceptance turns social psychology from an intellectual inquiry to a mechanical fact-gathering inquiry.

 The opposition to the power of the operational definition stems from a belief that fixed instruments of measurement cannot properly tap social representations, which are themselves intrinsically fluid phenomena: 'What is most striking to the contemporary observer is their mobile and circulating character; in short, their plasticity' (1984b, p. 18). The social scientist should be seeking to examine how social representations are created and how they are transformed through usage. Subtle processes of communication must be examined, as Moscovici (1976) illustrated in his major study of the way that psychoanalytic concepts were transformed as they passed from the technical language of psychoanalysts to become the common property of everyday reality. Such transformations of meaning, and the way that the transformed, or re-presented, psychoanalytic concepts in turn transformed the meanings of other elements of common-sense, cannot be captured in the thick netting of the standard opinion questionnaire. Moscovici was not interested in the percentage of respondents who might declare that they 'strongly support' or 'tend to oppose' psychoanalysis: he was concerned with the continually fluctuating meanings of psychoanalytic terms. To use the pollster's measuring devices to understand these meanings would be like trying to entrap the morning mist in an elephant net. It is for this reason that some theorists have predicted that field research is liable to supplant experimentalism in the new social psychology of social representations (Farr 1985).

Unthinking image of the thinker

Social representation theorists hold that current social psychology not only fails to study the 'thinking society' because it ignores the social: it also fails to understand thinking. The individual subject in the social psychological theory is far from the flesh and blood thinker in real life. Psychological theories deny the reality of the thinking individual 'by declaring that our minds are little black boxes, contained within a vast black box, which simply receives information, words and thoughts, which are conditioned from the outside in order to turn them into gestures, judgements, opinions and so forth' (Moscovici 1984b, p. 15). The problem is not merely that psychologists are adopting an individualist perspective, but that they are viewing thinking in terms of pre-programming. The devaluation of thinking can occur equally from a social perspective, for sociological theories can envisage an ideological pre-programming. Moscovici (1984b, p. 15) claims that social theories of ideology, just as much as individual theories of psychology, can devalue the thinking society by

... maintaining that groups and individuals are always and completely under the sway of a dominant ideology which is produced and imposed by their social class, the State, the Church or the school, and that what they think and say only reflects such an ideology. In other words, it is maintained that they don't as a rule think, or produce anything original, on their own: they reproduce and, in turn, are reproduced.

Rhetorical approach

Billig (1987) has argued for a rhetorical approach to the study of social psychology. In so doing he has advocated the revival of classical rhetoric, especially those ideas which emphasize the importance of argumentation in social life. Such a rhetorical approach would follow the social representation theorists in all three strands of criticism, which were outlined in the previous section. As regards individualism, Billig (1987) stresses that a rhetorical approach must move from a monologic to a dialogic approach. Moreover, the rhetorical approach, like the social representational one, emphasizes the social content of culture. Moscovici (1973) suggests that a social representation corresponds to a 'system of values, ideas and practices' (p. xiii). It would be possible to draw a parallel between this conception of a social representation and the *sensus communis* (the shared sense of the community) which classical rhetoricians claimed to provide the basic content of oratory. Similarly, a rhetorical approach would oppose a methodologically-dominated social psychology, in which quantitative means dominate the ends of theory. Of course, an opposition to the *dominance* of quantitative methodology should not be equated with an opposition to using quantitative techniques *tout court*. Lastly, the criticism of the unthinking image of the thinker has been a main theme in the rhetorical critique of cognitive social psychology (Billig 1985, 1987). Moreover, this critique has been specifically extended to theories of ideology: Billig *et al.* (1988) have criticized theorists such as Althusser, Mannheim, and Berger and Luckmann for envisaging ideology as a monolithic system which constrains, and indeed prevents, thinking. Billig *et al.* suggest that such theories ignore the dilemmatic aspects of social life, and consequently fail to show how ideology can provide the elements of everyday thinking.

There is a further aspect of the social representation approach which suggests how much the new social psychology of social representations should include the topic of rhetoric. When theorists stress the fluidity of social representations, they point to the importance of communication in the genesis, maintenance, and transformation of representations. Moscovici (1984a) suggests that the act of communication is integral to social representations: the term 'representation' should be reserved 'for a special category of knowledge and beliefs, namely those that arise in ordinary communication and whose structure corresponds to this form of communication' (p. 952). It is through communication that knowledge is transformed and 'social representations generally come into being during transformations of this kind, whether by an intervention of the mass media or by the act of individuals' (p. 964). Jodelet (1984) also links communication to the nature of social representations: 'Social representations are modalities of practical thought oriented towards the communication, comprehension and mastery of the social, material and ideal environment' (p. 361).

Since rhetoric is involved in acts of communication, the social representation approach, by stressing the importance of communication, is implicitly recognizing the centrality of rhetoric for social psychology. Moreover, social representation theory can be interpreted as recognizing rhetoric's importance for the social psychology of thinking. Moscovici (1984*b*) points specifically to the importance of conversation in the 'thinking society', for it is through conversation that 'thinking is done out loud' (p. 21). Although the social representation approach links social representations to communication, and thinking to conversation, it has not specified which forms of communication and conversation might be particularly related to the transformation of the social representations of common-sense. It is at this point that the rhetorical approach can make its distinctive contribution, for rhetoric does not treat all forms of conversation or communication equally.

It is the argument which is of the greatest rhetorical interest, because rhetoricians, in seeking to persuade, are arguing for a point of view and countering the arguments of opponents. Thus, Billig (1987) points specifically to the importance of the argument for an understanding of thinking. Thinking may be achieved out loud through conversation, but not equally by any form of conversation. The polite discourse, in which smiling agreement and the repetition of stock phrases are the norm, is not productive of public thinking, for such conversations merely rehearse what is known previously. By contrast, in argumentative discourse there is the element of unpredictability, as socially shared common-sense opinions find themselves opposed, in a way which provides a model for individual, internal deliberation. Therefore, the social representation approach, which aims to explore the thinking society, might be directed towards paying special attention to the argumentative aspects of communication. As will be suggested, this may involve developing certain key aspects of social representation theory, so that they are directly addressed to argumentation in particular rather than to communication in general.

Anchoring

Moscovici (1985) has emphasized that there is a *theory* of social representations, over and above a general conceptual framework. If there is a theory, then it must refer principally to the notions about the genesis of social representations. Moscovici has highlighted 'the two processes that generate social representations' (1984*b*, p. 28), these two processes being anchoring and objectification. According to social representation theorists, both processes operate to make the unfamiliar seem familiar. According to Jodelet (1984), anchoring and objectification 'illuminate an important property of knowledge: the integration of novelty which appears as a basic function of social representations' (p. 367).

Each of the two processes will be considered separately, with anchoring being discussed in this section and objectification in the following one. The discussion of the processes will be from a rhetorical perspective, and it will be suggested that each process represents only half of an incomplete opposi-tional pair of processes. From a theoretical point of view, each needs to be complemented by the recognition of a counter-process. This is necessary, if the social representation approach is to accord theoretical significance to the argumentative aspects of rhetoric, thereby analysing the thinking society in terms of a dialectic between criticism and justification.

According to Moscovici (1984b), anchoring is both a process and a mech-anism. He writes that anchoring is 'the mechanism' which 'strives to *anchor* strange ideas, to reduce them to ordinary categories and images, to set them in a familiar context' (p. 29, emphasis in original). Moscovici goes on to des-cribe anchoring as a 'process which draws something foreign and disturbing that intrigues us into our particular system of categories and compares it to the paradigm of a category which we think to be suitable' (p. 29). Anchoring reduces the threat of the unfamiliar by providing familiar classifications and names: — things which are 'unclassified and unnamed are alien, non-existent and at the same time threatening' (p. 30). Thus, Moscovici claims that 'classi-fying and naming are two aspects of this anchoring of representations' (p. 35). All in all, anchoring permits 'the cognitive integration of the repre-sented object in the pre-existing system of thought' (Jodelet 1984, p. 371).

There is a *prima facie* similarity between these remarks about the opera-tion of anchoring and the ways that cognitive social psychologists talk about the operation of categorization and schemata. Cognitive theorists assume that it is a basic property of thought that information, especially novel infor-mation, must be categorized in terms of pre-existing schemata (Fiske and Taylor 1984; Mervis and Rosch 1981). It is assumed that individual stimuli are perceived in terms of the general category, in order to permit the smooth processing of information (for example Rosch 1978; Taylor and Crocker, 1981). However, the process of categorization involves cognitive bias. In particular, cognitive theorists have suggested that schemata, or categoriza-tion systems, necessarily influence the judgement of stimuli, so that there is a tendency to make prejudiced or stereotyped judgements (Hamilton 1981; Hamilton and Trolier 1986; Tajfel 1981; Wilder, 1981). The same sort of notions can be found in social representation theorists when they describe anchoring. For example, the assumption of smooth operation is expressed by Jodelet (1984), when she writes that 'anchoring, permitting the rapid evaluation of available information, authorises rapid conclusions' (p. 377). Similarly it is assumed that such smooth functioning inevitably produces bias and prejudice. This assumption is contained Moscovici's (1984b) des-criptions of anchoring, especially if 'prejudice' is interpreted literally as 'pre-judgement': 'anchoring . . . involves the priority of the verdict over the trial' in a way that 'fosters ready-made opinions and usually leads to over-hasty decisions' (p. 32).

Nevertheless, the social representation theorists claim that there are

essential differences between their treatment of the topic of categorization
and that shown by schemata theorists. Moscovici (1984*b*) claims that standard cognitive studies of categorization and classification 'fail to take into
account the substrata of such phenomena or to realise that they presuppose
a representation of beings, objects and events' (p. 30). For present purposes,
this critical claim can be noted, rather than evaluated. Less contentious, on
the other hand, is the claim that the social representation theorists are far
more alert than the cognitive theorists to the cultural aspects of categorization. The social representation theorists pay particular attention to the
content of classifications and stress that this content is socially shared (Farr
1985). Cognitive theorists sometimes give the impression that individuals on
their own create their schemata to avoid the burdens of stimulus-overload,
but, by contrast, the social representation theorists locate categories in social
groups or cultures. If categories bias the perceptions of individuals, these
biases have group origins and are part of a whole cultural set of meanings:
'The images, ideas and language shared by a given group always seem to
dictate the initial direction and expedient by which the group comes to terms
with the unfamiliar' (Moscovici 1984*b*, p. 26). The social representation
theorists stress that what is represented in a social representation is a social
object. Anchoring, therefore, draws the individual into the cultural traditions of the group, while at the same time it continues those traditions.
The individual, whose thinking is anchored in social representations, not
only reduces personal uncertainty, but also partakes of cultural traditions.
In this sense, representation is rooted 'in the life of groups' (Jodelet 1984,
p. 372).

   The first point to note about the concept of anchoring is that it is a universal concept (Billig 1988*b*). Some concepts in the social sciences are universal,
in that they refer to phenomena, which are presumed to be found in all forms
of society and in all historical epochs. Other concepts are particular, in that
they describe phenomena, which are particular to some social arrangements
but not all. The distinction is necessary, because it has been argued that
the social representation theorists have used the concept of social representation in both universal and particular ways. Sometimes social representation
theorists suggest that social representations are to be found in all societies
and sometimes they claim that social representations are a particularly
modern form of social knowledge. It is not necessary to document these
different uses of the concept of social representation here (see Billig 1988*b*,
for details). Nevertheless, it is clear that anchoring is conceived to be a general process, or mechanism: in all cultures the unfamiliar will be anchored
into familiar cultural patterns of meaning. Moscovici's comment that the
theory of social representations 'excludes the idea of thought or perception
which is without anchor' (1984*b*, p. 36) confirms that anchoring is a universal
phenomenon. Again, a parallel can be made with cognitive social psychol-

ogy, for cognitive theorists assume that the possession of schemata and the categorization of incoming stimuli also are universal.

The assumption of universality is also made by the rhetorical perspective, especially when it seeks to portray the general forms of argumentation. For example, Aristotle's *Topica*, in outlining the different forms of argumentative propositions, was making a universal thesis. Aristotle was not detailing the sorts of arguments which might appeal to Athenians or to Thracians, but he was seeking to portray the structures of all arguments. Similarly, if thinking is seen as a form of argumentation, then it is assumed that argumentation is universal. All societies will be arguing societies, in so far as they are thinking societies, although they might not argue, or think, about the same things or in quite the same way. Despite the differences between types and contents of arguments, the same basic question can be asked, as was posed in Aristotle's *Topica*: how is argument possible?

In answer to this question, a rhetorical approach stresses the importance of the faculty of negation (Billig 1986, 1987). The capacity to negate is seen to be a basic constituent of human thought, and without negation deliberation would be impossible. Humans might share with animals the ability to categorize stimuli. It might even be possible to teach some higher mammals to associate sounds with certain categorizations of stimuli. Yet, naming does not constitute the essence of thinking from a rhetorical point of view. Thinking involves acceptance and rejection, criticism and justification, and without negation none of this is possible. Cognitive psychologists, who concentrate upon the process of categorization, often seem to end up talking about unthinking routines, for thinking involves more than the thoughtless classification of stimuli (Billig 1985). It is for this reason that the social representation approach runs the risk of missing the essence of the thinking society, if it places too much emphasis upon the process of anchoring. The resulting image of the thinker will be of someone who timidly can do little more than absorb incoming information to a pre-existing network of meanings. In other words, it is an image of a person who avoids thought, rather than contributes to the thinking society.

In order to avoid the image of the unthinking society, or of the unthinking individual, it is necessary to view cognitive processes in terms of opposing pairs. This insight can be derived from Aristotle's *Topica*, which arranged propositional judgements in contrasting pairs, each of which was the negation of the other. If categorization, or anchoring, is seen as a fundamental form of thought, it is difficult to see how the faculty for negation can also be seen as a basic cognitive faculty unless there is an assumption of an equally basic, but opposing, form to categorization. Billig (1985) argues that linguistic categorization is impossible, unless the speaker can also particularize, for the very process of categorization also intrinsically involves the process of particularization, such that the two processes entail each other dialectically. It is possible to see the process of particularization as being just as basic as that of categorization, or, to use the terminology of Aristotle, to see judgements of quality to be just as basic as judgements of quantity. If this is accepted, then any categorizing judgement is potentially negatable, for what has been categorized could have been particularized, or treated as a special case. In this way, categorizations can be seen as potentially controversial — for the very faculty which enables us to categorize, also enables us to criticize categorizations by suggesting particularizations or alternative categorizations.

This basic notion can be applied to the social representational conception of anchoring. The metaphor of the anchor can be pursued. Not only can anchors be dropped, but they can also be hauled in. In fact, this is intrinsic to the skills of anchoring, for the same anchor cannot be continually dropped without be raised. Moreover, the ship's crew can assemble on the foredeck to debate the most suitable position of the anchor. Similarly, it is not a necessary feature of the unfamiliar that it is suddenly and automatically embedded in familiar structures. One might hypothesize that the unfamiliar is likely to be a focus of controversy. There will be arguments about how anchors should be dropped, and whether new anchors need to be fashioned in order to deal with the special properties of the unfamiliar seabed.

It is a feature of arguments that they often seem to turn into arguments about words (Billig 1987). From a rhetorical point of view, and indeed for understanding the thinking society, this is of crucial significance. It means that the unfamiliar is not painlessly anchored, but that the dilemma of how to anchor the unfamiliar can lead to a debate about the meanings of the categories into which the unfamiliar will be inserted. The thinking society does not merely anchor unfamiliar particulars into more general categories, but through the dialectic between particularization and categorization, and between justification and criticism, it can turn around on its own categories. It is by recognizing the tensions between categorization and particularization that the social representation approach can avoid slipping into the sort of cultural determinism from which it seeks to escape. In consequence, thinking should not be seen in terms of a single process in which an anchor is forever thrown into a familiar patch of sea by timid sailors; the anchor can also be hauled up so that the ship can sail adventurously onwards.

Objectification

The second process, or mechanism, by which social representations are generated is that of objectification. Like anchoring, objectification serves to make the unfamiliar familiar. It produces a 'domestication' of the unfamiliar, in a way that is 'far more active' than anchoring (Moscovici 1984b, p. 38). Moscovici describes the way that 'objectification saturates the idea of unfamiliarity with reality, turns it into the very essence of reality' (p. 38). In particular, objectification transforms abstract concepts into familiar, concrete experiences and, in this way, objectification effects the 'materialization of an abstraction' (p. 38). According to Farr (1984), it is through objectification that the 'invisible' becomes 'perceptible' (p. 386). Moscovici's (1976) classic study of psychoanalysis provides the prototypical example of a social representation theorist illustrating the process of objectification (see Jodelet 1984, pp. 367–71). The abstract and technical concepts of psychoanalysis changed their nature when they were translated into ordinary, everyday discourse. Concepts such as neurosis and the unconscious came to resemble material, perceptual concepts in their journey from abstract science to common-sensical thought. Having undergone such an objectified transformation, they became socially shared, and much changed, re-presentations of the original scientific concepts.

The process of objectification differs from that of anchoring in that it is not a universal process. Whereas social representation theorists might assert that unanchored thinking is an impossibility, non-objectified thoughts are quite possible. Objectified thoughts are particular types of thoughts, rather than objectification being a constituent property of all thinking. By contrast, social representation theorists sometimes seem to suggest that objectification is a necessary feature of social representations. Although the concept of social representation has not been used consistently in this respect, it has been suggested that social representations are only, or principally, to be found in modern consciousness. For example, Moscovici has described social representations as constituting a 'specifically modern social phenomenon' (1984a, pp. 952–3). He claims that they 'are in certain respects, specific to our society' (1984b, p. 23). In such comments, Moscovici distinguishes between modern social representations and the common-sense of earlier epochs.

If social representations are peculiar to modern society, then their distinguishing feature cannot reside in anchoring. As has been seen, anchoring is considered to be a universal feature of thought and, therefore, cannot be held to be peculiar to modern consciousness. On the other hand, objectification, if it is understood in terms of the materialization of abstract scientific concepts, is not a universal property of social thinking. The argument is that it is because modern common-sense is objectified, that it is different from pre-modern consciousness. Thus, Moscovici (1984b) declares that 'now common-sense is science made common' (p. 29). He continues (Moscovici 1984a, p. 953) by claiming that when we observe modern consciousness

. . . we can observe a proliferation of original systems of concepts and images, which are born and evolve under our very eyes. Most of them are scientific in origin. They fill our minds and our conversations, our mass media, popular books and political discourses. At the same time they determine our world view and our reactions to people and things.

Moscovici is assuming that scientifically-originated concepts are beginning to fill the modern mind, and that the modern thinking society is using these concepts as it converses out aloud. Billig (1988b) has drawn a distinction between objectified consciousness, which has transformed the abstract to the material, and transcendentalized consciousness, which transforms the material into the abstract. If modern society is said to be dominated by objectified consciousness, then a traditional religious society might, by the same token, be said to possess a predominantly transcendentalized consciousness. This point is made, in order to emphasize that social representation theorists see the process of objectification as a peculiarly modern process, whose importance is continually growing, as we are said to progress towards the 'coming era of social representations' (Moscovici 1982).

However, there is a danger in the way that social representation theory characterizes modern common-sense or, to be more precise, the modern replacement of common-sense. There is the danger that too homogeneous a picture is being painted: all thoughts are being seen to possess a similar character, in that the mechanism of objectification is dominating the contents of modern consciousness. If this line of argument is pushed too far, and indeed much further than it is being pushed by social representation theorists at present, then the theory of social representations might come to resemble those theories of ideology, which Moscovici has criticized. Theories of ideology present an image of the unthinking individual, not to mention the unthinking society, when they assume that ideologies are fully homogeneous schemata (Billig *et al.* 1988). If all thoughts are systematized, and made domestically tame, then there is little to think about. Similarly, if the theory of social representations was to concentrate upon showing the common character of the thoughts which fill the modern mind, it would run the risk of overlooking the contrary themes, and conflicting elements, which are necessary for argumentation and thereby for thought.

By contrast, the rhetorical perspective stresses that argumentation depends upon conflicting themes and, in particular, on conflicting themes in common-sense. It is because the contents of common-sense, or the commonplaces of common-sense, can be brought into opposition that rhetorical argument is possible (Billig 1987). The discussion about anchoring suggested that opposing forms of thought are necessary conditions for argumentation. Now it is suggested that opposing content is also necessary. Clearly if one is considering arguments between groups, the opposition can be between contents of different common-senses. However, if one is talking about the thinking society, one is talking about the thoughts, and arguments, within a group. For these to occur there must be oppositions within common-sense or within social representations.

In consequence, one need not suppose that the translation of psycho-analytic terms into contemporary common-sense has led to a conceptual homogenization, by which unfamiliar concepts have become objectified so as to be similar to the other ideas that fill contemporary consciousness. The psychoanalytic concepts, in entering contemporary mass conscious-ness, have become elements which can be used in ordinary argumentation. Notions about neurosis and complexes are to be found alongside other maxims, proverbs, and bits and pieces of everyday wisdom. Some of these bits and pieces might suggest that individuals are not in control of their destiny, as they suffer from complexes or unconsciously desire this or that. Others of the bits and pieces will suggest that people are quite responsible for their own actions and should not seek excuses, and so on. Edelman (1977) has analysed the contemporary discourse on poverty, and found a similar mixture of sympathetic and blaming themes. These can be considered as modern variants of the old rhetorical dialectic between the common-places of mercy and justice.

The psychoanalytic terms may have become elements in modern dilem-mas, as people converse about morality and immorality, freedom, and neces-sity. Nor are these dilemmas merely the result of a conflict between modern concepts (such as psychoanalytic ones) and the maxims of a much older, pre-modern common-sense. New contradictory pairs of themes can enter modern discourse. Enlightenment philosophy simultaneously gave rise to new notions of freedom and necessity, with the same philosophers simul-taneously declaring the virtues of freedom and the reality of materialist necessity (see, for example, these themes in the writings of the Ideologues: Billig 1982; Head 1985; and indeed the comments by Gramsci 1971, about Freud being the last of the Ideologues). Moreover, the heritage of enlighten-ment has entered into everyday discourse so that philosophy — perhaps but not necessarily objectified — can create the preconditions of everyday argu-mentation. There is no reason for supposing that the argumentation must rest at an objectified level, but that ordinary people can turn around on their concepts to argue about what is meant by 'freedom' or 'responsibility' (Billig et al. 1988). Similarly the twin themes of freedom and necessity are contained within Freud's great contribution to the enlightenment. The Freudian dream of psychoanalysis, that ego should triumph where id now reigns, itself expresses the conflicting themes of freedom and necessity, while wishfully hoping for an end to the conflict.

The foregoing is not intended to be a criticism per se of the notion of objectification. It might be objected that conflicting themes in common-sense can themselves be objectified themes. However, the point is that if one seeks to understand the thinking society one must start from the assumption that the cultural elements of the society, which permit thought, must be oppositional. To explain all in terms of a single mechanism of objectification would be to run the risk of blurring the oppositions. It would suggest that a single explanatory process could account for theme and counter-theme. On the other hand, the sense of opposition would be maintained if pairs of opposing mechanisms, such as objectification and transcendentalization, were retained theoretically. This is not to say that an account which leaned heavily upon a single mechanism would necessarily be inaccurate. Nevertheless, it might end in an emphasis which stressed the homogeneity of cultural content and thereby overlooked the essentially argumentative nature of the thinking society.

Attitudes and social representations

It is also possible to say a few words from a rhetorical perspective about the relations between the concept of social representation and that of attitude, and about the latter's possible contribution to the study of the thinking society. At present, some adherents of the social representation approach see an opposition between the two concepts. For example, Jaspars and Fraser (1984) and Farr (1985) suggest that the study of social representations should supplant the study of attitudes. The argument is that the study of attitudes has been static and concerned with individual differences. Researchers have typically investigated attitudes solely from the perspective of the individual, and have sought to discover what functions the attitude serves for the individual attitude-holder. Jaspars and Fraser (1984) suggest that this sort of research strategy ignores the socially-shared aspects of beliefs. They argue that within a population attitude holders might manifestly differ in their attitudes, yet they might share the same representation of the topic or issue on which they are holding the attitude. Traditional attitude research, which concentrates upon finding differences between subjects, ignores such socially-shared aspects: 'A much better understanding can be achieved if we go beyond the manifest responses which Ss provide in many attitude surveys and concern ourselves with the representations which are implicit in these responses' (Jaspars and Fraser 1984, p. 122).

At its simplest level, a change from studying attitudes to studying social representations would involve a move from the search for differences between respondents in a sample to the search for commonalities. The studies by Hagendoorn and Hraba (1987) and Hraba *et al.* (1988) are a case in point. These researchers have looked at expressions of social distance towards ethnic minorities, as expressed by the majority population in the Netherlands. Instead of looking for differences between respondents (for example, between the prejudiced and the non-prejudiced, or between middle-class and working-class respondents), the researchers were concerned to discover whether the sample as a whole tended to have shared responses to the different ethnic groups. Although the questionnaire might have been a very traditional one (a modified social distance scale), the statistical analysis was not. The usual psychological statistics, which are useful for discovering what divides populations, were replaced by tests of commonality. On the basis of discovering commonality across the population in the way that respondents tended to arrange ethnic groups, the researchers claimed that ethnic hierarchy was a social representation. Thus, the claim that a social representation existed was based upon the commonality of responses within the population.

In consequence, the switch from attitudes to social representations might involve a methodological switch. Instead of searching for differences between respondents and often proclaiming small differences to possess great theoretical, as well as statistical, significance, social representation researchers will concentrate upon shared characteristics. According to Jaspars and Fraser (1984) such a change will mean a return to the earlier traditions of attitudinal research from before the concept of attitude was individualized by Gordon Allport. Jaspars and Fraser point to a notable piece of early research in which attitude was discussed in group, rather than individual, terms. Thomas and Znaniecki (1918) used the term 'attitude' in a similar way to the modern concept of social representation. Their understanding of 'attitude' was not an individualized one, but was related to the existence of social groups. They were concerned with the attitudes shared by members of groups, and if they studied attitudinal differences these related to the differences between the beliefs of different social groups. As Jaspars and Fraser write, one major consequence of this view is 'that one should not expect a strong relationship between attitudes and within-group differences in behaviour, because attitudes differentiate primarily between groups and not between members of the same group' (1984, p. 116).

However, one cannot merely dismiss the concept of attitudes as used in modern social psychology and return to a group conception, which can be relabelled as a social representation. As Moscovici has stressed, the notion of social representation has been designed specifically to deal with social beliefs in contemporary society. In this respect, social representations differ from Durkheim's notion of the *conscience collective*, which referred specifically to the social beliefs of traditional societies and for which religion was 'the primary form' (Durkheim 1972, p. 241). In modern societies, attitudes possess a social reality of their own, for people are expected to possess and express attitudes. Hundreds of thousands of people have been stopped by pollsters and have willingly partaken in the modern ritual by which they 'give' their 'attitudes'. Even more have read with interest the results of the attitude surveys, which are so regularly published in the newspapers. The concept of 'attitude' has, in the era of the mass media, been translated from the technical vocabulary of portraiture to the mass vocabulary of social beliefs. Significantly, Thomas and Znaniecki were studying a traditional society, that of the Polish peasant, and attitudes in the modern sense were not part of that social reality. If social psychologists aim to study the sorts of beliefs which are held in modern society, it would be curious if they were to turn their back on the study of attitudes.

The problem for the social representation approach is not whether or not to discard the concept of attitude, but how to study simultaneously both the shared and non-shared aspects of modern beliefs. To study only the shared aspects would be to ignore the social reality of attitudes and the division of public opinion. On the other hand, studying only the non-shared aspects would tie the social representation approach to the traditions of opinion surveying and, as Jaspars and Fraser point out, it would ignore the underlying similarities between attitudinal opponents, including their sharing of the concept, or perhaps the social representation, of attitude itself. A rhetorical perspective may be able to recast the concept of attitude in a way that accords simultaneous reality to both shared and non-shared aspsects. The basic oratorical situation illustrates this duality. Two orators oppose each other on an issue and, as such, they may be said to express different stances or attitudes — yet they call upon common rhetorical traditions as they appeal to the common-sense of a common audience (Billig 1987). The rhetorical situation cannot be understood, either purely in terms of the different psychological characteristics of the opposing orators, or solely with reference to the common oratorical training and learnt common-places, which both orators have absorbed. Instead, the oratorical situation represents a complexity of shared and opposed meanings.

If attitudes are seen in terms of rhetoric, there is one immediate conceptual move that must be made. Attitudes must be studied in terms of their rhetorical context, and this means recognizing that attitudes are primarily stances in matters of public controversy. Thus, attitudes are not to be seen solely as individual properties of the attitude-holder. By recognizing the controversial aspect of attitudes, one is stressing their social nature, but it is a socially-shared nature which features non-shared, or controversial, aspects. One might assert that the context of public controversy is a necessary part of an attitude, so that one would not properly have an attitude on a topic which was not a matter of debate. Thus, in contemporary Western society, one might have an attitude about capital punishment, or the teaching of religion in schools, but one does not have attitudes about the roundness of the earth or the desirability of money. Public pollsters recognize that only attitudes on matters of controversy are worth eliciting. For example, the 1984 British Social Attitudes Survey, which is repeated annually, asked respondents 'How important or unimportant do you think that it is for Britain to have a monarchy?' The results revealed that 'attitudes to the monarchy are strongly in the direction of uncritical support among all social groups' and, consequently, 'this question clearly need not be repeated annually' (Young 1984, p. 30).

One might say that, from a rhetorical perspective, what were revealed in the survey were not attitudes at such, but the absence of attitudes. However, it must also be stated that, as regards the monarchy, public opinion is more complex than the British Social Attitudes Survey suggests, and the complexity has definite rhetorical, or argumentative, dimensions (Billig 1988a, 1988c). If the perception of controversy is a necessary part of an attitude, then one might equate the possession of an attitude with a willingness to express a stance in a matter of controversy. This has an important social psychological implication. An attitude is not merely an expression of the attitude-holder's viewpoint; it is also an implicit, or explicit, opposition to a counter-viewpoint. The supporter of capital punishment who answers the pollsters' questions is not merely expressing some inner motive for a 'just world' or 'authoritarian aggression', as individualized approaches might suggest (such as Altemeyer 1981; Lerner 1980): the supporter is also expressing a willingness to enter into controversy with those of opposing attitudes. In this way, an attitude is both a stance in favour of a position and a stance against the counter-position. Consequently, the attitude-holder is not an isolated social atom, but is joined argumentatively to a wider, socially-shared but socially-dividing, controversy (Billig 1986, 1987).

This implies that social psychologists might study attitudes by examining them in their argumentative context. One means of doing this would be to examine the topics and processes of discursive conversation where two or more people argue their points of view against each other. Instead of exploring attitudes by means of the single respondent in an interview, whether formal or informal, the researcher would be studying the unfolding of arguments in discussion groups. The respondents themselves would be rhetoricians counter-posing their pros against the cons of opponents and in this clash of opinions the researcher could examine both the formulation and expression of attitudinal thinking.

Nevertheless, it should not be assumed that such a direct argumentative clash is a necessary condition for observing the argumentative dimensions of attitudes in discourse. Interesting argumentative aspects can be observed when people, ostensibly sharing a common view, discuss a topic of controversy. Billig (1990) presents an analysis of a family discussing the issue of monarchy: all members of the family are pro-monarchists, yet still their presentation of opinions was structured argumentatively. Even when they were combining to recreate common-sense assumptions about the monarchy, the form of their discourse was argumentative, as they combined to 'take into account' the relevant factors. Each relevant factor to be taken into account qualified, and thereby argued against, the previous factor: it was good to have a monarchy but, of course, privilege was wrong, yet royalty shouldn't be too ordinary, but they shouldn't be too superior, and so on. All the participants of the discussion shared these themes of common-sense, which argumentatively were reproduced in discourse, and the participants were reproducing internal arguments as much as arguing between themselves. If in the discourse the members of the family could be said to have been reproducing the social representation of the monarchy, then this representation was argumentatively structured around contrary themes. As such, common-sense itself could be said to be argumentatively structured. The theoretical implication is that rhetoric is not a means for expression of thoughts which themselves are essentially non-rhetorical; instead, the structure and content of thinking within the thinking society is essentially rhetorical.

The qualitative examination of discourse from discussion groups may provide a means for examining the rhetorical nature of attitudes and common-sense. However, it is not the present intention to prescribe any methodology as being *the* correct methodology for a rhetorical analysis: it is important that methodology should be a tool to serve the interests of theory, rather than providing an activity which becomes its own end. For this reason, it seems more appropriate at the present stage to clarify theoretical points, so that the questions of theory will determine where, and how, researchers look for the rhetorical dimensions of thought. One particular set of theoretical concerns relates to the ways in which changes in rhetorical context will produce changes in the way that points of view are expressed. Attitudinal stances, which are taken to oppose a particular set of counter-attitudes, are likely to be altered as the context of controversy changes and a different set of counter-attitudes are to be counterposed. Under certain circumstances, attitude-holders might appear to change their position entirely, in order to 'take the side of the other', and to adopt the rhetoric of former opponents to deal with the new argumentative challenge (Billig 1987, 1988c).

Observation of arguments would also permit the sort of discourse analysis which could analyse the use of social representations in the expression of attitudes. In this respect, one might point to the similarity between the concept of social representation and the old rhetorical notion of 'commonplaces', which were the socially-shared values and maxims of a particular rhetorical community (Perelman and Olbrechts-Tyteca 1971). Rhetorical opponents, in outlining their opposition, draw upon socially-shared notions, or representations. Supporters of capital punishment might use the discourse of justice, while opponents draw upon the common-places of mercy. As Eiser and Ross (1977) have shown, some odd effects can result if supporters and opponents are artificially denied access to their natural store of rhetoric. Much of this discourse is shared between opposing camps, to the extent that both supporters and opponents recognize in general the need for both justice and mercy. One might say that, as they argue, they draw upon common representations, only to interpret and instantiate them differently. In consequence, opposing camps will frequently end up arguing about words and the 'real' meaning of justice and mercy (Billig 1987).

A rhetorical approach would fulfil the demands of the social representation theorists that the study of social beliefs should not be a static one. One would be accepting that attitudinal expressions are not individually fixed, but can alter as the context of controversy alters. This is particularly so because attitudinal holders share common-places or the representations of common-sense: the individual attitude-holder need not be locked into using one particular set of attitudinal discourse (Potter and Wetherell 1987). For example, liberal opponents of capital punishment may feel the need to modify their discourse should they suddenly be challenged by a rising anarchist movement, which challenges the legitimacy of all punishment. Suddenly the old argumentative discourse or attitudinal positions, which served so well to combat the attitudes of the traditional supporters of capital punishment, are no longer equipped to combat the fresh argumentative challenge. In this new debate, the old liberals might find themselves drawing upon the rhetoric of justice, just as forcefully as their former opponents had. Such a switch in rhetoric does not indicate an individual change of heart, but illustrates the extent to which representations, which can be used to divide rhetorical opponents in one controversial context, can nevertheless be shared.

A social-representation approach might well benefit from developing rhetorical themes, for the rhetorical approach suggests a way out of the theoretical opposition between socially-shared representations and unshared attitudes. On a more general level, it is vitally important that the social-representation approach does not jettison the topic of attitudes, in order to concentrate exclusively on what is consensually and uncontroversially shared in modern society. If it were to do this, the approach would never be able to fulfil its aim of studying the thinking society. The wholly consensual society would be a society not only without attitudes, but also devoid of argumentation and the controversy of thought. It is, of course, a society which has never existed, except perhaps in the imagination of social theorists and some dictators. By contrast, it is through the rhetorical and argumentative study of attitudes that the complexity of modern social representations might be revealed. The very social existence of attitudes represents the sort of argumentative activity which is a constituent property of the thinking society.

References

Abric, J. C. (1984). A theoretical and experimental approach to the study of social representations in a situation of interaction. In *Social representations*, (ed. R. Farr and S. Moscovici), pp. 169–84. Cambridge University Press.

Altemeyer, R.A. (1981). *Right-wing authoritarianism*. University of Manitoba Press.

Billig, M. (1982). *Ideology and social psychology*. Blackwell, Oxford.

Billig, M. (1985). Prejudice, categorization and particularization: from a perceptual to a rhetorical approach. *European Journal of Social Psychology*, **15**, 79–103.

Billig, M. (1986). *Thinking and arguing: an inaugural lecture*. Loughborough University.

Billig, M. (1987). *Arguing and thinking: a rhetorical approach to social psychology*. Cambridge University Press.

Billig, M. (1988a). Rhetorical and historical aspects of attitudes: the case of the British monarchy. *Philosophical Psychology*, **1**, 83–104.

Billig, M. (1988b). Social representation, anchoring and objectification: a rhetorical analysis. *Social Behaviour*, **3**, 1–16.

Billig, M. (1988c). Common-places of the British Royal Family: a rhetorical analysis of plain and argumentative sense. *Text*, **8**, 91–110.

Billig, M. (1990). Collective memory, ideology and the British Royal Family. In *Collective remembering*, (ed. D. Middleton and D. Edwards), pp. 60–80. Sage, London.

Billig, M., Condor, S., Edwards, D., Gane, M., Middleton, D., and Radley, A.R. (1988). *Ideological dilemmas*. Sage, London.

Durkheim, E. (1972). *Emile Durkheim: selected writings*, (ed. A. Giddens). Cambridge University Press.

Edelman, M. (1977). *Political language: words that succeed and policies that fail*. Academic Press, New York.

Eiser, J.R. (1986). *Social psychology*. Cambridge University Press.

Eiser, J.R. and Ross, M. (1977). Partisan language, immediacy and attitude change. *European Journal of Social Psychology*, **7**, 477–89.

Emler, N. (1987). Socio-moral development from the perspective of social representations. *Journal for the Theory of Social Behaviour*, **17**, 371–88.

Farr, R.M. (1984). Les représentations sociales. In *Psychologie sociale*, (ed. S. Moscovici), pp. 379–89. Presses Universitaires de France, Paris.

Farr, R.M. (1985). The social and collective nature of representations. Paper given at Social Beliefs Conference, Cambridge, March 1985.

Festinger, L. (1957). *A theory of cognitive dissonance*. Stanford University Press.

Fiske, S.T. and Taylor, S.E. (1984). *Social cognition*. Random House, New York.

Gramsci, A. (1971). *Prison notebooks*. Lawrence and Wishart, London.

Hagendoorn, L. and Hraba, J. (1987). Social distance toward Holland's minorities: discrimination amongst ethnic outgroups. *Ethnic and Racial Studies*, **10**, 317–33.

Hamilton, D.L. (1981). Stereotyping and intergroup behavior: some thoughts on the cognitive approach. In *Cognitive processes in stereotyping and intergroup behaviour*, (ed. D.L. Hamilton), pp. 115–44. Erlbaum, Hillsdale.

Hamilton, D.L. and Trolier, T.K. (1986). Stereotypes and stereotyping: an overview of the cognitive approach. In *Prejudice, discrimination and racism*, (ed. J.F. Dovidio and S.L. Gaertner), pp. 127–64. Academic Press, Orlando.

Head, B.W. (1985). *Ideology and social science: Destutt de Tracy and French liberalism*. Martinus Nijhoff, Dordrecht.

Hraba, J., Hagendoorn, L., and Hagendoorn, R. (1988). Social distance in the Netherlands: the ethnic hierarchy as a social representation. Unpublished MS, University of Nijmegen.

Jaspars, J.M.F. and Fraser, C. (1984). Attitudes and social representations. In *Social Representations*, (ed. R.M. Farr and S. Moscovici), pp. 101-24. Presses Universitaires de France, Paris.

Jodelet, D. (1984). Représentation sociale: phénomènes, concept et théorie. In *Psychologie sociale*, (ed. S. Moscovici), pp. 357-78. Presses Universitaires de France, Paris.

Lerner, M.J. (1980). *The belief in a just world*. Plenum Press, New York.

McGuire, W.J. (1986). The vicissitudes of attitudes and similar representational constructs in twentieth century psychology. *European Journal of Social Psychology*, 16, 89-130.

McKinlay, A. and Potter, J. (1987). Social representations: a conceptual critique. *Journal for the Theory of Social Behaviour*, 17, 471-88.

Mervis, C.B. and Rosch, E. (1981). Categorisation of natural objects. *Annual Review of Psychology*, 32, 89-115.

Moscovici, S. (1963). Attitudes and opinions. *Annual Review of Psychology*, 14, 231-60.

Moscovici, S. (1973). Foreword. In *Health and illness*, (ed. C. Herzlich). Academic Press, London.

Moscovici, S. (1976). *La psychanalyse, son image et son public*. Presses Universitaires de France, Paris.

Moscovici, S. (1982). The coming era of representations. In *Cognitive approaches to social behaviour*, (ed. J.P. Codol and J.J. Leyens), pp. 115-50. Nijhoff, The Hague.

Moscovici, S. (1984a). The myth of the lonely paradigm. *Social Research*, 51, 939-67.

Moscovici, S. (1984b). The phenomenon of social representations. In *Social representations*, (ed R. Farr and S. Moscovici), pp. 3-70. Cambridge University Press.

Moscovici, S. (1985). Comment on Potter and Litton. *British Journal of Social Psychology*, 24, 91-2.

Moscovici, S. (1987). Answers and questions. *Journal for the Theory of Social Behaviour*, 17, 513-29.

Parker, I. (1987). Social representations: social psychology's (mis)use of sociology. *Journal for the Theory of Social Behaviour*, 17, 447-70.

Perelman, C. and Olbrechts-Tyteca, L. (1971). *The new rhetoric*. University of Notre Dame, Indiana.

Popper, K. (1960). *The open society and its enemies*. Routledge and Kegan Paul, London.

Potter, J. and Litton, I. (1985). Some problems underlying the theory of social representations. *British Journal of Social Psychology*, 24, 81-90.

Potter, J. and Wetherell, M. (1987). *Discourse and social psychology*. Sage, London.

Rosch, E. (1978). Principles of categorization. In *Cognition and categorization*, (ed. E. Rosch and B. Lloyd), pp. 28-48. Erlbaum, New Jersey.

Tajfel, H. (1981). *Human groups and social categories*. Cambridge University Press.

Taylor, S.E. and Crocker, J. (1981). Schematic bases of social information processing. In *Social cognition*, (ed. E.T. Higgins, C.P. Herman, and M.P. Zanna), pp. 84-134. Erlbaum, New Jersey.

Thomas, W.I. and Znaniecki, F. (1918). *The Polish peasant in Europe and America*. Badger, Boston.

Wilder, D. A. (1981). Perceiving persons as a group: categorization and intergroup relations. In *Cognitive processes in stereotyping and intergroup behaviour*, (ed. D. L. Hamilton), pp. 213–58. Erlbaum, Hillsdale.

Young, K. (1984). Political attitudes. In *British social attitudes: the 1984 report*, (ed. R. Jowell and C. Airey), pp. 11–46. Gower, Aldershot.

3 Studying social representations in children: just old wine in new bottles?

Nicholas Emler and Jocelyne Ohana

A cautionary tale

The research programme on which this chapter draws had its beginnings in a visit by the first author in 1981 to the Laboratoire de Psychologie Sociale of the Ecole des Hautes Etudes en Sciences Sociales in Paris, directed by Serge Moscovici. The former was interested in learning more about the social representations approach as it had been developed by Serge Moscovici and his colleagues in France. The latter, having learned something about Kohlberg's work on moral reasoning, was interested in applying the social-representations approach to children's development of moral judgements. The series of studies which emerged from this collaboration has examined the relationship between moral judgement and social representations.

The problem that struck us at the outset, however, was how our work was going to differ at all from the legions of already-published inquiries into children's socio-cognitive development. Others had interviewed children and discovered stages in the construction of cognitive structures. What method were we going to use now to discover something completely different, children's social representations? Would we ask children different questions, or ask the questions in a different kind of way? Would we do something completely different to bring forth data from the mouths of infants? Or would the novelty occur at the data-analysis stage? Was there a, 'social representations analyser' that one could wave over the data and make the social representations spring forth?

The first author knew that people in France, working with Moscovici, had been studying social representations for some time. He hoped during his stay in Paris to learn this new alchemy, to sit at the feet of the masters and acquire powerful new tools with which he could go forth and extract social representations from every nook and cranny. After all, there were plenty of examples of this happening to others — students went to Piaget to learn the *méthode clinique* and were then able to discover cognitive structures in every aspect of children's knowledge. They had gone to Kohlberg at Harvard to learn the system for analysing structure in moral reasoning which they would then be able to apply to any fragment of moral argument—an unrealized promise. They went to Paul Ekman to learn FAST and so make new discoveries in the field of emotions. They went to IPAR at Berkeley and learned personality-test construction and were then able to discover all manner of personality dimensions, as in earlier decades they had learned psychoanalysis, Rorschach interpretation, or TAT analysis and so been able to discover the structure of motives. So, surely, there was a method waiting in Paris, something that could push back intellectual frontiers and turn a base academic career into ground-breaking publications and golden achievements.

However, in Paris the mystery only deepened. Where was the social-representations analyser—not in any of the cupboards in the LEPS lab (once the room had been found). The laboratory, it turned out, was not a room full of equipment used to pursue this mysterious practice called European Social Psychology; it was, if anything, a concept, perhaps even a social representation! So, if the analysis of social representations was not equipment, was it a system? If so, where was the operating manual? Not on the shelves. Yet, before his eyes, *chercheurs* were looking at data and pulling out social representations, like rabbits from a hat. How was this conjuring trick performed?

His pursuit of this enigma led him deeper into Europe, the night train to Bologna on the eve of Christmas 1983. There, in a smoke-filled room, were brought together most of the European scholars who had apparently mastered this mystery—and they were gathered there to talk about methods of research in the study of social representations. At last he was going to find out how the trick was done.

But, of course, they fooled him again. As so often happens when people gather together to discuss methods, they end up talking about findings. They have just completed some research, the results look interesting, and they want to tell someone. They regard their methods as far less interesting. But, he thought, they'll still have to give something away, say something about how they did the research. His puzzlement only deepened. Evidently a large number of different methods had been used—rating scales, observation, account gathering, children's drawings, content analysis of published texts, questionnaires, semi-structured interviews, unstructured interviews . . . Most of the methods were familiar—in other contexts. They were the kind of procedures that others had used to study attitudes, beliefs, stereotypes, or socio-cognitive development.

He came to realize, of course, that his quest for a method was naive and misconceived; this 'Holy Grail' simply did not exist. But, like all such journeys of discovery, there were lessons to be learned. The first was that he had repeated a mistake others had made—and doubtless will make again—to suppose the only thing that lies between the scholar and the discovery of new truths is the absence of a method. This pursuit of enlightenment through methodology is illusory. If he had been wrong, quite possibly so had anyone who had gone to Harvard or Geneva or Berkeley expecting to learn no more than a method.

The second lesson was that much of the research which has been produced on social representations could indeed be little more than a relabelling exercise. Students of attitudes, stereotypes, or cognitive development might quite legitimately ask What are you doing that is different from us? Are you not simply applying the label "social representation" where we have used other terms — "attitudes", "beliefs", "stereotypes", and "cognitive structures"? In truth are you not studying the same phenomena we have been studying for years, but just calling them something different?, We would not say this is true of all research produced under the social-representation heading, but certainly of some.

The third lesson is that research cannot be method-driven alone; it should first and foremost be theory-driven. If one really wants to know how to study social representations one must to go back to the theory of social representation. This chapter is an attempt to show how a distinctive research strategy does emerge out of the theory. To this end we shall need to consider, if only briefly, a bit of the more recent history of enquiries into children's social development.

Problems of prior colonization

Up until the mid-sixties, the analysis of social development across childhood was the province of two kinds of psychological theory, psychoanalysis and behaviourism. The former asked questions about the structure of motives and sought answers in the quality and style of parent–child relations (for example Sears *et al.* 1957; Hoffman 1970). The latter asked questions about the origins of social and anti-social habits of behaviour and sought answers first in terms of general principles of learning (Aronfreed 1968; Eysenck 1964), supposedly as applicable to children as to other conditionable animals, and then in terms of the behavioural examples or models present in the child's environment (Bandura and Walters 1959). Social development was, in effect, socialization. It was the process whereby children come to resemble the adult members of their society, whether in character, motives, values, beliefs, or action tendencies. Within ten years, the diffusion of Piagetian ideas into English-language psychology had completely transformed the picture. By the mid-seventies the premise from which almost all students of social development began was that individuals think about their experience of social life and that this is the key to everything else. Neither children nor adults are simply, as psychoanalysis had it, creatures at the whim of unconscious or irrational inner compulsions. Nor, as behaviourism had it, are they biological machines reproducing acquired behavioural routines or automated responses to stimuli. On the contrary, they make choices and judgements, based on inferences and deductions. Therefore, if you wish to understand why people behave or feel as they do you must first understand why they think as they do. Actions and reactions arise from the intellectual interpretations persons make of circumstances; they arise from the way people think. Of course, the Piagetian revolution did not simply replace an interest in behaviour, motivation, or affect with an interest in cognitive process. It also established a particular view about the 'what' and 'why' of development itself.

It would be impossible to summarize in a few lines the fruits of all this endeavour, but one can one begin to see the dilemma presented in writing about children's social representations. In so far as we are concerned with moral judgement and social knowledge, this intellectual territory is already thoroughly colonized. Moreover, this prior colonization is well defended by a wealth of evidence apparently entirely consistent with its claims. Any student of this approach would surely say 'all our evidence indicates successive qualitative changes in children's social knowledge over age, and none of our evidence indicates any variations, whether in the structure of this knowledge or the sequence in which it is constructed, that could be attributed to culture. Both structures and sequences are under all social conditions the same.'

Furthermore, the precise methods that cognitive developmentalists use to generate data are indistinguishable from our own. How could we show, if at all, that we were studying children's social representations and not their cognitive development? This question can, of course, be turned around: what is to say that the constructivists have not been studying social representations all along? Indeed, is there really any difference between the two enterprises? And if there is not, are we just pouring old wine into new bottles?

Representations—individual or social?

The social-representations perspective does offer an analysis of social cognition at variance with cognitive developmental theory on a number of fundamental points of theory (Emler 1987). But the greatest difficulty would appear to be presented by an empirical claim. Jaspars and Fraser (1984) note that representations can be social in at least three senses, in that they are representations of some aspect of the social world, socially shared, and social in origin. For us, the third sense is the most important but this would seem to be an indefensible position if constructivists are correct in their claim that no social influences on the development of knowledge have been demonstrated.

Before attacking this crucial point of difference, let us consider the area of apparent agreement, namely that social knowledge is knowledge about the social environment. Work in the cognitive—developmental tradition has gradually extended and elaborated a definition of this environment. In the earliest research, it is no more than other people, undifferentiated and interchangeable. It subsequently became other people differentiated in terms of knowledge, age, gender, nationality, wealth, occupation, and societal role. Ultimately it has come to encompass different kinds of social rules, relationships, social activities such as politics and commerce, and institutions such as government and the law.

Our own work in this area reflects a conviction that gaps remain in these views about what constitutes the domain of social knowledge, and the gaps are there partly because psychology has traditionally been unsophisticated about social theory. Cognitive-developmental work typically begins with some aspect of adult social knowledge and asks 'what has to happen over the course of childhood to reach this point?' But when researchers have considered what the social environment is like to inhabit, what kinds of experience it presents to its occupants, and what its adult occupants 'know' to be true, they have most frequently consulted their own common-sense. There are few grounds for confidence that this will invariably be a reliable guide or a sufficient substitute for a social theory, and yet there are almost no references to the corpus of work on the nature of society contained in the sociological, anthropological, political-science, or social-psychological literatures.

Any attempt to analyse children's social knowledge must be part of a larger process which includes the construction of a theory of society. This might seem wildly ambitious but we do not claim instant success, and nor do we need to. It is sufficient to unite our enterprise with the broader work of social-theory construction and to recognize that hypotheses about children's social knowledge and its development are also hypotheses about the nature of society. Moreover, we can and should take advantage of the considerable work that has already been accomplished in the realm of social theory. Our views about those aspects of social knowledge deserving examination derive from this work. There are four aspects in particular:

1. Knowledge concerning how people can and should behave, which means in large part representations of social role performances, or representations of prototypes for various social roles.

2. Knowledge relating to institutionalized social practices, such as commercial or wage–labour relations. These first two reflect the view that participation in contemporary society is participation in a system of interlocking and more or less formal organizational structures. Obviously organizational theory and particularly Weber's (1947) analysis of bureacracy is a major influence here.

3. Knowledge relating to social controversies. This reflects an oppositional rather than a consensus view of society (compare Dahrendorf 1959), the idea that conflict is endemic and inherent in society and that there is ceaseless competition between powerful elites and minority interests for the intellectual allegiance of the majority. Notable exponents of this view in psychology include Billig (1986) and Moscovici (1976), though it also builds on notions of competitive social categories (Tajfel 1981).

4. Knowledge relating to the particularities of reputations and relationships. This derives from recent arguments in sociology and social anthropology about the survival of community in contemporary society, and the primacy of personal relationships between acquainted individuals as the interface between the person and the social order (for example Boissevain 1974; Fischer 1981; Mitchell 1969; Wellman 1979).

This, then, defines a kind of research agenda for the social-representations approach to social knowledge, though it is also one within which most previous work on socio-cognitive development can be located — for we believe it is more appropriately interpreted in these than in cognitive-developmental terms.

We have completed some work on the first agenda item. This includes studies of children's representations of the teacher as a prototypical institutional role, of institutional and non-institutional responsibilities, of relationships among children and between children and adults, and of hygiene standards (for example Calvert 1987; Emler *et al.* 1987). We would also place most of the moral judgement literature under this heading.

Regarding the second, we have carried out studies of representations of institutionalized inequalities embodied in the occupational structure of society (Dickinson 1986; Emler and Dickinson 1985; Emler and Luce l986). Under this heading we would also place Furth's (1978) and Jahoda's (1979) work on commercial transactions, and research into the development of political and legal concepts.

As yet, there has been little work relating to the third heading, representations of social controversies. A possible model for this, however, is research on representations among adults of the moral orientations of competing political categories (Emler *et al.* 1983; Reicher and Emler 1985).

So far as the fourth area is concerned, there is at present almost no empirical work, and we are only beginning to speculate about reputations as social representations (for example Emler 1987, 1990).

A theory-driven research strategy

Few would now dispute the constructivist claim that people think and even reason about their experience of the world. What is at issue is what people think and why they think it. Constructivists have defended their own position by arguing that the alternative is simply implausible. This alternative, as they present it, is 'societalism' (Gibbs and Schnell 1985), the proposition that society transmits arbitrary, culturally-relative, non-rational beliefs to its new members, children, who are the passive and compliant recipients of these beliefs. As Gibbs and Schnell note, this is a misleading caricature of the theoretical alternative to constructivism, but it has succeeded because it contains a grain of truth. It is in error, however, in suggesting that this is the only possible alternative. The theory of social representations provides a third alternative, we believe more plausible than either of the others.

This theory (compare Jodelet 1984; Moscovici 1961, 1982, 1984) emphasizes the content, and not just the structure, of thinking. It emphasizes the communicated character of thought — people do not just have reasons for their views or actions, they state reasons. It also emphasizes the socially-constructed and socially-sustained character of social knowledge: independent individuals do not construct knowledge, individuals in groups and as groups construct knowledge. We believe these points of difference between the theory of social representations and the theory of cognitive development provide the essential guides to research strategy. These can be encapsulated as the four Cs — communication, content, culture, and community.

Communication

Social representations are *communicated* ideas. The idea that language plays some part in the child's social development is peculiarly muted in psychology. One might have imagined that contructivism would have made the role of language central in this process. After all, it made conversation, or interrogation, the basic research instrument. Those interested in children's understanding of social phenomena or reasoning about social problems almost of necessity find themselves studying only children who can absorb and respond in kind to verbally-transmitted information, and the reports of this kind of research will often contain transcripts of these conversations. The evidence is contained in the words children utter, where previously it had been found in their behavioural responses.

However, it turns out that constructivists had in mind a different role for language; that role is largely in the mind. Language was treated as an instrument of private thought more than as a means of communication, or of sharing thought, and in the research process language was essentially a means for discovering the process of thought: cognition was, above all, internal mental activity. Children construct internal cognitive structures which allow them to generate interpretations of each experience they encounter. Hence, in this view, moral judgement is a process of, for example, making internal decisions as to whether one approves or disapproves of particular actions, how one should react to injuries received, or whether one should obey a particular rule on a particular occasion. Researchers have directed their energies towards discovering the nature of the decision processes and the ways in which they are organized in children's heads. Researchers have asked: 'What is the structure or mental organization underlying this process?' What children say about their judgements and the reasons they express are treated as clues to the internal mental process, means of access to the phenomena of interest, which are the cognitive structures in children's minds.

The theory of social representation offers a very different view of cognitive activity. People do not merely have reasons, they also give reasons. They do not simply think, they seek to share their thoughts. Where constructivists regard cognition as the internal generator of action, the social-representations perspective treats cognition as action, but action in the form of publicized, expressed, communicated representations. From this perspective, thoughts only have significance or existence as shared (and therefore communicated) ideas and images. Hence, the means by which they are communicated and shared become important, for they must be understood in some form by those who share them.The imperative of communication itself impinges on and reshapes ideas in making them into social representations. Piaget (1928), it should be recalled, discussed intellectual development in terms of the socialization of thought. He proposed that the internal coherence of thought depends on specifically social experiences, namely being confronted by others demanding justifications for judgements and opinions. But, if communication can encourage a complexity in thought which it would not achieve by itself, it can also enforce simplification. Ideas that enter the domain of public discourse may of necessity be simplified to meet the requirements of this form of exchange.

This brings us to a crucial difference between the respective research strategies of constructivism and social representation. Constructivists dissect children's utterances to discover an underlying mental structure in much the same way that chemists might examine the photographic plates produced in X-ray crystallography to discover the structure of molecules; or, closer to home, in the way that clinical psychologists once claimed that non-verbal behaviour provided them with clues to unconscious motives (Weiner *et al.* 1972). These are signs given off that there is something underlying. For constructivists, the vocabulary children use to express their judgements and give their reasons has never been particularly important in itself; what matters is what is revealed about the underlying structures which organize thought.

For the theory of social representations, utterances are not signs given off but signals given, intentional communicative acts. Since the words are being shared it is important to study the words themselves, the precise vocabularly and grammar children use to express their thoughts. Social representations are to be found at this level and not at some level of abstract structure discernible only to the trained eye of the developmental psychologist.

We have now begun to examine children's social representations in this way, in an initial study looking at the language children use in talking about issues of rules and responsibilities in school. Thus, Ohana (1986) has shown that children attending experimental schools in the Paris region, when compared to children attending more traditional schools in the area, talk about these matters in quite distinctive ways.

Children in the traditional schools represent the school's functioning as articulated around a rigid hierarchy. At the bottom is the child, followed by the teacher, then the head-teacher 'who governs the school', and then the inspector, 'the director who is above the head-mistress' (trad. 10-year-old). Social relations are based on obedience to formal or statutory authority. 'If the mistress says you must do it, you must do it' (trad. 11-year-old). Children assert the necessity of obeying rules: 'You cannot disobey the rules . . . you don't have the right.' (trad. 8-year-old); 'If that is the rule, it's obvious you can't do anything else' (trad. 10-year-old). They characterize teacher–pupil relations in authoritarian terms: 'A child cannot contradict the mistress; in relation to him she is always right.' (trad. 8-year-old); 'The mistress is in charge; the children can't tell her who she should help most; the mistress has the right to do what she wants.' (trad. 11-year-old).

Children in the experimental schools represent authority in terms of a hierarchical network with several levels; it involves dependence and the necessity of obedience on the part of those at the bottom in relation to those higher up. However, also present is representation of a capacity to bring pressure to bear and exert influence in the upward direction. Thus, in a situation in which a teacher refuses to let a child take a book from the school library: 'If he really wants the book, the mistress will give it to him and if not he can go and complain to the head teacher if he wants, he can go and tell his parents who would go and complain to the head.' (exp. 8-year-old).

Social relations appear to be organized in terms of *respect* for authority. 'The mistress must respect the law of the school; we respect it. We don't have the right to leave the school and not before the bell rings at 4.30. We respect it . . . because something might happen to us . . . it could even stop the school. Those who don't respect it are dressed down because we don't want it [the school] to be finished, or else the school would have to pay big fines., (exp. 10-year-old). These children also represented the functioning of the school and the transactions taking place within it as founded on a social *consensus* achieved through discussion and negotiation. Thus one child says: 'The head, when he has something to say, it's necessary that everyone agrees because if he is the only person in the school who agrees, it wouldn't work.' (exp. 8-year-old); another child represents resolution of conflicts in terms of discussion: 'If we don't share this opinion at all, we talk about it.' (exp. 10-year-old); yet another says 'What's good here is that the teachers, before deciding, always ask the children's advice and if we are against it we try to discuss it.' (exp. 10-year-old).

Among these children, the model of decision-making in the school and the class room is the majority vote: 'In the class we all take the decisions together; we suggest something and then we see what is the best, and then we vote.' (exp. 9-year-old). 'It's always the majority that counts, it's like when one is President . . . it's true that there are very [weak] majorities, ten against nine; well, then it is necessary to discuss and take the nine into consideration.' (exp. 11-year-old).

Although this is a brief example from a preliminary and somewhat unsystematic analysis of the data, and an example in which the original words and phrases have been translated into another language, we hope it gives something of the flavour of our point.

Content

Social representations are structured content. Cognitive developmental research has been driven by a problem-solving model of thought. Where behaviourism or psychoanalysis might have implied that socialized beings proceed through life directed by an internal gyroscope, operating according to a set of behavioural instructions sufficient for all occasions, constructivists assume that life is full of intellectual puzzles and choice points. Reflexes, habits, and rules will not do; each new situation requires thought, and individuals solve these problems by drawing upon the inner intellectual resources they have each developed. They literally reason their way to solutions. How better, then, to study these resources than by presenting individual children with further problems and observing the solutions their mentalities produce?

In the study of intellectual development, this has been the method of choice since Binet and Simon (1905), as in two of the most infamous puzzles in developmental psychology: 'Is there more liquid in this container?', and 'Was Heinz wrong to steal the drug?' The task of developmental psychology has become the description of the intellectual resources available at each stage of life to solve such problems.

There are several difficulties with this model: (i) it requires a straightforward distinction between cognitive structure, which refers to the problem-solving process, and cognitive content, which refers to its results; (ii) it fails to deal with the knowledge-based character of human problem-solving. (iii) it is applied to a domain in which it is not evident that an absolute distinction is possible between right and wrong answers; (iv) It probably misrepresents the way in which problems are solved; (v) and it does not recognize the extent to which society provides solutions and not problems.

The latter three difficulties will be considered in relation to our third and fourth Cs, culture and community.

The structure–content distinction

Constructivists regard this distinction as fundamental to their research strategy, for their theories are about form, not content (for example Furth 1978; Kohlberg 1976). One can think of instances when what is form is obvious enough. For example, Inhelder and Piaget (1958) describe the proportionality schema as a set of logical relations; these correspond to the physical operations that can be performed on a balance. The same logic (or structure) also underlies other cases. For example, Hook and Cook (1979) observe that it is contained in the equity formula for the distribution of rewards in accordance with inputs. It is also the principle underlying unit pricing of goods by supermarkets. But even the different cases introduce important modifications to this structure; for example, proportionality describes a necessary relation between the effects of weight and length in Inhelder and Piaget's balance problem but an entirely optional relation between work and wages.

In other cases, what is content and what is structure is even less obvious. Our suspicion is that there is no useful way of studying one without the other; there are few instances of pure form without content, and no content lacks form or structure. Moreover, the domain of human experience to which purely logical operations are applicable is probably quite limited (Billig 1986).

Note that we are not arguing that the content of social knowledge is not structured, suggesting that it is arbitrary, or denying that content exists at different levels, as for example in attitudes (or evaluative judgements) versus an underlying belief structure on which these judgements may draw. But, at no level is there any structure which can be specified without also referring to its content.

A related issue here concerns the logical versus psychological character of certain distinctions. Cognitive-developmental research often distinguishes between the descriptions children give and their explanations, and between their explanations and their judgements. Thus, logically, a question about what kind of work doctors do is distinct from one about why their pay is higher than that of other professions, and this latter question is distinct from one about whether it is right that this difference exists. But, as we have found, children often treat the questions as interchangeable. Description, explanation, and justification interpenetrate in their expressed views, which requires that we reconsider the kind of cognitive phenomenon revealed when children are asked questions of these kinds.

The truth, perhaps, is that they are not drawing on interrelated principles to decode answers according to their logical type and so generate answers

based on a logical classification of evidence: they are drawing on powerful cultural myths in which the purpose of description is justification, that
is, it is ideological. Descriptions of social phenomena are not simply dis-
interested factual observations. Constructivism appears to be based on a
quasi-scientific model of knowledge: individuals describe (represent) objects,
events, or processes to themselves in a spirit of dispassionate scholarly
inquiry — as a step towards understanding how the world works. The contrary view is that (i) knowledge (description) is not built up by direct observation but substantially provided by the human community in which one is
embedded, and (ii) it is provided for a purpose, the fundamental purpose
being justification. If we understand this, we can understand why description, explanation, and justification have no discrete boundaries in common-
sense or lay as opposed to scientific discourse. We can begin to understand
that all social knowledge is an answer not to the question 'what is this?', or
even 'why is this?', but 'should it be this and not something else?'

Knowledge-based judgement

We can begin to see the answer to this once we recognize the knowledge-
based character of problem solving. To take a simple and familiar case from
the moral judgement literature, what is going on cognitively when children
make a judgement about the culpability of a character whose actions result
in some damage or harm to others (compare Piaget 1932)? The stock answer
is that, at some point in development, children begin to apply the criterion
of intention; they ask 'Did the actor intend the consequences or not?' This
is supposedly a more rational principle than that of consequence ('How
much damage or injury was caused?'), on the grounds that people can be held
responsible only for what they intend because they have control only over
their intentions.

There are a number of possible objections to this idea: that the 'rationality'
of the principle depends on a socially-constructed notion of accidents, that
this is a philosophical position, a Judaeo-Christian notion of responsibility
which is ultimately no more rational than others, or that it is an ideological
position to prioritize intention over avoidable harm as the criterion of
culpability. Let us, however, concentrate on a more general point, the constructivist assumption that such cognitive processes operate on self-evident
facts. In studies of children's moral judgements, the 'facts' might be of the
kind: 'A large/small amount of injury results from an action' and 'The actor
intended/did not intend this result'. There is direct, unproblematic access to
these facts. The cognitive process is one of noticing these facts and applying
to them some principle which accords them differing weights. This principle
can be described in very general terms, for example: intentions are more
important than consequences.

We are labouring the point but the point is crucial: Constructivism treats judgement as a knowledge-free process. Moral judgements involve process-ing the direct factual evidence of specific cases in accordance with abstract principles. Social-representations theory assumes that this evidence is also normally processed in terms of knowledge or beliefs that are social in origin. That is, when children or adults make normal or real life judgements, these invoke or derive from all kinds of beliefs about the people involved. Moral judgements thus involve three components, not two: the facts of a case as understood, general principles applied to these, and knowledge already held by the individual and perceived as relevant. It is in this sense that we argue that moral judgements are a function of social representations as well as abstract moral principles, though the principles are also social in origin.

The knowledge and the principles together form theories about the social world. Thus, the theories people hold consist of beliefs (policemen are honest; Robert is greedy and selfish; doctors make a greater contribution to society than bus drivers) and socio-moral hypotheses or principles (intended harm is more reprehensible than foreseeable but unintended harm; officials should act impartially; rewards should be proportional to contributions). Neither can sensibly be considered without the other, though this is precisely what the formalism of cognitive-developmental theory encourages – it dis-cusses only the hypotheses. Here, intentionality and equity are hypotheses; the beliefs which invariably provide the context for these hypotheses are omitted. Knowledge in the form of beliefs has been almost completely ignored in the cognitive-developmental literature. It is regarded as uninteresting, unproblematic, or superficial. It does, of course, occasionally intrude into the data but when this happens it is redefined as form or dismissed as irrele-vant 'noise'.

Yet, of course, what people know or believe cannot be taken for granted; it is problematic. We still know next to nothing about the ways in which children come by this knowledge, let alone what it consists of, how it is organized, or how it is deployed in socio-cognitive processes such as moral judgement (the 'socio-' here emphasizes the view that these are public, communicative acts and not private mental events)

Judgements, then, are normally a function of prior beliefs as well as direct perceptions, but the normality of this is concealed by a research strategy which presents children with simplified, hypothetical cases so lacking in contextual detail that little remains to invoke social representations. So, there is a further methodological lessson here: if children's social representa-tions are to be examined, it is desirable to elicit as far as possible their views about the familiar, and not the abstract or hypothetical.

Culture

Social representations reflect an intellectual process at a cultural level and on a historical time scale. Cognitive-developmental theory is concerned with intellectual events which occur purely at the level of individuals and in the space of a few years. In Piaget's case it deals with the way in which each child discovers for itself principles of causality, conservation, or logical classification. It describes how, within fifteen years or so individual children construct the capacity for systematic hypothetico-deductive thought. Our position is not just that this does not apply to some other forms of knowledge; it is not even a sensible interpretation of the causal, conservation, logical-classification, or hypothetico-deductive knowledge which children display at different ages.

Let us again remind ourselves of the thinking that informs the constructivist position here. As an account of social development, its theoretical adversaries were seen to be psychoanalysis, learning theory, and functionalist theories in sociology and anthropology. These positions shared the assumption that beliefs are arbitrary, or at least that the reasons people become committed to them have nothing to do with recognizing their truth-value. If people believe that misfortunes arise from witchcraft, this is because the psychological and social mechanisms which produce beliefs in individuals are insensitive to the truth value of those beliefs. The same mechanisms can transmit any belief, true or false. A process of conditioning could generate the response 'five' as the habitual response to the stimulus. 'What is the sum of two plus two?' just as readily and in exactly the same way as it could produce the response 'four'. Conformity to majority opinion could lead individuals to believe that the world is flat or that the world is spherical.

Since we 'know' that one answer is right and the other wrong, in the arithmetical case at least, constructivists argue that these theories are insufficient to account for the nature of our knowledge or how we come by it. They might also add that it is unlikely that we learn the answer to every problem of addition by any mechanical learning process, simply because there are too many individual answers to learn. Instead, we learn a method for generating answers to all conceivable cases (just as we learn principles according to which words are combined to produce meaningful utterances, and this allows us to produce, or indeed comprehend, an infinite number of utterances).

There are three kinds of error in this line of argument. The first is to accept that there is no alternative to two rather extreme positions, one inhabited by constructivists, the other *necessarily* by all their theoretical opponents: either knowledge is not arbitrary and is therefore constructed independently by individuals, or knowledge is acquired by social transmission and is therefore arbitrary. A third position, perhaps also Piaget's true position, is possible: knowledge constructed independently by individuals is inclined to be arbitrary; any non-arbitrariness it possesses derives from the discipline of sharing thought with others. Only collective processes can produce non-arbitrary beliefs, though they do not invariably do so.

The second error has been to expand the importance in human affairs of 'knowing how' at the expense of 'Knowing that'. Constructivism in its purest form, Piaget's theory of logico-mathematical structures, is about a mental technique, a deductive problem-solving process. Having discovered the principle of multiplication, a child can apply its rules to any new instance and, in theory, arrive at the correct answer. However, the range of experience to which this kind of know-how is applied may actually be quite small. Most of the technical knowledge of which humanity makes use involves non-obvious connections discovered by a very mundane intellectual process, trial and error (Humphreys 1976). In Piaget's classic study of hypothetico-deductive thought, some children discover which combination of chemicals will produce a certain colour when mixed together (Inhelder and Piaget 1958, pp. 107–22). They do so by setting up and testing a logically-systematic set of hypotheses. We can be sure that the procedures for making coffee or soufflés could never have been discovered in this way. Piaget took a case in which the possibilities were finite and very limited and, one might add, dependent on the evolution of chemistry as a corpus of knowledge over several centuries, without which this limited set of possibilities could not have been defined and presented to children in the first place.

Most of the knowledge in which we share, not only could not have been discovered deductively, but also does not involve precise truths. Two plus two equals precisely four, and absolutely nothing else, but a variety of actions will produce a tolerable cup of coffee. As March and Simon (1958) have pointed out in another context, humans may be intendedly rational but they are more often 'satisficers' than they are optimizers, settling for solutions that are 'good enough' given the impracticality and perhaps impossibility of identifying ones which are perfect.

At the level of social practices, the possibility of identifying perfect solutions is even more remote. It is even more improbable that individuals exercising their independent intellects, however vast (Durkheim 1887), could deduce for themselves the greater logic of one set of arrangements over another, yet we are asked to suppose that children do precisely this (Nisan 1984; Gold *et al.* 1984). Rather, each of us is confronted with the imperfect, though far from arbitrary, solutions embodied in our culture — but we are not the blind prisoners of these solutions. We will argue about their merits and disadvantages as every previous generation has done, and so contribute to the process that created them (Billig 1986). MacIntyre (1981) talking about practices and traditions, makes a similar point:

A practice involves standards of excellence . . . To enter into a practice is to accept the authority of those standards and the inadequacy of my own performance as judged by them. Practices of course . . . have a history: games, sciences and arts all have histories. Thus the standards themselves are not immune from criticism, but nonetheless we cannot be initiated into a practice without accepting the authority of the best standards realised so far (p. 190).

and later:

. . . all reasoning takes place with the context of some traditional mode of thought, transcending through criticism and invention the limitations of what has hitherto been reasoned in that tradition; this is as true of modern physics as of medieval logic. Moreover when a tradition is in good order it is always partially constituted by an argument about the goods the pursuit of which gives to that tradition its particular point and purpose.

So when an institution—a university say, or a farm or a hospital—is the bearer of a tradition of practice or practices, its common life will be partly, but in a centrally important way, constituted by a continuous argument as to what a university is or ought to be or what good farming is or what good medicine is (p. 222).

A third error is to assume that mathematical knowledge or hypothetico-deductive thought are spontaneous discoveries in the course of ten to fifteen years of intellectual development from birth. On the contrary, these kinds of knowledge reflect over 2000 years of cultural endeavour. They are collective achievements and there is no inconsistency between their rationality and their social origins. Nor is there any between their social origins and the fact that they may be complex and difficult to penetrate or assimilate. Fifteen years is perhaps what it takes on average for contemporary society to construct these complex cognitive systems in new members.

To take another example, children have told us (for example Calvert 1987), and apparently Turiel (1983), that cleanliness is desirable because it reduces the risk of infection. This is an objective, non-arbitrary connection, but it is not, as Turiel implies, a discovery made directly by children themselves. Given that the discovery took many hundreds of years for medicine to make, we ought to be a little surprised if children spontaneously arrived at the same conclusion after only a few years of life. It is surely more plausible that they have assimilated a dominant interpretation within the culture to which they belong, an interpretation which owes its origins precisely to the development in medicine of a germ theory of disease.

The message here is that, in studying social knowledge, a vital piece of equipment in one's methodological tool kit is a bit of historical perspective. One may then be more inclined to recognize what are products of the collective history of culture and what the direct intellectual discoveries of individuals.

Community

Knowledge as social representation is knowledge that has a social existence and location. The implication of our foregoing argument is that children do not acquire particular interpretations of social reality, or come to advocate moral standards, simply because these are objective or rational ways of thinking or judging that would compel the commitment of any individual with sufficient intellectual powers. Children can only come to express these notions to the extent that these are currently employed and acknowledged ways of thinking — and that means talking — about the world within the community to which these children belong.

This recalls the second of Jaspars and Fraser's (1984) three senses of the 'socialness' of representations: these are ideas that are shared. Cognitive developmentalists do not dispute that social knowledge is shared, but this is sharing in the sense of 'have in common', not 'have distributed or disseminated among themselves'. If many eight-year-olds share the same view of moral obligations, this does not reflect any social process; it is because they have arrived at this point in development through the independent exercise of the same mental processes. This kind of agreement is actually taken as evidence for the operation of cognitive universals in developmental psychology.

Constructivism implies that each child is faced anew with the task of making sense of the world and starts from scratch. It does not allow that cultures may be systematized ways of ordering life, solving problems, and explaining the world, which are presented to the child. But if our alternative scenario is correct, it raises three important issues. First, it argues that development entails the emergence of self-conscious ignorance or, in other terms, awareness of the social distribution of knowledge, that is, recognizing that the community of which one is a part contains knowledge, and that it contains more than oneself. There may also be other inequalities or specializations within the community, and perhaps what is distinctive about the modern world is consciousness of knowledge *beyond* one's immediate community. But, the more basic point is that children's knowledge is not merely defined by what they know about things, it is also defined by what they know about knowledge. This is not meta-cognition in Flavell's (1985) sense, but knowledge of their own ignorance as a relative state; that is, it means knowing that others do know what one does not. Second, it implies that children do not interact directly with the objects of experience but with socially-constructed representations of that experience. Third, it is a claim that knowledge development must be a social and not merely a cognitive process; it must involve the transmission of knowledge, not just its construction by individual children.

From this follows a basic premise of the theory of social representations: social representations of the world may be different in different communities (Moscovici 1984). One therefore needs to study communities. Psychologists have never been sufficiently interested in sampling issues: one human being is much like another, a representative of the species *Homo sapiens*, exhibiting species-specific cognitive characteristics (Flavell and Ross 1981), and that is all that matters.

There is a clear implication here for research strategy: sample from different communities, and be sure that they *are* communities (not just contrasting
social categories), and different. This has been our general approach and we
find differences in representations that cannot simply be attributed to
developmental differences.

This may not take things very far but it is none the less a vital step in establishing the legitimacy of social-representations theory. Cognitive developmentalists will ask 'If there are social influences on knowledge, if knowledge
differs from one cultural group or community to another, why have years
of research failed to pick these up?' The simple answer is that researchers
have not been especially interested in looking for them, but there are several
reasons why such differences may have gone unnoticed: lack of historical
perspective, ignorance of differences, failure to notice the knowledge-based
character of judgement, interpreting differences as developmental, failure to
ask the right question, and ignoring quantitative differences.

Lack of historical perspective

As already observed, without sufficient historical perspective one is not
likely to notice the relativity of currently widespread beliefs. We have
already considered the instance of hygiene rules. To take another example,
preference for certain forms of procedural justice may seem rational and
logically defensible (Demetriou and Charitides 1986; Gold *et al.* 1984), but
in different times and places other very dissimilar procedures have seemed
equally sensible and rational. Armed combat was once regarded as a reasonable way to resolve disputes: it was thought to be a way of submitting the
argument to the judgement of God. In another century, witchcraft trials
were held to be equally reasonable procedures for settling questions of guilt
and innocence.

Differences have been ignored

A notable example of this tendency is the contemporary presentation of
Piaget's (1932) moral judgement research, particularly his findings concerning retributive justice. All children supposedly proceed from the view that
it is right to retaliate directly against others to the view that it is wrong, and
this is a consequence only of their developing rationality as social problem
solvers. But this is not at all what Piaget's own data show. These indicate that
boys were far more likely than girls to favour retaliation in kind and that this
belief was still predominant amongst the oldest children Piaget questioned.
Some years later, Durkin (1961) claimed that a belief in retaliation is abandoned much earlier by both boys and girls. Is it not possible that these findings reflect the values of quite different cultures, Switzerland in the 1920s
versus America in the 1950s?

In our own research on children's views about retaliation, we compared children in Scotland and France, children at different ages (six, eight, and ten years), children in working- and middle-class communities, and children at different kinds of school (traditional and experimental). These children offered various remedies for a victim of an injustice, including discussion with the culprit to resolve the situation, appeal to authority, direct action (recover one's property by force if necessary), and punitive action or physical retaliation. The proportions recommending direct or punitive action showed no changes with age, but the French children were more enthusiastic about direct action than the Scottish. Children's views also clearly reflected their social class backgrounds — children from working-class backgrounds were significantly more likely to recommend direct or punitive action.

We believe that an interpretation consistent with these findings is not that each child constructs increasingly rational, internally-consistent solutions to this kind of problem, but rather that each community contains various recommendations for response to a common occurrence, being victimized. In different communities, perhaps as a consequence of historically-shared experiences, certain of these solutions are more strongly endorsed than others. Thus, for example, the experience of the working class may well be that authorities have seldom responded sympathetically to their grievances and so direct action is the only effective remedy open to them (see also Black 1983; Emler and Reicher 1987).

Failure to notice the knowledge-based character of judgement

The knowledge or beliefs about the world on which judgements draw will itself be culturally variable. We found (Emler *et al.* 1987) that children's judgements about the actions of teachers drew upon beliefs about the nature of the teacher's role and the teacher's responsibilities in that role. Both French and Scottish children asserted that teachers' personal preferences should not influence the way they discharge their professional duties, but the French and Scottish children had different expectations about how teachers behave in practice, for example, in rewarding effort versus success: the French children believed that teachers are more influenced by whether pupils are successful than by whether they try hard. While Scottish children were inclined to believe that teachers were bound to comply with superior orders, French children believed that these orders could be disgarded by teachers if they conflicted with the requirements of fairness.

To take another example (Emler and Luce 1985) we found that American children, as compared to Scottish children, had different beliefs about what doctors do to deserve their higher income as compared to various other occupational groups. Where the Scottish children emphasized how hard they worked, the American children made reference to their investment in education. This example also illustrates the next point.

Interpreting differences as developmental

In the developmental literature on distributive justice, there is broad agreement that belief in a strictly-equal division of resources gives way with age to a belief in distribution according to some standard of relative deservingness, whether bases on effort or contribution—the equity principle (Damon 1978; Hook and Cook 1979; Enright *et al.* 1980, 1981; Nisan 1984), or on relative need (Damon 1978; Piaget 1932; Siegal 1981).

Occasional social-class differences have been reported, with working-class children more likely to endorse parity or strict equality (for example Enright *et al.* 1981). In these cases, researchers have assumed that working-class children simply lag behind their middle-class peers in the development of more rational distribution principles. Similar interpretations have been made about the findings from developmental studies of perceptions and judgements concerning social inequalities. The common finding is that older children are more likely than young children to regard inequalities in wealth as justified, normally by differential contributions to society (for example Baldus and Tribe 1978; Connell 1977; Cummings and Taebel 1978; Leahy 1983). In other words, in matters of social justice, children appear naturally inclined to become equity theorists.

However, we found that when somewhat different questions were asked, clear social-class differences did emerge (Emler and Dickinson 1985; Emler and Luce 1985). We asked children about the earnings of people in different occupations and about the fairness of the differentials they perceived. Most children agreed that the differentials were fair, and this tendency was unrelated to class background. We also asked whether it would be preferable to equalize incomes. This produced both age and class differences. This suggestion was more likely to be rejected by the older children (the age range was 6–12 years) and by the middle-class children.

A cognitive-developmental view of these findings would be that working-class children lag behind middle-class children in their development of a concept of equity. Our interpretation is rather different (Emler and Dickinson 1985). Equity is part of a powerful social myth within the culture we studied. In effect, it is part of an explanation and justification for inequalities. Among the middle class (more likely to be the beneficiaries of equity), this myth is more extensively developed and their members are more fully committed to it.

Consistent with this interpretation were two other social-class differences. Middle-class children gave significantly more explanations and justifications for inequalities. They also possessed a much more realistic representation of the scale of these inequalities, as well of as their consequences.

This leads to an important observation. Not all differences between communities or social groups will take the form of possessing one kind of belief rather than another. In some matters the differences will be of degree, for knowledge, like wealth, is unequally distributed in society. Knowledge about the socio-economic and class structure of society is distributed among people in terms of their own social-class position. Children growing up in the middle class have more differentiated representations of inequalities, more extensive justifications for them, and are more committed to them.

Our findings are also consistent with the idea that society provides solutions and arguments for solutions, as much as it provides problems to be solved. The cognitive-developmental version of equity theory asks one to believe that children examine inputs (contributions) and then calculate what the rewards should be, ultimately according to the principle: rewards should be proportional to inputs (Hook and Cook 1979). So, in the case of earnings in different occupations, they examine the relative contributions, determine outcomes, and then agree that the status quo is consistent with their conclusions.

This is hardly credible. There is virtually no way in which inputs could be quantified to meet the requirements of the equity formula. It is surely more plausible that the status quo represented by established income inequalities is supported by various socially-disseminated arguments, and that children reiterate the arguments that have currency in their respective communities. In the case of incomes, society presents children with solutions in terms of existing differentials and arguments for these in terms of relative contributions. Different societies present different solutions or different arguments or both.

Nothing in the equity formula specifies which contributions are to be regarded as relevant to outcomes. So, if equity theory predicts that children will eventually prefer incomes to be distributed according to relative contributions, it does not predict which contributions they will invoke, yet this is all-important. As Dickinson (1986) has shown, the nature of the justifications (the contributions regarded as relevant) shifts with the nature of the comparison. For one kind of comparison, a child might mention differences of responsibility, for another kind differences in social contribution, and for another kind differences in skill or training required. Moreover, across cultures different contributions are introduced to justify the same inequalities, as noted above. It is hard to see how independent processes of intellectual development, untouched by culturally-supported myths, could produce these differences.

Recently, some researchers have reported cultural differences in the emphasis on equity (Nisan 1984; Mann et al. 1985), differences which suggest that support for equity as a distributive principle has as much to do with a cultural emphasis on competition as with the individual child's age or level of intellectual sophistication (Emler 1991).

Another difference commonly regarded as developmental is commitment to principled as compared to conventional morality (Kohlberg 1976). This commitment varies as a function of educational level (Rest and Thoma 1985) and culture (Snarey 1985). Our own evidence indicates that it may be even more directly a function of political identity (Emler *et al.* 1983; Emler 1990; Reicher and Emler 1985). This particular case raises another issue.

Failure to ask the right question

Cognitive developmentalists commonly ask about children's understanding of a general principle. For example, they may ask 'At what age does the child understand the general principles underlying social rules?' (for example Piaget 1932). They discover that by the age of about eleven years, children recognize that rules are the products of mutual agreements and can be modified on this same basis. However, the relevant question may not be 'Can the rules be changed?', but 'Who has the power to change them in a particular context?' We found, for example, that children were increasingly likely to believe that individual teachers were *not* able to change school rules (Emler *et al.* 1987). Another example of the limitations of past practice has been the tendency to ask children what *they personally* believe, yet our knowledge of the social world includes knowledge about what other people and groups believe, and this in turn shapes our own intellectual and moral commitments.That is, our beliefs reflect the way in which we locate ourselves in an ideological space that we occupy with others. To return to the case of conventional and principled moral beliefs, we asked people what beliefs they thought other types of people held (Emler *et al.* 1983). We found very clear representations of the types of moral beliefs held by people of contrasting political persuasions. It may be that the basic level at which moral beliefs are structured is not, as Kohlberg suggested, specific moral theories corresponding to his stages, but an ideological space which contains these various 'theories' as contrasting positions. People then locate their own commitments within what they represent to be the range of options available.

It would be interesting to extend this work to children, much as Yussen (1976) has done in eliciting children's representations of the moral theories of policemen and philosophers.

Ignoring quantitative differences

The constructivist tradition has fostered the view that only qualitative changes in social cognition matter, thus only qualitative cognitive differences between groups would count as demonstrations that social influences do operate. But, it is not evident to us that this is a sensible or even a meaningful restriction. The intention/consequence distinction mentioned above has been shown to be a matter of the relative weight that older and younger children attach to these two criteria, not an absolute choice of one versus the other (Weiner and Peter 1973). Similar quantitative differences have frequently been observed between social groups. To take just one example, Hamilton and Sanders (1983) have shown that Japanese and American adults differ in the relative weights they attach to deeds versus role obligations in their moral judgements.

Summary and concluding observations

In this chapter, we have argued that there are no technical tricks which will give researchers access to the social representations of children. Instead, the most important methodological guide is a theory of the phenomenon under consideration. As a perspective on social knowledge and its development in childhood, the theory of social representation provides four sets of pointers to research strategy.

First, it directs attention to the fact that social representations are communicated ideas and images. One should therefore study the precise terms in which these ideas are communicated. Undoubtedly the most important of these is the language, literally the words, that children use to express their knowledge.

Second, social representations are representations *of* something. They are defined by their content, even if that content is structured. It is therefore necessary to study the content of children's knowledge, and not merely to try to identify general structures which might be typical of a variety of contents.

Third, social representations are socially constructed and sustained forms of knowledge. What individual children know, they know as members of groups, communities, societies, or cultures. It is important to appreciate the timescale over which the social process of constructing knowledge occurs, and to recognize when children are revealing their assimilation of collective intellectual achievements and when they are demonstrating spontaneous intellectual discoveries of their own.

Fourth, social representations are shared and as such are properties of social groups and not isolated individuals. It is important, therefore, to recognize the kinds of social groups to which children belong, the relations between these groups and others, and the ways in which groups and relations, between them, shape representations. This has several implications for methodology, the most basic of which is the need to sample from, and to compare, truly distinct social groups. Another is to recognize that the views expressed by individual children are samples of the representations contained within the groups to which they belong. In a sense, therefore, the group and not just the individual is a proper unit of analysis. A third implication is the desirability of identifying topics, issues, contexts, or circumstances which form an important part of the experience of a social group. Or, in other terms, children should be asked about what is familiar and significant and therefore likely already to be represented in their collective discourse. Finally, children may have knowledge about the differences between social groups themselves: it could be as relevant to ask children what others believe as to ask about their own beliefs.

This chapter has been substantially an exercise in 'product differentiation'. Just as advocates of a constructivist interpretation of social development began by making their case through a critique of psychoanalysis and behaviourism, so we have found it necessary to subject constructivism to critical scrutiny. We have argued that it does not tell all there is to know about the development of social knowledge in childhood. In particular we believe it is limited by its problem-solving emphasis, its stress on logic, and its assumption that the child's intellect independently constructs itself.

In the longer run, overcoming this cognitive individualism will require a closer relationship between developmental and social psychologies, for the development of social knowledge is as much a matter of the former as of the latter psychology. We have in the event said little about the processes by which children acquire knowledge in this chapter, but we believe that the constructivist's repertoire of cognitive mechanisms — equilibration, cognitive conflict, and so on — can provide only half the story. The other half will be provided by social processes, such as social influence, intergroup relations, socio-cognitive conflict, and social comparison.

Acknowledgements

We would like to acknowledge the involvement of many people in the research and development of the ideas on which this chapter draws. These include Sandra Calvert, Julie Dickinson, Terry Luce, Stephen Reicher, and Kerry Stace. A particular debt of gratitude is owed to Serge Moscovici for his key role in developing and guiding this research, and we are also grateful for his comments on an earlier draft of this chapter. The research was supported by the ESRC and CNRS through the Franco-British programme in the form of grants Nos HG 11/24/11 and 95 5219 respectively.

References

Aronfreed, J. (1968). *Conscience and conduct*. Academic Press, New York.
Baldus, B. and Tribe, V. (1978). The development of perceptions and evaluations of social inequality among public school children. *Canadian Review of Sociology and Anthropology*, **15**, 50-60.
Bandura, A. and Walters, R.M. (1959). *Adolescent aggression*. Ronald Press, New York.
Billig, M. (1986). *Arguing and thinking*. Cambridge University Press.
Binet, A. and Simon, T. (1905). Methods nouvelles pour le diagnostic du niveau intellectuel des anormaux. *L'Annee Psychologique*, **11**, 191-244.
Black, D. (1983). Crime as social control. *American Sociological Review*, **48**, 34-45.

Boissevain, J. (1974). *Friends of friends: networks, manipulators and coalitions.* Blackwell, Oxford.

Calvert, S. (1987). Children's representations of hygiene. Unpublished doctoral thesis, University of Dundee.

Connell, R.W. (1977). *Ruling class, ruling culture.* Cambridge University Press, Melbourne.

Cummings, S. and Taebel, D. (1978). The economic socialisation of children: a neo-Marxist analysis. *Social Problems,* **26**, 198–210.

Dahrendorf, R. (1959). *Class and class conflict in an industrial society.* Routledge and Kegan Paul, London.

Damon W. (1978). *The social world of the child.* Jossey Bass, San Francisco.

Demetriou, A. and Charitides, L. (1986). The adolescent's construction of procedural justice as a function of age, formal thought and sex. *International Journal of Psychology,* **21**, 333–53.

Dickinson, J. (1986). Children's social representations of inequality. Unpublished doctoral thesis, University of Dundee.

Durkheim, E. (1887). La science positive de la morale en Allemagne, *Revue Philosophique,* **14**.

Durkin, D. (1961). The specificity of children's moral judgements. *Journal of Genetic Psychology,* **98**, 3–14.

Emler, N. (1987). Socio-moral development from the perspective of social representations. *Journal for the Theory of Social Behaviour,* **17**, 371–88.

Emler, N. (1990). A social psychology of reputation. In *European Review of social psychology,* Vol. 1, (ed. W. Stroebe and M. Hewstone), pp. 179–93. Wiley, Chichester.

Emler, N. (1991). What do children care about justice: culture and cognitive development in the development of a sense of justice. In *Social justice in human relations,* Vol. 1 (ed. H. Steensma and R. Vermunt), pp. 123–50. Pergamon, New York.

Emler, N. and Dickinson, J. (1985). Children's representations of economic inequalities: the effects of social class. *British Journal of Developmental Psychology,* **3**, 191–8.

Emler, N. and Luce, T. (1985). Social class background and perception of occupation-related income differences in middle childhood. Unpublished MS, University of Dundee.

Emler, N. and Reicher, S. (1987). Orientations to institutional authority in adolescence. *Journal of Moral Education,* **16**, 108–16.

Emler, N., Renwick, S., and Malone, B. (1983). The relationship between moral reasoning and political orientation. *Journal of Personality and Social Psychology,* **45**, 1073–80.

Emler, N, Ohana, J., and Moscovici, S. (1987). Children's beliefs about institution roles: a cross-national study of representations of the teacher's role. *British Journal of Educational Psychology,* **57**, 26–37.

Enright, R., Enright, W., Manheim, L., and Harris, B.E. (1980). Distributive justice development and social class. *Developmental Psychology,* **16**, 555–63.

Enright, R., Enright, W., and Lapsley, D. (1981). Distributive justice development and social class: a replication study. *Developmental Psychology,* **17**, 826–32.

Eysenck, H. (1964). *Crime and personality.* Routledge and Kegan Paul, London.

Fischer, C. (1981). *To dwell among friends: personal networks in town and city.* University of Chicago Press.

Flavell, J. (1985). *Cognitive development*, (2nd edn). Prentice Hall, Englewood Cliffs, NJ.

Flavell, J. and Ross, L. (1981). *Social cognitive development: frontiers and possible futures*. Cambridge University Press.

Furth, H. (1978). Young children's understanding of society. In *Issues in childhood social development*, (ed. H. McGurk), pp. 228–56. Methuen, London.

Gibbs, J. and Schnell, S. (1985). Moral development 'versus' socialization: a critique. *American Psychologist*, **40**, 1071–60.

Gold, L. J., Darley, J. M., Hilton, J. L., and Zanna, M. P. (1984). Children's perceptions of procedural justice. *Child Development*, **55**, 1752–19.

Hamilton, V. L. and Sanders, J. (1983). Universals in judging wrongdoings: Japanese and Americans compared. *American Sociological Review*, **48**, 199–211.

Hoffman, M. (1970). Conscience, personality and socialization techniques. *Human Development*, **13**, 90–126.

Hook, J. and Cook, T. (1979). Equity theory and the cognitive ability of children. *Psychological Bulletin*, **86**, 429–45.

Humphreys, N. (1976). The social function of the intellect. In *Growing points in ethology*, (ed. P. P. G. Bateson and R. A. Hinde), pp. 303–17. Cambridge University Press.

Inhelder, B. and Piaget, J. (1958). *The growth of logical thinking from childhood to adolescence*. Basic Books, New York.

Jahoda, G. (1979). The construction of economic reality by some Glaswegian school children. *European Journal of Social Psychology*, **9**, 115–27.

Jaspars, J. and Fraser, C. (1984). Attitudes and social representations. In *Social representations*, (ed. R. Farr and S. Moscovici), pp. 101–23. Cambridge University Press.

Jodelet, D. (1984). Representations sociales: phenomenes, concept et theorie. In *Psychologie sociale*, (ed. S. Moscovici), pp. 357–78. Presses Unversitiaires de France, Paris.

Kohlberg, L. (1976). Moral stages and moralization: the cognitive developmental approach. In *Moral development and behaviour: theory, research and social issues*, (ed. T. Lickona), pp. 31–69. Holt, Rinehart and Winston, New York.

Leahy, R. (1983). Development of the conception of economic inequality: II. Explanations, justifications, and concepts of social mobility and change. *Developmental Psychology*, **19**, 111–25.

MacIntyre, A. (1981). *After virtue: A study in moral theory*. Duckworth, London.

Mitchell, J. C. (1969). *Social networks in urban situations*. Manchester University Press.

Mann, L., Radford, M., and Kanagawa, C. (1985). Cross-cultural differences in children's use of decision rules: a comparison between Japan and Australia. *Journal of Personality and Social Psychology*, **49**, 1557–64.

March, J. G. and Simon, H. A. (1958). *Organizations*. Wiley, New York.

Moscovici, S. (1961). *La psychanalyse: son image et son public*. Presses Universitaires de France, Paris.

Moscovici, S. (1976). *Social influence and social change*. Academic Press, London.

Moscovici, S. (1982). The coming era of representations. In *Cognitive analysis of social behaviour*, (ed. J. P. Codol and J. P. Leyens) Nijhoff, The Hague.

Moscovici, S. (1984). The phenomenon of social representations. In *Social representations*, (ed. R. Farr and S. Moscovici), pp. 3–69. Cambridge University Press.

Nisan, M. (1984). Distributive justice and social norms. *Child Development*, **55**, 1020–9.

Ohana, J. (1986). *Educational styles and social knowledge.* Interim Report to CNRS.

Piaget, J. (1928). *Judgement and reasoning in the child.* Harcourt Brace, New York.

Piaget, J. (1932). *The moral judgement of the child.* Routledge and Kegan Paul, London.

Reicher, S. and Emler, N. (1985). Moral orientation as a cue to political identity. *Political Psychology*, **5**, 543–51.

Rest, J. R. and Thoma, S. J. (1985). Relation of moral judgment development to formal education. *Developmental Psychology*, **21**, 709–14.

Sears, R., Maccoby, E., and Levin, I. (1957). *Patterns of child rearing.* Row, Peterson, Evanston, Illinois.

Siegal, M. (1981). Children's perceptions of adult economic need. *Child Development*, **52**, 379–82.

Snarey, J. (1985). The cross-cultural universality of socio-moral development: a critical review of Kohlbergian research. *Psychological Bulletin*, **97**, 202–32.

Tajfel, H. (1981). *Human groups and social categories: studies in social psychology.* Cambridge University Press.

Turiel, E. (1983). *The development of social knowledge.* Cambridge University Press.

Weber, M. (1947). *The theory of social and economic organisations.* (ed. A. M. Henderson and T. Parsons). Free Press, New York.

Weiner, B. and Peter, N. (1973). A cognitive developmental analysis of achievement and moral judgments. *Development Psychology*, **9**, 290–209.

Weiner, M., Devoe, S., Rubinow, S., and Geller, J. (1972). Nonverbal behaviour and nonverbal communication. *Psychological Review*, **79**, 185–214.

Wellman, B. (1979). The community question: the intimate networks of East Yorkers. *American Journal of Sociology*, **84**, 1201–31.

Yussen, S. (1976). Moral reasoning from the perspective of others. *Child Development*, **47**, 551–5.

4 An ethnographic approach to social representations

Gerard Duveen and Barbara Lloyd

Introduction

A characteristic of much contemporary social and developmental psychology is the desire to analyse psychological activities in relation to the contexts in which they occur. From this point of view, a purely formal account of psychological, or cognitive, processes is inadequate, and new procedures need to be developed which are capable of expressing the relations between psychological processes and their contexts, as well as clarifying the notion of context itself. Whatever else the context may include, it certainly incorporates collective systems of meaning, and the growing interest in social representations centres on the possibilities that this concept offers for a description of the psychological structure and influence of collective systems of meaning. However, social psychologists are still not clear about the ways in which the notion of social representations may be conceptualized, articulated, and incorporated into empirical research. There is a general idea of the role which the concept ought to play, but we are still struggling to make the transition from programmatic statements to substantive accounts.

The methods to be used for describing social representations have presented a recurrent problem. Moscovici has maintained that the theoretical concept ought not to be tied to any particular empirical procedure; rather, he suggests that the theory needs to encompass a 'methodological polytheism' (Moscovici 1982; compare Hearnshaw 1987). While there is an admirable clarity in this empirical liberalism, there is also the corollary that each research project needs to establish in its own terms which methods for describing social representations are appropriate to the specific object of research. In our present research, we have felt it necessary to produce an ethnographic description as part of our investigation of social representations of gender in primary school.

In this chapter, we review the reasons which led us to this decision and illustrate the role that it has played in the project as a whole. First, we present the theoretical background to our research. We then describe our project in more detail and explain the framework we have developed for organizing our ethnographic material. Next, we consider the relationship between ethnographic and socio-psychological investigations; ethnography may also have more general applicability for the description of social representations. In the conclusion, we consider the circumstances in which it may be appropriate.

Social representations

Moscovici defines a social representation as '. . . a system of values, ideas and practices with a twofold function'. On the one hand, social representations establish a consensual order among phenomena and on the other they enable 'communication to take place among the members of a community by providing them with a code for social exchange' (Moscovici 1973, p. xiii). Thus, social representations constitute collective systems of meaning which may be expressed, or whose effects may be observed, in values, ideas, and practices.

The notion of 'ideas' which Moscovici includes in his definition of social representations requires some clarification. For many psychologists, particularly contemporary cognitive psychologists, ideas are understood as having a propositional structure with a verifiable truth value. This is not at all the conception which Moscovici intends. The ideational component of social representations is combined with the evaluative component in beliefs of one kind and another. In his recent work on *The Age of the Crowd*, Moscovici (1985) clarifies what he takes to be the nature of beliefs. 'Beliefs', he notes, 'act as forms' (Moscovici 1985, p. 115) capable of organizing groups of people. Because of this social-psychological role, beliefs are not open to empirical validation, nor does their articulation respect the law of non-contradiction. Moscovici identifies the essential features of beliefs as 'dogmatism and utopianism' (Moscovici 1985, p. 119). There is a closer similarity, between beliefs and the classical Freudian description of unconscious ideas, than between beliefs and any notion of ideas as propositional structures. Beliefs may include inconsistent and mutually contradictory elements; and in analysing social representations we cannot assume from the outset any primary motivation for logical consistency in the expression of beliefs. Nevertheless, beliefs serve to organize groups of people; indeed, what makes a group is the existence of a shared set of beliefs among its members, beliefs which will be expressed in the practices of the group, whether these are linguistic practices, preferences, activities of one kind or another, and so on.

The developmental dynamics of social representations can be considered from two points of view. First there is the process through which novel social representations emerge, or through which existing social representations are modified or transformed: here, development concerns the structure of the social representations themselves, and the relevant concepts are those of objectification and anchoring discussed by Moscovici (1981). But, there is also the process through which non-group members come to share the characteristic social representations of a group: here, development concerns transformations in the representational structures of individuals as they adapt to existing social representations. This process can be investigated in adult contexts (see, for example, De Paolis 1990), but it is also a central problem in the study of development through childhood. It is this latter problem with which we have been particularly concerned.

In an earlier paper (Duveen and Lloyd 1986), we linked the concept of social identity to Moscovici's notion of social representations. Social representations are collective products, the properties of groups. As such they pre-exist the birth of the human infant, and to become able to participate in social life the child must gain access to these collectively-held social representations. That is, social representations are internalized by individuals in the course of their development, a process which enables people to locate themselves in relation to groups, as well as furnishing them with an interpretive framework for construing the world. We proposed that as social representations are internalized, individuals gain access to social identities which enable them to situate themselves in relation to social groups and to participate in social life.

Our particular focus has been the gender system (Lloyd 1987; Lloyd and Duveen 1989). In all human societies, physical sex differences are given meanings associated with the social categories of male and female, that is, they are elaborated as social representations of gender. At birth, it is obligatory to assign an individual to one of the two mutually-exclusive gender categories. All individuals develop *social gender identities* which locate them in relation to the gender system of their culture. Initially, these social gender identities are held by the adults and others around the child; they are the ones who locate the infant in society, and whose social representations of gender provide the scaffolding which enables the infant to internalize a social gender identity. Through this social-developmental process children gain access to a particular gender system and acquire the resources which enable them to participate independently in social life. The assertion of gender-marked social identities indicates that children have internalized the social representations of gender in their community, and are able to mobilize these resources for social interaction.

The concept of social-gender identities takes a more sociological view of the phenomena which are discussed in the psychological literature as gender- or sex-role stereotypes. Moscovici's (1976, 1981) criticism of the notions of opinion and attitude in traditional social psychology parallels the reasons we prefer to talk of social gender identities rather than stereotypes. The notion of stereotype has come to mean a way of processing information through which category membership implies specific characteristics. Such schemata are construed as the property of individuals. What we have been concerned to stress is that such processes are always located in the wider context of the individual's participation in social life. Individual psychological processes need to be understood in terms of the social relations in which the individual participates rather than as autonomous sets of information-processing rules. In addition, the concept of stereotypes has been considered as a process invoked by individuals to categorize others, particularly in situations where there is a minimum of information available. As internalized social representations, social identities provide interpretive rules for the actor's understanding of themselves as well as of others.

The impact of schooling on the development of social gender identities

As a societal institution, the school presents a set of social representations of gender to children, and it does so in ways which distinguish the school from the family as an ecological context for children. It may be helpful to consider the contrast between these two contexts in terms of Habermas's theory of communicative action (compare Habermas 1984; Furth 1983). Habermas distinguishes the field of communicative action, which is personal and consensus-orientated, from that of strategic action, which is systematic and success-orientated. He also suggests that a central developmental process is the uncoupling of systematic strategic action from personal communicative action.

It would be an oversimplification to associate the family exclusively with the field of communicative action, and the school with the field of strategic action. There are systematic aspects to family life, and also communicative aspects to school experience. Nevertheless, from the developmental point of view, that is with respect to the the process through which gender is uncoupled as a system from the field of personal communicative action, the school has a particular role to play. As an institution, the school not only represents gender to children as a 'system of values, ideas, and practices', but it also legitimizes this social representation of gender in relation to the social world beyond the family. Categorizations which remained implicit within the personal relationships of the family nexus become explicitly elaborated in the context of the school.

The contrast between home and school as ecological contexts for the child suggests that the period of children's entry into formal education may be a particularly interesting moment in the development of social gender identities. Of course, children bring to school the social gender identities which they have already developed. The guiding hypothesis for our project is that as they enter formal schooling, children encounter social representations of gender embedded in novel contexts, and that children need to adapt to these social representations in the course of their first year at school. Our project aimed, therefore, to examine the reconstruction of social gender identities through the first year of formal schooling (see Lloyd and Duveen 1992).

To achieve this aim, we needed a description of the ways in which gender functioned as an organizer of classroom activities. Our first objective, therefore, was to describe the social representations of gender presented to children in primary schools. This is a task for which the more usual interview- or questionnaire-based methods seemed inappropriate for two reasons. Firstly, communicative competence is itself developmentally organized, so that only very limited types of discourse can be elicited from young children. Secondly, our research interests focussed not only on the ways in which teachers and other adults connected to the school might speak about gender to us as interviewers, but, more importantly, the ways in which gender featured in their ordinary activity and discourse within the classroom. Consequently, ethnography appeared to offer the most appropriate approach to describing the ways in which gender is articulated in the beliefs and practices associated with school.

There is a considerable body of ethnographically-inspired research on schools (Burgess 1984 and Hammersley 1986 provide two collections of studies), though for our purposes this material was limited in two important respects. For the most part, this research concentrated on junior and secondary schools, where classroom organization is much more formal than in the context of the primary school. The focus for a good deal of this work has been the analysis of classroom interaction, and specifically the processes of instruction and learning (for example Streeck 1983; Edwards and Mercer 1987). While gender has been a theme in some of this ethnographic research (compare Delamont 1980; Delamont and Hamilton 1984; Wilcox 1982), the organization of the junior or secondary school classroom presents a significantly different context from the reception classes in primary schools.

The second limitation of existing research was apparent in the few ethnographic studies of primary schools which do exist. While the influence of a number of social categories has been considered, gender as a systematic influence disappears from most accounts. Despite its absence, it is clear from some of the recorded comments that gender does have an importance and significance in primary schools. In Ronald King's (1978) book, for instance, he reported that a number of teachers explained to him that that they always try to deal with children as particular individuals rather than as boys and girls. Nevertheless, when he examined these same teachers' various ratings of their pupils, it was clear that on a number of dimensions they divided the children between boys and girls, In other words, gender was an organizing feature of classrooms. King (1978, p. 68) also reported that teachers explained the educational and behavioural problems of boys in terms of 'taken-for-granted natural sex differences'. It appears that gender-related patterns are so pervasive and expected that they are absorbed into the realm of the natural, rather than the cultural. (An exception to the systematic neglect of gender is Corsaro's (1985) ethnography of peer relations in an American kindergarten, which does consider questions of gender. However, the ethnographic context for this study, is quite distinct from that of British primary schools.)

The disappearance of gender from ethnographic accounts is a particular instance of a well-known feature of ideologies; cultural phenomena are represented as natural facts. However interesting this may be for a consideration of social representations of gender in primary school, it also means that existing ethnographies offered us very little in the way of description relevant to our interests. By force of circumstance, therefore, we took on the role of ethnographers. An advantage of doing so was the possibility of grounding our observations of children's practices in a detailed ethnographic account of the contexts for these activities.

The project as a whole was divided into two phases. The first phase consisted of observations of the first year of school with the aim of generating a description of the potential resources available to children for the organization and regulation of their social-gender identities. The second phase consisted of quantitative observations which provided a longitudinal study of social gender identities through the first year of school. Questions about individual and group variations in the use of resources for social gender identities are more adequately addressed through an analysis of this quantitative data. The present chapter concentrates on the first phase, and later we present some of our qualitative data describing the potential resources available to children for the expression of social gender identities.

Both phases of our work were located in two different schools. Although only a few kilometres apart they present contrasting sociological characteristics. One school (A) serves primarily a middle-class community and is housed in modern buildings; it is also a large school, with three classes in each year. The other school (B) is set in a predominantly working-class area and housed in an older, Victorian building. In this school there is only one class in each year.

The policy of the local education authority allows children to enter school in September if they will be five years old by the end of the following August, though they are only able to attend full-time from the beginning of the term in which they will be five. In school A, the three first-year classes are divided according to age, so that one class consists of children attending full-time in September, another of those children who become full-time in January, and the third of those who do not attend full-time until after Easter. It is this third class which we have observed. For the first two terms the children are divided into two groups, with one attending the morning session and the other the afternoon session. In school B the first-year class consists of some children who attend full-time from the beginning of the year in September, and others who attend the morning sessions only at first, and become full-time in either the spring or summer terms.

The class in school A consisted of 18 children in each of the groups during the first two terms, though when they were combined into a single full-time class some children were transferred into other first-year classes, leaving a total of 32 children for the summer term, 18 girls and 14 boys. The teacher for this class was female; an auxiliary helper, also female, was present for most of the time. In the class in school B there were 24 children, 11 girls and 13 boys; in addition to the class teacher, a woman, a female student teacher was also frequently present.

Motivated ethnography

Our ethnographic description assumes that social life revolves around collective systems of meaning, and that it is through the interrogation of the beliefs and practices of a community that these systems can be analysed. These presuppositions are also common to the theory of social representations; it is this common ground which establishes ethnographic description as appropriate for the study of social representations.

It is possible to argue that all psychological research proceeds from some ethnographic interpretation on the part of the investigators, that they begin with some intuition about psychological processes drawn from participation in their own culture. Generally, this ethnographic moment remains hidden in formal accounts of research procedures (Herzlich 1972 makes a similar point about the unacknowledged role of social representations in psychological research). What is novel in our research is that this ethnographic moment has not only become explicit, but also systematic. Indeed, the research project as a whole was dependent on the autonomous ethnographic study of social representations of gender within the school. It provided the descriptive framework which made possible the interpretation and assessment of individual actions.

In contemporary usage, especially by sociologists, ethnography has been taken to refer to participant observations combined with interviews undertaken in field settings. From these observations and their work with informants, ethnographers construct an interpretation of events. Through the course of their fieldwork, ethnographers also seek to test the adequacy of their interpretations through triangulation, in which emerging interpretations are re-presented to informants for comment and discussion. However, as Agar (1986) makes clear, this enterprise has been conducted using many different interpretive procedures and many different terminologies for describing the process.

How, then, should ethnography be characterized? We can consider the practices of ethnographers themselves. Their activities can be described in two ways. First we could describe the activities of the ethnographer in the field, observing the society under study and interviewing informants, but ethnography is more than the academic poking of a nose into other people's cultures. The ethnographer is aiming through these procedures to describe the collective life of a society — to articulate, among other things, the beliefs which are shared by the members of this culture.

The two kinds of description contained in this brief account may be contrasted using the distinction drawn by Gilbert Ryle (1971) between *thin* and *thick* descriptions. The former description portrays the observable activities of the ethnographer, and in this sense is thin. The latter description highlights the intentionality of the ethnographer's endeavour and to that extent is a thicker description. (It is also the case that the thick description may not correspond to anything observable, or it may be something which the ethnographer does while sitting in a tent, at the office, or even at home. The ethnographer would then resemble more closely Rodin's sculpture *Le Penseur*, which is the example given by Ryle.) Clearly the notion of thin description as pure observation is an ideal type. All description implies some interpretation, however minimal it may be. Equally, there can be no single thick description which exhausts the interpretive possibilities for any given situation. In a practical sense, it is only possible to distinguish degrees of thickness in particular descriptions. Nevertheless, this contrast between thin and thick descriptions has been used by Geertz (1973) to characterize ethnography as an interpretive procedure aimed at generating thick descriptions of a culture, which will articulate the collective systems of meaning that sustain a culture as a particular set of social relations.

In his discussion of ethnography, Geertz stresses the interpretive (or hermeneutic) aspect of this activity. Starting from their observations and interviews with informants, ethnographers generate various accounts which form the basis for interpretation. Very often, as Geertz notes, this actually means that they are dealing with second- or third-hand accounts passed on to them by their informants. All of this is to be expected, but it does strike a warning note as well as indicating the need for ethnographic research to range across a variety of sources. The situation of ethnographers becomes more complex, however, when they undertake field work within their own culture. They can no longer maintain the fiction of being outsiders trying to gain an insider's view; on the contrary, they are insiders with an interest in gaining an outsider's sense of wholeness.

Ethnography, then, can be characterized as the description of social phenomena and, in Geertz's terms, the more interpretive the description becomes the thicker it will be. As such, ethnography is not tied to a specific methodology. While participant observations and interviews with informants have been the most common sources of data, ethnographic descriptions have also been derived from textual sources, both historical and contemporary. Our own ethnography drew primarily on observations of classroom life, our conversations with children in the classroom, and discussions with teachers. From these data we constructed an interpretation of the role of gender in the organization of social relations in the classroom. In considering ethnography as an empirical approach to social representations, we take it to refer to an interpretive description based on observational and conversational data. As with any interpretive procedure which aims to recover the intentions informing the activities of social actors, no claim for objectivity can be sustained for ethnographic accounts. Intentionality is not an objective phenomena; it cannot be directly observed, so that any event is open to a multiplicity of interpretations. It is possible, however, to consider the adequacy of the interpretation offered by an ethnographic account. As well as providing a coherent and consistent account, an adequate interpretation needs to refer to a specified range of social phenomena; the account ought to provide a means for distinguishing relevant from irrelevant phenomena.

The setting for our research was primary schools, and the children in them were a particular focus for our work. This raised some special problems. As a social institution the school is a focus for diverse representations. There are those held by the parents, as well as those held by the local authority, and so on. All of these impinge in some way on social life within the school and the social relations within the classroom, and need to be considered in an ethnographic study. It would be impossible to give a description of children's culture which did not incorporate elements of the adult community in which the children lived. One characteristic of adult communities is that a part of their culture consists of representations of children, that is, expectations of how children will behave at different ages, of what they will be able to understand, and of the communicative competence to be expected at each age level (compare Chombart de Lauwe 1984: D'Alessio 1990). It would be misleading to give the impression that representations of childhood form a kind of monolithic block within our own culture; they do not. Like every representation, they exist within the context of other representations and are influenced by them. We noted above that in our two schools there are differences in the representations of childhood. We also noted that teachers' representations of children differentiate between the genders, though this differentiation is more apparent in the practice of teachers towards children than in their discourse about childhood and education (indeed, gender is often described as a hidden curriculum in education).

In our own case, this kind of reflexivity of representations goes a step further. As developmental psychologists we hold some specific representations about children which have consequences for how we approach ethnographic research. A particular issue concerns children's ability to achieve in practice solutions to problems which they are not able to explain theoretically, a phenomenon which Piaget (1977) described as the grasp of consciousness. As developmental psychologists, then, one of our representations of children suggests that there are developmental limits to their cognitive ability to communicate an adequate understanding of their practice. This clearly has ethnographic significance, for it means that we did not expect children to be in a position to act as ethnographic informants about their culture in the same way as adult informants. Indeed, this representation of childhood has been translated into our strategy for ethnographic work. A large part of our ethnographic work was observational; we kept diary records of what we had seen and of the interactions to which we had been party.

Our work also differs from traditional ethnographic procedures in that it is motivated by two specific concerns. First, we selected gender *a priori* as the theme of our observations; we did not go to the field ready to work on whatever material came up in the course of research. We went to the field with the belief that gender was a significant phenomenon in the organization of social life within the school, and our knowledge of contemporary collective representations of gender in our culture provided the initial framework for our interpretations of events in the school. Secondly, in terms of the project as a whole, the ethnographic work was instrumental to the development of psychological instruments. We were looking, as it were, for gendered phenomena which would provide suitable material for the construction of observation schedules and interview questions. Because of these concerns, we describe our method as *motivated ethnography*.

For the research project as a whole, the motivated ethnography served a dual function. In the first place it aimed to bring into view the phenomena we wished to investigate by providing a descriptive account of social representations of gender in the primary school. An essential strand of this account was the description of the activities and processes through which these social representations are articulated or made manifest. We refer to the collection of these activities and processes as the resources available for the expression of social gender identities. The second function of motivated ethnography follows on from the first: the ethnographic description also provided the basis for constructing psychological instruments capable of evaluating hypotheses about individual and group variations in the development of children's use of such resources. In the language of psychological research methodology, this second function can be expressed by saying that the ethnography provided the external, or ecological, validation for these measures. These two functions of ethnography correspond to the two phases of the research project, and in the following section we give some further details about these two phases.

Ethnography of gender marking

The aim of our ethnographic work was to provide a description of the structure of the social representation of gender in the classroom as it is articulated in the marking of various aspects of the setting. Wherever gender is marked, the possibility exists for the expression of a social gender identity, and in this section we present an analysis of the means through which gender is marked within the classroom. As well as the persons involved and the relations between them, a description of settings also needs to take account of the kind of activities being undertaken, the objects being used, the spatial location, and so on. In order to organize our ethnographic material, we tried to construct a taxonomy which distinguishes those different aspects of settings which can be used to mark gender. The semiotics of the gender system are such that different elements within settings are used to mark gender.

Before outlining this taxonomy we need to make two methodological comments. First, observational methods only allow us to record what children actually do. This tells us when they are able to mark gender in a particular manner. When gender is not marked, or when children disregard the rules of gender, we cannot conclude that they are ignorant of the conventions of the gender system. Thus, this analysis of our ethnographic material provides an overview of the potential resources available to children for marking gender. Secondly, although these observations concern the social practices of children and adults in the classroom, it is important to distinguish between different modes of activity in these practices. At times gender is marked in the practical activities of these people, at other times gender marking is primarily articulated through their verbal discourse. This verbal discourse may include reflections upon the gender system. Disjunctions may occur between the representations of gender articulated through these different modes of activity.

Each of the six aspects of settings which we identify below can be marked according to the rules of the gender system. In some cases, the marking of gender was explicitly made by the children and adults we observed; in other cases, the marking was made in our interpretation of an observation. Some of these aspects can also be marked in terms of other social categories (particularly age relationships). Although they do not form an exhaustive list, these aspects of settings do highlight those dimensions which allow children to express their knowledge of the gender system. These six aspects are not independent; many of our observations illustrate the interdependence among these aspects, but in some cases particular aspects are more salient than others. As a whole, these six aspects describe the parameters which we observed being used to mark gender, and thus provide potential opportunities for the expression of social-gender identities. The six aspects on which we focussed were: social categories, group composition, material culture, activities, space, and behavioural styles.

Social categories

In invoking social categories in the organization of interaction, although gender is a fundamental category (male, female), other categorizations are also salient, particularly age (child, adult). The cross-categorization of gender with age produces the four terms: boy, girl, man, and woman.

Categorization is a ubiquitous phenomenon of school life, with children being organized into groups for one reason or another. Although it is often the teacher who establishes the groups, children also categorize their peers. In some cases, the criteria used to define categories may be arbitrary (as, for example, when teachers organize children into groups on the basis of the kinds of shoes they are wearing), but they may also articulate some parameter of social organization in the classroom. Gender, of course, is an example of such a rational categorization, though other instances would be friendship groups, or work groups.

Teachers frequently make gender salient to children as a social category by using gender groups to organize school life. The registers, for example, divide the children's names according to gender, so that when the teacher in school B called out the list of names it was the boys' names which were called first and the girls' names second. In both schools the categories of boys and girls were frequently invoked in the teachers' discourse to the children. A typical example comes from school B when the teacher was getting the children ready for playtime: 'Let's see if the girls are ready and the boys are ready.' Children also used these categories in their relations with their peers. An observation from school A provides an example. The class is lining up to go into assembly and, although the teacher has not organized the line according to gender, there is a group of five girls jostling with each other at the end of the line saying 'I don't want to be by a boy', because the girl at the front of this group would have to stand next to a boy.

Group composition

Interpersonal settings can be described in terms of the combinations of the social category memberships of the participants. The people engaged in a reading lesson, for instance, can be described as a woman, two boys, and a girl, or as a teacher and three pupils. The gender and age composition of groups can be a powerful influence on interaction. Consider, for example, the following observation from school A.

Two boys C and D are playing on the carpet with a game which consists of pieces which fit together to make a slide for marbles. The boys have been busy for a little while, but none of the other children, neither boys nor girls, have shown any interest in what they are doing. One of the boys runs across to the teacher to say 'Look what we've done', and the teacher comes across to see what they've been doing. While she's talking to them, two girls, R and G, come over and stand and listen. The teacher draws them into the game by encouraging one of the girls to take a turn at letting the marble drop. When the teacher leaves the two girls stay on and all four children play together. After a minute or two, however, one of the girls drifts off, but R stays. D is busy explaining to her just how the game works. The other boy, C, however, also leaves.

In this example the composition of two same gender groups was modified through the presence of the teacher. First of all the boys' group was changed with the arrival of the teacher, but her presence effected a second change with the subsequent arrival of the two girls. The teacher is often a source of attraction for children, and this instance also shows how the teacher often mediates between boys and girls. With her departure, the group of four children had only a limited stability and two of the children soon left. The teacher's participation had, however, modified the gender composition of the group, a modification which persisted after her departure.

Material culture

Examination of the material culture (toys, games, and so on) may yield information about gender marking. Objects such as baby dolls are usually construed as feminine, while guns and vehicles are often described as masculine.

An example of the marking of material culture came from school A. S, a boy, is dressing up in some of the clothes from the home corner. He selects an orange nightie, and although he has some trouble in putting it on he finally succeeds. He then picks up a white tutu which he tries to put on as well. This is much more difficult for him to manage. The only other child to take any notice of what he's doing is C, a girl, who is also in the home corner. She looks at him struggling to put on the white tutu and says 'It's not for you, S'. S looks a bit bemused but continues struggling with the tutu. Finally he takes it across to the teacher and asks her to put it on him. She responds by saying 'Oh no, S, that's the smallest dress we've got — you won't fit into it. Let's look for something else.' Together they return to the clothes rack and S selects a skirt. The teacher says 'That's nice', but also encourages him to put on a waistcoat.

In this example, S was persistent in his determination to dress up in women's clothes. This was an unusual event, since by and large the children dressed up only in clothes appropriate to their own gender. In this case the reason why S should want to assert a feminine identity at this point was not clear, but the reactions of others were. The girl, C, explicitly stated the inappropriateness of S dressing up in feminine-marked clothes. The teacher, by contrast, avoided saying anything explicit about the appropriateness or otherwise of S's choice, but when she encouraged him to put on a waistcoat she was also encouraging him to add something marked as masculine to his outfit.

Activities

Activities, scripted play, and rituals may be marked for gender. The use of construction toys and the home corner, for instance, are often assumed to be marked respectively as masculine and feminine. The roles and objects evoked in scripted pretend play may also carry gender markings; roles are associated with social categories and objects form part of the material culture.

The most elaborate kinds of scripts these children produced were those which evoked domestic scenes, as in this example from school A. Two girls, H and S, are crawling about near the book corner. The observer asks them what they are playing, and they say 'Babies'. They take turns saying 'goo-goo'. A boy, F, comes over and says 'Don't be silly'. H says that F can be a baby, but he says that he's not a baby, he is a daddy. S says to him 'Good morning daddy. I am going out' and F replies 'Bye-bye'. Variations on this theme of greetings are repeated several times. Another boy, C, comes over and they agree that he can be the big brother.

In this evocation of domestic life, both F and the two girls recognized that F has chosen a domestic role congruent with had membership of the male gender category. As we have noted elsewhere (Duveen and Lloyd 1988), the scripted pretend play of young children is more elaborate when they evoke domestic rather than occupational scenes. While they may know about many occupations, children at this age have only limited knowledge of what people actually do in performing these roles.

Space

Space can be used as a sign denoting gender, although this may be the most fluid aspect of gender marking. While there may be very few, if any, fixed markings of spaces for gender within the classroom, the use of particular areas for particular activities involving specific objects may lead to the recognition of certain areas as gender marked. There may be a temporal dimension to the way in which spatial locations are marked for gender; the marking may persist only as long as a particular activity continues.

This example comes from school B. The teacher sends five boys to play in the playroom adjoining the classroom. No girls go, none ask to go, and none are sent. A few minutes later when one of the girls does ask to go the teacher says to her 'No, not yet. Let the boys finish first'. A few minutes later, there is a complete gender separation between the two rooms. All seven boys are now in the playroom where they are running around playing with the trucks or engaged in rough and tumble play. In the classroom, all the six girls are on the carpet with the teacher giving a tea party for the dolls.

In this instance, it was the teacher who initiated and sustained a division of space according to gender, a division which the children completed.

Behavioural styles

Behavioural styles are also given gender meanings. Thus, forceful or assertive activities are often labelled masculine, while passivity or compliance are construed as feminine. Our observations included many instances of both boys and girls acting in masculine and feminine styles. In these cases, the marking of behaviour styles for gender is a feature of our interpretation, though the following example from school A illustrates adults explicitly marking behavioural styles.

Several children are building a rocket from the wood blocks in the space by the door. As well as several boys there are also two girls involved in this group, K and Z. Z is so frequently involved in these games with the boys that she is recognized by both the teacher and the children as a tomboy. Both the teacher and the auxiliary are with other children in the main part of the room and they do not have a clear view of the rocket game. Both of them ask the the rocket group to be quieter. The auxiliary finally gets up and goes across to see what's going on. She comes back and says to the teacher 'It's K and Z as well.' The teacher replies 'K as well? I knew it was Z. Why do we always think it's the boys?' The auxiliary grins in recognition.

From ethnography to psychology

As a semiotic system, gender is realized through the signifying practices of children, teachers, and other adults in the context of the school. It is these practices which were the focus of our ethnographic investigations, and we interpreted these practices as expressions of social gender identities, that is, as expressions of children's internalizations of social representations of gender. Our ethnography provided a description of the potential resources available for marking gender in the social life of the classroom. These resources constituted the elements available for the expression of social gender identities, and the second phase of our research consisted of a study in how these potential resources were actually used, and particularly of variations in their use between individuals and groups through the course of the first year of school.

The study in the second phase required the construction of measures sensitive to individual variations in the use of resources for marking gender. From our ethnography, it was also apparent that such measures needed to take account of the different modalities of action which could be employed in marking gender. To meet these requirements we elaborated a series of three interlinked measures. These consisted of (i) spot observations of each child's activity at a given moment; (ii) detailed written observations of interactions within the classroom which could be coded for the various aspects outlined above; and (iii) interviews with children in which they were presented with tasks requiring them to reconstruct the use of particular resources. The first of these measures provided an overview of individual children's engagements with other children and adults, where these interactions were located, the material objects used, patterns of talk, and the degree to which activities were coordinated among children. The second measure provided more detailed information about the way in which different resources were employed in the various modalities to express social gender identities in particular interactions. The third measure concerned children's ability to represent (in the strictest sense of the term) the use of resources to mark gender. These measures were employed in a longitudinal study of the first-year classes in both of the schools. They provided data for evaluating our hypotheses by allowing us to examine changes in the organization of social gender identities through the first year of schooling.

Each of the measures we have devised draws directly on our ethnographic work. The categories for the spot observations, the coding frame for the written observations, and the themes for the interview task all found their external validation in that ethnography. This is the solution which we found for the problem of moving from ethnographic to psychological modes of investigation. In some respects, this solution is specific to the particular research problem with which we were concerned. Different techniques of psychological investigation might be more appropriate in other cases. In general, though, it would be the case that ethnography plays the same dual role as it has for our own research. Ethnographic research should bring the social phenomena under investigation into view, and thereby provide external validation for the appropriate psychological methods.

Conclusions

As we noted in the introduction to this chapter, the theory of social representations adopts a 'methodological polytheism' rather than specifying particular methodological procedures. In commenting on Moscovici's proposal, Hearnshaw notes that this implies a 'certain methodological diversity and tolerance . . . embracing at one end precise quantitative techniques and at the other shading off into the weighing of evidence and the hermeneutical interpretation of meanings' (1987, p. 302). Ethnography is concerned with not only the interpretation of meanings, but also the description of the social practices through which meanings are constructed and communicated. We have indicated the role which ethnography played in our own research concerned with social representations of gender. In this conclusion, we want to consider the wider issue of the use of ethnography in the investigation of social representations.

Most studies of social representations have analysed the structure of representations through the medium of verbal or written discourse; typically these analyses have considered responses to interviews or questionnaires, or the content analysis of newspapers and periodicals. By focusing on practical activity as a modality of social practice, the use of observation to construct an ethnographic description of social representations expands the range of media accessible to analysis. In the particular case of our research, a consideration of practical activities was, in part, necessitated by the limited capacity of young children for reflection and self expression in verbal discourse. Analysing social representations through the medium of practical activities has the benefit of emphasizing the significance of this modality within the ensemble of social practices through which social representations are articulated.

The systematic investigation of practical activities from the perspective of social representations raises some important issues; in particular it demands a more interpretive approach to observational data than has generally been the case in psychology. As with any hermeneutic procedure, the objectivity and generality of an interpretation is always open to question. While the internal coherence and consistency of an interpretation is always open to rational criticism, the adequacy of an interpretation as an account of the phenomena can only be assessed through a continuing confrontation with the data. In social anthropology, this latter question has usually been treated through various triangulation techniques within the fieldwork itself. In such cases, both the interpretation and its triangulation are undertaken by the same investigators. However, the adequacy of an interpretation could also be examined by different investigators undertaking studies of similar phenomena. While it would be difficult to undertake a replication in the strict sense of the term, studies of similar phenomena in different contexts create the possibility for examining the generality of any particular interpretation.

Clearly, the use of ethnography in the description of social representations depends upon the practical activities associated with the representation being accessible to the investigator. This is not always the case: there may be instances where practical activities are simply inaccessible to an investigator, or it may be the case that a social representation carries no practical consequences for the expression of social identities. This consideration raises the problem of making distinctions between types, or varieties, of social representations, an issue which has not yet been tackled by the theory of social representations.

There are, for example, important differences between social representations of, say, gender, and those of psychoanalysis. One way of contrasting these two types of social representation is to note that, whereas in relation to psychoanalysis individuals can exercise a choice in the degree to which they become involved with psychoanalytic themes, no such choice is possible in relation to gender. Membership in certain social categories is an inescapable part of social life. One cannot be just a human being, one is either young or old, male or female, and so on; and these categories provide social locations for individual subjects which are among the most basic prerequisites for participation in social life. One could choose to have nothing to do with psychoanalysis, but one would then have no basis for participating in the professional life of psychoanalytical societies. With gender there is no choice: to become human means to become male or female.

Thus, social *gender* identities are always an active element in everyday life, and hence readily open to observation. These circumstances contrast with the voluntary engagement of individuals with psychoanalysis. People may develop social identities in relation to social representations of psychoanalysis, but there is no compulsion. In his study of psychoanalysis, Moscovici (1976) employed questionnaires and the content analysis of magazines as his tools. One could imagine that for some of his communist or catholic subjects psychoanalysis may also have been an observable feature of their daily life. They too might have had their daily 50-minute hour. But, for the most part, psychoanalysis would have had no identifiable part to play in the daily lives of these people; they would have no active social identity in relation to social representations of psychoanalysis. This is not to say that an ethnography of social representations of psychoanalysis based on observations would be impossible, only that it would have to be restricted to those groups for whom psychoanalysis figured as a daily reality. There would remain, however, the problem of the accessibility of psychoanalytic practice to a prospective investigator. Janet Malcolm (1982, 1984), for instance, presents accounts of psychoanalytic practice and relations between psychoanalysts. As an ethnographic study of the social representations of psychoanalysis held by analysts themselves, these books draw on her interviews with various informants.

The minimum conditions for an ethnographic description of social representations can, then, be stated as follows. Wherever individuals actively assert a social identity, ethnography can provide an appropriate way of reconstructing the social representations informing their activities. Where particular social representations are not articulated in active social identities, ethnography will yield little descriptive information. Equally, where the practical activities through which social identities are expressed remain inaccessible to an investigator, ethnography based upon observation and interview would not be a suitable approach for investigating the social representations held by the participants themselves.

Acknowledgements

This research was supported by a grant to the authors from the Economic and Social Research Council (No. C0023 2321). Nicholas Barley and Marion Smith were part of our research team and contributed to the development of this work. We are grateful to our colleagues in Social Psychology and Social Anthropology at the University of Sussex who have discussed this work with us on a number of occasions. We owe a particular debt to the children, teachers and parents of the two schools for the cooperation which they extended which made this work possible.

References

Agar, M.H. (1986). *Speaking of ethnography*. Sage, Beverly Hills.
Burgess, R.G. (Ed.) (1984). *The research process in educational settings: ten case studies*. The Falmer Press, London.
Chombart De Lauwe, M.J. (1984). Changes in the representation of the child in the course of social transmission. In *Social representations*, (ed. R.M. Farr and S. Moscovici), pp. 185–209. Cambridge University Press.
Corsaro, W. (1985). *Friendship and peer culture in the early years*. Ablex, Norwood, N.J.
D'Alessio, M. (1990). Adolescents' representations of infancy and childhood. In *Social Representations and the development of knowledge*, (ed. G. Duveen and B. Lloyd), pp. 70–90.
Delamont, S. (1980). *Sex roles and the school*. Methuen, London.
Delamont, S. and Hamilton, D. (1984). Revisiting classroom research: a continuing cautionary tale. In *Readings on interaction in the classroom*, (ed. S. Delamont), pp. 3–37. Methuen, London.
De Paolis, P. (1990). Psychologist: vocation or profession? In *Social representations and the development of knowledge*, (ed. G. Duveen and B. Lloyd), pp. 144–63.
Duveen, G.M. and Lloyd, B.B. (1986). The significance of social identities. *British Journal of Social Psychology*, **25**, 219–30.
Duveen, G.M. and Lloyd, B.B. (1988). Gender as an influence in the development of scripted pretend play. *British Journal of Developmental Psychology*, **6**, 89–95.
Edwards, D. and Mercer, D. (1987). *Common knowledge*. Methuen, London.
Furth, H. (1983). A developmental perspective on the societal theory of Habermas. *Human Development*, **26**, 181–97.
Geertz, C. (1973). *The interpretation of cultures*. Basic Books, New York.
Habermas, J. (1984). *The theory of communicative action*, Vol. 1. Beacon Press, Boston.
Hammersley, M. (Ed.) (1986). *Case studies in classroom research*. Open University Press, Milton Keynes.
Hearnshaw, L.S. (1987). *The shaping of modern psychology*. Routledge and Kegan Paul, London.
Herzlich, C. (1972). La représentation sociale. In *Introduction à la psychologie sociale*, (ed. S. Moscovici), pp. 303–25. Librairie Larousse, Paris.

King, R. (1978). *All things bright and beautiful*. John Wiley, UK.
Lloyd, B. (1987). Social representations of gender. In *Making sense: the child's construction of the world*, (ed. J. Bruner and H. Haste), pp. 147–62. Methuen, London.
Lloyd, B. and Duveen, G. (1989). The re-construction of social knowledge in the transition from sensorimotor to conceptual activity: the gender system. In *Cognition and social worlds*, (ed. A. Gellatly and J. Sloboda), pp. 83–98. Oxford University Press.
Lloyd, B. and Duveen, G. (1992). *Gender identities and education: the impact of starting school*. Harvester-Wheatsheaf, Hemel Hempstead.
Malcolm, J. (1982). *Psychoanalysis: the impossible profession*. Vintage Books, New York.
Malcolm, J. (1984). *In the Freud archives*. Jonathan Cape, London.
Moscovici, S. (1973). Foreword to *Health and illness*, C. Herzlich. Academic Press, London.
Moscovici, S. (1976). *La psychanalyse, son image et son public*. Presses Universitaires de France, Paris.
Moscovici, S. (1981). On social representation. In *Social cognition*, (ed. J. Forgas), pp. 181–209. Academic Press, London.
Moscovici, S. (1982). Perspectives d'avenir en psychologie sociale. In *Psychologie de demain*, (ed. P. Fraisse), pp. 137–47. Presses Universitaires de France, Paris.
Moscovici, S. (1985). *The age of the crowd*. Cambridge University Press.
Piaget, J. (1977). *The grasp of consciousness*. Routledge and Kegan Paul, London.
Ryle, G. (1971). *Collected papers*, Vol. II. Hutchinson, London.
Streeck, J. (1983). *Social order in child communication*. John Benjamins Publishing Company, Amsterdam.
Wilcox, K. (1982). Ethnography as methodology and its applications to the study of schooling: a review. In *Doing the ethnography of schooling*, (ed. G. Spindler). pp. 456–88. Holt, Reinhart and Winston, New York.

5 Vikings! Children's social representations of history

David Uzzell and Linda Blud

Making the familiar unfamiliar

Central to the idea of social representations is the proposition that abstract scientific and ideological concepts filter through to people in general and become 'common-sense' general knowledge. Moscovici (1976) makes the distinction between the 'sacred' sphere of science and the 'profane' sphere of ordinary life which is central to his perspective. He refers to these as different worlds of meaning, which he calls the reified and consensual universes. The sciences are the means by which we understand the reified universe, and social representations deal with the consensual. Moscovici sees this distinction as a relatively modern phenomenon, unique to our culture: 'Science was formerly based on common sense and made common sense less common, but now common sense is science made common.' (Moscovici 1984, p. 29).

Moscovici attempts to show how the representations that we develop are the result of our attempts to make usual that which is unusual (that is to fit the abstract notions of science and ideology into a more concrete and familiar framework) and he argues that in this sense social representations work in opposition to science, which attempts to make the usual everyday things in life more unusual (that is to turn the ordinary world into abstract scientific and ideological concepts).

The museum environment is an interesting setting in which to examine these ideas, because it is here that we can observe how Moscovici's two universes interrelate. Museums attempt to present the reified universe to the general public, to make the abstract scientific world available to everyone. In this respect museums are unique, since their directors see them primarily as learning establishments, implying the competence, hierarchy, and sacred nature of the reified universe. As part of the reified universe their aim would be, in Moscovici's terms, to make the familiar everyday world more unfamiliar. Yet, clearly, most directors of modern thematic museums would argue that their intention is to make the unfamiliar familiar. Museums are concerned with transmitting knowledge to the general public in a relaxed and informal manner. Thus, while they may be seen as representing the reified world of science, their influence will be directly on the consensual world of people's social representations — visitors to a museum are free to select and discuss whatever they like.

The changing role of museums

The traditional role of museums has been the collection, conservation, and presentation of historical artefacts, providing a rich and important record of man's cultural and natural heritage. It has been appreciated in recent years, though, that this role could and should be extended. For example, the presentation of artefacts is no longer confined to displays in glass cases, but extends to interpretation and environmental education programmes for schoolchildren.

In Britain and elsewhere in recent years there has been an immense growth of interest in preserving and interpreting the past. Museums, heritage and visitor centres, industrial trails, restored mines and mills, and archaeology and countryside centres have proliferated. The function of such interpretation is to bring the past to life and to make more meaningful something not within our experience. In social representation terms, it is to make the unfamiliar, familiar. There are, of course, psychological difficulties with presenting, or rather representing, the past. Freeze-framing our heritage ignores the psychological reality that neither those who provide interpretations of the past nor those who receive these interpretations can avoid loading them with their own twentieth-century perspectives. We cannot recreate the past or provide an authentic experience, since visitors' perceptions of the past will always be influenced by their present-day attitudes and values. As David Lowenthal points out, 'The press of numbers also inhibits a sense of the past: it is hard to suspend disbelief about the seventeenth century with hundreds of other twentieth-century folk milling about' (Lowenthal 1985, p. 298).

It has also been recognized by many museums that they need to market and promote themselves more effectively, thereby implicitly casting themselves in the role of tourist and visitor attractions as much as the scholarly repository of the nation's heritage. This alliance between conservation, education, and tourism has led to what Hewison (1987) has termed the 'heritage industry': 'Instead of manufacturing goods, we are manufacturing *heritage*, a commodity which nobody seems able to define, but which everybody is eager to sell . . .' (p. 9). This obsession with the past is seen as a new cultural force of which museums are just a part.

The presentation techniques used today in museums are very different to those which were used at the beginning of the century. The Natural History Museum, when it opened in 1881, presented an impressive but static collection of objects which were expected to speak for themselves. Nowadays the same museum recognizes the need to actively encourage and facilitate learning, and emphasis is placed on the importance of interpretation, categorization, and interaction, in an effort to maximize understanding.

Consequently, there would appear to be great potential for encouraging learning in such environments, although the learning may be different from that experienced in a classroom or from a book, and the individual motivations to learn may vary widely.

Informal education, according to Laetsch (1979), is characterized by free choice, lack of prerequisites and credentials, heterogeneity of learner groups in background and interests, and the importance of social interaction, rather than individual effort. In addition, informal education centres like museums, science centres, and zoos, offer primary evidence. Seeing the 'real thing' as opposed to some representation of it is inherently more interesting and stimulating. Moreover, the kind of visual evidence offered by a museum or zoo can be useful at all levels of age and ability. Limited literacy skills need not inhibit or frustrate an individual's understanding in the way that it might at school.

Learning in museums

Despite the burgeoning growth of museums and interpretive centres throughout the world, with their plethora of educational and entertainment technology to enhance visitor understanding and enable learning, it would seem from research on the effectiveness of museums and exhibitions that visitors to museums actually do not learn very much (Shettel 1968; Borun 1977; Screven 1975). Typically, the assessment of learning in museums has been undertaken by the measurement of cognitive gain in terms of the number of facts and concepts remembered by individuals. It has to be questioned whether the methodologies currently used to assess learning and enhanced understanding are sensitive enough or even appropriate in these settings (Uzzell 1988). Visitors to museums are given what amounts to a comprehension test, whereas for research and planning purposes one is invariably more interested in whether the structure of visitors' thinking has changed. That is, does the museum or exhibition experience lead to more differentiated and discriminating ways of understanding and conceptualizing the interpreted material (Lee and Uzzell 1980)?

The purpose of the research reported here is to establish a social-psychological framework for evaluating informal learning in museums, so that the focus is shifted from individual cognitive processes to the social and interpersonal aspects of learning. Because of the essentially social and informal nature of museums, an examination of people's understanding of exhibitions in terms of social representations would appear to be a more valid exercise than attempting to measure more formal and individual types of cognitive gains.

Research on learning in museums has been confined largely to the investigation of adult visitors. However, the two main groups of visitors to museums are school groups and family groups (Laetsch *et al.* 1980). Very little research has investigated children's learning in a museum and, in particular, little is known about learning in either the school group or the family group. Yet for both groups the museum offers a unique learning experience, although research indicates that most people visiting a museum see it as primarily a social event, rather than an educational trip (see, for example, Borun 1977).

Research into learning in museums has generally been influenced by theoretical and methodological approaches drawn from cognitive-experimental psychology and formal education theory and, as a result, learning has been perceived in terms of individual cognitive processes. This would seem to be questionable in terms of the principal social groups which visit museums. There has been very little research on the influence of social interaction in relation to learning in museums (Gottesdiener 1988; McManus 1989).

This research aimed to explore alternative theoretical and methodological approaches, drawn from social psychology, in an attempt to provide a more valid framework within which learning in an informal setting can be examined. In addition, the literature indicates only that adults do not learn very much from a museum visit. We wanted to see if this applied to children as well.

The Viking setting

This study examines childrens' understanding of an historical theme of the Vikings, before and after a visit to a museum which endeavours to present a non-stereotypical view of Vikings. The word 'Viking' conjures up in the popular imagination an image of a bloodthirsty, brave, but merciless race of seafarers, sporting beards and horned helmets.

The Jorvik Viking Centre is a modern museum which portrays Viking life in York by presenting a reconstruction of a Viking settlement with houses, workshops, and a wharf, brought to life not only through the use of life-size models but also through sounds and smells. In addition to the reconstructed settlement, the Jorvik Viking Centre also portrays the archaeological process which led to this reconstruction, showing parts of excavated buildings with pits and hearths exposed, in the actual location where they were discovered, and reconstructed site sheds and a laboratory showing what archaeologists do. The final part of the museum has artefacts in glass cases, more like a conventional museum. The artefacts displayed relate to the Vikings' domestic and cultural life rather than their raids and explorations. For the first part of the visit, visitors are transported through the museum in four-person battery-driven 'time-cars', each of which has a pre-recorded tape commentary.

In comparison with a conventional museum, the Jorvik Viking Centre appears highly original. However, Chabot is more sceptical, arguing that the Jorvik Viking Centre presents an exhibition which is 'technologically innovative, but, academically traditional, in that it presumes an unintelligent and passive public' (1988, p. 73).

The Jorvik Viking Centre aspires to present a very different picture of Vikings than is typically portrayed, focusing instead on the domestic side of their life. This is not as unproblematic as it may seem. Despite assurances by Dr Peter Addyman, Director of the York Archaeological Trust, that: 'the Viking figures are based on living Yorkshire people and therefore all the activities in which they are engaged are easily recognisable' (Caldwell 1985), we are not as sure about social roles and relationships amongst the Vikings of Jorvik as we are about the current inhabitants of York. A close analysis of the exhibition suggests that twentieth-century gender stereotyping has been uncritically transferred to the representation of the tenth century (Chabot 1988). Such views are redolent of Hewison's comment that many of the products of the heritage industry are '. . . fantasies of a world that never was; not simply because at a deeper level it involves the preservation, indeed reassertion, of social values that the democratic progress of the twentieth century seemed to be doing away with . . .' (Hewison 1987, p. 10).

The Jorvik Viking Centre is of particular interest in terms of a social-representations perspective, since it purports to present accurate historical details in a way which should be easily assimilated by the public. It does this by creating an atmosphere of tenth-century life through the use of life-size figures, sounds, and smells. In social-representation terms there is an attempt to make the familiar unfamiliar, and then the unfamiliar familiar. Market research by the York Archaeological Trust has, it is claimed, enabled the exhibition planners to understand the Viking 'image in the popular mind' (Addyman 1986, p. 4). As a consequence, visitors are taken through an orientation tunnel on their way to the 'time-cars' in order to 'implant pre-requisite knowledge, and remove misinformation' (ibid.). The familiar is thus made unfamiliar as popular myths and representations are challenged. As visitors travel on the 'time-cars' through a reconstructed Viking settlement, then through a reconstructed archaeological site, and finally through a reconstructed archaeological laboratory, so does the scientific and the unfamiliar become revealed, intelligible and familiar.

The research

This research looks at the image of the Vikings which children bring with them to the museum, questions whether they have a shared representation image, and how effective the museum is in shaping and altering this image. Two methods were used: content analysis of texts and the gathering of accounts and drawings. These techniques were used to establish whether beliefs about the Vikings are shared social beliefs which have their origins in historical reality, but may have become altered or shaped in some way in order to coincide and assimilate with consensual understanding.

The kinds of representations presented in historical accounts are representations which are formulated mainly (but not exclusively) in formal academic contexts. However, within academic history there are often competing constructions of the past, and those representations which are successful in gaining public acceptance are not necessarily historically accurate. They may be stereotypical constructions or myths as the Popular Memory Group (1982) point out. For example, images of the Second World War in Britain have developed into a plethora of fact and fiction influenced more by the traditions of masculine romance inherent in movies and in today's superhero cults than by historical writing. It is important, therefore, to examine the kind of images presented in historical accounts aimed at children in order to see how these relate to the images reproduced by children.

In order to examine any shared images which the children held, their drawings and accounts of the Vikings were examined. In addition, the portrayal of the Vikings in historical accounts aimed at children were examined to provide indications of the type of information available to children and to establish a framework for coding the children's descriptions.

Content analysis of text

Three books on the Vikings were selected because they were widely available in primary schools and public libraries. The books were all factual and intended for school work as well as recreational reading. A thematic analysis was undertaken on the three books (*A closer look at Vikings*, Archon Press; *Great civilizations: the Vikings*, Longman; *Ladybird great civilizations series: The Vikings*; Ladybird) using the context unit of a paragraph (each paragraph was considered separately), and the recording unit of a theme (each theme within a paragraph was noted: a paragraph might contain several overlapping themes).

From an initial reading of the texts, two aspects emerged. There were many explicit and implicit references to the Viking character: what the Viking was like, what personal qualities he possessed, and how indigenous people reacted to the Viking. In addition, there were many references to the Viking way of life.

Two coding frames were developed to analyse children's drawings and accounts: one for the Viking character (Table 5.1) and the other for the Viking way of life (Table 5.2). The Viking character coding frame had two

Table 5.1　Coding frames: Viking character

Internal qualities	
Moral	Good/bad
	Honest/dishonest
	Obedient/disobedient
Social/emotional	Kind/cruel
	Peaceful/aggressive
	Civilized/uncivilized
	Adventurous/cautious
Egoistic	Skilled/unskilled
	Strong/weak
	Appearance positive/negative
	Humble/Pride
External qualities	
Influences	Character moulded by the environment
Effects	Fear/fearless
	Welcoming/avoidance

Table 5.2　Coding frames: Viking way of life

Culture	Law/class
	Money
	Writing
	Art/craft
	Religion/myth
Domestic	Houses
	Food
	Clothes
	Animals/pets
	Work
	Leisure
War/sea	Ships/sea
	Raids/explorations
	Armour/weapons
	Horns
	Slaves

main codes: 'internal qualities' and 'external influences and effects'. The internal qualities code had three sub-codes to cover the references to Viking qualities:

(1) moral aspects (moral qualities of the Vikings as a race);
(2) social/emotional aspects (characteristics which affect relationships with others);
(3) egoistic aspects (personal qualities such as bravery and skill).

Each of these sub-codes had several categories (all with positive and negative poles).

The external codes refer to:

(1) environmental influences — the idea of the Viking character as being moulded by the environment was a strong theme in the books;
(2) the reactions of others towards the Vikings.

The Viking way of life coding frame covered all aspects of Viking life mentioned in the books and these could be classified into three main areas — culture, domestic, and sea/war. These three sub-codes also contained several sub-categories.

To assess the validity of these coding frames, a small sample of accounts and drawings of the Vikings were analysed. These descriptions were obtained from two groups of children, one from a school in the north of Scotland and the other from a school in London. Both coding frames were used for the accounts, but only the Viking way of life coding frame was used for the drawings, and several modifications were made to this — including extra categories for 'fighting' in the war/sea sub-code and two extra codes referring to 'male figures' and 'female figures and children'.

Since 'horns' appeared in almost all the drawings and many of the accounts, it was included as a category in its own right in the coding frame. However, there is no evidence at all that Vikings had horns on their helmets.

Main study

One hundred and twelve children from four schools took part in the main study, producing 175 accounts and drawings (both before and after their visit). The schools were selected from a list of schools booked to visit the Jorvik Viking Centre. The age range of the sample was from 7 years to 11 years 6 months. One school (7–8 year olds) produced drawings only, one school (9 years 6 months–11 years) produced accounts only, the other two schools (one young group, one older) produced both accounts and drawings.

The school which only produced accounts had received extensive formal educational instruction on the Vikings prior to their visit. These lessons began before the pre-visit accounts were obtained. The other schools only had lessons relating specifically to their visit, and these did not begin until after the pre-visit accounts were obtained.

All the children were asked by their own teacher in class to think about the word 'Vikings' and to draw a picture, or write a short paragraph on the topic, putting down whatever the word brought to mind. They were asked: 'What do you think of when you hear the word "Vikings"? Draw a picture to show what the word means to you.' This was carried out approximately four weeks prior to and again four weeks after their visit.

Accounts

Inter-judge reliability for the coding of the accounts was 0.86 (Viking character) and 0.88 (Viking way of life). Tables 5.3 and 5.4 show the percentage of subjects using the principal codes in the two coding frames before and after their visit.

It can be seen that there is an emphasis on war/sea themes at pre-visit (94 per cent of the accounts contained references to warlike aspects) but a much more balanced picture emerges at post-visit.

Similarly, the children had a very negative view of the Viking character before their visit (Table 5.4). Eighty-one per cent of the children referred to the negative characteristics of the Vikings before their visit, while only 19 per cent mentioned any positive aspects (mainly referring to bravery and skill). Again, after the visit a more balanced view emerges (59 per cent negative, 41 per cent positive).

There was little attribution by the children to external influences and effects, although these had been quite strong themes in the literature. The books emphasized the effect of the harsh environment of Scandinavia on the Vikings, making them tough and hard and encouraging invasions of other lands. This was not something the children appeared to appreciate. For example, one 10 year old wrote prior to the visit: 'My image of a Viking is a ruthless bloodthirsty vicious man who has no pity gives no mercy and will destroy towns and villages just for something to do. They are proud but have

Table 5.3 Percentage of subjects using various themes of the Viking way of life in accounts of Vikings before and after a visit to the Jorvik Centre

	Before visit	After visit
Culture	20	60
Domestic	51	79
War/Sea	94	71

Table 5.4 Percentage of subjects using various themes of qualities of the Viking character in accounts of Vikings before and after a visit to the Jorvik Centre

	Before visit	After visit
Internal		
Moral positive	0	0
negative	41	12
Social positive	8	13
negative	81	55
Ego positive	19	38
negative	31	18
External		
Environment	7	2
Effects positive	0	2
negative	18	7

nothing to be proud of.' The implication is that the Vikings were motivated by greed rather than necessity.

Although warlike and negative aspects of the Viking appear to be dominant themes at the pre-visit time, over half the children also used references to domestic aspects before their visit to Jorvik. Chi-squared analyses were performed to see if there were differences between the schools, or between the age groups, in the use of the various themes both before and after the visit. Differences between the schools before the visit could be due to the different amounts of formal educational input the school children received, as well as age differences. It was important to establish the influence of school and any age-related differences before the effects of the museum visit could be assessed.

Table 5.5 shows the percentage of themes used by the various schools at pre- and post-visit. School A has children in the youngest age group (7–8 years), schools B and C have older children (school B 9:4–11:6 years; school C 9:3–10:10 years). School B received much more extensive instruction on the Vikings prior to their visit than either of the other two schools. Since schools B and C have a similar age range, the differences between the children in these two schools should be due to the influence of school lessons. Whereas schools A and C both received minimal lessons on the Vikings, differences between these two schools should be due to the fact that school A's pupils were considerably younger.

Table 5.5 Percentage of subjects from each school using themes from Viking Way of Life Code and Viking Character Code in their accounts taken at 4 weeks pre-visit and post-visit, showing differences due to formal education input

	School A*		School B*		School C*	
	Before	After	Before	After	Before	After
Way of life						
Domestic	11	22	91	98	7	93
Culture	3	55	37	73	0	40
War	96	37	95	86	89	70
Character						
Positive	8	5	30	60	7	26
Negative	81	15	88	77	67	63

*School A 7–8 year olds; schools B and C 9–11 year olds.

The chi-squared analyses on the pre-visit data revealed that there were significant differences between the schools before the visit. However, there were no differences with respect to mentioning items in the war/sea theme: all the schools used this theme quite extensively.

There were differences in relation to the other themes in the way of life code, and in the use of positive character references. These differences do not appear to be related to age, however, since there is little difference between the younger group (A) and the older group (C) in this respect. Both groups used the culture and domestic themes very infrequently and made very few references to positive aspects of character. The difference would appear to lie with school B, and thus be explicable in terms of the difference in school instruction. For example, they used the domestic theme as much as the war theme at the pre-visit stage.

However, after the visit the differences between the two older groups (schools B and C) were greatly reduced (for example in the use of the domestic theme after the visit). The differences which are most apparent at post-visit appear to be related more to age than schooling, since the youngest group (school A) differs from the other two schools in their use of the various themes. There are still differences between schools B and C, but the greatest differences are between school A and the other two schools.

In terms of these age differences, what appears to have happened is that the younger children still adhere to one theme only (in respect to the Way of Life code). Some still use the war theme, but others have dropped this and taken up one of the other themes. The older children, on the other hand, appear to use all three themes. Similarly, with regard to the Character code, the younger group appear to have dropped references to character altogether, whereas the older children balance their references to negative aspects by including more references to the positive aspects of the Viking character.

Drawings

Two of the schools (A and C) also produced drawings, as did another group of 7–8 year olds (school D). School B, which had received the most comprehensive instruction on the Vikings, was excluded from this analysis. Therefore all the children in this sample had only received minimal briefing lessons prior to their visit. Arguably the exclusion of school B drawings data results in representations more typical of the images of the naive visitor. Inter-judge reliability for the coding of the drawings was 0.95. Table 5.6 demonstrates that the differences between pre- and post-visit are even more dramatic. Furthermore, the consensus which exists at the pre-visit stage is more apparent than in the accounts data.

The data has been broken down by age, with the sea/war theme and the domestic/culture themes shown separately. No differences are apparent at the pre-visit stage. *All* of the subjects used categories from the sea/war theme in their drawings, and very few drew anything in addition to this theme. However, differences appeared after the visit. The younger children appeared to have dropped one theme in favour of another, whereas the older children used elements from all of the themes.

The difference in the use of categories for pre- and post-visit descriptions indicates that the image of the Viking does undergo change after a visit to the Jorvik Viking Centre. The pre-visit descriptions by the whole sample (with the exception of school B) contain a fairly narrow set of variables,

Table 5.6 Percentage of subjects in each age group producing elements from War/Sea and Domestic/Culture themes in drawings of Vikings

	7 years	8 years	9 years	10–11 years
War/sea				
Pre-visit	100	100	100	100
Post-visit	13	40	78	77
Domestic/culture				
Pre-visit	18	13	0	8
Post-visit	37	76	43	54

whilst in the post-visit descriptions a wider and more diverse range of items are included.

However, examining the data simply in terms of frequency distributions does not allow one to make informative statements about any systematic individual differences which may exist, in terms of the processes underlying the data. To overcome this problem, a multidimensional scaling procedure was used.

Multidimensional scalogram analysis

Multidimensional scaling (MDS) procedures provide geometric representations of relational data. These can be useful in dealing with open-ended data, such as accounts and drawings. The MDS procedure used here is the Multi-Dimensional Scalogram analysis (MSA-1) (Shye 1978). This is a non-metric analysis which makes no assumptions about the distribution characteristics in the data and operates entirely on categorical data.

The MSA-1 computer program presents the results in a pictorial display which is easily interpreted. It creates a geometrical representation of the multivariate distribution (a scalogram), taking into account the interrelations among the items. No *a priori* demands on the distribution characteristics of the items or of the relationship between them is made. Instead, every subject is represented as a point in geometrical space of an appropriate dimensionality, in such a way that for each item there will be a clear partition of the space into several regions according to the categories of that item. These regions are typically called contiguity regions (Zvulun 1978).

MSA-1 does not depend on the concept of statistical significance but attempts to find a spatial solution which minimizes the distortion between the pattern embedded in the data matrix and its spatial representation. It produces a 'best fit' solution. The level of distortion is given by a coefficient of contiguity, with a value lying between +1 and −1. Usually a coefficient of 0.9 is considered satisfactory for a two-dimensional solution (the MSA-1 programme maximizes the fitness of the representation using iterations until a satisfactory coefficient of contiguity is obtained).

In this case, the categories to which each item could be assigned were 1 (denoting the presence of that attribute/item in the subject's description) and 0 (denoting the absence of the attribute/item). Each subject is shown as a point in space which represents their position on all the variables. A profile is built up for each subject on the basis of the presence/absence of each of the variables used in their descriptions. The distance between any pair of points (that is, subjects) in the space corresponds to the size of the correlation between them, so that the higher the correlations the closer the points are in the space (hence the more similar the profiles).

Each subject was entered into the MSA-1 programme twice, firstly in

relation to their pre-visit profile (all of the descriptions or attributes produced before the visit to Jorvik) and secondly in relation to their post-visit
profile (all of the attributes produced after their visit). The MSA-1 plot was
examined in order to establish whether the pre-visit profiles for each age
group were distinct from the post-visit profiles. That is, is there a difference
in the configuration of points representing the same subjects before and
after the visit? Where a clear partition of the space can be identified, a line
can be drawn to divide off different regions.

In many cases, of course, not all variables will give rise to clear regions.
However, the MSA-1 programme also provides plots for each variable or
attribute used (such as armour/weapons; fighting; ships/sea). The configuration of points (subjects) on these plots is identical to the initial profile
plot. However, on each attribute plot an indication is given of that particular
attribute's presence (denoted by a 1) or absence (denoted by a 2) in each
subject's description. These attribute plots can be used to establish whether
identifiable regions exist for each variable and whether these regions correspond closely to pre-visit or post-visit regions, to indicate other underlying
dimensions of difference or similarity between the subjects, or fail to give
rise to a clear partitioning of the space.

The aim here is to examine more fully whether a common image can be
identified in the children's descriptions, and which attributes contribute to
this image. Those attributes which give rise to a partitioning of the space
which is identical or very similar to the pre-visit or post-visit profile of a
particular age group may be seen as contributing strongly to the pre-visit
or post-visit image of the Viking. It is argued that if several attributes
contribute to the pre-visit (or post-visit) image of all the children, this may
indicate that these attributes constitute a social representation of the Viking.
The disposition of these attributes in multidimensional space can be regarded
as a graphical representation of a social representation. In addition, any
changes which occur between pre- and post-visit descriptions can be more
clearly identified, and the underlying dimensions of conceptualization can be
examined.

The accounts and drawings of each age group (7–8 year olds, 9 year olds,
10 year olds, and 11 year olds) were analysed separately. This was necessary
because the MSA-1 programme cannot deal with large numbers of subjects.
More importantly, it was desirable to identify any differences between the
age groups. A two-dimensional solution provided the closest fit in each
case. The regions occupied by the pre- and post-visit profiles of the subjects within each group were found to be clearly differentiated. The two-
dimensional space was partitioned into regions to demarcate subjects'
post-visit descriptions.

Further plots, showing the attributes used in the descriptions separately,
were also produced. These plots indicate which subjects used each of the

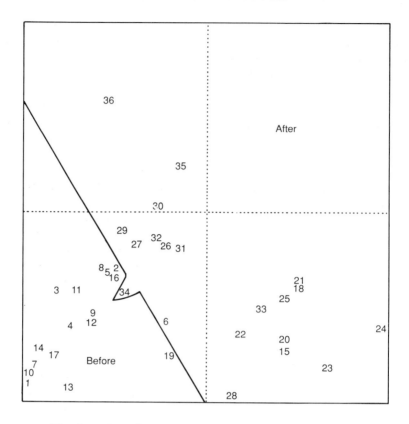

Fig. 5.1. Drawings of 7–8 year olds, before and after

attributes. The pattern of distribution for each of the attributes were compared with the 'before' and 'after' profiles.

The MSA-1 results are illustrated by the drawings of the youngest age
group (7–8 year olds) only, since the pattern seen here was generally reflected
throughout the sample.

Figure 5.1 shows the profile plots for the 7–8 year olds (accounts and
drawings shown separately). In several cases, subjects had identical profiles
and so several subjects are represented by a single point. In each case, all the
pre-visit profiles fall on one side of the line, and all the post-visit profiles on
the other: thus, clearly differentiated regions can be identified.

The transmission of a social representation

In attempting to assess whether the transmission of knowledge about the
Vikings can be seen in terms of the transmission of a social representation

to the children, any sources of information about the Vikings to which the children had access were of interest. All the children had some formal instruction on the Vikings at school, using books similar to those used in the text analysis. However, the text analysis produced categories which were inadequate to accommodate all the descriptions given by the children prior to the museum visit, and this suggests that they were subject to other sources of information. In particular, the Vikings are not portrayed as sporting horned helmets in any of the books examined, yet horns were a major feature of all the children's pre-visit descriptions.

The accounts were further examined for any references to sources of information which appeared. Only two children in the school sample made any reference to a source of information in their pre-visit accounts, compared to 37 per cent in the post-visit accounts. Several explicit references were made to museums (including museums other than the Jorvik Viking Centre), books, and archaeological finds. In addition, mention was made of Hagar the Horrible, a cartoon character appearing in a tabloid national newspaper and in advertisements for Danish lager on television. There were also several implicit references to an old adventure film (*The Vikings*) which coincidentally was shown on British television during the period of the data collection. This was not specifically referred to by the children, but they described several scenes which clearly emanated from this source. The Viking, as portrayed in the cartoon and the film, is the classic horn-helmeted villain. The fact that these sources of information appeared in the post-visit descriptions of the Viking, although the horns have been eliminated, suggests that the children had become more aware of sources of information about history in general as a result of their museum visit. It is also clear that these sources of influence had shaped their pre-visit descriptions. The museum visit was effective in dispelling some of the myths surrounding the Viking, so that in the post-visit descriptions the categories used by the children related more closely to those found in the texts.

Figures 5.2–5.10 show the plots for individual attributes used in the 7–8 year olds' drawings. Only those attributes which divided the space into clearly identifiable regions (present/absent) are shown. On the attribute figures (Figs 5.2–5.10), the hatched area indicates a region which contains all the subjects using that particular attribute in their descriptions (individual points representing subjects are not shown, but the distribution of points is identical to that shown in Fig. 5.1). The boundary line indicates the partitioning of pre-visit and post-visit regions. Where several attributes constituting a group partition the space in a similar way, these attributes can also be seen as contributing to the same underlying dimension. Ideally, this would be indicated by identical patterns of orientation for certain sets of attributes. While this does not occur in all cases, attributes can be identified. In addition, there are clear differences between the attributes, and the underlying

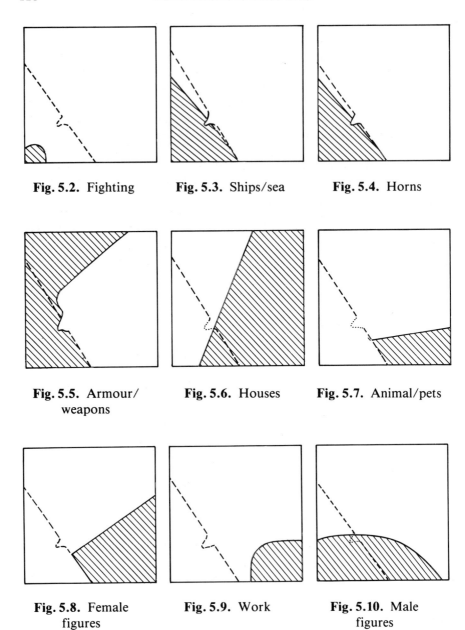

Fig. 5.2. Fighting

Fig. 5.3. Ships/sea

Fig. 5.4. Horns

Fig. 5.5. Armour/ weapons

Fig. 5.6. Houses

Fig. 5.7. Animal/pets

Fig. 5.8. Female figures

Fig. 5.9. Work

Fig. 5.10. Male figures

dimensions which these attributes indicate, appearing in the descriptions before the visit and those appearing after the visit.

In the 7–8 year olds' drawings, two attributes were identical in spatial delimitation with the pre-visit region — sea/ships and horns (Figs 5.2 and 5.3). These two attributes were used by all the children prior to the visit, and none of the children after the visit. Fighting also appears only in the pre-visit region. These three attributes do not appear at all in the drawings produced after the visit. Armour/weapons also occupies the entire pre-visit space, but this attribute also persists after the visit. These four attributes can be seen to share a warlike connotation, which is shared by all the children before the visit, and largely disappear after the visit. The spatial relationship between the four attributes shown in Figs 5.6–5.9 (houses, animals/pets, female figures, and work) form a separate grouping which corresponds largely to the post-visit space and does not occur in the pre-visit drawings. Taken together, these attributes contrast sharply with the 'war' dimension identified in the pre-visit descriptions, and would appear to indicate an opposing underlying dimension of 'peace'.

Male figures (Fig. 5.10) are situated in a clearly identifiable region. However, the relationship between this attribute and the two underlying dimensions identified above is not clear, since this attribute is associated with a different partitioning of space. Considered separately, male figures would appear to be closely related to the war dimension on the pre-visit plot, and the peace dimension on the post-visit plot.

It is also interesting to consider the relationship between male figures and armour/weapons, and how this relationship changes as a result of the museum visit. Before the visit, the two attributes occur in the same region of the space, whereas after the visit they occupy clearly separate regions. This suggests that before the visit armour and weapons are always perceived as part of the male image, whereas after the visit armour weapons are not associated with men at all, but are seen as a separate entity.

In the descriptions given by the older children, the distancing of the accoutrements of war from the figure of the Viking is even more apparent. Indeed, in the two oldest age groups, armour/weapons becomes part of a separate orientation, together with the attributes art/craft and clothes. This third dimension appears only in the post-visit descriptions of the older children and could be interpreted as an 'ornamentation' dimension.

Conclusion

While the frequency data indicate that the Jorvik Viking Centre was successful in influencing children's knowledge about Vikings, it does not really answer the question as to whether one can see historical themes like this in terms of social-representations theory. Although a strong and cohesive image prevailed at the pre-visit, differences did exist between the individual schools, as well as between different age groups. This is not inconsistent with a social-representations view, but does highlight one of the problems in this approach, as outlined in a critique of the theory by Potter and Litton (1985). They suggest that the notion of consensus across representations fails to take into account intra-group differences and that different layers of consensus may exist. They also note the problem of the researcher's role in identifying the social categories of interest. If a researcher is interested in examining the social representations of schoolchildren, the implicit assumption is that this can be regarded as a cohesive group. Yet, leaving aside obvious age differences, other social dimensions such as class or race may be more influential. In the light of these problems, the MSA-1 analysis of the data may be more useful in identifying the elements which comprise the social representation of the Viking.

Overall, what emerges from the MSA-1 is a differentiation between 'war' and 'peace' as the underlying conceptualization of the Vikings. The war theme emerges most clearly and relates closely to the pre-visit descriptions. The peace theme emerges most strongly in the descriptions produced after the visit to Jorvik, but is less cohesive. In all age groups the post-visit profile comprises several themes, including some aspects of war which persist from pre-visit, and notably a new dimension which has been referred to above as the 'ornamentation' dimension. This ornamentation element appears to encompass aspects of Viking life which do not involve judgemental processes (making inferences about Viking character in terms of positive or negative aspects), but instead relates to more aesthetic aspects of Vikings' life, for example, their culture and crafts.

One purpose of the MSA-1 analysis was to examine in more detail the nature of change which occurs between pre- and post-visit, and to relate these changes to the underlying differences in cognitive structures which might be expected at the different age levels. A clear differentiation between pre- and post-visit descriptions is most clearly seen in the youngest age group. As the children get older, the distinction between pre- and post-visit responses becomes less clear, and the underlying representation of the Viking becomes more sophisticated and differentiated. For example, the 11-year-old group see the seafaring theme as separate from the war theme.

The 9-year-olds presented the least clear picture. This may indicate that this age group is experiencing changes in their underlying cognitive structures. The clear-cut division between pre- and post-visit perceptions begins to break down, and the underlying conceptualization is less clear. In the drawings, the distinction appears to be between 'male' and 'female' aspects rather than 'war' and 'peace'.

By 10 years of age, a more consolidated view has been achieved and a wider range of variables contribute to the underlying cognitive organization.

The perception of the Viking would appear to be less directly influenced by single events, such as a museum visit. The blurring of the distinction between pre- and post-visit themes may indicate that the children are developing the ability to consider various aspects of the Viking character simultaneously, which is not the case with younger children.

The 11-year-old group shows the most sophisticated cognitive structures, and the beginning of more abstract processes of conceptualisation. This emerges in implicit internal and external themes which can be identified here. The 11-year-olds' accounts revealed two major opposing concep-tualizations, similar to those appearing in all the children's descriptions. One dimension included the attributes fear, horns, aggressive appearance, and raids/exploration, relating most closely to the pre-visit region. A second group of attributes linked ships/sea, skill, and art/craft, and was most closely related to the post-visit region. Whilst these could be interpreted as similar to the war and peace themes identified in the descriptions of the other age groups, another interpretation might be in terms of external and internal aspects. External aspects relate to appearance (aggressive appear-ance, horns) and the way in which the Vikings impinged on the lives of others (fear, raids), whereas the second grouping refers to more positive and inter-nal qualities of skill and achievement. This differentiation into external and internal aspects can be compared to the kind of conceptualization being portrayed in the texts, where an emphasis on external influences and effects was counterbalanced by the appreciation of internal strengths and qualities. Although an awareness of these two contrasting aspects did not emerge explicitly in the children's descriptions, they appear to be underlying features of this group's accounts, and perhaps imply the development of more abstract modes of thinking in the 11-year-old group.

The more differentiated conceptualization characteristic of the post-visit descriptions of all the age groups suggests that intra-group differences, which are not evident at pre-visit, have emerged at the post-visit stage. It is especially interesting to note that male figures appear to be closely related to the war dimension on the pre-visit plot, and the peace dimension on the post-visit plot. One interpretation of this is that male figures domi-nate the exhibition. This is paradoxical, because although there are fewer female figures represented in the exhibition, Chabot (1988) has noted that during a visit to the Jorvik Viking Centre it seemed that there were even fewer female figures than were actually depicted. Chabot argued that there were two possible explanations. First, the females figures may have been situated more frequently in the background and therefore have been less likely to command the visitor's attention. Alternatively, while the female figures are portrayed as doing things which we 'expect' women to do (such as cook or weave), the male figures are portrayed as engaging in unusual pursuits, at least for a museum exhibition (such as sitting on the lavatory). The women thus become 'invisible'.

In addition to indicating more clearly the nature of the changes which occur, the MSA-1 is also useful in suggesting which perspective on Viking life is shared by all the subjects and where differences emerge—which attributes contribute to a social representation of the Viking. The attributes which best describe the pre-visit space for all the age groups are horns and ships/sea. Raids/exploration, armour/weapons, and fighting also correspond closely with the pre-visit image. Since these five attributes are common across the majority of the whole sample (above 70 per cent), it would appear that the predominant image of the Viking is that of the warlike adventurer. No similar cohesive correspondence emerges in the post-visit descriptions.

Interestingly, the image of the Viking which emerges contains few elements from the Viking character coding scheme (for example good/bad, kind/cruel, skilled/unskilled). Very few of the character attributes divided the MSA-1 space into clearly-identifiable regions, and none were common across the different age groups. The image of the Viking which is shared by all the children is essentially a very concrete and visual image, and the Viking emerges as merely a symbol of war and adventure, rather than a real historical figure with a particular personality, feelings, or characteristics.

Thus, the evidence is that a social representation of the Viking does exist, and children visiting the Jorvik are likely to bring with them a fairly strong representation of the Viking race as a hoard of fierce, seafaring warriors, sporting horns. The contrasting image which Jorvik presents would appear to be fairly effective in modifying this representation, in that an awareness of an alternative representation is evident in many of the post-visit descriptions. In particular, the emergence of an ornamentation dimension in many of the children's descriptions indicates that the museum is effective in encouraging some awareness of cultural aspects of Vikings' life, as well as an appreciation of their domestic lifestyle. For many, though, the warlike image persists.

Discussion

The results indicate that the museum visit did enhance the children's understanding of the Vikings. At the simplest level, learning can be seen to have occurred in that factual misconceptions have been corrected (for example, in relation to horns). Of greater significance is that it appears that more complex cognitive structures underlie the post-visit descriptions. Thus, the older children's descriptions suggest an ability to appreciate several contrasting points of view, and the use of more abstract dimensions of categorization. Even in the young group, there is evidence of the beginning of more complex cognitive structures after their visit.

The data here also suggests that children visiting Jorvik may already have a strong representation of the Vikings. When thinking about ways of exploring learning in historical museums, clearly one must take into account the pervasiveness of historical representations which may be founded more on myth than truth. Any investigation of learning in a museum must recognize the existing knowledge and misconceptions which visitors bring with them, and this may be most usefully investigated using a social-representations perspective.

A social-representations framework has been used in this study to examine learning and images of the past, in order to go beyond an investigation of the simple recall of facts, and to examine how knowledge of our cultural and historical past is represented in our current consensual understanding. Knowledge of our past is social knowledge, based on shared cultural-belief systems and representations. Any examination of the transmission of such knowledge must acknowledge the social-contextual factors involved, and develop methods of investigation which can take this into account.

One problem with the approach adopted here is that it is static and, while reflecting process, it really provides only a descriptive snapshot in time. No account is given of either the origins or the development of these representations. An assessment of social representations without such a historical analysis is at best only partial. Surprisingly few studies within psychology attempt to do this (Moscovici 1976, Uzzell and Summers 1987). Those undertaking social-representation studies could do no better than to look to disciplines, such as history, which have used historical analyses to examine contemporary psycho-historical phenomena such as the creation and maintenance of invented traditions (Hobsbawm 1983). Case studies, such as Trevor-Roper's (1983) study of the creation of the 'Highland tradition' in Scotland, or Morgan's (1983) investigation into the origin and mutating mythology of Welshness to serve cultural and political purposes, provide enlightening examples.

The social-representations approach has generally been used to investigate how people explain and interpret their social worlds. The subjects which have been explored have usually focused directly on current major research areas and preoccupations within social psychology, such as social identity and group membership. However, it should not be assumed that because the object of study is the past, then this has little or no relevance for our appreciation of the present.

It is not difficult to see the central role that invented traditions can play in the origin and development of social representations. Furthermore, social representations of the past and their interaction and relation to invented traditions can have a functional significance for current social psychological processes. Social representations comprising the history, myths, and traditions of social, industrial, religious, or political groups and communities can have a profound functional value in establishing or symbolizing social cohesion on their members and outsiders. Trades unions, the Mormons, the Boers, and the IRA provide examples of such groups where the interaction between representations of the past and current attitudes and behaviour is highly significant. A museological example of an extension of this process might be the role of military and regimental museums, which act as a socializing force inculcating the traditions, value systems and conventions of behaviour into new recruits. Finally, institutions as well as power and authority relations often acquire legitimacy through historical precedence and images of the past, as exemplified by reference to the parliamentary and the democratic tradition. Myth-making and socially constructed representations of the past are obviously a vital element in our understanding of contemporary phenomena and social psychological processes.

References

Addyman, P. (1986). *Reconstruction as interpretation*. Paper presented at the World Archaeological Congress, University of Southampton.

Borun, M. (1977). *Measuring the immeasurable: a pilot study of museum effectiveness*. Association of Science–Technology Centers, Washington, DC.

Caldwell, C. (1985). *Jorvik: the public response*. Unpublished BA dissertation, University of Sheffield.

Chabot, N. J. (1988). The women of Jorvik. *Archaeological Review from Cambridge*, 7 (1), 67–75.

Gottesdiener, H. (1988). Visitors' interaction in front of a computer game in an art exhibition. Paper presented at symposium *A social approach to exhibition evaluation*, British Psychological Society London Conference, 20th December 1988.

Hewison, R. (1987). *The heritage industry: Britain in a climate of decline*. Methuen, London.

Hobsbawm, E. (1983). Inventing traditions. In *The invention of tradition*, (ed. E. Hobsbawm and T. Ranger), pp. 1–14, Cambridge University Press.

Laetsch, W. M. (1979). Conservation and communications: a tale of two cultures. *South-East Museums Conference Journal*, March, 1–8.

Laetsch, W. M., Diamond, J., Gottfried, J. L., and Rosenfeld, S. (1980). Children and family groups in science centres. *Science and Children*, March, 14–17.

Lee, T. R. and Uzzell, D. L. (1980). *The educational effectiveness of the farm open day*. Countryside Commission for Scotland, Battleby.

Lowenthal, D. (1985). *The past is a foreign country*. Cambridge University Press.

McManus, P. (1989). What people say and what they think in a science museum. In *Heritage interpretation, Vol. II*, (ed. D. L. Uzzell), pp. 156–65 Belhaven Press, London.

Morgan, P. (1983). From a death to be a view: the hunt for the Welsh past in the romantic period. In *The invention of tradition*, (ed. E. Hobsbawm and T. Ranger), pp. 63–100, Cambridge University Press.

Moscovici, S. (1972). Society and theory in social psychology. In *The context of social psychology: a critical assessment*, (ed. J. Israel and H. Tajfel), pp. 17–68, Academic Press, London.

Moscovici, S. (1976). *La psychanalyse: son image et son public*, (2nd edn). Presses Universitaires de France, Paris.

Moscovici, S. (1984). The phenomenon of social representations. In *Social representations*, (ed. R. Farr and S. Moscovici), pp. 3–69 Cambridge University Press.

Popular Memory Group (1982). Charms of residence—the public and the past. In *Making histories*, (ed. R. Johnson), Centre for Contemporary Cultural Studies/ Hutchinson, London.

Screven, C.G. (1975). *The measurement and facilitation of learning in the museum environment: an experimental analysis*. Smithsonian Institution Press, Washington DC.

Shettel, H.H. *et al.* (1968). *Strategies for determining exhibit effectiveness*. American Institute for Research, Pittsburgh.

Shye, S. (1978). *Theory construction and data analysis in the behavioural sciences*. Jossey-Bass, San Francisco.

Trevor-Roper, H. (1983). The invention of tradition: the highland tradition of Scotland. In *The invention of tradition*, (ed. E. Hobsbawm and T. Ranger), pp. 15–41 Cambridge University Press.

Uzzell, D.L. (1988). The interpretative experience. In *Ethnoscapes, Vol. II: Environmental policy, assessment and communication*, (ed. D. Canter, M. Krampen, and D. Stea), pp. 248–63 Gower, London.

Uzzell, D.L. and Summers, K. (1987). Changing attitudes and ideology in pregnancy and childbirth. Conference on *Health psychology*, Wessex and Wight Branch of the British Psychological Society, University of Surrey.

Zvulun, E. (1978). Multidimensional scalogram analysis: the method and its application. In *Theory construction and data analysis in the behavioural sciences*, (ed. S. Shye), pp. 237–64 Jossey-Bass, London.

6 Discourse analysis and social representations

Andy McKinlay, Jonathan Potter, and Margaret Wetherell

Introduction

In a number of recent publications, the theory of social representations has been criticized on analytic, operational, and theoretical grounds. Nevertheless, the perspective embodies certain important features which we see as being a crucial part of an effective and radical social psychology. In this chapter we will overview these problems and qualities and argue that a discourse analytic approach (Potter and Wetherell 1987), although being somewhat more qualified in its theoretical objectives, captures many of the best features of the theory while avoiding its central problems. The final part of the chapter will illustrate, using practical examples, how discourse analysis develops a social approach to the phenomenon of representation.

Social representations: the qualities

A social theory in social psychology

Social-representations theory provides a form of analysis which deals with the specifically social aspects of activity. This is probably its most important contribution to social psychology. By emphasizing the way in which groups and communities make joint sense of their world, the social-representations theorist can highlight the importance of the effects of social phenomena on individual activities. Unlike its more individualist rivals, such as attitude theory and attribution research, the social-representations research strategy explicitly makes room for the influence of factors which seem outwith the usual explanatory reach of the individualistic perspective.

There are at least three senses in which the theory is distinctively social, although it is only the first which is free of difficulties. First, social representations are linked to communication processes, the most important of these being unstructured everyday talk; as Moscovici puts it, 'representations are the outcome of an unceasing babble and a permanent dialogue between individuals' (1984b, p. 950). This emphasis on the primacy of the mundane conversation — gossip, pub arguments, and family reminiscences — for the genesis of social understanding allies social representations to thinkers such as Sacks in the conversation-analytic tradition (Heritage 1984; Sacks 1984). However, this theoretical emphasis makes the lack of analytic concern for this topic within social-representations research particularly disappointing.

The second social dimension to the theory is the idea that social representations provide a theoretically-principled way of distinguishing between social groups. The fact that social representations offer a code for communication and are basic resources for making sense of the world, means that those who share representations will agree in their understanding and evaluations. Representations are thus a unifying and homogenizing force; indeed, the theory suggests that social representations are the very thing that makes groups what they are (Moscovici and Hewstone 1983).

Thirdly, representations provide an agreed code for communication. To the extent to which people share common representations, they will understand what other people are talking about and be able to have fluid and intelligible conversations. Moscovici's classic work on the representation of psychoanalysis illustrates this phenomenon; it shows that psychoanalytic concepts, such as repression, became a popular currency for understanding human behaviour.

A constructivist theory in social psychology

Social-representations theory offers an explanation of thought, and to a lesser extent language, which stresses their constructive roles. Just because we do see the world in terms of what has already been given to us by our social background, we find ourselves creatively constructing sense out of what might otherwise be puzzling, incoherent experience. Put another way, meaning does not reside 'out in the world'; rather the world of the individual is only meaningful to the extent that social representations give it meaning (Moscovici 1984a). Indeed, it is the construction of meaning, through the processes of anchoring and objectification, which allows people to come to terms with and assimilate the new and unfamiliar.

The theory of social representations is just one of a number of constructivist positions available in social psychology, and it is important to be wary of treating them as a unified stance (Gergen 1985). For example, there are major differences between the constuctivisms in the ethnomethodological (Coulter 1979), social studies of science (Latour and Woolgar 1979), and ethogenic (Harré 1979) traditions, and each of these is different in turn from the constructivism in social-representations theory.

Most notably, for Moscovici, social-representations theory takes construction to be an essentially cognitive phenomenon, made to happen through anchoring and objectification, while other constructivist positions place far more stress on the role of language. Indeed, later in the chapter we will argue for a linguistically-orientated constructivist position. Despite this caveat, social-representations theory is making an unusual and welcome step in social psychology in taking up this general stance.

Social representations: the problems

The qualities of the theory have to be weighed against a number of severe problems in both the metatheoretical assumptions of theory (McKinlay and Potter 1987*a*) and its practical deployment (Billig 1988; Eiser 1986; Parker 1987). There is not space to explore all these in detail here. We will merely take up two lines of criticism to elucidate the rationale behind our analytic suggestions which follow.

We will first outline a set of criticisms concerning the way in which the theory has been put into practice (Litton and Potter 1985; Potter and Litton 1985; Potter and Wetherell 1987) exploring the relation between social groups and social representations; the notion of consensus and agreement assumed by the theory; and the way in which the theory coordinates the realms of cognition and language. Secondly, we will argue that contemporary analyses of social representations have adopted simplistic assumptions about the status and process of representation *per se*. We can then start to indicate the direction that a more fruitful analytic practice might take.

Operationalizing social representations

Relating social groups and social representations

In the theory, as expressed by Moscovici, social groups are constituted by their social representations. As we have indicated, social-representations theory holds that what makes a group into a group is the fact that its members share a set of representations. It is offered as a virtue of social-representations theory that it can provide a principled way of distinguishing different social groups, thus providing a novel and sophisticated solution to one of social psychology's perennial problems (Turner *et al.* 1987). This solution runs into considerable difficulties when it is implemented in practice, however (Potter and Litton 1985).

Empirical studies typically start with a relatively well-defined social group and then try to sort out what their representations are. There are two problems with this. On the one hand, it *presupposes* that representations mark group boundaries, that is, it enters a vicious circle where representations are identified from the group, and then representations are said to define the group. This, of course, means that social representations cannot be used as a principled criterion of separating groups.

On the other hand, there is a related problem — how can researchers identify psychologically-meaningful social groups independently of participants' social representations of those groups? Given this difficulty, a damaging inconsistency results; for researchers are treating group categories as naturally-occurring phenomena which are a stable base for research conclusions and, *at the same time*, they are treating group categories themselves as social representations.

This can be illustrated with an analytic example. Say we wish to research a protest movement which is split between 'hard-line militants' and 'moderates' (compare Di Giacomo 1980). As social-representations researchers, we wish to find out which representations separate the two groups. Yet, in taking 'militants' and 'moderates' as natural, out-there-in-the-world groupings, we have already accepted one representation or version of the protest movement. Yet, research on social categories in discourse reminds us that there are almost certain to be other available versions of the movement (Gilbert and Mulkay 1984, Chapter 6; Jayyusi 1984; Potter and Wetherell 1987, Chapter 6).

These alternative versions might characterize the same categories differently: 'militants' will be talked of as 'radicals' and 'moderates' as 'right-wingers'. However, participants are just as likely to split the movement up into different kinds of groups altogether; for example, two 'sound factions', a 'group of Trots', some 'politically-inexperienced social democrats', and so on. These alternatives are not just abstract classification schemes; categorizations of this kind are part of the framework of broader arguments and ideologies (Billig *et al.* 1988; Jayyusi 1984; Potter and Reicher 1987), and particular kinds of evaluative work and motive attribution (Potter 1988; Watson 1978; Watson and Weinberg 1982; Wetherell and Potter 1992; Wowk 1984; Yearley 1984).

The general point is that there is no way of talking about groups independently of social representations; there is no version that is free of its own specific versionality. The theory cannot just be switched on when needed and ignored when it is inconvenient. The broader implication is that when social-representations theory is combined with an unselfconscious use of social-category discourse it runs the risk of becoming inadvertently embroiled with the evaluative and argumentative work of the participants.

Consensus and agreement in social representations

The second major area of problems with operationalizing-representations theory focuses on the issues of agreement and consensus. Moscovici and other advocates have persistently stressed that representations are consensually shared across groups of people. That is, as we have just noted, not only do the edges of representations mark the edges of social groups, but within groups there is an agreed adoption of the representation. At first sight this idea seems relatively clear-cut; but complexity multiplies when we come to think about what is involved in practice.

When we examined some empirical studies of social representations it became clear that rather than researching the issue of consensus it was simply being presupposed (Potter and Litton 1985). Techniques were being used which smoothed over the internal diversity in samples' responses and exaggerated consistency. Such techniques — averaging, some forms of multidimensional scaling, and some forms of interpretative analysis — have been used with great effect elsewhere in psychology, so it is not at all surprising that they should be deployed here also. However, as consensus is exactly what is at issue here, their use is rather more problematic.

Part of the problem stems from the notions of consensus and agreement. Our everyday notion of consensus is usually deployed in contexts where groups of people are publicly expressing views on specific issues — a unanimous vote can indicate a consensus has been *achieved*. Moreover, 'agreement' typically implies that people are aware of each other's positions — that they have a mutual understanding — and it is this dimension which is stressed in the legal usage of the term 'agreement'. Statistical preponderance measured by questionnaire implies neither of these things, and yet it is the most commonly-used measure of consensus in social-representations research (compare de Rosa 1987; Palmonari *et al.* 1987; Verges 1987, for recent examples).

Furthermore, even the question of how far participants are using the same explanations and versions is fraught with difficulties when dealing with actual discourse (Litton and Potter 1985). In a study of a set of accounts of the 'St Paul's riot' of 1980 we found that we needed to make a number of distinctions before our study of shared explanations could even get off the ground. In particular, we had to distinguish between 'use', 'mention', 'theory', and 'practice'. An explanation is mentioned if it is referred to as available, but not supported. This idea should be very important in social-representations theory, as it stresses that what a person disagrees with is as important as what they agree with. Newspaper accounts commonly use constructions such as the following (*Daily Telegraph* 5 April 1980, cited in Litton and Potter 1985):

the advice givers have made a great chorus of 'Amenity'. Is it really supposed that a craving for table tennis and coffee bars is at the bottom of [the uprising]?

This account, which 'mentions' an explanation, can be contrasted with one which straightforwardly 'uses' one (Participant on BBC TV *Nationwide* discussion, 3 April 1980, cited in Litton and Potter 1985):

I don't believe you can separate race from the explosion and it is not just coincidence. I think that the reason the violence was directed at the police is that the police are the representatives of the white establishment.

When explanations are 'used' in this way this is not the end of the complication. At one extreme, explanations can be espoused in theory, without even giving a single exemplar. (*The Guardian* 3 April 1980, cited in Litton and Potter 1985):

There is no form of perfect race riot, although in different forms they usually contain a confrontation with authority in the form of the police.

Towards the other extreme, explanations can be developed with a very specific application (black 17-year-old respondent cited in Reicher and Potter 1985):

Well, the police niggled us and when they started pushing us around we just got carried away.

The crucial point for social-representations theory is that the degree to which explanatory resources are shared across a sample of people could be assessed at each of these different levels. If we are to count instances, we could count all the mentions, all the uses in theory, or all the uses in practice — and each would give a different idea of the overlap. Clearly this is a recipe for considerable confusion.

Allied to this is the implicit notion of conflict adopted in social-representations theory: conflict is something that happens between those holding differing representations; where representations are shared conflict need not happen. This idea is sustained by the failure to explicate the notion of consensus, by the loose use of the notion of agreement with its overtones of psychological harmony, and by social-representations researchers' resistance to examining natural discourse. The existence of generalized representations, rules, or versions always opens the possibility of dispute over their practical application (compare Mulkay 1979; Wieder 1974; Zimmerman 1971) or simply over their meaning in the abstract (Billig 1987). Both discourse analysts (Litton and Potter 1985; Potter and Wetherell 1987) and rhetoricians (Billig, Chapter 2 of this book) have stressed that representations are as much a site of conflict and argument as of harmony and agreement. Overall, this suggests that the notion of social representations as an agreed code seriously underplays the conflictual possibilities inherent in social life.

Coordinating language and cognition

The problem of coordinating the cognitive and linguistic realms becomes crucial when attempting to operationalize social representations in practice. This difficulty applies particularly to the level at which operationalization is meant to take place. Moscovici (1984a, p. 38) states that representations are made up of both abstract and concrete elements; that is, social representations are part concept and part image. However, in practice researchers are almost inevitably faced with discourse of some kind. This is true both of 'traditional' methods, where we might have responses to questionnaires or experimental check lists, and more 'radical' interpretative approaches, dealing with transcripts of open-ended interviews or records of naturalistic interaction (Potter and Wetherell 1987).

The central problem lies in the extrapolation from discourse to the concepts or images that go to make up the social representation, given the action orientation of discourse. That is, discourse is no easy pathway to mental furniture because it is constructed in highly context sensitive ways to accomplish a whole variety of practical tasks — as work in discourse analysis, pragmatics, and semiotics has documented in great detail (for example Heritage 1984; Levinson 1983; Potter and Wetherell 1987; Barthes 1975). Discourse is designed to do particular jobs and is organized in such a way that certain practical consequences are likely to follow.

For example, in the riot accounts we studied (Litton and Potter 1985; Potter and Reicher 1987; Wetherell and Potter 1989; Potter and Halliday 1990), positions were justified and undermined, people and groups were blamed and mitigated, and police decisions were supported or attacked. These were the significant issues for the participants, and we suggest that it is therefore these activities, rather than mental images or processes such as anchoring and objectification, which are most analytically pertinent in making sense of discourse. We will return to this point later in the chapter.

The concept of representation

Many of the problems with social-representations theory in practice arise from the conception of social representations as pseudocognitive phenomena — mental representations — which have objective causes and effects. In this section, we will indicate some of the difficulties with this cognitive notion of representations, noting problems created in analytic practice.

Representation as images

According to Moscovici (1984a) representations are cognitive mechanisms which have two facets: the symbolic and the iconic. The representing aspect of social representations stems from the iconic element of these representations — in a large part, representations represent by depicting aspects of the world in a pictorial fashion (Moscovici 1984a, p. 38). As an example of how this idea of social representations as images might be used, consider the notions of anchoring and objectification.

Representation is a system of classification in which novel experiences are 'anchored' to existing frames of thought in such a way as to make the 'unfamiliar' 'familiar'. The process of classification requires the thinker to locate an aspect of the world within a particular class of phenomena. One aspect of such classes is that they contain members which can be regarded as prototypical. If we are to regard representations as images in the way that Moscovici suggests, we will have to think of such classes as providing a 'photo-kit' which represents a 'test-case' for class membership, summing up the common features of the member cases. This 'photo-kit' will be an iconic matrix of observable features. The iconic matrix is inspected or processed by the mind's eye and the appropriate decision as to class membership is then made for each given experience. Moscovici offers as an example of such a photo-kit the image of a Frenchman as an undersized, beret-wearing, French-loaf carrier.

There are important problems with this idea. If social representations are cognitive images, when we understand the unfamiliar by assimilating it to the familiar we represent an unfamiliar experience to ourselves as being like a picture which is already before our mind's eye. However, this still leaves the crucial thing to be explained; namely, how the thinker's image can be thought of as a classificatory mechanism depicting events in some specific way. In other words, we need to know what it is about the image which guarantees that the thinker 'sees' it in the correct way. There is no room in the current conception of the theory for an account of how the thinker sees the image as depicting events in one specific way rather than another.

The problem is that there is a process of interpretation required in order to make sense of an image as a classificatory mechanism — as depicting events in one specific way rather than another — but the theory itself offers no account of what this further interpretative process might be. It is, naturally, open to the theorist to claim that the thinker's view of the image through the mind's eye is itself a matter of representation, that the image is *represented* as being such and such or so and so. But, what would then seem to be required is another image which will allow the thinker to correctly classify the first image (Blackburn 1984)! This idea thus leads to a damaging regress.

Seeing in the mind

There is, additionally, a worry about taking the notion of seeing images with the mind's eye to be an explanation of what it is to represent something to oneself. To begin with, such an explanation offers no account of how the mind's eye sees the image. An ordinary account of seeing will refer to the use we make of our eyes, to perspectives, to viewing conditions, and to the possibility of being mistaken. None of this holds for seeing images with the mind's eye. More importantly, perhaps, the cognitive social-representations theory of representing offers no account of when two images are the same image. According to the theory, whenever the thinker assimilates experience to some given class, he or she likens it to the image associated with that class. This leaves open the question of how, on two different occasions, the thinker can be certain that he or she has hold of the same image as on the previous occasion. There are checks which can be performed when one wishes to ascertain whether the object seen now is the same object as the one seen previously, but these will involve precisely the kinds of empirical investigation which are unavailable in the case of trying to establish whether two images are the same (Peacock 1983). The best the thinker can do in ensuring that two images are the same is to ensure that they represent the same thing. However, this presupposes that we have a means of establishing the identity of things, which is, in principle, independent of our conception of them via social representations — and such a form of 'direct' conception of the environment is explicitly ruled out by cognitive social-representations theory.

Social basis of representational images

Social representations theory needs to explain how the process of representing through images can possibly constitute a social phenomenon. Moscovici's claim is that images are necessary for social communication. The process of representing which establishes an individual's social representations likewise establishes his social persona. A thinker will take himself to share the same world view as another just when he or she is convinced that that other shares his or her social representations. On the model of representing offered by Moscovici, this means, in part, that the thinker's communication and social involvement with others is dependent on a common stock of images — but this relies on the assumption that images could so much as be even a part of the communicative process, and there is good reason to cast doubt on this assumption.

To see the nature of such a doubt, suppose we accept the claim that most of our words and all of our ideas are linked up to images which play a central role in communication. This still leaves the question of the role that such images play among individuals. No individual has direct access to the images 'inside the head' of another individual. All that each individual has to go on, in interpreting the behaviour of others, is the outward consequences of the experiences, thoughts, conceptions, and so on of those individuals. This seems to indicate that if a process is essentially social, then its explanation must rely not on phenomena such as images which, if they exist at all, are of necessity hidden, but on phenomena which are themselves essentially social (Hacker 1986). But this suggests that, far from being an essential part of social communication, the images conjured up through representing experience are exactly the kind of phenomena which are ruled out in providing an explanation of how such communication functions. To conclude, it seems that the cognitive social-representations theorist ought not to appeal to the idea of social representations as cognitive images.

From social representations to discourse analysis

These various difficulties imply that the notion of social representations as representational, cognitive states should be abandoned, but this does not mean that the social scientist need abandon the general attempt to make sense of social phenomena from a genuinely *social* viewpoint. Nor need we abandon interest in the notion of *representation*. The concern with the production of representations, or versions, and their effects is an important one which can be sustained without the need to appeal to an 'in the head' notion of representational, cognitive states. For the rest of this chapter, we intend to demonstrate the utility of an alternative social perspective concerned with representational practices, namely, discourse analysis.

Discourse analysis can best be understood through its interconnected central concepts of function, variation, and construction and the analytic unit the interpretative repertoire. We will take these in turn, indicating their advantages over comparable social-representation ideas as we do so.

Function

As we have noted above, recent theoretical developments in the study of language stress the action orientation of language use. Language use can best be understood in terms of three broad bipolar dimensions: intended/ unintended, interpersonal/ideological, and explicit/hidden.

First, as we noted, people do things with their discourse; they make accusations, ask questions, justify their behaviour, and so on. At the same time, these developments show that there is another side of the coin — we need to modulate and supplement the study of the performative dimensions of language use with work on unintended consequences. A particular form of discourse may have consequences which have not been formulated or even understood by the speaker or writer. Put simply, we need to study how people use discourse and how discourse uses people.

Secondly, we can think of a very rough continuum running from more interpersonal functions such as blaming, explaining, and excusing, which formulate the local discursive context, to the wider purposes that discourse might serve; for example, where an account might have a particular ideological effect in the sense of legitimating the actions of one interest group in a society. At times, there may be different levels in the same materials, such as in Atkinson and Drew's (1979) study of accounts made by Royal Ulster Constabulary members to the 1972 Scarman Tribunal, where at one level the officers were excusing and mitigating their own actions and, at another, defending the reputation of a crucial state body.

Thirdly, functions may be explicit or hidden. A ship-naming, for example, is an explicitly-meant speech act. In the appropriate circumstances, in the presence of the dignitaries, spectators, and the ship, the utterance of the naming will be, explicitly and unambiguously, the act of naming. Many language functions — requests, excuses, and accusations — will be manifest in this way. However, these same functions on other occasions may be hedged or inexplicit. For example, Drew (1984) has shown that speakers often make requests in a highly indirect manner so that the recipient can rebuff them without making the rebuff a public issue. Moreover, it is self-evident that speakers are often unaware of the kinds of broader unintended consequences that their discourse may have.

For these reasons, discourse analysis should not be understood as a straightforward study of functions, because for much of the time functions are simply not available for study. Discourse rarely comes ready-labelled with its functions. Instead, discourse analysis often involves developing *hypotheses* about the purposes and consequences of language. Thus, the elucidation of function is one of the end-points of discourse analysis; functions are the findings rather than the data.

The notion of function in social-representations theory is completely undeveloped. The functions which are specified are characterized in the standard rhetoric of cognitive processes; thus, social representations make the unfamiliar familiar, anchor onto prototypes, objectify novel phenomena, and so on. Not only does this mechanistic language abound, but the focus is almost entirely on social representations as sense-making devices — they allow the participant to see. The reflexive and knowing dimension of language use, where versions are produced to create argumentative effects or to legitimate positions, is absent. More generally, social representations are not understood as fully part of the world of human activity — for blaming, questioning, and warranting — but as part of the rarefied abstract world of cognitive processes.

Given that discourse analysis is centrally concerned with the explication of activities and functions, the question now becomes 'How can these things be revealed?' There is no single answer to this (see Potter and Wetherell 1987, Chapter 8). However, one important response is that function is revealed through a study of variation.

Variation

The fact that discourse is action-orientated means that it will be highly variable — what people say or write will be different according to what they are doing. If you take an event, say, or a social group or policy initiative, it will be described in many different ways as the function changes from, for example, excusing to blaming, or from forming a positive evaluation to a negative one. Speakers give shifting, inconsistent, and varied pictures of their social worlds. Variability is a phenomenon that discourse analysts have repeatedly identified in a wide range of discursive contexts (see references in Potter and Wetherell 1987). Often, one of the most striking things about an interview transcript is the way in which inconsistencies develop over time (Potter and Wetherell 1988). Discourse which sounds perfectly reasonable on a first hearing reveals all sorts of twists and turns when it is examined more closely.

This variability is important for analysis because of its close relation to function. As function leads to variation, so variation can be used as an analytic clue to what function is being performed in a piece of talk. By identifying variation, which is a comparatively simple analytic task, we can work towards an understanding of function. We can predict that function will lead to certain kinds of variation and look for those variations (Gilbert and Mulkay 1984; Mulkay and Gilbert 1982; Potter and Mulkay 1985). It is important to stress again that this variability need not be a consequence of deliberate or intentional processes. Much of the time, people will not be strategically planning or self-consciously adjusting their discourse in a machiavellian fashion, but just 'doing what comes naturally' or stating what 'seems right' for the situation.

Given that social-representations theory has such an undeveloped notion of function, it is not surprising that it has not formulated variability as an issue. Nevertheless, many of the problems with consensus and agreement described above arise as a direct consequence of the failure to accommodate to the fact that functional usage leads inexorably to discursive variability. In a sense, there is a large black hole in social-representations theory, where some construal of participants' practices should be. The simple notions of consensus and agreement paper over this hole, but can quickly be shown to be inadequate when compared to actual discursive materials.

Construction

The fact that discourse is orientated to particular functions, which in turn throw up a mass of linguistic variation, tells us that discourse is being used *constructively*. As we noted at the start, both discourse analysis and social-representations theory are constructivist approaches. However, while social-representations theory takes construction as an essentially cognitive phenomenon — sense is mentally constructed by the representation — discourse analysis takes construction as a phenomenon of language. Discourse is put together (constructed) for purposes and to achieve particular consequences. Thus, variation is an index of both function and the different ways in which accounts can be manufactured.

The notion of construction is appropriate for three reasons. First, it cues the analyst to the point that discourse is manufactured out of pre-existing linguistic resources with properties of their own, much like a bridge is put together with girders, concrete, and so on. Secondly, it reminds us that active selection is going on, and that out of many resources available some will be used and some not. Thirdly, the notion of construction alludes to the fact that much of our lives depends on dealing with events and people which are experienced only in terms of specific linguistic versions. In a profound sense, then, discourse can be said to construct our lived reality.

We can sharpen up this difference between construction at the cognitive and linguistic levels by comparing the social-representations theory notion of objectification with the linguistic notion of nominalization. Objectification follows the process of anchoring when people are dealing with unfamiliar ideas, experiences, or objects. After the unfamiliar is anchored to a prototypical category at the heart of a social representation, its essential elements are said to be reproduced in pictorial form in the minds of group members. This image is amalgamated with the images of more familiar ideas, and then these become the reality of the group (Moscovici 1984a, p. 40; see McKinlay and Potter 1987a for critical overview). In this way, the realm of the unfamiliar is transformed into familiar and concrete experience.

This may be acceptable as a piece of speculative cognitive psychology; however, what phenomena indicate that a process of this kind is taking place? One recurrent discursive process which is superficially analogous to objectification is nominalization which, put simply, occurs when actions or processes are treated in terms of nouns. Kress and Hodge (1979) give the example of 'picketing' which is the nominal form of 'strikers picket factory'.

The transformation of processes into concrete objects in this way would, on the face of it, appear to be just the kind of evidence that Moscovici might desire to substantiate the process of objectification. Yet, the differences between the way the two processes are understood is very instructive. For social-representations theory, the main role would be one of mentally taking-hold, of incorporating awkward phenomena by turning them into familiar images. The process is basically perceptual. In contrast, discursive studies of nominals such as picketing, violence, and community relations suggest that these constructions are drawn upon to accomplish very specific kinds of ideological and/or interactional tasks, most commonly the obscuring of patterns of agency and causality (Kress and Hodge 1979; Potter and Reicher 1987). Trew (1979) has demonstrated how a newspaper can assimilate a problematic version of events into a standardized and less politically-awkward explanatory form, partly with the aid of nominalization. Problematic patterns of agency and causality (in this case, police gunning-down unarmed protesters) can be transformed into nominal form ('sad loss of life') and then reconnected into other kinds of causal processes ('tribalism'), and in this way the assignment of blame away from the police and on to more traditional targets for racist thinking can be accomplished. Another way of looking at this would be to say that processes of anchoring and objectification would be better understood in the context of rhetoric than in the context of cognition (Billig 1988).

Interpretative repertoires

The suggestion that discourse is variable because speakers are constructing their talk differentially according to function, does not imply that discourse is random and irregular. Regularity does not necessarily appear at the level of the individual speaker. Rather, there is regularity in variation itself. Inconsistencies and differences in discourse can be understood as part of broader differences between relatively internally consistent, bounded language units which we have called interpretative repertoires, following Gilbert and Mulkay (1984).

Interpretative repertoires can be seen as the building blocks that people use for constructing versions of actions, cognitive processes, and other phenomena in their discourse. Any particular repertoire is constituted out of a restricted range of terms used in a specific stylistic and grammatical fashion. Commonly, these terms are derived from one or more key metaphors and the presence of the repertoire is often signalled by particular tropes or figures of speech.

For example, we have examined 'community' talk in these terms. It can be seen to be organized around central metaphors — communities are conceived of in organic and agency terms and with specific spatial organization. Thus, a community can grow, evolve, and be close-knit. Furthermore, it is generally used with an implied oppositional status — thus community policing is contrasted with other forms which are potentially heavy handed, uninformed, or insensitive. The community repertoire is a resource which participants can use in the performance of a variety of disparate tasks, such as blaming or warranting, and can be identified through its recurring pattern in different materials.

There is no space here to give a full and detailed account of the application of the notion of interpretative repertoires to a body of data. Examples are given elsewhere: in scientists' discourse (Gilbert and Mulkay 1984; Mulkay 1985; Mulkay and Gilbert 1983; McKinlay and Potter 1987b; Potter 1984, 1987; Potter and Mulkay 1982; Yearley 1985); for the use of the notion of community as in community policing and community relations (Reicher and Potter 1985), community leaders (Potter and Halliday 1990), and community care (Potter and Collie 1989); for racist discourse (Wetherell and Potter 1992); and for gender discourse (Wetherell 1986; Marshall and Wetherell 1989; Wetherell et al. 1987).

The concept of interpretative repertoire does some of the same sort of explanatory work as social-representations theory. That is, it is an analytic concept designed to help illuminate the construction of representations in discourse and to help make sense of phenomena which social psychologists have traditionally understood in terms of attitudes, stereotypes, beliefs, and attributions. However, the notion has the advantage of being moulded in the test-bed of analytic practice. It is not handicapped by the presupposition of a one-to-one correspondence with group boundaries and it eschews the sorts of speculative cognitive science which has contributed so much to the vagueness of social-representations theory.

Furthermore, the analyst of interpretative repertoires is not wedded to a simple notion of consensus in the sense that some group members will always use a particular repertoire. As the basic level of analysis is a functional one, and as functions can be accomplished by using a range of different discursive resources, we will expect considerable variation in the way that repertoires are used. While certain repertoires may indeed be recurrently used to achieve certain tasks (for example Mulkay and Gilbert 1982), in other cases several different repertoires might be adequate to the job (Wetherell and Potter, 1992).

In the final section of this chapter, we wish to move the argument closer to some actual examples. The point will be to show in more detail how a number of representational phenomena which might be viewed in cognitive terms within social-representations theory can be more straightforwardly understood as features of discourse. We stress that these examples are not intended to be a full analysis of discourse — rather, they are intended to show in a preliminary fashion how representations can be understood in discursive terms.

Representing as a phenomenon of language: craft and selection

The following excerpts are taken from the transcript of a set of regular meetings in which a selection committee of Craftsmen and Craftswomen assess the work of applicants to a County Craft Guild. The assessment takes the form of the committee examining and evaluating the quality of items of the applicant's work. During this examination, the committee discuss the relative merits of the pieces presented, and each assessor then gives an evaluation of the work. On the basis of these evaluations, a joint decision is agreed as to whether the applicant ought to be accepted into the Guild. In effect, then, the Guild Craftsmen and Craftswomen are engaged in a 'gate-keeping' task. Their joint responsibility is to offer skilled membership criteria, through which they will judge the merit of each applicant for membership of the Craft Guild.

This is an ideal database for the study of the role of representations in practice. The task of the group is predefined, as their role is to provide assessments, and their focus is predefined as a limited range of craft objects which all of the members have currently available for inspection. The setting is a conversational one, where members can talk as much as they wish about the quality and status of these artefacts; they can formulate representations, and we have access to any acts of agreement or disagreement they may make about these.

Example one

The first extract is taken from a discussion which centres on an applicant who has submitted, as examples of his work, a number of items of furniture.

Extract one

01	*Joan*:	And he didn't do the upholstery. But all this
02		is a restoration job.
03	*Beth*:	What was there before he started on it though?
04	*Joan*:	Well [laughs] maybe it just needed doing up.
05	*Beth*:	He's painted it.
06	*Brian*:	Yes.
07	*Beth*:	It's all hard to know, isn't it? Perhaps he's
08		made some of the parts.
09	*Joan*:	It may have been it may have been bits missing
10		or knocked about. I don't know.
11	*Beth*:	We can't judge it if we don't know, can we?
12	*Joan*:	No.
13	*Chris*:	We don't go in for that sort of thing anyway.
14	*Peter*:	We don't want people that restore, do we?
15	*Joan*:	Don't we? Oh, I see. So it's immaterial.
16	*Peter*:	Well that aspect of it. I mean if we =
17	*Beth*:	If that's a restoration job we aren't even
18		looking at it.
19	*Peter*:	No.
20	*Joan*:	So it's out.

As the recorded conversation develops in this extract, a query arises about whether the items of furniture submitted by the candidate are original or merely restorations. This allows the Craft Guild assessors to represent the applicant's work in a specific way — they agree on viewing 'restored-ness' as an important feature of the candidate's work (lines 1–2 and 11–20). In doing so, they establish a particular representation of the candidate's work: it is a 'restoration job' (line 17). Having established this particular representation of the candidate's work, the Craft Guild assessors use it in coming to a decision about the candidate's application. Chris states that they 'don't go in for that sort of thing' (line 13), and Beth ends by saying that they will not even look at 'a restoration job' (lines 17–18), a view with which Peter agrees (line 19). So as a result of the constructive efforts of the assessors and their formulation through a specific representation, the candidate's work is deemed not of a level required of members of the Craft Guild.

This first example demonstrates that it is possible to examine the way in which people utilize joint representations without positing the existence of cognitive, representing states and without, therefore, attempting to estimate the form and content of such states. Instead, the analyst examines the way that a particular phrase, expression, metaphor, or whatever, is recurrently drawn upon throughout a discussion in order to achieve a particular result. Furthermore, here we see agreement over a representation actively done by participants rather than presupposed by the analyst.

Example two

A central aspect of representing, in social representations theory, as we have seen, is the production of images which act as 'iconic matrices' to which experience is assimilated in a pictorial fashion. Phenomena of this kind can be understood in discursive terms. In the next short example, this picturing process can be seen at its most basic. In this section of the transcript, the work presented by the candidate is made up of soft fabrics — cushions and items of clothing:

Extract two

01 *Brian*:   I'm a bit dubious about them [the candidate]
02   going into clothes, mm, basically because I
03   think that looks like a cushion with arm-holes.
04   [laughs]
04 *Paul*:   [laughs]
05 *Beth*:   [laughs]

Brian puts across his impression of the low standard of the clothes submitted by the applicant by representing one of the garments using a simple evocative picture: the garment looks like the cushions which accompany it in the applicant's submission. The local effectiveness of this representational feat is suggested by the accompanying laughter and the negative assessments of the clothes offered by all the other participants later in the discussion.

Whether or not its rhetorical effectiveness was crucial to the discussion, this example illustrates well the way that discourse analysis can provide one sort of account for the picturing aspect which is a major feature of social representations stereotyping functions. In their representational work, people recurrently conjure up particular pictures or arresting images. However, there is no need to revert to a problematic discussion of cognitive states or mental images in order to give an explanation of the way that such picturing processes help the speaker to achieve his or her conversational goal, or to indicate the role of particular versions of events in warranting evaluations.

Example three

The claim that representations are fluid and dynamic is also a central part of social-representations theory. Within a group, renegotiations should occur when individuals differ as to whether a particular event fits a specified representation. One of the strengths of the discourse approach is that it can start to document dynamic processes of this kind. To give a flavour of such an analysis, consider the following extract, in which the Guild assessors are discussing the work of an applicant who produces pottery.

Extract three

01	*Beth*:	I think a lot of it is tremendous fun, but I
02		think the effect of all of it is very ugly.
03	*Brian*:	But you could say that with a lot of them. I
04		mean if you put just one piece, you know, I can
05		sort of see it in the home, sort of person who
06		would buy that. But if you put, say, the
07		Millseys' work all together =
08	*Beth*:	= Mm
09	*Brian*:	You know, it's really sort of — and, and
10		Jolanada's as well. And Caroline's =
11	*Beth*:	Mm.
12	*Brian*:	One piece on its own is much nicer, I think you
13		have to see it all in you know the light of
14		that =
15	*Beth*:	Mm. I think — I'm thinking obviously of the
16		context of a Guild exhibition on a stand.

In this extract, two competing representations of the applicant's work are canvassed. On the one hand, Beth suggests that the pieces of applicant's work should be considered simultaneously — what matters is 'the effect of all of it' (line 2). On the other hand, Brian suggests that it is more important to consider each piece in its own right — 'just one piece, you know' (line 4). In the course of discussion, each offers further specification of the representation. They refine their respective representations by offering an identifiable image. The 'all together' representation carries with it the picture of work gathered together at an 'exhibition on a stand' (line 16). The 'just one piece' representation carries with it a picture of a single item of the applicant's work in someone's home (lines 3–6). What this extract reveals, then, is a dynamic process of renegotiation and refinement of competing representations.

Clearly, the limited space available has allowed only the briefest sketch of how discourse analysis might start to use materials of this kind. However, we have been able to gain an initial glimpse of the way in which jointly-produced representations were used by the Guild assessors in order to fulfil their group 'gatekeeping' role. At times, the assessors produced generalized verbal labels ('restoration job') under which they subsumed an applicant's work. At other times, they produced representations, in part, by means of the creation of specific images.

Such representing procedures can have a fluid, dynamic character as different individuals offer competing representational accounts. Social-representations theorists make the general claim that social representations are dynamic, rather than static. However, they have been notably unsuccessful in documenting this facet of representations in action. Indeed, despite recent attempts (de Rosa 1987; Verges 1987), what is generally striking about social-representations analyses is that they produce static analyses which give no clue to either processes of change in the short term or of large scale historical development. Without in any way wishing to imply that this is a straightforward goal to achieve, it is clear that one source of the failure to encompass dynamic processes is the failure to accommodate to natural interaction sequences, most centrally conversation. It is in this arena that conversation analysts have been most successful in explicating some of the basic dynamic structures of interaction (see for example Levinson 1983; Atkinson and Heritage 1984).

We would also stress that our discussion of the three extracts above did not require examining the form and content of putative mental states. Instead, a close attention to the way that people constructively drew on ordinary linguistic resources was sufficient as a means of gaining an (at least initial) understanding of the way that representations are used to create sense in everyday life.

Summary and conclusion

In this chapter, we have attempted to raise some of the analytic issues which arise when taking a social approach to the study of representations. In particular, we have concentrated on the analytic problems of the version of social-representations theory expounded by Moscovici and the way in which discourse analysis deals with those problems.

Social-representations theory has the virtue of offering a strongly social perspective at a time when social psychologists are increasingly attracted by cognitive reductionism. It also presents a thoroughgoing constructivist alternative to traditional approaches, although it is a constructivism which maintains certain cognitivist biases. Furthermore, it brings the important issue of representation to centre stage in psychology; it directs attention to the way that people construct versions of the world and the role that those versions play in social life.

Important problems arise in practice. When used in particular research projects, the theory suffers a number of difficulties with its understanding of social groups. In particular, the theory is often used inconsistently, its radical constructivism switched on in parts of the analysis but then switched off when the researcher wishes to give a clear-cut realist operationalization of the relevant social groups. The often-touted consensus in social representations turns out to be much simpler to conceptualize in theory than in practice, where the whole notions of agreement and consensus become problematic.

Social-representations theory also suffers from a number of difficulties of both a practical and conceptual nature, as a consequence of its specification of social representations as cognitive phenomena such as images, prototypes, or sets of concepts. In practical terms, the location of social representations in this way leads to difficulties in separating out cognitive-representational phenomena from linguistic-representational phenomena. Conceptually, there are difficulties because (i) images themselves do not make sense, they just move the problem of interpretation and sense-making further back into the individual; (ii) the whole notion of iconic images and seeing with the mind's eye provides a rather ill-explicated core to the theory; and (iii) there are difficulties with the idea that social representations are largely iconic images and that they are social phenomena.

We have argued that the discourse-analytic approach embodies the constructivist and social emphasis which are so valuable in theory, while avoiding or at least minimizing the practical and conceptual problems. It avoids the contradictions in operating with both realist and representational versions of groups at the same time; it resists the global notions of consensus and agreement; and it makes a clean break with the speculative cognitive theorizing about images, processes of anchoring, and so on, which are the source of many of the theory's problems. The analytic examples presented toward the end of the chapter started to give a preliminary illustration, in more concrete terms, of the way in which the notion of representation can be applied to bodies of data without the need to start peering under the skulls of the actors.

Acknowledgment

We would like to express our gratitude to the members of the Craft Guild who put up with the intrusions of researchers in their meetings and allowed their discussions to be used for research purposes. We would also like to thank the University of St Andrews Faculty of Arts for financial support and Liz Barratt for transcription.

References

Atkinson, J.M. and Drew, P. (1979). *Order in court: the organization of verbal interaction in judicial settings*. Macmillan, London.

Atkinson, J.M. and Heritage, J. (ed.) (1984). *Structures of social action: studies in conversation analysis*. Cambridge University Press.

Barthes, R. (1975). *S/Z*. Jonathan Cape, London.

Billig, M. (1987). *Arguing and thinking: a rhetorical approach to social psychology*. Cambridge University Press.

Billig, M. (1988). Social representation, objectification and anchoring: a rhetorical analysis. *Social Behaviour*, **3**, 1–16.

Billig, M., Condor, S., Edwards, D., Gane, M., Middleton, D. and Radley, A. (1988). *Ideological dilemmas*. Sage, London.

Blackburn, S. (1984). *Spreading the word*. Oxford University Press.

Coulter, J. (1979). *The social construction of mind*. Macmillian, London.

de Rosa, A.S. (1987). The social representations of mental illness in children and adults. In *Current issues in European social psychology*, Vol. 2, (ed. W. Doise and S. Moscovici), pp. 47–138. Cambridge University Press.

Di Giacomo, J.-P. (1980). Intergroup alliances and rejections within a protest movement (analysis of social representations). *European Journal of Social Psychology*, **10**, 329–44.

Drew, P. (1984). Speakers' reportings of invitation sequences. In *Structures of social action: studies in conversation analysis*, (ed. J.M. Atkinson and J. Heritage), pp. 129–51. Cambridge University Press.

Eiser, J.R. (1986). *Social psychology: attitudes, cognition and social behaviour*. Cambridge University Press.

Gergen, K. (1985). The social constructionist movement in modern psychology. *American Psychologist*, **40**, 266–75.

Gilbert, G.N. and Mulkay, M. (1984). *Opening Pandora's box: a sociological analysis of scientists' discourse*. Cambridge University Press.

Hacker, P.M.S. (1986), *Insight and illusion*, (revised edn). Oxford University Press.

Harré, R. (1979). *Social being: a theory for social psychology*. Blackwell, Oxford.

Heritage, J. (1984). *Garfinkel and ethnomethodology*. Polity Press, Cambridge.

Jayyusi, L. (1984). *Categories and the moral order*. Routledge and Kegan Paul, London.

Kress, G. and Hodge, B. (1979). *Language as ideology*. Routledge and Kegan Paul, London.

Latour, B. and Woolgar, S. (1979). *Laboratory life: the social construction of scientific facts*. Sage, London.

Levinson, S. (1983). *Pragmatics*. Cambridge University Press.

Litton, I. and Potter, J. (1985). Social representations in the ordinary explanation of a 'riot'. *European Journal of Social Psychology*, **15**, 371–88.

McKinlay, A. and Potter, J. (1987*a*). Social representations: A conceptual critique. *Journal for the Theory of Social Behaviour*, **17**, 471–87.

McKinlay, A. and Potter, J. (1987*b*). Model discourse: interpretative repertoires in scientists' conference talk. *Social Studies of Science*, **17**, 443–63.

Marshall, H. and Wetherell, M. (1989). Talking about career and gender identities: a discourse analysis perspective. In *The social identity of women*, (ed. S. Skevington and D. Baker), pp. 106–29. Sage, London.

Moscovici, S. (1984*a*). The phenomenon of social representations. In *Social representations*, (ed. R. Farr and S. Moscovici), pp. 3–69. Cambridge University Press.

Moscovici, S. (1984*b*). The myth of the lonely paradigm: a rejoinder. *Social Research*, **51**, 939–67.

Moscovici, S. and Hewstone, M. (1983). Social representations and social explanations: from the 'naive' to the 'amateur' scientist. In *Attribution theory: social and functional extensions*, (ed. M. Hewstone), pp. 98-125. Blackwell, Oxford.

Mulkay, M. (1979). Interpretation and the use of rules: the case of norms in science. In *Science and social structure*, (ed. T. F. Gieryn). Transactions of the New York Academy of Sciences, Series III, **39**, 111-25.

Mulkay, M. (1985). *The word and the world*. Allen and Unwin, London.

Mulkay, M. and Gilbert, G. N. (1982). Accounting for error: how scientists construct their social world when they account for correct and incorrect belief. *Sociology*, **16**, 165-83.

Mulkay, M. and Gilbert, G. N. (1983). Scientists' theory talk. *Canadian Journal of Sociology*, **8**, 179-97.

Palmonari, A., Pombeni, M. L., and Zani, B. (1987). Social representation and professionalization of psychologists. In *Current issues in European social psychology*, Vol. 2, (ed. W. Doise and S. Moscovici), pp. 231-70. Cambridge University Press.

Parker, I. (1987). Social representations: social psychology's (mis)use of sociology. *Journal for the Theory of Social Behaviour*, **17**, 447-70.

Peacock, C. (1983). *Sense and content*. Oxford University Press.

Potter, J. (1984). Testability, flexibility: Kuhnian values in psychologists' discourse concerning theory choice. *Philosophy of the Social Sciences*, **14**, 303-30.

Potter, J. (1987). Reading repertoires: a preliminary study of some techniques that scientists use to construct readings. *Science and Technology Studies*, **5**, 112-21.

Potter, J. (1988). Cutting cakes: a study of psychologists' social categorizations. *Philosophical Psychology*, **1**, 17-33.

Potter, J. and Collie, F. (1989). 'Community care' as persuasive rhetoric: a study of discourse. *Disability, Handicap and Society*, **4**, 57-64.

Potter, J. and Halliday, Q. (1990). Community leaders as a device for warranting versions of crowd events. *Journal of Pragmatics*, **14**, 725-41.

Potter, J. and Litton, I. (1985). Some problems underlying the theory of social representations. *British Journal of Social Psychology*, **24**, 81-90.

Potter, J. and Mulkay, M. (1982). Making theory useful: utility accounting in social psychologists' discourse. *Fundamenta Scientiae*, 3/4, 259-78.

Potter, J. and Mulkay, M. (1985). Scientists' interview talk: interviews as a technique for revealing participants' interpretative practices. In *The research interview: uses and approaches*, (ed. M. Brenner, J. Brown, and D. Canter), pp. 247-71. Academic Press, London.

Potter, J. and Reicher, S. (1987). Discourses of community and conflict: the organization of social categories in accounts of a 'riot'. *British Journal of Social Psychology*, **26**, 25-40.

Potter, J. and Wetherell, M. (1987). *Discourse and social psychology: beyond attitudes and behaviour*. Sage, London.

Potter, J. and Wetherell, M. (1988). Accomplishing attitudes: fact and evaluation in racist discourse. *Text*, **8**, 51-68.

Reicher, S. and Potter, J. (1985). Psychological theory as intergroup perception: an illustration using 'professional' and 'lay' accounts of crowd events. *Human Relations*, **38**, 167-89.

Sacks, H. (1984). Notes on methodology. In *Structures of social action: studies in conversation analysis*, (ed. J. M. Atkinson and J. Heritage), pp. 21-7. Cambridge University Press.

Trew, T. (1979). Theory and ideology at work. In *Language and Control*, (ed. R.

Fowler, B. Hodge, G. Kress, and T. Trew), pp. 94–116. Routledge and Kegan Paul, London.

Turner, J., Hogg, M., Oakes, P., Reicher, S., and Wetherell, M. (1987). *Rediscovering the social group*. Blackwell, Oxford.

Verges, P. (1987). A social and cognitive approach to economic representation. In *Current issues in European social psychology*, Vol. 2, (ed. W. Doise and S. Moscovici), pp. 271–306. Cambridge University Press.

Watson, R. and Weinberg, T. (1982). Interviews and the interactional construction of accounts of homosexual identity. *Social Analysis*, **11**, 56–78.

Watson, R. (1978). Categorization, authorization and blame-negotiation in conversation. *Sociology*, **12**, 105–13.

Wetherell, M. (1986). Linguistic repertoires and literary criticism: new directions for the social psychology of gender. In *Feminist Social Psychology* (ed. S. Wilkinson), pp. 77–96. Open University Press, Milton Keynes.

Wetherell, M. and Potter, J. (1988). Discourse analysis and the identification of interpretative repertoires. In *Analysing everyday explanation: a case book*, (ed. C. Antaki), pp. 168–83. Sage, London.

Wetherell, M. and Potter, J. (1989). Narrative characters and accounting for violence. In *Texts of identity*, (ed. J. Shotter and K. Gergen), pp. 206–19. Sage, London.

Wetherell, M. and Potter, J. (1992). *Mapping the language of racism: discourse and the legitimation of exploitation*. Harvester, Hemel Hempstead.

Wetherell, M., Stiven, H., and Potter, J. (1987). Unequal egalitarianism: a preliminary study of discourses concerning gender and employment opportunities. *British Journal of Social Psychology*, **26**, 59–72.

Wieder, L. (1974). *Language and social reality*. Mouton, The Hague.

Wowk, M. (1984). Blame allocation: sex and gender in a murder interrogation. *Women's Studies International Forum*, **7**, 75–82.

Yearley, S. (1984). Proofs and reputations: Sir James Hall and the use of classification devices in scientific arguments. *Earth Sciences History*, **3**, 25–43.

Yearley, S. (1985). Vocabularies of freedom and resentment: a Strawsonian perspective on the nature of argumentation in science and the law. *Social Studies of Science*, **15**, 99–126.

Zimmerman, D. (1970). The practicalities of rule use. In *Understanding everyday life*, (ed. J. Douglas), pp. 221–38. Routledge and Kegan Paul, London.

7 Debating social representations

Willem Doise

Introduction

Several ways of commenting on the foregoing chapters are possible, and I have chosen to comment on them one by one. But, when I started writing my comments, I very rapidly realized that a more general approach was necessary. After all, most of the chapters brought me back to the basic question I have already tried to answer several times (Doise 1985, 1988, 1989*a*, *b*): what is meant by social representations? I concluded that it was necessary first to present my answer to this question before taking issue with the single chapters.

The grand theory of social representations

Most authors in this book seem to admit that the theory of social representa-tions is rather vague and still under construction, but that processes such as anchoring and objectification have already been theoretically defined and empirically studied. That is an important point: descriptions of processes can stimulate and even orientate investigations of researchers even when they are embedded in a general theory which is considered to be vague. I would be ready to defend such an eventuality, but I do not have to do so in the present case.

The theory of social representations is not vague. It basically is a general theory about a metasystem of social regulations intervening in the system of cognitive functioning. As few authors mention this very explicitly, I will quote some passages from Moscovici (1976) on this basic theoretical princi-ple, which was already very clearly devised in his book on the social representations of psychoanalysis.

While studying adults' thinking on psychoanalysis, Moscovici noticed several characteristics of their thinking which were similar to characteristics usually ascribed to children's thinking—such as, for instance, incorrect use of fragmentary information, frequent contradictions and repetitions, causal interpretations of mere concomitances, and frequent reformulations of premises in order to make them fit with conclusions that one holds for other reasons, instead of drawing conclusions from premises. How does one explain these similarities or common characteristics between children's and adults' thinking?

The question has been phrased in this way by Moscovici (1976, p. 284): 'Does the cognitive system of social representations take the form observed because our (adult) reasoning harbours within it intellectual structures belonging to our earlier (childish) years? Or is it because it corresponds to a collective situation or interaction to which it is well adapted? One might show that fundamentally there is no contradiction.'

In childish thought, as in adult thought, two systems are involved and these underlie their common characteristics. Moscovici wrote in 1961: '. . . we see two cognitive systems at work, one which operates in terms of associations, inclusions, discriminations, that is to say the cognitive operational system, and the other which controls, verifies and selects in accordance with various logical and other rules; it involves a kind of metasystem which re-works the material produced by the first' (Moscovici 1976, p. 254).

The metasystem is constituted by social regulations, considered to be 'normative regulations which control, verify and direct' (ibid.) cognitive operations. The organizing principles of the metasystem vary across different domains of adult thought; they can require a rigorous application of logical principles, as in the scientific domain, or be directed primarily at maintaining social cohesion, as in controversies of various kinds. 'Natural thought is articulated around directional and "controversial" communication'; particular positions are defended by recourse to forms of arguments which would be judged logically unacceptable in the framework of other debates, for instance in scientific discussions or in judicial arguments. The same individuals are guided in their reasoning by different metasystems on different occasions.

Mastering of cognitive competences by individuals in no way implies '. . . that these operations would be applied to no matter what content. Even when they have mastered their physical and ideological universe, children or adolescents are still a long way from making general use of their intellectual tools. Society does not ask it from them.' (Moscovici 1976, p. 284).

It is incumbent upon social psychologists in particular to study the links between social regulations and cognitive functioning in order to answer the question: which social regulations engage which cognitive functions in which specific contexts?

It is the analysis of the relations between the social metasystem and the cognitive system which constitutes the study of social representations. According to social positions in specific networks of relations, demands of the metasystem change; they can, for instance, require rigorous application of logical principles during scientific activity, or aim above all to defend group cohesion during a conflict with a hostile group. In both cases, the cognitive functioning is in fact governed by different social regulations, by 'normative regulations which control, verify and direct' (to take the terms of Moscovici) the cognitive operations.

A privileged instance for studying this double dynamic in social representations is found in systems of communicative relationships.

It is in the second part of Moscovici's (1976) book on social representations of psychoanalysis that one finds, from my point of view, the best example of a study on the insertion of representations within the organization of symbolic relationships between social actors. The general aim of the book is the study of the transformation of a scientific theory into common sense, while the second part is more specifically on the way that the French press of the 1950s dealt with psychoanalysis.

Three kinds of publications were analysed: the press related to the communist party, the press related to the Catholic church, and the newspapers with a large circulation. These three sectors of the French press do not have the same relationships with their readers and with their social and cultural environment. Therefore, three different communicative relationships will be described.

Diffusion is characterized by a lack of differentiation between the source and the receivers of the communication. In journals with a large audience, journalists pass on the information which they have usually received themselves from the specialists. Their principal aim is to create common knowledge and to adapt themselves to the interests of their readers. The *propagation* report of communication is established by members of a group who rely on a well-organized world vision, who have a belief in propagation, and who aim to accommodate contents of other doctrines to their own well-established system. In the example chosen by Moscovici, the question under study is how communication emanating from the Catholic church accommodates psychoanalytical knowledge to the principles of religion. *Propaganda* is a form of communication that is embedded in conflicting social relations. The aim of the communication is to clearly differentiate false and true knowledge, to entertain an antagonist vision, an incompatibility between the source's own vision and the mystified vision attributed to the defenders of psychoanalysis.

The cognitive organizations of messages in various communication modalities are different. In the diffusion system, themes are not strongly integrated, and given standpoints can be different and sometimes contradictory. Depending on the case, psychoanalysis can be treated seriously, with reserve, or even with irony, and one may associate psychoanalysis with other subjects in fashion. Without necessarily looking for change in behaviour, one makes a new subject fashionable while accepting the fact that opinions on it can differ.

A more complex organization of contents characterizes propagation. The writings of Catholics on psychoanalysis advocate moderation and prudence.

They envisage its use in educational settings but dispel the notion of libido as a general explanatory concept. Instead, a positive role is attributed to affectivity and to therapeutic practices of analytical inspiration. In contrast to positivism, psychoanalysis is supposed to elaborate a more integrated comprehension of the human being as it affords an important place to symbolism, and can therefore further a revival of a spiritualist vision. The origins of such interpretations of psychoanalysis are to be sought in an assimilation into the religious message. For the rest, no global acceptance or global disproof is advised.

Propaganda, on the contrary, recommends a global refusal of a rival conception. In the communist newspapers of the cold-war period, psycho-analysis is considered to be nothing more than a pseudoscience imported into France from the USA. Systematic oppositions in society and in politics are related to oppositions in psychology. The Soviet Union is presented as the country of peace, and the USA as the one of war and social exploitation; the Soviets develop a heuristically- and scientifically-valid psychology, whereas the Americans propose a psychoanalysis which, only in appearance, seems to be scientific but which, in reality, reflects a mystifying ideology.

Of course, the current representations of psychoanalysis have changed. Moscovici (1976), in a new edition of his book, shows this for the communist press, where the articles on psychoanalysis reveal, nowadays, more pro-pagation than propaganda dynamics. But, the general conclusion of Moscovici (1976, p. 497) remains valid when he proposes an integrative framework for research on opinions, attitudes, and stereotypes: 'Consider-ing from the angle of structure of messages, elaboration of social models, relation between senders and receivers, behavioural aims, the three systems of communication maintain their singularity. Therefore, it is specifically their particularity that allows us to link term to term diffusion, propagation and propaganda to opinion, attitude and stereotype.'

This conclusion is important: it implies above all that definitions of social representations in terms of consensus are insufficient. Only stereotypes are consensually shared within a given group or subgroup; attitudes result from various efforts of assimilation into an already complex and varied system and therefore give rise to new variations, opinions fluctuate and follow fashions. More than consensual beliefs, social representations are therefore organizing principles of various kinds, which may imply common reference points. The study of social representations advocated by Moscovici necessitates intertwining complex systems of relations at the individual level with complex systems of symbolic relations between social actors. Other patterns than those of diffusion, propagation, and propaganda can be envisaged; they can originate other structures of representations based on other organizing principles.

This new definition of opinions, attitudes, and stereotypes has unfortunately not been retained by social psychologists working in these fields. This is surely not a coincidence, because few researchers work at the articulation between systems of communication and systems of cognitive organization.

To conclude this section: I have borrowed from Moscovici a theory on social representations which is not only heuristically useful for analysing complex phenomena, but also able to reorganize theoretically traditional domains of studies in social psychology. Of course, by reporting these ideas of Moscovici I do not consider that they exhaust his theoretical contribution on social representations. However, they are the general principles which have orientated his thinking on more specific processes and which offer a more general framework for the detailed analyses of the three communication dynamics just described. I consider, therefore, that the concepts of system and metasystem are the essential concepts of a kind of grand theory.

In my view, grand theories in human sciences are general conceptions about individual and/or societal functioning which orientate the research effort. They none the less are to be completed by more detailed descriptions of processes which are compatible with the general theory, but which may also sometimes be compatible with other theories. In this sense, for instance, the Piagetian ideas on accommodation and assimilation are part of a grand theory, but more detailed descriptions of the acquisition of symbolic thinking, of cognitive operations, and of formal thinking offer specific models which constitute Piaget's main contribution to developmental psychology. If Piaget had not worked at this more specific level, his theory on accommodation and assimilation would have been considered only as another version of a kind of Bergsonian philosophy. The same distinction can be drawn for constructivist theories or for our own social definition of the intellect.

The readers who are familiar with the literature on social representations will probably have been struck by the fact that I did not present in this section the concepts of anchoring and objectification. There are several reasons for that omission. First of all, I wanted to underline the special status of Moscovici's thinking on system and metasystem, as this part of the theory is currently neglected, whereas many recent writings, among them various chapters of this book, deal with anchoring and objectification. Furthermore, I think that Moscovici's various writings on objectification and anchoring only receive their full meaning in the light of his general ideas on system and metasystem. Finally, I think that in some sense the basic ideas of system and metasystem, and the embedding of social representations in networks of symbolic or communicative relationships, are the theoretical postulates which are to be clearly expressed at the beginning of a debate on social representations. In a certain sense they are the main issue at stake and, if the debate does not evolve aroud them, then it is not a debate on social representations — however interesting the arguments may be.

Theoretical positioning of the six approaches

I now will start discussing the usefulness of Moscovici's theory for the specific issues raised by the chapters on which I was asked to comment. The order of the chapters in the book will be followed, and I will almost exclusively analyse the theoretical status afforded to social representations by the authors. The principles described and illustrated in the previous section will, of course, offer me the main guidelines for this exercise in theoretical positioning; but I will also call in more idiosyncratic conjectures when necessary.

The main argument developed by Farr approaches the problem of social representations at the level of grand theories. He underlines the contribution of social-representation theory to the study of culture and, more specifically, to the study of that subpart of culture which is psychological science. I cannot but agree with his thesis that social representations also orientate psychological research as such, and that, for instance, the laboratory is to be considered 'a *direct* consequence of representing psychology as a branch of natural science'. Indeed, many authors insist on the study of social representations downstream from the scientific activity, but social representations also intervene upstream and during scientific activity itself: the theory 'ought to apply at the level of the research community itself'. I have tried such an application showing that, concerning the Piagetian school, dynamics of diffusion, propagation, and propaganda have interfered with its scientific work (see Doise 1987). Chapter 1 by Farr offers an example of such an interference when he enhances the opposition between the French-speaking and the English-speaking scientific culture. Reality is more complex, as I have seen behaviourists at work in France and interpretatively-orientated psychologists in Great Britain and the USA!

Of course, I agree totally with Farr when he stresses the diversity of methodological approaches which characterize research on social representations: the grand theory as such does not stipulate, unlike behaviourism, a preferred method for its illustration. That experimental work can be compatible with the grand theory is also my opinion. In fact, all other chapters propose different methodological paradigms for studying-social representation; at least they do not reject the usefulness of the idea of social representations as McKinlay, Potter, and Wetherell tend to do in Chapter 6.

Billig in Chapter 2 very strongly argues in favour of a 'rival approach', based on the study of rhetoric, suggesting 'that social representation theorists will need to give due attention to these features (i.e. the rhetorical features of social life) if they are to fulfil their ambitious intellectual aims.' In a certain sense, he pleads for a re-evaluation and a re-adjustment of some key concepts 'because the social representation approach was not initially formulated to deal specifically with rhetorical issues'. The key concepts under discussion are the notions of anchoring, objectification, and attitude.

Billig adopts a strategy of propagation in Moscovici's terms: he tried to convince us that social-representation theory should be adapted to his rhethorical approach. I am also in favour of propagation, in the sense that Billig's approach should be adapted to social-representation theory. A mutual assimilation and accommodation between social-representation and argumentation theories has recently been carried out by Grize *et al.* (1987) in their study on argumentation of employees about new technologies. These authors consider it necessary to refer to social-representation theory in order to explain the issues under argumentation. Billig also points to common ground on which his theory and social-representation theory already meet each other: the concern to overcome 'conventional social psychology's individualism, its static nature, its unthinking image of the thinker'.

It is not my intention to comment here on Billig's own research and more specially to evaluate to what extent it takes into account the dialectical relationships between a metasystem of social regulations and the evolution of argumentation. I will limit myself to commenting on the three main criticisms which he addresses to social-representation theory. These criticisms bear not on the general principles of the grand theory, but on the more specific concepts of anchoring, objectification, and attitude.

I take the point of Billig 'that the social representation approach runs the risk of missing the essence of the thinking society, if it places too much emphasis upon the process of anchoring' and I consider Billig's ideas on negation and particularization as further developments in the study of the ways in which representations attract but also repulse each other, to use Durkheimian terms. It is certainly the case that anchoring is not necessarily a smooth process and that, as Zeegers (1988) suggests, the anchoring of a given social practice in another one (for instance psychoanalytic treatment in the Catholic, practice of confession, or sexual relations in friendship as in the personal advertisements studied by our Dutch colleague) results often in important changes not only in the practice which is anchored but also in the anchor itself.

In his remarks on objectification, I think that Billig considers it too unilaterally as a 'materialization of abstract scientific concepts'. It is true that it has been studied in this way by Moscovici in his book on psychoanalysis, and that other authors (for instance, Roqueplo 1974) seem to locate objectification only downstream from scientific activity. But, according to Moscovici (1988*a*), it certainly is not the only position to locate objectification, as he describes money as a typical example of an objectified social representation which, of course, existed long before it was studied by economists. What is most typical of the objectification process is that it isolates concepts or social constructs from the network of conceptual or social relations in which they were originated. This is not necessarily a symptom of an 'unthinking society', but can also be the result of such processes as 'méconnaissance' which Burdieu thinks to be necessary for a given society, or subpart of a society, to function (see Doise and Lorenzi-Cioldi 1989).

A third concern of Billig is that, as a result of the switch from attitudes to social representations, 'researchers will concentrate upon shared characteristics' and therefore 'it is vitally important that the social representation approach does not jettison the topic of attitudes, in order to concentrate exclusively on what is consensually and uncontroversially shared in modern society.' Billig rightly reminds us that 'the oratorical situation represents a complexity of shared and opposed meanings'. I share this concern and will come back to it later, but I have already mentioned that, among the three dynamics of representation, only propaganda results in consensual stereotypical thinking and that diffusion and propagation allow for much variety. On several occasions, Moscovici (1988b) has explained that the change in terms from collective to social representations meant for him that he was interested in explaining the diversity and plurality of representations in modern society.

At the cost of repeated travel to the continent and dangerous contacts with tobacco smoke, Emler is now in a position to bear witness that social-representation researchers do not cultivate methodological orthodoxy, and that they probably do not bother too much about theoretical orthodoxy either. Therefore, I do not take much of a risk in asserting that I find the ideas developed in Chapter 3 by Emler and Ohana fully compatible with social-representation theory, as well as their description of the theory: 'This theory . . . emphasizes the content, and not just the structure of thinking. It emphasizes the communicated character of thought — people do not just have reasons for their views or actions, they state reasons. It also emphasizes the socially-constructed and socially-sustained character of social knowledge: independent individuals do not construct knowledge; individuals in groups and as groups construct knowledge.

These characteristics of social representations mean that they cannot be studied by the traditional theoretical tools developed by most researchers on cognitive development, even if they claim to be constructivists. Researchers on social representations are not looking so much for underlying mental structures as for communicative structures. Fundamentally, the authors consider 'that hypotheses about children's social knowledge and its development are also hypotheses about the nature of society'. To many developmental psychologists, this statement may seem provocative, but — let me try an analogy to show them that it is not. Recently, much progress has been made in the study of recognition of phonemes by babies of a few days old, and it has been verified that they are capable of discriminating between phonemes characteristic of the family language but not between phonemes which belong to foreign languages. Could one ever think of discovering such subtle differences without a comparative theory about phonemics? Why, then, think that one could study children's thinking about social issues without a theory about these issues?

Theoretically-founded societal knowledge is necessary to follow Emler's and Ohana's advice for studying social representations: 'sample from different communities, and be sure that they are (i) *communities* (not just contrasting social categories) and (ii) *different*. This has been our general approach and we find differences in representations that cannot simply be attributed to developmental differences' This is indeed a very favourable condition for studying links between characteristics of representations and patterns of social regulations.

Duveen and Lloyd also highlight the methodological liberalism of the social-representation theory. The authors have chosen an ethnographic approach as Jodelet (1989) did for her study of social representations of mental illness. Their ethnography is motivated in the sense that it focuses on gender as an organizing principle of the social life in the school and that the final aim is to construct research instruments in the form of observation schedules and interview questions. It is also important to notice that, on a general level, the study of social representations is linked to the study of communicative relationships and more specially to Habermas's (1984) distinction between communicative action which is personal and consensus orientated and strategic action which is systematic and success orientated. The family setting would rather further the former and the school setting would rather further the latter. If this difference could be tested and related to different contents of gender representations, it would be a nice illustration of the necessity to study different communities as advised by Emler and Ohana.

Meanwhile, Duveen and Lloyd report the structuring effect of gender marking in six different aspects of school life. This leads us to the important question of the links between social representations and social actions. I have elsewhere defined (Doise 1987) social representations as organizing principles of symbolic relations between social actors which are to be studied in relation to the specific positions that these actors occupy in a societal framework. Of course, these symbolic relations have material and behavioural components and as such I consider the six aspects studied by Duveen and Lloyd to be manifestations of social representations. To continue this line of thought, I would be less firm than the authors in denying truth value to social representations: 'For many psychologists, . . . ideas are understood as having a propositional structure with a veritable truth value. This is not at all the conception which Moscovici intends. . . . "Beliefs", he notes, "act as forms" . . . capable of organizing groups of people. Because of this social-psychological role, beliefs are not open to empirical validation, nor does their articulation respect the law of non-contradiction.' Is the truth value of social representations and their empirical verification not to be sought in their embedment in social relationships, in their capacity for organizing groups of people? The law of non-contradiction is to be sought in their role of preserving given social relationships even by arguments which may appear logically incoherent.

Chapter 5, by Uzzell and Blud, expands further the range of settings which can be considered appropriate for studying social representations: the whole domain of representations of the past. If, for instance, Chombart de Lauwe (1986) insists on studying adult thoughts about children as a way of thinking about the relationships between individual and society, and if Herzlich (1986) also considers that representations of illness can be considered as representations of societal relationships, it is also likely that our vision of the past is function of our contemporary vision of societal relations. Unfortunately, the authors remind us only about this possible societal embedment at the end of their paper. They regret also that learning in the museum has been 'perceived in terms of individual cognitive processes', and that is considered to be questionable in terms of the principal social groups which visit the museum (families and schools), but they do not give evidence about interactions going on except for the teaching interaction in one of their groups.

The problem then becomes: are they studying social representations? Without doubt the phenomenon in which they are interested can be studied as a social representation, for instance as a manifestation of a form of ethnocentrism, enhancing the difference between the contemporary national ingroup and primitive invaders, or even as a form of sexism. It should be possible to formulate more precise hypotheses about the change of these representations in terms of an adaptation of current hypotheses on the effect of new information on intergroup stereotypes. In a certain sense, an imaginary warlike relationship seems to be substituted by a family encounter that looks more real-life during the museum visit. It is certainly interesting to notice that the younger children are more sensible to the new concrete information than the older ones, who apparently have already more strongly-anchored representations. In its present state, however, their research could as well be considered as research in the area of social cognition, as is the case for many empirical investigations of social representations. Many authors do not hesitate, without any further justification, to identify factor scores with social representations, but Uzzell and Blud are perhaps the first to represent social representations graphically: 'The disposition of these attributes in multidimensional space can be regarded as a graphical representation of a social representation'. The process of objectification is indeed also detectable in scientific writings.

In the first part of Chapter 6 McKinlay, Potter, and Wetherell welcome social-representations theory as a constructivist innovation in social psychology. Their intention is to capture in the net of their own approach 'many of the best features of the theory while avoiding its central problems.' This is, of course, a commendable intention for scientists, but the rest of the chapter shows that they enter the debate on social representations rather in a spirit of propaganda. Apparently, they try to introduce an antagonism between the social-representations approach and their conception of discourse analysis.

It is true that unsupportable allegations and attacks on men of straw often abound in scientific debates. It is not the most pleasant side of our activity to fight such windmills. Nevertheless, I do believe that sociocognitive conflict can be an important motor of intellectual advancement, but for sociocognitive conflict to be efficient it is necessary that opposed approaches deal with the same issue. I think basically that McKinlay, Potter, and Wetherell do not deal with social-representations theory when they address two specific criticisms to the theory: circularity in the definition of the group and simplistic assumptions about the status of representation as a mental image.

Social-representations theory is said to enter 'a vicious circle where representations are identified from the group, and the representations are said to define the group'. This would be true only if social-representations researchers did not accept that other approaches can identify groups, but nothing in the theory urges them to reject this possibility. Moscovici himself, for instance, did not have to use his theory to define the sample of journals which were linked to the Catholic church or to the communist party. In the research by Di Giacomo (1980), referred to by the authors, it would have been possible to define membership of the student committee and to compare their representations with the representations of the other students, but that was not the scope of the investigation.

Of course, group categories can be studied as social representations, but that does not mean that they cannot be determined in another way. I can study representations about gender categories or about Swiss nationals and immigrants given by members of either sex, or by Swiss natives and immigrants, and use their identity cards for determining to which category interviewees belong. It is also not true that 'Moscovici and other advocates have persistently stressed that representations are consensually shared across groups of people'. We have seen that consensus was only postulated in the specific circumstances of a propaganda dynamic. When the authors refer to de Rosa (1987), Palmonari et al. (1987), and Verges (1987) for recent illustrations of their allegation that 'statistical preponderance measured by questionnaire . . . is the most commonly used measure of consensus in social representations research', I state very explicitly that none of these authors has claimed to measure consensus and that consensus or agreement is not an issue dealt with in their papers. At least these researchers have not persistently stressed that representations are consensually shared across groups of people.

Where I do agree with McKinlay and his colleagues is when they write 'that representations are as much a site of conflict and argument as of harmony and agreement'. When reading the part of Moscovici's book on propaganda, it is not difficult to reach this conclusion and even to understand better his theory on minority influence which is, in a certain sense, a prolongation of the last chapters of the social-representations book.

Is it necessary to comment on what McKinlay and his colleagues write about social representations as mental images? Let me only reassure them that social-representation theory does have to invent a 'mind's eye' because images are directly related to known social practices (such as making love or going to confession; Moscovici 1976, p. 5) and it is the proof of the social interaction which will decide on the adequancy and the persistence of the use of some images.

It is again not true that 'the notion of function in social-representation theory is completely undeveloped'. I refer again to Moscovici's analyses of diffusion, propagation and propaganda, but also to more recent research as, for instance, the research by Mugny and Carugati (1985) who intend to show how some representations of intelligence serve the parents' need for a positive identity, and the research by Jodelet (1989) on how representations of madness allow for distinctions between people with whom social intercourse is practicable or not.

The 'central problems' which McKinlay and colleagues try to avoid are neither central nor theoretically real. However, discourse analysis can indeed enrich social-representations studies and the most obvious meeting ground will probably be the study of interpretative repertoires. Therefore, I agree with van Dijk (1990, p. 165) who has this to say of relevance to our colleagues: 'Thus, whereas I share the recognition of the fundamental role of discourse in social psychology with the authors of the only book on the subject (Potter and Wetherell 1987), I differ from these authors in my approach to cognitive social representations or attitudes, which they tend to "explain away" by reducing them essentially to properties of social discourse. In my opinion, no sound theoretical or explanatory framework can be set up for any phenomenon dealt with in social psychology without an explicit account of socially shared cognitive representations. Whereas discourse is of course of primary importance in the expression, communication and reproduction of social representations . . ., this does not mean that discourse or its stategies are identical with such representations.'

Conclusion

I am aware that I have, perhaps, taken my British colleagues by surprise in relying so extensively on earlier writings of Moscovici. But, judging from their reference lists, it is also a well-known book across the English Channel.

Above all, it contains the most complete exposure of social-representation theory, and it is certainly this original version of the theory which has orientated most of the subsequent research. Unfortunately, the second part of the book is not as widely quoted as the first. A very simple explanation can be offered for this asymmetry: the concepts of the first part, such as anchoring and objectification, are more easily assimilable by the more dominant social-cognition approach. But, during this process of assimilation, they have lost much of their original meaning. Indeed, also in the first part of the book, Moscovici insisted on the necessity of studying social representations as embedded in communicative relationships: In other words, to grasp the sense of the term social, one can better put the accent on the function to which it corresponds than on the circumstances and entities which it reflects. This function is central in so far as the representation exclusively contributes to the processes of formation of behaviour and orientation of social communications' (Moscovici 1976, p. 75).

In summary, I consider it an excellent proof of the vigour of a theory in social sciences when its main principles remain innovative proposals in a lively debate about thirty years after their initial formulation.

References

Chombart de Lauwe, M. J. (1986). Liens entre les représentations véhiculées sur l'enfant et les représentations intériorisées par les enfants. In *L'étude des représentations sociales*, (ed. W. Doise and A. Palmonari), pp. 96–117. Delachaux et Niestlé, Paris.

de Rosa, A. S. (1987). The social representations of mental illness in children and adults. In *Current issues in European social psychology*, Vol. II, (ed. W. Doise and S. Moscovici), pp. 47–138. Cambridge University Press.

Di Giacomo, J. P. (1980). Intergroup alliances and rejections within a protest movement. *European Journal of Social Psychology*, **10**, 329–44.

Doise, W. (1985). Les représentations sociales: définition d'un concept. *Connexions*, **45**, 243–53.

Doise, W. (1987). Pratiques scientifiques et représentations sociales: que faire de la psychologie de Piaget? *Cahiers du Centre de Recherche Interdisciplinaire de Vaucresson*, **3**, 89–108.

Doise, W. (1988). Les représentations sociales: un label de qualité? *Connexions*, **51**, 99–113.

Doise, W. (1989a). Attitudes et représentations sociales. In *Les Représentations Sociales*, (ed. D. Jodelet), pp. 22–38. Presses Universitaires de France, Paris.

Doise, W. (1989b): Cognitions et représentations sociales: l'approche génétique. In *Les représentations sociales*, (ed. D. Jodelet), pp. 341–62. Presses Universitaires de France, Paris.

Doise, W. and Lorenzi-Cioldi, F. (1989). Sociologues et psychologie sociale. *Revue Européenne des Sciences Sociales*, **27**, 147–96.

Grize, J. B., Vergès, P., and Silem, A. (1987). *Salariés face aux nouvelles technologies. Vers une approche socio-logique des représentations sociales.* Editions du CNRS, Paris.

Habermas, J. (1981). *Theorie des Kommunikativen Handelns.* Suhrkamp, Frankfurt am Main.

Herzlich, C. (1986). Représentations sociales de la santé et de la maladie et leur dynamique dans le champs social. In *L'étude des représentations sociales*, (ed. W. Doise and A. Palmonari), pp. 157–70. Delachaux et Niestlé, Paris.

Jodelet, D. (1989). *Folies et représentations sociales.* Presses Universitaires de France, Paris.

Moscovici, S. (1976). *La psychanalyse, son image et son public*, 1976 (2nd edn). Presses Universitaires de France, Paris.

Moscovici, S. (1988a). *La machine à faire des dieux.* Fayard, Paris.

Moscovici, S. (1988b). Notes towards a description of social representations. *European Journal of Social Psychology*, **18**, 211–50

Mugny, G. and Carugati, F. (1985). *L'intelligence au pluriel: les représentations sociales de l'intelligence et de son développement.* Delval, Cousset.

Palmonari, A., Pombeni, M. L., and Zani, B. (1987). Social representation and professionalization of psychologists. In *Current issues in European social psychology*, Vol. II, (ed. W. Doise and S. Moscovici), pp. 231–69. Cambridge University Press.

Potter, J. and Wetherell, M. (1987). *Discourse and social psychology.* Sage, London.

Roqueplo, P. (1974). *Le partage du savoir.* Editions du Seuil, Paris.

van Dijk, T. A. (1990). Social cognition and discourse. In *Handbook of language and social psychology*, (ed. H. Giles and W. P. Robinson), pp. 163–83. John Wiley and Sons, Chichester.

Verges, P. (1987). A social and cognitive approach to economic representation. In *Current issues in European social psychology*, Vol. II, (ed. W. Doise and S. Moscovici), pp. 271–305. Cambridge University Press.

Zeegers, W. (1988). *Andere tijden, Andere mensen. De sociale representatie van identiteit.* Uitgeverij Bert Bakker, Amsterdam.

8 The problems of investigating social representations: linguistic parallels

David Good

Introduction

The conceptual and practical difficulties which face those who take on the empirical challenge of studying social-representations theory arise from one of the few definite things that one can say about it. For all workers in this field, it is axiomatic that a social representation (SR henceforth) can only exist where there are social relationships between the members of a society. These interactions and relationships may take many forms, and do not necessarily depend on face-to-face contact. SRT is the study of the 'thinking society', and social interaction is the *sine qua non* of society. SRs must, therefore, pervade every interaction, but saying how is the heart of the problem. Consider, for example, the case of just two members of a society interacting with one another on one occasion where they are discussing the recent psychiatric breakdown of a colleague. In their discussion, the SR of psychiatric disorder will necessarily figure, but where is it located? There will be both private and public processes and products enabling, or deriving from, this engagement, and each of these can be seen as related to, or part of, the SR of psychiatric disorder.

On the private side, it is clear that these two individuals must have certain basic cognitive processes and a set of relevant beliefs and representations, if they are to perform as competent social actors. Unless they can say and do a relevant thing at an appropriate time, they will not be part of the social fabric. Through such saying and doing, these individual memories might be changed, thereby providing a private product of the exchange. On the public side, ordinary conversational processes and routines must be followed if the interaction is to be well-formed, and, through the public claims and statements that the conversation includes, a public product is created.

These processes and products can be easily indicated in this way, but it takes only a moment's reflection to realize the extent of that which has thereby been nominated. For example, just consider what might be included under the heading 'basic cognitive and conversational processes'. To be socially competent, it is necessary to know how to construct intelligible utterances, to remember things in the appropriate way, to be able to move one's body in the right way at the right time, and so on. Those who cannot do these things properly often have their participation rights impaired, as many studies of the impact of stigma and handicap have shown. Alternatively, consider how the content of the exchange will depend upon not only the participants' ideas about psychiatric disorder, but also their related ideas about health and sickness, what counts as appropriate behaviour at work, their mad colleague's previous behaviour, and so forth. Indeed, if we pursue this exercise only a short way, it begins to seem almost as if all of human life is present in every exchange, and needs to be understood *in toto*, if we are to understand any of it. In many respects, this is an observation of some antiquity (see, for example, the discussion in Garfinkel (1967)), but the enormity of the agenda which it reveals, and which is seemingly present in the growing theoretical literature on SR, makes it easier to understand why there seems to be such a diversity of methods and foci in the empirical work in this area.

Not surprisingly, no single researcher or group of researchers has chosen to take on this whole agenda — most have been happy to work on some small part of it. The obvious necessity of the individual processes, beliefs, and representations has led many of these (for example, all the contributors to Part II of this volume in one way or another) to study individual judgements and memories. However, this focus has resulted in the charge that the definition of SR thereby offered is inherently individualistic, and thus inconsistent with the SR manifesto. Yet, there are good theoretical and practical grounds for an individualistic focus provided that the larger picture of which it is part is not forgotten. This argument will be structured around a consideration of the scope of the verb 'to represent' as ordinarily used in English — partly because I believe that the understanding of that ordinary use is relevant to understanding many of the moves which SR researchers have made, and partly because considering the sentence frame in which the verb might be placed makes it easier to see how the public and the private, and the individual and the social, are closely intertwined. This exercise by itself should be read not as an attempt to define what a SR is or what SRT should be about, but more as an attempt to illuminate the implicit definitions which are in play at the moment. Having argued for this position, I will then consider two particular problems which nevertheless arise for those who choose to focus on the individual.

To represent

The verb 'to represent ' is a five-argument predicate, the essential form of which is given in (1). An example of the kinds of values that A–E might take in a rather mundane case is given in (2).

1. A represents B by C to D for a purpose E.

2. An underground railway company (A) represents its system (B) by means
    of a map (C) to travellers (D) so that they might plan their journeys (E).

This characterization emphasizes the separation of the five arguments, but
it is easy to see how each might affect the others, and most importantly how
variability in A, B, D, and E will produce variability in C. C is of particular
interest here because it corresponds to a social product. Consequently, I will
consider each of the arguments in turn with the aim of elaborating the nature
of this relationship between C and the rest.

In producing a representation, its author (that is, A) will reflect his or her
understanding of the object being represented, and variations in the quality
of that understanding will have consequences. For example, the designers
and builders of a subway will have a much more extensive and complete conception of the network than will any individual traveller. If we asked a
traveller to draw a map of the system, the quality of the map produced would
depend upon his or her skills and knowledge, and a partial, imperfect, or
even misleading representation is a possible outcome. The map produced by
the system designers, builders, or operators is likely to be quite different, and
would reflect this greater knowledge.

In the case of SRs, it would seem that there are no *a priori* reasons
why there should not be an impact on what is said of variability in the
knowledge and expertise of the persons involved, even though identification of the precise locus of the variability is not so straightforward. Given
the dialogic emphasis offered in many of Moscovici's writings, one might
characterize any two-party conversation as having two co-producers and two
co-interpreters (that is A and D in (1) above) of what is said, but this does
not endow them, either individually or jointly, with omniscience. For example, it is easy to see how two different pairings of subjects from Zani's
or Purkhardt and Stockdale's studies (Chapters 15 and 13 of this volume)
could have quite different versions of my imaginary dialogue about a mad
colleague. It would seem odd to resist the conclusion that some of that
variability was due to variations in the beliefs and memories of the participants, and the idiosyncracies in the semantic structure of the relevant
parts of their respective lexicons. Purkhardt and Stockdale provide procedures for tracking this variation, as does Hammond (Chapter 10 of this
volume). He offers further techniques for investigating what it is that
individuals have in common by way of shared beliefs, to what degree they
share them, and how those beliefs are structured.

One reply to this observation would be that many different dialogues are
possible on the same topic, even between the same pair, and that this
variability is of interest because it provides access to the wider aspect of the
SR of psychiatric disorder. The source of the variation is unimportant; all
that matters is charting its extent. If that is the concern though, then one is
faced with a hopeless prospect as the set of all possible dialogues which

contain this variability is indefinitely large, if not infinite. Any observations of actually-occurring dialogues will necessarily be restricted to a small subset and, by examination of these alone, one could never be sure that the range had been properly assessed. By comparison, individual variability is relatively restricted, and the alternative is to collect data about this using a multiplicity of techniques to investigate this more restricted range.

It should also be borne in mind that in looking at these elements of individual variability in this way, the investigator is not examining something asocial. It is clear that these cognitive resources, while located at any one point in time in the individual, are not simply an individual creation — they are derived from the individual's previous social experiences. This is necessarily the case for the beliefs and representations, because this is the only possible source for them, but, of course, those experiences will not leave a simple imprint. Their nature in memory will be a function of other related memories, and the general character of human memory processes. These processes, together with various psycholinguistic capacities, might be thought to be simply individual. However, there is a growing body of opinion that these intellectual capacities have their evolutionary origin in the demands of our ancestors' social life (see Byrne and Whitten (1988)), and it has often been argued that their precise structuring in the individual members of any one society will reflect the culture of that society.

In other circumstances, the object which is represented (that is, B in (1)) would seem to offer many constraints on the nature of that representation, but it would be wise not to overestimate the strength of this constraint. Consider, for example, the relation between the London Underground ('tube') map and the actual distribution of the stations and the lines throughout the Greater London area. The linear distances between stations on the underground map does not correlate very well with the actual distances, and anyone who sought to find the lines by following its scheme would not be very successful. This is no surprise, as the map was designed to help tube-travellers move through the system, and not to guide maintenance men who wish to repair it. The way in which a representation is constrained by its subject matter will depend upon the purpose that it is designed to serve, and the audience to which it is orientated. I will return to these two points below, but for the moment I will draw attention to the specific problems of the constraints which exist for objects which are socially constructed, or which have a socially-constructed facet.

In certain respects, all objects come into this category in one way or another, but it would seem reasonable to suggest that they vary in the extent to which they are contingent upon states of the physical world. Representations of God in western Europe tend not to be so constrained in any significant way, but beliefs about what constitutes female circumsion practices in Sudan are (see Hammond, Chapter 10 of this volume). For those objects which are relatively independent of physical states, it is clear that powerful constraints on new versions of a representation do come from the existing variants, and this is also true to a lesser extent of those social entities which have a physical aspect. This point emphasizes the importance of studying the representations themselves, and to do so over a long timespan. However, it also indicates the need to study two other issues which ultimately lead us back to a focus on the individual.

First, there are the processes by which these representations are transmitted from generation to generation. A child's acquisition of a representation of, for example, the religion of its community will depend upon how it is presented to him or her, and also his or her own capacity for appreciating what is said and the criteria to which he or she attends in evaluating the information. This suggests that we must look on the one hand at the changing cognitive capacities of the child, and on the other at the relationship between what parents and their children hold to be the case.

Secondly, it becomes important to consider the other parts of the conceptual universe to which any particular representation is linked, because change in one representation will have implications for related entities. For example, a SR of work will inevitably include elements concerning the different roles of men and women, and these in turn will link to the SR of gender in general. One could study this relationship between different parts of the conceptual universe of the members of a society by examining what people ordinarily say in the normal course of events but, for the reasons outlined in the previous section, it makes sense to study their individual views too.

I have already noted that A and D (that is, the intended audience for C) are interchangeable, and thus they can have, similar effects on C. There is another aspect of D which should be borne in mind, though, which can increase variability in C. This derives from the common observation that speakers adjust their style and the content of their contribution to any conversation with reference to the addressee. This phenomenon produces two effects. First, speakers have a strong tendency, as Levinson (1987) has put it, 'to understate and oversuppose' when talking, so that they rarely say what they believe is known mutually by themselves and their addressees. Thus, certain aspects of a SR within a closely-knit community may never be articulated in the ordinary conversations between members of that community, because there is no need to do so. If they all know the relevance of some belief or idea at some point in a conversation, and each knows that the others know it and that this knowledge is widespread, then its expression is otiose. This could have several consequences, but it is tempting to think that the very variable lexical resources of different linguistic groups reflects, in part, the operation of this minimization principle in areas where a high level of mutual knowledge may or may not be assumed.

Secondly, within the range of what is said, a speaker will adjust the content of his or her contribution in the light of its perceived intelligibility to the addressee. This can be seen in an extreme fashion in the way that parents talk to their children, but also in the way that teachers speak to students, experts to novices, and so on. It might be objected that I am offering here a somewhat idealized account of conversational practices, and that speakers often fail to take account of their audience or even seek to deliberately mislead them. I would not wish to deny this; in some respects, this tendency would serve to reinforce my argument that the characteristics of D could lead to variation in C.

The final element in (1) (that is, E, the intended purpose of the representation) is one which has rarely had much attention paid to it in the research literature, even though the effects of SRs and their value to the members of a society are central in Moscovici's original theorizing. If we return for a moment to my London Underground example, it is clear that the purpose of the standard tube map is to help travellers; it is not to aid those who wish to dig down through the streets to find tunnels. Different representations serve different purposes and these are reflected in what an author will choose to include in and exclude from a representation. This is not to say that it cannot be used for other purposes, but these other subsequent uses will not figure in the original determination of the form and content.

This loose talk about an author's intentions may be fine if we are analysing the production of maps, but in certain respects it seems irrelevant when we consider SRs. They have no author as such, and thus there can be no intended purpose of this type. It would be foolish to disagree with this observation, even in cases such as Moscovici's (1961) original work on psychoanalysis. Freud was clearly the origin of this SR, but to construe him as the author of it in the sense that I have just used, the term would attribute to him a degree of prescience and power that even his most fervent admirers refrain from proposing. This does not mean, though, that questions of purpose and authorship are irrelevant to the nature of an SR.

SRs can serve some very clear purposes in sanitizing the presentation of an event so that it does not conflict with the requirements of the prevailing ideology. Discovering what these purposes are, though, is never a simple matter, and that should come as no surprise — a transparent purpose of this type is unlikely to remain unchallenged for very long. Similarly, the origins of the beliefs which a SR proposes may be obscured to further inhibit challenges. This may sound an odd thing to say, but reasons for believing are an issue and often proposed to lie in the natural order of things, or to be the result of divine will. For example, Breakwell (1990), in discussing gender, observed that, in most everyday discussions, gender distinctiveness was explained as a natural consequence of the physical world. Thereby, questions concerning whose interests were being served, and whether or not this was a way of construing the world rather than some veridical reflection of it, are avoided.

Two problems

Hopefully, in the preceding section, I have provided support for the position that a multiplicity of methods and foci is necessary in the study of SRs if we are ever to get a good grasp of the subject matter in any one area. However, this theoretical and empirical ambition does not come without problems, and it is to two of these that I will now turn.

The first point to raise, concerns the problem of the interconnectedness of all that we wish to study. This problem arises no matter whether we examine only the conversational products which are the consequence of social interaction, or the properties of those individuals which produce it. If we are following the latter strategy, then we often restrict the range of questions posed so that they all fall within in some predefined area such as gender, work, madness, or the like, and so that we can examine that area in depth. Usually, these categories have some social reality, but how we treat them necessarily produces a segmentation by topic of the world, and this may hide many important, and perhaps crucial, interconnections.

A standard reaction to this problem is to work with semi-structured, or even unstructured, questionnaires, but this then leads to the complementary problem which those who analyse the content of naturally-occurring talk must face: namely, that any conversation will include talk about a wide variety of issues, and the participants may not say very much about any single one. Thus, one would be sacrificing depth for breadth. This is not to say, though, that conversationalists do not orientate to a notion of topic, nor that some conversations are not highly focused. Intuitively, they do, and highly-focused dialogues do occur. There are many analyses which support this intuition with their description of the procedures for topic introduction, for example Sacks and Schegloff (1973), or topic suspension, for example Jefferson (1972), but specification of what a topic is, has always been too difficult to achieve. Also, it is not clear that the participants' notion of the topic of a particular conversation relates to the categories of talk which the SR theorist might believe to persist across a number of encounters.

This segmentation problem, of choosing a topical focus, recurs when we consider how we might time-limit a study, and who we include in the reference group. SRs almost certainly change over time and, on the same topic, they may vary between groups. Indeed, the inter-group variation may well be central to the definition of the group, as many have proposed. Again, any segmentation which is chosen can be hard to motivate in terms of the social-psychological reality of the topic, and in a non-circular way.

A rather different problem arises when we take the results of studying individuals, and attempt to make sense of them in SR terms. No problem arises if we assume that the way in which our subjects respond is simply part or all of the relevant SR, and all that needs to be done is to organize those responses by the use of appropriate statistical procedures. However, if we do not think that the relationship between what these individuals say and the SR is so straightforward, then we must develop a logic for inferring the SR from this data, and for integrating the data from various sources. In many respects, the various statistical procedures offered in Part II of this volume represent an attempt to provide this logic.

Conclusion

The two problems above, and others, are reminiscent of the conceptual and procedural difficulties which have confronted studies of human language at different times. The segmentation problems are similar, in one respect, to the difficulties that the dialectologist has in defining a speech community, and in another respect to the problem of language change and whether or not linguistics should adopt a synchronic or diachronic perspective. In a third respect, they are similar to how different levels of the linguistic hierarchy should be demarcated, for example, where syntax ends and semantics begins. The problems of individual variability also arise in linguistics, as does the concern with how one studies an entity like the language system, which is clearly dependent for its existence on the instantiation of the rules in the head of the individual members of society, but is dependent on no single instantiation.

Linguistics has been in existence for much longer than SRT (or social psychology, for that matter) and it is unsurprising to discover that the discipline has developed positions which enable its practitioners to solve or circumvent such problems. Not all linguists agree on the viability of specific solutions, and there are very many different schools of thought within the discipline. Nevertheless, by comparison to the current state of affairs in SRT, the problems produced are minor. These disagreements concern clearly-articulated positions, something which is not currently available in SRT, and the bases of the disagreements are relatively clear. It is tempting to sympathize with Moscovici that to adopt clear definitions in the way that linguistics has, would too easily inhibit the theoretical imagination, and allow the empiricists to reify the SR concept into something uninteresting; but this need not be the outcome.

In most other branches of academic life, it is believed that clarity of definition, even at the cost of certain inexactitude, is preferable to indeterminacy because it permits the critical imagination to gain greater purchase on the substantive issues. Arguably, we have reached the stage with SRT where such certainty would serve us better, and it is clear that unless this happens a multitude of empirical redefinitions of the concept will arise with the same uninteresting outcome that Moscovici wishes to avoid.

Farr, in chapter 1 of this volume, recognizes this point very clearly. The agenda provided by the literature on SRT is a very large one, and one is tempted to say that if we are to study the 'thinking society', then we are proposing to study all of human life. In such a case, it is easy to believe that whatever investigations we conduct, we are revealing something worthwhile. However, unless we operate within a clear frame of reference, with a clear idea of how the various findings are to be related to one another as a function of both their topic and their methodological precepts, we will simply accumulate an amorphous and ultimately uninformative set of observations. One need not agree with Farr's specific proposals in order to agree that we need a more articulated relation between theory and method in the light of better-defined concepts.

References

Breakwell, G. M. (1990). Social beliefs about gender differences. Paper to the ESRC workshop on Social Beliefs, Madingley Hall, Cambridge, March 1985. Revised version in *The social psychological study of widespread beliefs*, (ed. C. Fraser and G. Gaskell), pp. 210–25. Oxford University Press.

Byrne, R. and Whitten, A. (1988). *Machiavellian intelligence*. Oxford University Press.

Garfinkel, H. (1967). *Studies in ethnomethodology*. Prentice-Hall, Englewood Cliffs, New Jersey. (Re-issued 1987 by Polity Press, Cambridge.)

Jefferson, G. (1972). Side sequences. In *Studies in social interaction*, (ed. D. Sudnow), pp. 294–338. Free Press, New York.

Levinson, S. C. (1987). Minimization and conversational inference. In *The pragmatic perspective*, (ed. J. Verschueren and M. Bertuccelli-Papi), pp. 61–130. *The pragmatic perspective*, John Benjamins, Amsterdam.

Moscovici, S. (1961). *La psychanalyse: son image et son public*. Paris: Presses Universitaires de France, Paris.

Schegloff, E. A. and Sacks, H. (1973). Opening up closings. In *Ethnomethodology*, (ed. R. Turner), pp. 233–64. Penguin, Harmondsworth.

9 Integrating paradigms, methodological implications

Glynis M. Breakwell

Doise, in Chapter 7 of this book, emphasizes that researchers have focused empirical work on only one aspect of the theory of social representations. They have been mainly concerned either with describing the content of existing representations or with examining how anchoring and objectification operate. They have left largely unexplored Moscovici's hypotheses concerning the ways in which, at the level of the metasystem, social groups generate representations which serve group purposes. Representations serve different types of group interest, and Moscovici describes three: diffusion, propagation, and propaganda. Representations serving these three communicative purposes have different structures and organization. They differ particularly in the extent to which they are consensually shared within a group or a subgroup. The defining property of a social representation is not simply that it should be shared: the predicted internal structure of the representation and the extent to which it is dispersed within a recognizable group or social category will depend on the functions that it is serving.

This has major implications for the empirical approaches which should be adopted when exploring social representations. It suggests that intra-group dynamics and inter-group relations will direct or channel the formation of any specific social representation. This requires that the theorist should formulate clear predictions concerning the structure of a representation as revealed in the thought, utterances, and action of the individual in relation to that individual's position in a group. It calls for the analysis of likely implications of changes in group structure for the representation. It necessitates consideration of the inter-group processes which promulgate the social representation and afford it a venue in which to be used. It emphasizes that representations are embedded in complex representational networks and that they are liable to change, whether in a subtle or a global way, as a result of their relationships to each other.

The empirical implications of this theoretical agenda range from the need to design studies differently, through issues concerning the appropriate type of data to collect, to questions about the optimal forms of data analysis. In order to illustrate the full range of the empirical implications of examining that part of the theory of social representations which focuses upon the

metasystem, it is necessary to first discuss some of the theoretical propositions which might be generated.

Social-identity theory and social-representation theory

Having emphasized the importance of intra- and inter-group processes in
shaping social representations, it is hard to avoid asking whether it is now
timely to seek to integrate the theory of social identity (Tajfel 1978) and the
theory of social representations. In their original forms, these two theories
represent two distinct paradigms. The word 'paradigm' is used loosely by
psychologists: we talk about paradigms which are models of methods of
discovery and about those which are models of description or explanation.
In both senses, social-identity theory and social-representation theory reflect
different paradigms.

Social-identity theory, while it attempts to explain inter-group relationships, is a model which focuses upon individual needs and motivation (the
need for a positive social identity) as the means of fundamentally explaining
interpersonal and inter-group dynamics. Social-identity theory represents a
formal model, in that it presents definitions of the constructs it uses and
clearly describes their relationship to each other. Social-identity theory
makes direct predictions of behaviour; it is an explanatory, not a descriptive,
model. Social-identity theory has been tested primarily using experimental
or quasi-experimental methods. In contrast, social-representations theory, in
describing how people come to interpret their world and make it meaningful,
is a model which focuses upon processes of interpersonal communication as
the determiners of the structure and content of the belief systems which are
called social representations. Moscovici at least (though not some of his
followers) has shunned formal propositional elaboration of the model. He
has rejected the need for formal definitions of the constructs he uses in the
model, and avoids prediction on the basis of the model. Social-representation
theory is concerned largely with describing the content of representations,
not with predicting what that content will be in any particular group context.
It is primarily a functionalist model; much attention is paid to explaining
the purpose of representations. Social-representations theory has occasionally been tested using experimental methods but researchers have chosen
primarily to collect representations using survey techniques — sometimes
using in-depth interviews, other times using questionnaire formats.

Social-identity theory and social-representation theory have characteristics which set them apart as quite distinct paradigms. Neither could be
regarded as having introduced a paradigm shift (in the Kuhnian sense) into
social psychology. Both have venerable ancestors within the discipline. They
reflect the social cognition–social construction debate which has haunted
social psychology since its inception. Social-identity theory and the theory

of social representations could be linked to create a more powerful explanatory model of action and could mark a step towards a real paradigm shift
in social psychology.

Integrating the two theories could make both more ready to face their
critics. Integrating them could also produce a generic theoretical framework
which might replace, or at least contextualize, a large number of social-
psychological models, each of which has been created to explain a narrow
range of social behaviour in highly specific settings.

Social-identity theory (Tajfel 1978) could benefit from the alliance with
social-representations theory because it has been too narrowly focused on
explaining inter-group conflict and differentiation (Tajfel and Turner 1986).
By addressing the issues of social representation, it can provide a model of
the broader role of identity processes in directing the social construction of
what passes for reality. The liaison may ultimately even encourage the
integration of social-identity theory and self-schema theory, since recent
work on schema has been shifting towards a recognition of the essential role
of social processes in cognition (for example Deaux (1992), Gurin and
Markus (1989), and Abrams (1992)).

The advantages for the linkage of social-identity theory and social-
representations theory would not be one-sided — social-representation theory
benefits, too. One of the major problems currently with the theory of social
representations is that it cannot explain why a particular social representation takes the form that it does. Social representations, at one level, are
cognitive structures which function to facilitate communication between
members of a collectivity because of their shared or consensual form. For
the individual, their role is to give meaning to novel experiences (whether
people, objects, or events) by setting them in a contextual frame that makes
them familiar (Moscovici 1981, 1984, 1988). At another level, social representations are public rhetorics used by groups to engender cohesiveness and
to manoeuvre relative to other groups. What is unclear in the theory is any
process which determines the actual form which the representation takes, or
the likelihood that any one individual will be able to reproduce or accept it
in its entirety. Social-identity theory could help to describe the processes
which might be at work both in shaping the form of the representation and
then determining the work it is made to do above and beyond simply making
the new familiar.

In presenting here some preliminary explorations of how identity processes might be linked to processes of social representation, it is useful to
start with questions about groups and representations.

Groups and social representations

The relationship between social identity and social representation is
undoubtedly dialectical; their influences upon each other are reciprocal. It

should also be acknowledged that while in any one instance they may be causally linked, in others the relationship may be non-causal (both being determined by some external variable or complex network of variables). But, to analyse the potential relationship between social identities and social representations, it is necessary to take one step back and examine how social representations are tied to groups. Of course, Moscovici has acknowledged in some of his writings that social representations are intimately related to group processes (Moscovici 1981, 1984). The problem has been pinning down quite how they are connected.

Production, differentiation, and function

In examining the connection, it is important not to confuse *a* social representation with the process of social representation which produces it. Group processes affect both the process of social representation and the form of a social representation.

In considering the relationship of group dynamics and social representations, there is, firstly, the question of ownership. Obviously, a group may be the producer of a social representation. Alternatively, and equally obviously, it can be produced outside the group. Often, more interestingly, a social representation will be co-produced by different groups, with executive producers changing over time as the social representation develops. The tendencies to see social representations as the property of either unstructured concatenations of individuals communicating without a goal or a single, highly goal-orientated conglomerate are both misleading. There is no reason to believe that social representations are less likely to be generated over great periods of time, with contributions from many different sources who are motivated by quite different objectives. This is clearly most true of the development of those social representations which equate with political ideologies. It is also evident where social representations are, as it were, 'borrowed' by one group from another. An illustration of this comes from the work of Palmonari *et al.* (1987), who showed how psychologists seeking to professionalize themselves integrated into their representation of the professional psychologist images common to other professional groups.

To the extent that structured groups *are* the producers of social representations, their form and development will not be controlled by any simple intra-individual, or even interpersonal, processes of anchoring and objectification. The form will serve group objectives. The task of theorists now is to show how group dynamics influence the operation of the processes of anchoring and objectification at both the intra-personal and inter-personal levels. Moscovici has failed to specify how these processes operate, not in terms of their cognitive underpinnings, but rather the systematic biases which social influences introduce into their operation.

Power differentials are only one such influence which might be examined empirically. Inter-group power differentials will have an important impact upon the development of social representations. The acceptance of alternative social representations of a single event is likely to be greatly affected by the relative power of the two groups generating them. This power may lie in the ability to propagandize the representation through the media. The alternative social representations of Iraq's invasion of Kuwait in 1990 which emanated from the parties involved in the conflict provide a suitable example. In the early days of the occupation, descriptions of the Iraqi removal of babies from life-support machines in Kuwait were used cogently to symbolize and make concrete, even familiar, the horror of the situation. It became known later, after the land war had removed the Iraqi forces, that the machines had not been stolen. The power to manipulate the social representation of the invasion during the lead-up to the war was significant in readying whole nations for action. It was interesting to see that the social representation generated on US media, with the active involvement of the exiled Kuwaiti ruling family, was differentially accepted across Europe. The Germans were particularly hesitant to accept the social representation which had taken hold of the US people.

The implications of the need to consider inter-group power relations for those studying social representations are significant. It requires, firstly, that the analysis explicitly establishes what power hierarchies exist which are pertinent to the representation. This often means going beyond the target group for the study, and sampling members of sometimes very distant outgroups simply to verify assumptions about which groupings are relevant. Secondly, it will frequently require a historical analysis of the relationship between groups and their changing use of representations over time. Such an analysis may use a diverse array of sources and data types (for example autobiographical, archival, or legal). Thirdly, it will demand that the distribution of a representation within the group is discovered. A powerful group may be able to impose a representation on some members of a less powerful group, but not on all of them. Only by developing sophisticated indices of the diffusion and degree of acceptance of the representation across the subordinate group is it possible to test fully assertions about the effects of power. All of these considerations militate against using minimal-grouping experimental paradigms, since establishing arbitrary and recognizably-transient power differentials cannot be expected to reveal much about the operation of representational processes within real hegemonies.

Just as the relative power of groups is significant, the relative power of individuals in the group is also important. It may be these individual power differentials which explain why, even in homogeneous groups, not all members will reproduce the same representation of a target. Social representations may be most simply defined by their 'shared' status, but it would be ignoring the facts to assume that large numbers of people share identical representations. Even when the representation is meant to be consensual, as in the case of stereotypes, there are still differences between individuals in the details and organization of the representation. As Potter and Wetherell (1987) have said, Moscovici has not specified what level of consensus or sharing must be attained before a social representation can be said to be shared within a group. Many of the early empirical studies (Di Giacomo 1980; Hewstone *et al.* 1982) used methods which ignored diversity or individual differences in representation. The implications of integrating the identity and representation paradigms is that methods used must allow the description of both consensus and diversity. This means that data must be collected from individuals, not simply from aggregates. It also means that sampling within the group should include individuals from different statuses or roles. Analysis should focus upon similarities between people but not to the exclusion of establishing their dissimilarities. Many of the statistical techniques for doing this are described in Part II of this book.

Differences in the extent to which a representation is available to, and used by, any one individual must be something to do with the individual's position in the group, but it is also linked with their relationship to the target of the representation and the context in which the representation is elicited. This has recently been clearly recognized where research on stereotypes is concerned (Billig 1985; Hewstone 1989; Hraba *et al.* 1989; Kleinpenning and Hagendoorn 1991) and, of course, stereotypes have been argued to be one type of social representation (Abrams and Hogg 1990; Hogg and Abrams 1988). If correct, this is important for the design of research. It means that greater care needs to be taken in establishing the significance of the representational target to the individual. It suggests that an inevitable question in any research on representations should be, 'What is the significance of X to you personally?' (where X is the target of the representation). Recognizing the relevance of context of elicitation also changes the shape of data collected: a structured analysis of the context in which people are asked to express their representations would be required.

The functions which the social representation serve for the group will also affect the processes of anchoring and objectification. At least, the functions served should affect the prior systems of representation chosen to act as the anchor for anything new, or any development of the old. They should shape the objects which will be chosen as the frame of reference or referent points for familiarization which permits objectification. It is interesting when exploring the social representations of AIDS/HIV that new beliefs about the disease were not, in the early years, tied to representations of other sexually-transmitted diseases but to rather less secular comparitors: it was widely represented as the plague meted out as divine punishment of homosexuals. This representation clearly served many intergroup prejudices.

In social-identity theory, Tajfel (1981) argued that stereotypes serve three types of function:

(1) social causality — scapegoating;

(2) social justification;

(3) social differentiation.

By extrapolation, one can assume that social representations serve these functions, but the emphasis in echoing Tajfel is too one-sided: it suggests that the form of a social representation will be determined by group needs. Yet, this ignores the possibility that over time a social representation will constrain the group's range of options in seeking legitimation or differentiation. Lyons and Sotirakopoulou (1991) illustrated how established representations can constrain and channel attempts to achieve positive differentiation for the ingroup. They showed that not even the most ardent British nationalist would claim Britain to be superior to France in food or fashion (though they were also unwilling to acknowledge inferiority). Traditional social representations constrict any gambit for improving the group's position, by determining what will be credible as a claim. This is rather more than saying that the new social representation is anchored in the old. The issue here is credibility, not necessarily ease of information storage or retrieval, and not even the search for familiarity.

The functions identified by Tajfel focus upon the group's manipulation of facts and their interpretation in the service of self-interest in inter-group comparisons. But, social representations obviously serve other types of function for the group. Groups can also use representations to foster common consciousness among members which need not be associated with the inter-group context. Basically, this is merely to emphasize that social representations serve group functions at the intra-group level. Sharing the representation can become the badge of membership and the precursor of understanding the reason for sharing common goals. Some recent work on environmental-social representations illustrates that novices in green movements are virtually 'educated' into particular representations of the issues (Ashford and Breakwell 1992). Moscovici and Hewstone (1983) argued that social representation contributes to group-identity formation in the sense that merely by sharing a social representation, group members come to feel a common identity since they have a common 'world view'.

It is important to recognize that one implication of this power of social-representation processes to engender a common sense of identity will be that social representations, once created, are very persistent but, more importantly, that the processes themselves will not disappear or fade away. There is a very clear illustration of this point in the breakdown of the Soviet Union and the resurrection of ethnic and religious identities. The old social representations are as vivid as ever; they may have been lying low for nearly five decades or longer, but they are still there.

One of the most obvious empirical implications of integrating the social-identity and social-representation paradigms is that this relationship between group identity and representational processes becomes a key issue. The methods used will need to take account of the longevity of representations tied to groups. Historical analyses would seem potentially valuable. Within the representation research tradition, they are already used to some extent. But, this would be a significant addition to the empirical armoury of social-identity theorists.

The function served by social-representation processes must be recognized as distinct from the function of the specific social representation which is then generated. There are actually two levels of function that we are dealing with here, the function of the process of representation and the function of a specific representation. The process of representation may function to anchor and objectify novel experiences and understandings. Knowing that anchoring and objectification occur does not help us to predict the actual shape of the representation which results or the action which it will motivate. Group dynamics and individual needs determine the function of the specific representation and consequently its actual structure. Only modelling these effects will help us to explain the forms which action actually takes.

Targets of representation

The second issue concerning the relationship between representation and group dynamics is the question of the object, or target, of the social representation. The connection of groups and social representations can come through the relationship of the group to the object of the representation rather than to the way in which it is produced.

A group may in reality be the object of the social representation either directly, because it is characterized in the representation, or indirectly, because its recognized out-groups are characterized in the representation. Either way, the social representation can come to reflect the existing group identity or posit an alternative identity for the group (affecting the defining properties of the group). The work which Jodelet (1989, 1991) has done to unearth the representations of mental illness illustrates forcefully the power that representation has in a community to create an identity for a social category.

Yet, a social representation may be significant to a group not because the group produces it or because it directly defines the boundaries of the group identity; it may simply be targeted upon an object which is important to the group at a specific time. An example can be drawn from the research conducted by a social geographer, Matthews (1981, 1983). A community group from an inner-city neighbourhood which included a red-light district and was facing redevelopment found the broader community's social representation of the prostitutes in the area important. The broader community (the city council) wanted to redevelop the area in such a way as to eliminate the sex-industry enclave, based upon a strong negative representation of the effects of the male and female prostitutes working in the area. The proposed redevelopment adversely affected the interests of the community group (such as by breaking up a long-established working-class neighbourhood in an unsympathetic way). The social representation of prostitution in the area became a vital fulcrum for renegotiating the redevelopment plan.

Another example would come from the representation of genetic engineering by society. This is clearly significant for those who suffer from genetically-transmitted diseases. Legislative decisions affecting potential offspring are based upon reactions to the social representation of genetic engineering which dominates. This example shows that the representation does not have to be about people — it can be about a scientific process. Moreover, it shows again that social representations held by a powerful few (legislators) can have tremendously significant effects for those who may have no effective route to influence the representations.

Any research which takes the distal impact of representations seriously will have to tackle two problems which will affect its methodology. First, it must actively explore which groups of people are likely to be affected by the representation, other than the group producing it. Having identified them, they will have to be sampled. Sampling appropriately will depend upon having some criterion for inclusion, such as potential range of diffusion of the representation effects within the group. Whatever criterion for sampling is chosen, it needs to be explicit. One of the great problems in research in this area is that samples tend to be opportunistic. This means that when any questions which concern the extent of diffusion of the representation or its impact in the group are asked, it is difficult to know to what extent strong generalizations can be made. If the sampling is inadequate or inappropriate, it is obvious that any conclusions, but particularly those about diffusion or consensus, are invalidated. At least, if researchers specify the criterion used in sampling, it is possible to deduce the level of assurance with which generalizations are made. It can also help in interpreting apparent disparities in representations produced by members of a group over time.

The second empirical problem to be faced concerns the time-frame for the research. Distal effects of representations may be long-term consequences, not immediately apparent when the representation is produced. This means that studying the groups potentially affected at the same time as studying the group generating the representation may be fruitless. The empirical problem lies in guessing the sensible time-frame to adopt. One way around the difficulty is to employ a time series design: collecting similarly structured information on a number of different occasions from the same population but not necessarily the same sample.

Salience of representations

The third issue to address in analysing the relationship of representations and group dynamics concerns the importance of a social representation to the functioning of the group. In understanding the role that group membership has in shaping the process of social representation for an individual, it is important to look not only at the part that the group plays in the production of the representation, or the relevance of the target of representation to group definition and objectives, but also to consider how significant or salient the representation is for the group. The same social representation will vary in its actual importance to the group over time and across situations. The relative importance of different social representations will similarly vary with circumstance. It should actually be possible to develop at least a crude model of the factors which will affect the importance which a social representation has for a group. This has not been attempted yet.

One fairly uncontentious prediction would be: the more significant the social representation is to the group, the more likely it will be that group membership will affect the individual's involvement with the representation. This prediction can be tested in very simple quasi-experimental designs.

Relationships between representations

Finally, in considering groups and representation, there is the question of the networking of social representations. It is notable that most empirical research on social representations has chosen single targets for representation and treated the resulting representations in isolation (for example representations of health, mental illness, the city, a student protest, or the family). Yet, we all know that a social representation of one target relates to that of another (this is actually implicit in the notion of anchoring). The problem empirically lies in knowing when one finishes and another begins, and the decision may ultimately be arbitrary. Sotirakopoulou (1991), in her longitudinal study of the nature of anchoring, has shown empirically (in relation to the changing representations of the unification of Europe) how difficult it is to talk about one discrete social representation being anchored to a separate discrete but prior representation. It seems reasonable to suggest that groups can often dictate to members which are the appropriate linkages between representations for them to make, constraining the individual degrees of freedom in association.

Several of the chapters in Part II of this book examine how it might be possible statistically to distinguish the boundaries between representations. It is worth noting that these approaches impose structure without reference back to the individuals who provided data. A complementary approach to exploring relationships between representations would be to build into the data-collection an opportunity for individuals to provide representations of different targets, and then to describe how they perceive the connections between them. This approach does not prevent the researcher from subsequently analysing the structure statistically, but the two accounts of structure can be compared. It also provides more than one representation from each individual, so it is possible to do a meta-analysis of the structure of representations independent of their target. Such a meta-analysis is necessary if we are to examine empirically the generic structure of representations.

Social identity and representational processes

For the purposes of this chapter, Tajfel's (1978) original definition is used, of social identity as that part of the self-concept derived from group memberships with the value attached to those memberships. It could be extended to include Turner's rather broader notion of a group which includes any category recognized by the individual (even one without material existence—as in minimal-grouping experiments). Turner talks about self-categorization rather than social identity (see Turner (1991) for a review of his work). The term social identity is used here, but what is said would equally well apply to self-categorization. Since social identities are a product of group or category memberships, there are a number of ways in which social identity might influence processes of social representation.

Exposure

Memberships will first affect exposure to particular aspects of a social representation, as well as to the target of the representation itself. Groups ensure that members are informed about, or engaged with, social representations which are central to group objectives and definition. Out-groups ensure that members are presented with other aspects of social representations which may be rather less in keeping with the in-group's interests. Additionally there are, of course, many other purveyors of social representations (the media, the educational establishment, and the government). Memberships may influence exposure to these not directly but indirectly, influencing the level of attention paid to particular social representations, or affecting opportunities to interact with them.

The effects of exposure can be examined in developmental perspective. Augustinos (1991) has argued that age, in so far as it equates with length of exposure to a group's repertoire of social representations, will relate to the degree to which the individual shares with others of the same age a social representation. She tested this notion by examining teenagers' representations of different groups in Australian society. She showed that while individual differences were present in all age groups, they reduced systematically with age. This line of enquiry is clearly worth taking further; it has echoes of Vygotsky's claims concerning the role of social influences upon apparent cognitive development.

Acceptance

Memberships will affect acceptance (or rejection) of the social representation. They do this sometimes by establishing the extent of the credibility of the source of the social representation, or at other times by explicit commentaries on the representation. Failure to accept the group's verdict on a social representation can put the individual at risk of censure or even rejection. The consequences of rejecting the group's preferred representation of an object clearly vary with the importance that it has for the group. The consequences will also depend upon the individual's power within the group.

It would be foolhardy, however, to overemphasize the tendency towards conformity within a group concerning social representations. Moscovici has shown that groups are capable of encompassing considerable divergence of representations among their membership. The problem of modelling the extent of the group's tolerance for disagreement is, in my opinion, very pressing.

Use

Memberships will affect the extent to which the social representation is used. Definition of 'use' in this context is difficult but would include: the frequency with which the social representation is reproduced (that is, communicated to others) and addressed (that is, used as a point of reference in making decisions, assimilating new information, and evaluating a situation).

Obviously, the importance of the social representation to the group and its relationship to the group's objectives and self-interest will affect the extent of the individual's exposure, acceptance, and use.

Some illustration of the relationship between social identities and social representation can be garnered from research on the political and economic socialization of 16–19 year olds (Banks et al. 1991). This project involved a longitudinal study of two cohorts of teenagers (15–16 and 17–18 at the start of the study) over a period of two years. One of the central concerns of the researchers was the exploration of political-party identification over this period when young people first officially participate in politics.

The first thing to say is that the representation of the political system which these young people held was clearly related to their political involvement. Those who had some consistent party preference – that is to say, those who identified themselves as consistently Conservative or consistently Labour over a period of three data collections taken at annual intervals – were more likely to represent the political system as responsive to the electorate, essentially as democratic. More importantly, those who had a consistent political-party preference were more likely to reproduce coherently in their own representations the pattern of policy-related ideology which separates Left from Right in British politics. This was expressed in their opinions about taxation, welfare rights, nationalization, and other policy issues.

These data seem to indicate that consistency in political self-categorization is the key to coherence in reproducing the current party ideologies. It should be noted that direction of self-categorization is not significant. Labour and Conservative alike were more able to generate the coherent pattern than those who were inconsistent. It is notable that the data show a very marked trend: those who are totally inconsistent over three surveys are least systematic in reproducing party ideologies; those with total consistency are most likely to mimic the party line.

There is an obvious question: is it coherence which is causal, or consistency? Unfortunately, this cannot be answered. The relevant measures which might have permitted comparison of ideological sophistication across time were not taken at the start of the study. For the purposes of the current illustration, the question of causality is secondary anyway. The significant finding is that consistency in self-categorization is tied to ideological coherence. Consistency in self-categorization is linked to the coherent reproduction of a social representation of political issues matching that espoused by the political party preferred. It is possible that consistency allows for greater exposure to the party's ideology; consistency is likely to be reinforced if the ideology is found to be acceptable, and may encourage more intense use of it over time. It was certainly the case that those who were consistent were more likely to report engaging in more frequent discussion of politics.

Not just the stability of a social identity, but its centrality to the overall self-concept or self-schema, will affect exposure, acceptance, and use. There are many indirect illustrations of this point in the literature. For example, Gurin and Markus (1989), in a fascinating exploration of the cognitive consequences of gender roles for women, showed that women would espouse more intense representations of the gender inequalities in society where a non-traditional gender role was for them a central social identity than where it was not central.

Moreover, centrality of a social identity to the self-concept often motivates the active search for exposure to group-relevant representations. Some of the work done by Coyle (1991) on the development of gay identity shows a clear pattern of significant and unqualified self-definition as gay, being followed by a period of seeking affirmation from other gay men and the adoption of specific patterns of social representation.

While centrality of the social identity to the self-concept will affect the exposure to and acceptance of a social representation, one would expect that the centrality of the social identity will change across situations and thus affect the differential use of the social representation. Even if a social representation is very salient to a group and thus to a social identity, it is unlikely to be used in a particular situation unless that social identity is seen to be relevant to the situation. The repertoire of social representations which can be addressed or used in any given situation is broad. The ones chosen will be influenced by the social identities pertinent to the situation. Kleinpenning and Hagendoorn (1991) illustrate this in the use of ethnic stereotypes, showing them to be context-specific and dependent on the group significance of the situation.

These effects of social identity upon social representations would imply that there will be considerable individual differences in any specific social representation which one cares to elicit. This is borne out empirically. Social representations, though shared, do not seem to be shared in their entirety — even within relatively homogeneous samples. Individuals customize their social representations to suit personal goals: in identity terms, these would include self-esteem, continuity, and distinctiveness (Breakwell 1986). This does not always work in the way that one might expect. Sometimes, social representations with a negative impact upon the individual's social identity are accepted and used. For instance, in the early 1980s unemployed young people were found to accept and reproduce aspects of the very negative social representation of unemployed youth common at the time (Breakwell *et al.* 1984). They did, however, add elements to it which set their version apart from the general one: combining self-recrimination for lack of ability and effort with a strong fatalism which was not present in the common version of the representation.

While social representations play a part in shaping social identities (both their content and their evaluation) through defining group identities and boundaries, social identities in turn, through influencing exposure, acceptance, and use of social representations, can shape their development. It does not take much imagination to see how a new idea might be stifled and never become a shared representation if group dynamics restricted its exposure, acceptance, and use.

The integration of the social-identity and social-representation paradigms puts these issues surrounding exposure, acceptance, and use forward as prime targets for empirical exploration. No methodological constraints are involved in pursuing them except the need to have data from individuals which is both pertinent and open to systematic analysis which will reveal individual differences.

Traits and social representations

In considering the relationship between social identities and social representations, it becomes evident that one really also needs to consider personality traits as potential determinants of individual differences in involvement in the processes of social representation.

There is no need to go into the tired old argument about the distinction between personal and social identity (Breakwell 1986; 1987). The term trait is used here to refer to a psychological characteristic which is long-lived and, though differentially manifested across situations, can be said to relate to behaviour in a systematic manner. This definition would include as traits such facets of self-concept as self-efficacy (Bandura 1989) and psychological estrangement (Breakwell, 1992).

Clearly, traits and social identities, from the viewpoint of the entire biography of an individual, are not always so discrete and separate. Traits can become a part of self-categorization. For example, having the trait of shyness can lead to self-definition as part of some conceptual grouping of shy people; it may even lead to seeking out the company of other shy people and, thereby, to group membership. Traits certainly lead to classifications imposed by other people. The shy person is identified as such and whole domains of social behaviour are no longer expected of her. In contrast, group membership may call forth or intensify certain traits: membership of a women's group might actively promote assertiveness, while membership of the Conservative party might actually nurture Conservativeness.

From the perspective of the entire biography, traits may, therefore, not be so clearly separable from social identities. Yet, taken at a single moment or over a brief period in the person's development, when a social representation is to be acquired, evaluated, and applied, it may be useful to look at traits. It may be particularly useful to consider those self-evaluative traits, like efficacy, self-esteem, and estrangement, which actually may systematically influence the way group memberships are chosen and enacted.

At this point, it is not necessary to consider the potential relationships between traits and social identities. For clarity, they can be dealt with separately in relation to processes of social representation, yet it will become clear that there is a great deal of similarity between their respective links to social representation processes.

There are two sorts of ways in which traits relate to social representation processes:

1. Traits as *psychological states* shape the individual's exposure to, acceptance of, and use of a social representation. Moscovici argues that social representations are a product of inter-individual communication/interaction and many personality traits would recognizably influence the course of such interaction. To go back to our shy person, shyness could prevent participation in many areas of communication necessary either to acquire or to influence a social representation. There are other examples. The trait of curiosity has a self-evident relationship to gaining exposure to a variety of social representations. In our research on the public images of science and

scientists, we have shown that curiosity is also related to a general proclivity to accept and use, as well as access, novel ideas (Breakwell and Beardsell, 1992).

2. Traits as *self-conscious self-definitions* also shape readiness to expose oneself to, accept, or use a social representation. In so far as at this level traits are self-categorizations, it could be argued that they are also social identities. However, they still need to be treated as different from those social identities which are derived from group memberships. This is particularly relevant since identities derived from memberships will be subject to group-determined pressures towards particular types of social representation which are absent where self-ascribed traits are concerned.

The importance of self-attributed traits can be illustrated with data from research conducted on the sexual activities of 16–21 year olds (Breakwell and Fife-Schaw, 1992, Breakwell *et al.* 1991). The work is a cohort-sequential longitudinal study involving postal surveys of an initial achieved sample of about 3000 young people, drawn randomly from all those in the relevant age cohorts in three districts of England. One facet of the findings can be used to illustrate the current point. A series of questions were posed to elicit aspects of what might reasonably constitute a representation of AIDS/HIV: knowledge of the routes of transmission, beliefs about people with AIDS, convictions concerning the possibility for discovering a cure, and feelings about personal chances of contracting the virus (including levels of fear). An extensive set of questions about sexual activity (for example, age of first intercourse, numbers of partners, condom use, and patterns of sex acts ranging from kissing to anal intercourse) were also asked. Additionally, self-descriptions of traits, which included willingness to take risks, were elicited.

The trends in this data are clear: self-professed riskiness is correlated with less 'safe' patterns of sexual behaviour (basically, more partners and less use of condoms). One could argue that people responding to the questionnaire in this way are using both the trait descriptions and the report of behaviour to self-categorize as risky. There is no need to claim here that the behaviour reported is determined by the trait; for the purposes of this argument, what matters is the relationship of both behaviour and trait to the representation of AIDS/HIV. Riskiness (defined in terms of self-ascribed behaviours and trait) was positively correlated with a representation of AIDS/HIV which effectively diminishes the risks attached. So, risk-takers are more likely to feel that a cure is feasible, to think it is possible to identify a person with AIDS by looking at him or her, and to think that having sex with only one partner will prevent infection.

No indisputable reasons for this relationship between a self-ascribed trait and aspects of a representation can be offered here. It may be that the representation is just a justification or rationalization for risky acts, generated either before or after they occurred. The point is merely that this sort of relationship between self-description, representation, and action exists and that researchers need to adopt the empirical approaches which will allow it to be explored.

The argument does not require that all traits affect the adoption of every social representation. It merely suggests that when examining the differential adoption of a social representation, either in its entirety or in some part, it is necessary to consider the role of personality traits. This is a somewhat unfashionable stance in social psychology. Yet, it is supported by the recent work of Gecas and Seff (1989, 1990) which has shown how closely related self-categorization (in terms of social class, for instance) and traits (namely self-efficacy and self-esteem) actually are. There is now reason to believe that the underlying trait of self-efficacy (as defined by Bandura) is fundamentally important in predicting not only action but also the acceptability and use of patterns of social representation.

Treating personality traits as important in the study of social-representational processes has significant implications for the type of empirical approach which is feasible. Clearly, the data source for both traits and representations must be at the level of individuals. Sampling must allow for individual variations in the target trait, and the form of data analysis chosen must permit exploration of individual differences. This effectively means that the analysis will have two apparently conflicting objectives. It will look across individuals for communalities in the structure of representations. It will also seek to pinpoint the patterns of differences between individuals and how these relate to trait variations.

It would be interesting to see how far it is possible to track the role of an individual in the generation of a social representation. Social identity clearly has a role to play in dictating the significance of any one individual (power differentials, networks, and so on) but it would also be intriguing to see how personality traits relate to involvement in developing a representation. At the moment, there appears to be no research on this type of issue and it is alien to the recent tradition of social-representation research. Yet, it is an arena where it would be possible to go that one step further in uniting the cognitive traditions in social psychology with the social-analysis movement in social psychology.

The empirical implication of the need to track individual inputs to the development of a social representation lies largely in the time-frame for the research. It requires a design which is, in one way or another, longitudinal — either continuously following the individual over some period which is predicted to be formative in the development of the representation, or time-sampling the relationship between the individual's activity and the structure of the representation.

The relationship between personality traits and social representation can be examined in reverse of course. It could be argued that, in so far as traits are socially-constructed domains (prototypes), they are a product of social-representation processes. This notion that the dimensions of personality are socially-constructed segments, with a socially-determined meaning and significance, is attractive. It does not mean that the trait possessed by an individual is any less real, but it gets us away from assumptions that traits are individualistic and non-social explanations for action.

Action, identity, and social representations

Social representations relate to both individual and group actions. They often specify objectives for action and the course that it should take. The major problem in explaining, worse still predicting, individual action in any particular situation lies in the fact that the person will be characterized by several social identities and their attendant social-representational baggage at the time. These identities may push towards different, even conflicting, forms of action.

The emphasis which is nowadays placed upon notions of centrality or salience and contextualization of identities is meant to overcome this problem. The identity salient in the context will direct action, or so the line of argument goes. The problem is then that it is usually impossible to establish, except *post hoc*, that a particular identity is salient in the situation.

The other approach to this problem has been to examine the interactive effects of group memberships. This recognizes that identities do not have separate existences, like individual ice-cubes segregated from each other in their plastic tray, but interact; their interaction changes their implications for both representational processes and action decisions. The research which has explored these issues of 'multiple-category membership' or cross-category membership (Doise 1978; Deschamps and Doise 1978; Vanbeselaere 1987; Hagendoorn and Henke 1991) is in its infancy. It is, however, clear that attributional aspects of social representation are much influenced by such interaction of category memberships. One would expect action decisions to be similarly affected by it.

The research on cross-category memberships has so far tended to rely upon rather stylized pairings of memberships (Muslim–non-Muslims/high–low-class; male–female/arts–science students) and to explore them as if their interaction was global (without variations across individuals or situations). Moreover, it ignores the fact that there are different sorts of groups. This is hardly likely to produce a robust model for predicting action. The empirical problem lies in catching the implications amidst the fluidity of transitions in the relative importance of each membership. Billig (Chapter 2 of this volume) in analysing situated rhetoric, the arguments which disclose both identifications and social representations, may be getting closer to tapping into this flow. There may be another type of solution to the problem empirically. Instead of attempting to control for the interaction of group memberships by setting up relatively arbitrary experimental cross-classifications, the impact of these multiple memberships upon representations could be examined statistically. The multivariate statistical approaches adopted in several of the later chapters in this book illustrate how, assuming that the sample size is large enough and the relevant information collected, it is possible to partial-out the effects of disparate networks of group memberships. Given the right indices of group salience, this approach could also allow researchers to explore the salience-related processes linking multiple memberships to representational preferences.

It would, clearly, be foolish to jump to the conclusion that there will be inevitably some high correlation between the requirements of identity, trait, or social representation and action. It is actually necessary to specify the conditions under which they do predict action (and are not merely *post-hoc* rationalizations for action taken, generated by the individual who has acted).

There is one pointer from recent analyses which could be pursued further. Skevington (1989) suggested that we should remember emotion when talking about the effects of social identity. She argued that the theory had omitted all reference to emotion and its impact upon action and social representation. Emotion could be more seriously analysed by social psychologists as an inevitable part of their models of action, predicted either by identity dynamics or by representational processes.

One of the clearest examples of the importance of emotion comes from research on fear. There is the enormous literature on the impact of fear upon persuasion, which must be pertinent when considering how social representations are propagated. We know that levels of fear are related in a complex manner to the facility with which people assimilate and act upon new understandings. The exploration of the effects of fear upon social-representation processes in inter-group contexts, where discrimination can be rather more realistically threatening than is reflected in the differential allocation of points in a minimal-group experiment, is important. At the level of individual action, fear can be an important factor in determining how a social representation is translated into action. Again, research on sexual activity provides an example. In intensive interviews, the young people studied would sometimes describe how their fear of alienating a partner would prevent them from suggesting that a condom should be used during sexual intercourse, despite the fact that they were fully aware of the dangers of AIDS/HIV and the social representation of what constitutes safer sex.

Taking emotion seriously in research on social representations would have some implications for the empirical approach adopted. First, it would suggest that manipulative designs (either experimental or quasi-experimental) would need to be used so that the researcher could be assured that the target emotion was present. If a manipulative design was not used, it would be necessary to collect structured information on the emotional context in which the representation was elicited or observed. Secondly, it would require that systematic measurement of emotional state should be used. This would entail indexing the target emotion but also any other concurrent emotion. Thirdly, it would require a time-frame for the study which allowed any change in representation related to changes in emotional state to be monitored. Finally, it would need forms of analysis which would delineate both correlation and change in the representation and the emotion.

Conclusion

Integrating the social-identity and social-representation paradigms has a number of methodological implications. None of these involve the imposition of any single methodological orthodoxy. In fact, the theoretical integration calls for a parallel diversity of empirical approaches. The choice of method of data collection or analysis in any particular study should be determined by the theoretical proposition to be tested. In virtually all cases, a variety of methods will be needed to address the theoretical question fully. The real problem lies in relating findings drawn from different methods to each other. In studying the genesis of a representation, it may be important to use a historical analysis of the relative power of the groups producing it and affected by it. In looking at its spread within a group, it may be necessary to use surveys with carefully chosen samples. In assessing its persistence, time-series sampling may be utilized. There is no question of homogenizing or layering data from these different sources in some bland soup or, even, laying one upon another in some rather more substantial lasagne. They should be related to each other via the theory used. The empirical findings are not an end in themselves. They are valuable in so far as they can test and develop the theory. Integration is not at the level of empirical findings, but at the level of theoretical conclusions.

References

Abrams, D. (1992). Processes of social identification. In *The social psychology of identity and the self concept*. (ed. G.M. Breakwell), pp. 57–99. Academic Press/Surrey University Press, London.

Abrams, D. and Hogg, M.A. (eds.) (1990). *Social identity theory*. Harvester Wheatsheaf, Brighton.

Ashford, P. and Breakwell, G.M. (1992). *Social change and social challenge: proenvironmentalism and group dynamics*. Paper presented at the European Association of Experimental Social Psychology East–West Meeting, Munster, Germany, 27 May–1 June.

Augustinos, M. (1991). Consensual representations of social structure in different age groups. *British Journal of Social Psychology, 30*, 193–205.

Bandura, A. (1989). Perceived self-efficacy in the exercise of personal agency. *The Psychologist, 2* (10), 411–24.

Banks, M., Bates, I., Breakwell, G.M., Bynner, J., Emler, N., Jamieson, L., and Roberts, K. (eds.) (1991). *Careers and identities*. Open University Press, Milton Keynes.

Billig, M. (1985). Prejudice, categorisation, and particularisation: from a perceptual to a rhetorical approach. *European Journal of Social Psychology*, **15**, 79–105.

Breakwell, G. M. (1986). *Coping with threatened identities*. Methuen, London and New York.

Breakwell, G. M. (1987). Identity. In *Psychological Survey No. 6*, (ed. H. Beloff and A. Coleman), Leicester: BPS, 94–114.

Breakwell, G. M. (1992). Processes of self-evaluation: efficacy and estrangement. In *Social psychology of identity and the self concept*, (ed. G. M. Breakwell), pp. 35–55. Academic Press/Surrey University Press, London.

Breakwell, G. M. and Beardsell, S. (1992). Gender, parental and peer influences upon science attitudes and activities. *Public Understanding of Science*, **1**, 183–97.

Breakwell, G. M., Collie, A., Harrison, B. and Propper, C. (1984). Attitudes towards the unemployed: effects of threatened identity. *British Journal of Social Psychology*, **23**, 87–8.

Breakwell, G. M. and Fife-Schaw, C. R. (1992). Sexual activities and preferences in a UK sample of 16–20 year olds. *Archives of Sexual Behavior*, **21** (3), 271–93.

Breakwell, G. M., Fife-Schaw, C. R. and Clayden, K. (1991). Risk-taking, control over partner choice and intended use of condoms by virgins. *Journal of Community and Applied Social Psychology*, **1**, 173–87.

Coyle, A. (1991). The construction of gay identity. Unpublished PhD Thesis, Department of Psychology, University of Surrey.

Deaux, K. (1992). Personalizing identity and socializing self. In *The social psychology of identity and the self concept*, (ed. G. M. Breakwell), pp. 9–33. Academic Press/Surrey University Press, London.

Deschamps, J. C. and Doise, W. (1978). Crossed category membership in intergroup relations. In *Differentiation between social groups*, (ed. H. Tajfel), pp. 141–58. Academic Press, London.

Di Giacomo, J. P. (1980). Intergroup alliances and rejections within the protest movement (Analysis of social representations). *European Journal of Social Psychology*, **10**, 329–44.

Doise, W. (1978). *Groups and individuals: explanations in social psychology*. Cambridge University Press.

Gecas, V. and Seff, M. A. (1989). Social class, occupational conditions, and self-esteem. *Sociological Perpectives*, **32** (3), 353–64.

Gecas, V. and Seff, M. A. (1990). Social class and self-esteem: psychological centrality, compensation and the relative effects of work and home. *Social Psychology Quarterly*, **53** (2), 165–73.

Gurin, P. and Markus, H. (1989). Cognitive consequences of gender identity. In *The Social Identity of Women*, (ed. S. Skevington and D. Baker), pp. 152–72. Sage, London.

Hagendoorn, L. and Henke, R. (1991). The effect of multiple category membership on intergroup evaluations in a North Indian context: class, caste and religion. *British Journal of Social Psychology*, **30** (3), 247–60.

Hewstone, M. (1989). Intergroup attributions: some implications for the study of ethnic prejudice. In *Ethnic minorities: social psychological Perspective*, (ed, J. P. Oudenhoven and T. M. Willemsen), Swets and Zeitlinger, Amsterdam.

Hewstone, M., Jaspars, J., and Lalljee, M. (1982). Social representations, social attributions and social identity: the intergroup image of 'public' and 'comprehensive' schoolboys. *European Journal of Social Psychology*, **12**, 241–71.

Hogg, M. A. and Abrams, D. (1988). *Social identifications*. Routledge, London.
Hraba, J., Hagendoorn, L., and Hagendoorn, R. (1989). The ethnic hierarchy in the Netherlands: social distance and social representation. *British Journal of Social Psychology*, **28**, 57–69.
Jodelet, D. (ed.) (1989). *Les representations sociales*. Press Universitaires de France, Paris.
Jodelet. D. (1991). *Madness*. Harvester Wheatsheaf, Hemel Hempstead.
Kleinpenning, G. and Hagendoorn, L. (1991). Contextual aspects of ethnic stereotypes and interethnic evaluations. *European Journal of Social Psychology*, **21** (4), 331–48.
Lyons, E. and Sotirakopoulou, K. (1991). *Images of European countries*. British Psychological Society Social Psychology Section Annual Conference, University of Surrey.
Matthews, J. A. (1981). Social identity and cognition of the environment. Unpublished PhD Thesis, University of Sheffield.
Matthews, J. A. (1983). Environmental change and community identity. In *Threatened identities*, (ed. G. M. Breakwell), pp. 215–37. Wiley, Chichester.
Moscovici, S. (1981). On social representation. In *Social cognition: perspectives on everyday understanding*, (ed. J. Forgas), pp. 181–209. Academic Press, London.
Moscovici, S. (1984). The phenomenon of social representations. In *Social representations*, (ed. R. Farr and S. Moscovici), pp. 3–69. Cambridge University Press/Maison des Sciences de l'Homme, Cambridge/Paris.
Moscovici, S. (1988). Notes towards a description of social representations. *European Journal of Social Psychology*, **18**, 211–50.
Moscovici, S. and Hewstone, M. (1983). Social representations and social explanations: from the 'naive' to the 'amateur' scientist. In *Attribution theory: social and functional extensions*, (ed. M. Hewstone), pp. 98–125. Blackwell, Oxford.
Palmonari, A., Pombeni, M. L., and Zani, B. (1987). Social representation and professionalization of psychologists. In *Current issues in European social psychology*, Vol. 2, (ed. Doise, W & Moscovici, S.), pp. 231–69. Cambridge University Press.
Potter, J. and Wetherell, M. (1987). *Discourse and social psychology*. Sage, London.
Skevington, S. (1989). A place for emotion in social identity theory. In *The social identity of women*, (ed. S. Skevington and D. Baker), pp. 40–58.
Sotirakopoulou, K. (1991). Processes of social representation: a multi-methodological and longitudinal approach. Unpublished PhD Thesis, Department of Psychology, University of Surrey.
Tajfel, H. (ed.) (1978). *Differentiation between social groups*. Academic Press, London.
Tajfel, H. (1981). Social stereotypes and social groups. In *Human groups and social categories*, (ed. H. Tajfel), pp. 143–61. Cambridge University Press.
Tajfel, H. and Turner, J. C. (1986). The social identity theory of intergroup behaviour. In *Psychology of intergroup relations*, (ed. S. Worchel and W. G. Austin), Nelson-Hall, Chicago.
Turner, J. C. (1991). *Social influence*. Open University Press, Milton Keynes.
Vanbeselaere, N. (1987). The effects of dichotomous and crossed social categorizations upon intergroup discrimination. *European Journal of Social Psychology*, **17**, 143–56.

Part II

10 The descriptive analyses of shared representations

Sean Hammond

This chapter is not intended as a didactic account of a particular procedure, although it may well be read as such, but rather as a series of observations of a plausible set of procedures for the empirical exploration of social representations. I would emphasize the exploratory component and state at the outset that they are not intended to give unequivocal answers to our questions but, rather, to provide a descriptive framework from which we can develop relevant questions.

Moscovici's (1973, 1984*a*, 1984*b*) use of the term 'social representation' lacks a clear operational meaning. This is argued (Moscovici 1983) to be a ㄴ6 strength of the concept, since it deters the formation of simplistic and categorical paradigms which are then dependent upon the arbitrary whims of academic fashion. He argues most clearly (Moscovici 1984*b*) that the concept of social representations is an emergent end-product of an accumulation of ideas in sociology, psychology, and anthropology, and that it is still in the process of being shaped.

Given this vagueness, it may seem somewhat presumptuous to propose a method for examining the application of measurement to context-specific social representations. Yet, the shaping of any concept of descriptive worth cannot rely entirely upon abstract theorizing if it is to have any scientific credibility. The purpose here is to attempt to provide a set of procedures which will remain sympathetic to the exploratory and cumulative aims of social representation research. However, before detailing these procedures further it will be necessary to explore, very briefly, those assumptions and ideas upon which they depend for their utility.

Social representations may be variously defined (Moscovici 1984*a,b*; Jaspars and Fraser 1984; Harre 1984; Potter and Litton 1985). Indeed, there is even variation across the definition for the separate terms 'social' and 'representation' (Harre 1984; Sperber 1985). Nevertheless, a common theme appears to be the existence of some form of shared ideation across some group or plurality. This, of course, would imply an aggregation of ideas across individual units of analysis, usually people. Such a view would seem to contradict Durkheim's (1897) position that a *'représentation sociale'* is more than simple aggregation and, indeed, describes a cultural imperative which is largely autonomous of the individuals that inhabit that culture.

Harre (1984) draws a clear distinction between distributive and collective pluralities. While distributive plurality is a function of simple aggregation, collective plurality describes a more structural quality. The latter is more closely related to the Durkheimian concept and, for Harre, better describes the concept of social representation. My view is that such distinctions are more apparent than real and, while they raise diverting philosophic questions, the pragmatic elements of social-psychological research serve to blur such neat discriminations. Thus, the existence of a collective plurality predicts a shared set of beliefs and knowledge across individuals. Of course, it is somewhat more of a moot point to posit, as Thomas Kuhn (1970) did, that commonality among individual representations come to represent the 'shared ties of a community'. It is certainly feasible to examine the structural elements of a culture, but an understanding of the meaning of that structure must surely rest upon individual perceptions and representations.

It would appear from the literature of social representations that there is an implicit support for distributive elements; this is acknowledged by Moscovici (1984*b*) in his reply to Harre, although he cites the work of Jodolet on representations of mental illness as an exception to this rule. It is worth noting that, in this rejoinder to Harre, I find the clearest account of what social representation entails. I hold this as evidence of Moscovici's contention that the concept is still in the process of formation, a process encouraged by dialogue.

Accounts of cultural milieux which do not utilize the individual representations abound in the disciplines of history and political philosophy. Thus, Lukacs (1971) describes in great detail the cultural concomitants of early Nazism in Germany by an in-depth analysis of the political structure of Europe at that time. Dumont (1986), attempting to describe German culture as some kind of entity in its own right, utilized an analysis of German literature and philosophy.

These approaches are limited in providing a precise picture of social representations, since they rely upon unrepresentative information. There is no reason to suppose, as Heidegger (1968) argues, that philosophers are representative of a culture and, although slightly more contentious, I see no reason to believe that governments and political movements are either. This position is aggravated by the growing plurality of modern culture, and while such supra-individual approaches must assume a strong degree of *Gemeinschaft*, most sociologists would acknowledge the rapid counter-growth of *Gessellschaft* in modern society (Tonnies 1974; Simmel 1968).

Sperber (1985), in a fascinating article from the anthropologist's point of view, clearly states that cultural representations may be observed in the prevalence and distribution of individual representations. He takes the approach of using epidemiology as a methodological metaphor for the explanation of these cultural representations. Thus, representations, like viruses, infect individuals and the degree of spread reflects the strength of cultural representation. The manner in which such representations spread may be studied in much the same way that epidemiologists study the spread of disease. Of course, this epidemiological approach to social knowledge is not new and is the starting point for the mathematical model of cultural transmission proposed by Cavalli-sforza and Feldman (1981).

In this chapter, I intend to draw upon Sperber's logic and to pronounce at the outset that the methods I espouse here are based upon the distributive premise of social representation. This does not reflect a rejection of Harre's important account of the collective plurality but, rather, reflects some doubts as to its empirical accessibility. Moscovici (1984b, p. 940) talks of representations as communicable 'images' and states that:

Explaining the content and dissemination of such a common 'image', what it conveys, these are all approaches to the study of social representations.

Since there is such diversity of opinion of what constitutes the legitimate meaning of the term 'social representation', and since I wish to emphasize the consensual aspect of the concept, I will henceforth use the term 'shared representation' to describe the conceptualization accepted here. By a shared representation I refer to a set of knowledge, beliefs, and attributions concerning a given phenomenon, which are jointly held or expressed by some form of plurality be they persons, groups, or media artefacts.

Any method for the exploration of shared representations must be sufficiently flexible to reflect the unspecific nature of the concept. A very real problem in psychological research concerns the reification of method over theory to the point where the techniques we use assert a Procrustean influence upon the very questions we attempt to ask of our data. Classic examples are the rigidly-linear models of factor analysis and multiple regression, and our heavy dependence upon arbitrary probability levels (Guttman 1977, 1982). For this reason, the procedures described here do not emphasize the fitting of data to a specific model. The intention, rather, is to provide some heuristic tools for the exploration of shared representations and, while not entirely model-free, these procedures should be sufficiently descriptive so as not to dictate, but to enrich, theory.

It has been pointed out that one of the main aims of social-representation research is the accumulation of knowledge, rather than the categorical acceptance or rejection of specific hypotheses (Moscovici 1984b). Thus, the emphasis may be considered exploratory rather than inferential. Shye (1978, p. 4), in the introduction to his book on theory construction and data analysis, states:

Unfortunately, social and psychological investigators, in their attempt to attain the rigour of the physical sciences, often report prematurely to quantitative trimmings in their studies while neglecting another feature essential to all empirical science: formulating a reliable definitional basis for carrying out observations. Thus, elaborate statistical methods are often used to analyse observations whose (usually unexplicated) definitional basis is extremely weak. As a result, meaningful replications of empirical studies are usually impossible and little knowledge is actually accumulated towards the formulation of scientific laws.

We are here concerned with a definition of social representations that is distributive, and our primary objectives are therefore taxonomic. The following procedures are designed to employ the simplest intuitive logic to this definitional basis. The resulting empirical analysis should then produce a picture of the data which may lead to the evolution of theory and the accumulation of knowledge.

Moscovici (1984b) has argued that the methods required to analyse social representations must be compatible with those which explore psychological phenomena, in order to accommodate the cumulative enterprise. However, there is an important superficial difference between psychometric approaches and those necessary to examine shared ideation. Psychologists have been traditionally concerned with the notion of individual differentiation. Thus, psychological phenomena are identified by variation across individuals, whereas shared representation is observed by consensus or the lack of variation between individuals.

We start from the assumption that the data received from an analysis of social representation will be categorical. It is obvious that this is the point at which some degree of operational definition of the phenomenon under study is required, and that this will vary with the researcher's orientation. Typically, such data is the result of some kind of content analysis. These data may be from a wide variety of sources, for example, verbal behaviours (Gottschalk and Gleser 1969), newspaper editorials (De Sola Pool 1952), artwork (Brown et al. 1987), or advertisements (Sommer and Sommer 1978).

The actual source of these data is, for our purposes, irrelevant — they may be taken from individuals, groups, or media artefact, but we will here describe them as the 'sources'. We now assume that the categories that emerge from the content analyses represent attributes which are identified as part of a specific phenomenon. Thus, Brown et al. (1986) asked young children to draw pictures of nuclear power stations and her subsequent content analysis of these paintings indicated a number of attributes that the children associated with the phenomenon of nuclear power such as 'weaponry' and 'radiation'. In this case, the children are the 'sources' and the categories are the 'attributes'.

Our data, then, may be viewed as dichotomous. Each source is assessed for the presence or absence of a particular attribute. Note that we do not, here, expect to be dealing with graded values, simply presence–absence, one–zero, binary codes. Thus, the complex verbal or iconic information needs to be decomposed into a rectangular data file with, for example, sources as rows and attributes as columns. Every value in the data file will be zero or one.

The problem now is to derive a means of assessing the consensus by which these attributes are held to belong to the phenomenon of interest. Clearly we can take each attribute separately and examine the frequency with which it is cited by our sources. This may be very useful in attempting to interpret the meaning of the phenomenon but it does not allow us to measure the general consensus across sources and so gives us no insight into the strength of the representation.

The first step in this endeavour is to identify a means of assessing the overall agreement of our sources. The problem is well known in psychometric theory where the idea is to assess the overall homogeneity of a set of questionnaire items. In this case, we are concerned to assess the homogeneity of our sources.

When we wish to construct a questionnaire to measure some latent psychological variable (such as attitude toward smoking), we are at great pains to select our items so that they tap a common theme. Should we prove successful in this endeavour, the empirical result will be that all the items of our questionnaire are at least moderately inter-correlated. Such a finding may inform us that the items were sampled from a homogeneous psychological domain, such as smoking attitudes. The mean correlation ($\bar{r}$) gives us a measure of the degree of homogeneity. Incidentally, the reliability of our measurement may be said to depend upon this homogeneity, since the Cronbach alpha coefficient may be estimated by the following formula:

$$\alpha = \left[\frac{n}{n-1} \right] \cdot \left[1 - \frac{n}{n + 2(\Sigma r_{ij})} \right],$$

where Σr_{ij} = sum of the inter-variable correlations
$\quad\quad n$ = number of variables.

Clearly then, a logical extension of this idea to the analysis of shared representation is to form a correlation matrix, not of questionnaire items across people, but of sources across attributes. Again, the strength of the mean correlation would represent the degree of homogeneity across our sources and may be extended to describe the strength of shared ideation within the group.

Unfortunately, this approach, which may lead on to such multivariate taxonomic procedures as G analysis (Holley 1966) or Q-factor analysis (Stephenson 1953), is not appropriate for the data to which we are heir, simply because we cannot legitimately utilize the product-moment correlation. To do so would imply that our sources must have a linear relationship with each other which makes little sense given our data and imposes an unnecessary methodological constraint. Perhaps even more problematic, however, is the fact that our data is likely to be too sparse for correlational procedures. In order to carry out Pearson correlation we need to assume a normal distribution of scores which, in the dichotomous case, is represented by a 50/50 split of zeros to ones. We would be naive to assume that such a distribution would be observed from a content analysis of open-ended data.

Also, we have the problem of what to do with the situation when two sources have both neglected to cite a particular attribute. Does this joint absence constitute a measure of agreement? I would argue that it does not, since the failure to produce an attribute does not imply that it is necessarily absent from the representation of that source.

When interrelating two sources which are likened according to a number of dichotomous attributes it is useful to examine the simple two-way contingency table:

| | Source 1 | |
	Present	Absent
Source 2 Present	a	b
Absent	c	d

The value a represents the number of times that sources 1 and 2 have jointly cited an attribute; b represents the number of times that source 2 cites an attribute but source 1 does not; c represents the number of times that source 1 cites an attribute but fource 2 does not; and d represents the number of times that neither source cites an attribute.

The formula for the Pearson correlation of dichotomous data is:

$$\phi = \frac{ad - bc}{\sqrt{(a + c)\,(a + b)\,(b + d)\,(c + d)}}$$

From this, we can see that the value d, which represents joint absence, has an equal weight in the formula as a, which is the value representing the number of times that two sources agreed in attribute citation. Clearly this is not satisfactory, and we will need to discover an alternative way of assessing agreement between sources which does not utilize d. This problem has been one that has worried ecologists and biologists for many years (Sokal and Sneath 1963; Jansen and Vegelius 1981) and happily there is a solution in a coefficient devised for biological taxonomy in the early part of the century by Jaccard (1908). Jaccard's coefficient (J) has the formula:

$$J = \frac{a}{a + b + c}$$

This coefficient has the advantage of extreme simplicity, which is one of our primary aims, as well as clear utility, since it is not mediated by joint absence and it always ranges between 0 and 1. So, if all the attributes are present for two sources, b and c would equal 0 and Jaccard's coefficient would thus equal 1. If, on the other hand, two sources failed to agree on any attributes, then a would equal 0 and Jaccard's coefficient would thus equal zero.

We may now calculate a matrix of inter-source Jaccard coefficients and the overall mean will represent our degree of homogeneity. Since there is no known distribution as yet for the mean Jaccard coefficient, this value is of purely descriptive value. If we were to stop there, of course, little would be gained, but we are now in a position to iteratively maximize our measure of shared representation by systematically refining our data set.

Let us start by identifying those sources that do not seem to agree with the others. This is done simply by calculating the mean Jaccard coefficient of each source with all the others. This value is then a measure of the individual source homogeneity with the group. The sources can be rank ordered, and those with lowest values may be eliminated from the data matrix and the overall homogeneity may be recalculated. Of course, it is very important to note those sources which are being jettisoned, as their failure to conform to the distributive norm will probably be indicative of some interesting feature. In other words, we are embarking upon an extremely simple procedure for identifying outliers. This is precisely equivalent to the procedure proposed by Ray (1972) for defining the psychometric domain of questionnaire items.

Once we have identified our outlying sources, we should return to look at the attribute counts without these sources. we may decide to drop some attributes from our domain simply because they are not cited often enough to justify them as elements of the representation. The process is iterative, in that we can move to and fro between examination of attribute counts and source homogeneity.

Of course, we can also carry out the same procedure upon our attributes. That is, we would obtain an inter-attribute agreement-coefficient matrix and perform a similar 'outlier' analysis. This analysis would identify a tight group of interrelated attributes to aid the description of the content of the representation.

The process that we have described here should enable not only an empirical definition of the shared representation under consideration, but also some descriptive insights into the structure of the representation. Specifically, it seeks to identify a tight consensus from which some idea of the shared meaning of the phenomenon may be implied by those attributes ascribed to the representation in question. We may now proceed further to examine the structural nature of the representation.

As we have a means of generating an inter-source matrix of agreement coefficients, there is no reason why the structure of this matrix may not be explored by well-established multivariate methods of data analysis. So, for example, a hierarchical cluster analysis may be performed in order to classify the sources into subgroups. We might then explore the notion that these subgroups represent some forms of subordinate representations, and it should be possible to explore the structural breakdown of the superordinate shared representation. Alternatively, we may perform some form of multi-dimensional scaling in order to portray the relationships between sources in Euclidean space. Thus, it becomes possible to explore the structure of our shared representation by exploring the regional patterns in our data.

It may be tempting for us also to attempt a principle-component analysis upon the inter-source agreement matrix and, while we would tend to suspect the linear assumptions underlying such an analysis, it should be pointed out that our choice of the Jaccard coefficient allows us this option. This is because the coefficient, although not a product-moment correlation, may be viewed as a scalar product of two vectors within Euclidean space. Thus, it satisfies the geometric requirements which underlie the eigen structure approach of principle component analysis. Indeed, the Jaccard coefficient is one of very few so called E coefficients (Vegelius 1978) which manifest this property.

We have been talking here exclusively about structural analyses of the inter-source agreement matrix, but there is actually no reason why the same analysis may not be also performed upon the inter-attribute matrix. Such analyses may give us insights into the relationship between attributes and so enlighten us further on the meaning and structure of the shared representation.

We will now give a brief, and somewhat trivial, numerical example of the procedures upon some simple fabricated data, and then give a brief discussion of an analysis using real data. In Table 10.1 we see some hypothetical data from ten sources and six attributes. We may assume, for example, that the sources represent popular weekly magazines and the attributes represent themes observed in their editorials. Equally, we could assume that the sources represent individual children who have been asked to write a story concerning a trip to the doctor and the attributes the themes derived from a content analysis of these stories.

We can see from this Table 10.1 that attribute A6 is cited only twice and, at this stage, we may decide to drop this attribute from our analysis since it manifests little consensual power. This does not suggest that this attribute is not interesting in its own right, but simply that our distributive definition of a shared representation does not include this attribute as a powerful exemplar. Again, it is worth noting that no statistical guidance is given for the rejection of attributes, and it should be borne in mind that we are not testing a theory or model but, rather, constructing one. It is envisaged that

Table 10.1 Hypothetical data from ten Sources and five attributes

Attributes							
Sources	A1	A2	A3	A4	A5	A6	Sum
S1	1	1	1	0	1	1	5
S2	1	0	1	0	1	0	3
S3	1	1	1	0	0	0	3
S4	1	1	0	0	1	0	3
S5	0	0	1	1	1	0	3
S6	0	0	0	1	1	0	2
S7	0	1	0	1	0	0	2
S8	0	0	1	0	0	0	1
S9	1	0	1	1	1	1	5
S10	0	1	0	1	1	0	3
Sum	5	5	6	5	7	2	28

many exploratory iterations will be performed before the researcher is satisfied. It may be a legitimate argument to say that if an attribute is used by more than one person then it merits inclusion. A multidimensional scaling (MDS) analysis of the inter-attribute agreement matrix might reveal its marginal nature.

In Table 10.2 we see the inter-source matrix of Jaccard coefficients, based on attributes A1–A5, after dropping A6 from the analysis. We see that the overall measure of homogeneity is 0.35. It is worth noting that this homogeneity value is identical to the mean of the 5×5 matrix of inter-attribute Jaccard coefficients. Thus, we are viewing the homogeneity of the entire data set and not just source homogeneity. I will leave it to the reader to calculate the 5×5 inter-attribute Jaccard-coefficient matrix and test this assertion. Suffice it to say that this illustrates the interchangeability of source and attribute homogeneity.

Source 8 is obviously less integrated than the other nine, and after removing this source the overall homogeneity rises to 0.38. We could now view the attribute counts again and we could find that attribute 3 has been weakened by the loss of source 8. Figure 10.1 shows us a smallest-space analysis (SSA) (Guttman 1968) of the nine remaining sources. It is apparent from this that there are two distinct groupings which indicate the presence of two subordinate representations.

Obviously, the above example is somewhat trivial and does not reveal the full potential of the method. We will now turn to more practical data taken from a pilot study of an on-going investigation into the representations of

Table 10.2   The inter-source matrix

	01	02	03	04	05	06	07	08	09	010	$\bar{r}$
01	1.00										0.47
02	0.75	1.00									0.42
03	0.75	0.50	1.00								0.34
04	0.75	0.50	0.50	1.00							0.37
05	0.40	0.50	0.20	0.20	1.00						0.42
06	0.20	0.25	0.00	0.25	0.67	1.00					0.31
07	0.20	0.00	0.25	0.25	0.25	0.33	1.00				0.23
08	0.25	0.33	0.33	0.00	0.33	0.00	0.00	1.00			0.16
09	0.60	0.75	0.40	0.40	0.75	0.50	0.20	0.25	1.00		0.47
010	0.40	0.20	0.20	0.50	0.50	0.67	0.67	0.00	0.40	1.00	0.39

Mean Jaccard coefficient = 0.35; mean Jaccard coefficient without source 8 = 0.38.

young people concerning drugs and drug use (Hammond and O'Rourke 1987). The data reported here is far from perfect and contains a number of methodological weaknesses, but it will serve us for illustrative purposes.

Two hundred and eight young people between the ages of 14 and 17 filled in a questionnaire containing a number of open-ended questions. The question we will consider here was 'What do you think of people who take drugs?' The responses to this question were subjected to a rudimentary content

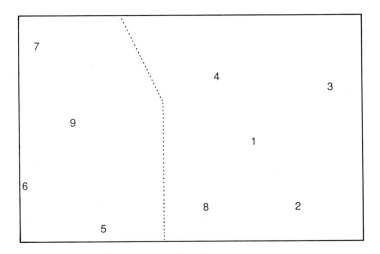

Fig. 10.1. Two dimensional smallest-space analysis (SSA) plot of nine remaning sources (Guttman–Lingoes coefficient of alienation = 0.04

Table 10.3 Attributes of drug users supplied by 208 schoolchildren

Attribute	Citation (per cent)
Dirty	32.3
Evil	27.6
Unhealthy	26.6
Frightening	22.2
Dangerous	15.8
Exciting	30.6
Uninteresting	19.7
Victimized	36.5
Romantic	18.4
Tragic	42.4
Stupid	47.7

analysis which identified 28 attribute categories. These were reduced to 11 by using the arbitrary cut-off that they must be cited by at least 10 per cent of the sample. They are listed in Table 10.3.

The 208 × 208 inter-person matrix was calculated and the mean Jaccard coefficient was found to be 0.11. We then proceeded to reduce the subject pool by excluding outliers and, after 50 exclusions, the mean Jaccard coefficient rose to 0.30. At this point we stopped and examined the outliers. It was interesting to note that, of the 23 young people admitting to some current drug use, 21 were in the excluded group. This indicates, very tentatively, that children with drug experience do not share the common representation of their inexperienced peers. Such a finding may be trivial, but it indicates how theory may be built from such a study. It was also interesting to note that the outliers, when taken as a separate group, do not appear to share a coherent alternative shared representation (mean Jaccard = 0.09; $N = 50$) but, rather, appear to be somewhat individualistic in the representations they adopt.

In addition to the open-ended questions, each young person filled in a self-report questionnaire designed to tap feelings of adolescent estrangement (Hammond 1985, 1988a). This measure was developed to assess the psychological concomitants of anomie (Durkheim 1897) (a quality variously termed 'anomia' (Srole 1956) and 'anomy' (McCloskey and Schaar 1965)). Thus, it was interesting to observe that the 50 outliers manifested a significantly higher mean on this measure than the homogeneous group ($t = 3.09; p < 0.01$). Additionally, the individual mean Jaccard coefficient for each person was correlated with the individual score on the estrangement measure. A very high correlation of −0.51 was observed, which is quite suggestive of the idea that estrangement is concomitant with the absence of homogeneous shared representations. Convergently, it also supports the use of mean Jaccard coefficients as an index of individual cohesiveness toward a common representation.

Of course, there are problems with this analysis since we have ignored a number of extraneous variables, most notably age. We do not draw strong conclusions here, as a more detailed analysis is currently on-going. The aim is to show how these purely descriptive analyses may serve to direct our focus as the study continues.

Since there were 208 sources and it would be troublesome to attempt an interpretation of the structural relationships between so many (though by no means impractical), we reproduce the SSA plot, for the 11 attributes based upon the 158 people remaining after outlier exclusion, in Fig. 10.2. It is fairly clear that the shared representation explored here includes both victim and offender themes as subordinate facets.

This set of procedures is designed not to give easy answers to the researcher but rather to provide an exploratory heuristic. As Moscovici has said of methods for exploring social representations:

Hence one should judge them not by 'what can be done with them' but by 'what can be thought with them'.

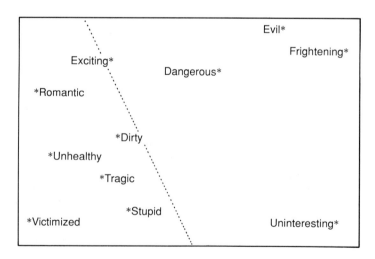

Fig. 10.2. Two-dimensional smallest-space analysis (SSA) plot of attributes of drug users supplied by 208 children (Guttman–Lingoes coefficient of alienation = 0.21; Jaccard coefficient of consensus = 0.30)

Once these procedures have been utilized, we should begin to have before us the following food for thought:

(1) some empirical-descriptive basis for defining the content of the shared representation;

(2) some empirical-descriptive criteria for judging the strength of the shared representation;

(3) some empirical-descriptive information regarding the structure of subordinate representations.

This cognitive nutriment may then form the basis for approaching more powerful, model-driven, analyses. A type of technique that we have found particularly useful is commonly known as optimal scaling and has been developed variously as dual scaling (Nishisato 1981), correspondence analysis (Benzecri 1971), homals (Gifi 1981), or multiple scalogram analysis (MSA) (Lingoes 1968; Guttman 1985). These procedures are designed specifically for the analysis of qualitative data.

We will finish here with a brief example of one application of correspondence analysis. We will not describe the mathematical or statistical background of the method, since excellent English language descriptions are available in Greenacre (1984) Lebart and *et al.* (1984). Suffice it to say that an appropriately-conditioned two-dimensional contingency table may be subjected to a singular-value decomposition (Eckart and Young 1936; Hill 1976). This allows a coordinate space to be identified into which the columns and rows may be jointly projected as points in this space.

Thus, suppose we have identified a number of subordinate groupings among our sources by means of cluster analysis, MDS, or *a priori* rationalization. We would now aggregate our sources into these groupings and record the total number of times that each attribute is cited by each group. Our data now becomes a two-dimensional contingency table, with source groupings in columns and attributes in rows. The numbers in the cells are now the frequencies with which the attributes have been cited by each group.

As an example, we will examine data collected by Hassan (1986) as part of a study leading to a masters degree in medical psychology at the University of Surrey. She was concerned to investigate representations of the phenomenon of female circumcision. The data was collected from 230 interviews with Sudanese individuals from rural areas of Sudan and the urban region of Khartoum. She also interviewed a number of British people. Full details of the sample are available in Hassan (1986). Clearly, then, groups may defined *a priori* as:

(1) rural Sudanese;

(2) urban Sudanese;

(3) British.

Of course, we could also group them according to other demographic features such as sex and age, but for the purpose of this illustration three groups will suffice. Certainly an understanding of the representations that different groups hold toward the practice has implications for health-education planning. One of the questions that Hassan asked was 'What is meant by female circumcision?'

A content analysis of this question resulted in seven categories of response. These were defined by the degree of knowledge expressed. Not surprisingly, perhaps, the British sample produced a high number of people who did not know what female circumcision was while no Sudanese inter-viewee professed ignorance. The content categories reflect non-specific responses (removal of sex organs) to more specific (removal of the clitoris) as well as knowledge of the milder Sunna practice (excision of labia minora) to the more severe type of practice known as the pharonic procedure (total exision of the vulva). Thus, with three groups and seven categories, the contingency table for this data is reported in Table 10.4.

A correspondence analysis programme (CORRES), written by the author (Hammond 1988b), was applied to this matrix and the resultant spatial plot is reported in Fig. 10.3. The space may be divided into three broad regions, each exemplified by one of the groupings. Clearly the British group, occupying the western region, is represented by lack of knowledge—which is much as we might expect. Additionally, we may observe that pharonic and infibrillation practices are most closely associated with the rural group in the north-east region. The urban group appears to be associated with greater precision and a tendency to cite the somewhat less severe Sunna type of practice.

Table 10.4 Contingency table of response categories across three groups to the question 'What is meant by female circumcision?'

Category of response	British	Urban Sudanese (per cent)	Rural Sudanese
Don't know	25	0	0
Removal of the clitoris	31	72	30
Removal of the labia (non-specific)	12	52	19
Removal of the labia minora	4	13	2
Removal of the labia majora	8	12	2
Removal of the sex organs (non-specific)	18	37	89
Sew up the sex organs	27	77	87

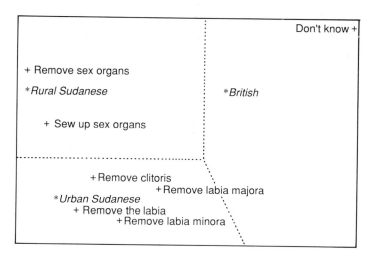

Fig. 10.3. A spatial plot of answers to the question 'what is female circumcision?'

Thus, we may tentatively conclude that the rural groups still maintain a strongly-traditional representation of female circumcision, while the urban group manifest a more precise but less severely-traditional representation. We also observe that the British group is marked by the presence of a weak representation.

This dual-scaling procedure relies upon a strong canonical model and therefore carries with it a number of methodological concerns such as the use of appropriate constraints (Goldstein 1987) and the seemingly indeterminate problem of true distances between row and column points in joint space (Greenacre 1984; Nishisato 1981). Nevertheless, as a descriptive tool it offers great scope for theory construction.

In summary, it must be re-emphasized that the perspective on social representation adopted here is distributive rather than structural, a perspective perhaps best described by use of the term 'shared representation'. A set of procedures has been described which are designed to illuminate these representations, given empirical data of the phenomena in question. These procedures are all descriptive in essence and are designed as an aid to interpretation and theory construction rather than model testing. The simplicity of the techniques is intended to ensure that the researcher is never far from her own data.

Since these methods are designed to help in the formation of theory and models, it may be reasonably argued that they may also have some relevance to the exploration of representational structures. Clearly, the identification of super- and subordinate representations within a given sample provides the

220 Sean Hammond

basis for thinking about structural models of shared representations. Thus, it may be hoped that the discrepancy between distributive and structural features of social representations may, with careful juxtaposition of descriptive empirical evidence and theoretical rigour, be resolved into a testable model.

References

Benzecri, J.P. (1973). *L'analyse des données. II. L'analyses des correspondances.* Dunod, Paris.
Brown, J., Henderson, J., and Armstrong, M. (1987). Childrens' perceptions of nuclear power stations as seen through their drawings. *Journal of Environmental Psychology*, 7, 184–8.
Cavalli-Sforza, L.L. and Feldman, M.W. (1981). *Cultural transmissions and evolution: a quantitative approach.* Princeton University Press, New Jersey.
De Sola Pool, I. (1952). *Symbols of democracy.* Stanford University Press.
Dumont, L. (1986). Are cultures living beings? German identity in interaction. *Man*, 21, 587–604.
Durkheim, E. (1987). *La suicide: étude de sociologié.* Alcan, Paris.
Eckart, C. and Young, C. (1936). The approximation of one matrix by another of lower rank. *Psychometrika*, 1, 211–18.
Gifi, A. (1981). *Non-linear multivariate analysis.* Department of Data Theory, University of Leiden.
Goldstein, H. (1987). The choice of contrasts in correspondence analysis. *Psychometrika*, 52, 207–15.
Gottschalk, L.A. and Gleser, G.C. (1969). *The measurement of psychological states through the content analysis of verbal behaviour.* University of California Press, Los Angeles.
Greenacre, M.J. (1984). *Theory and applications of correspondance analysis.* Academic Press, London.
Guttman, L. (1986). A general nonmetric technique for finding the smallest coordinate space for a configuration. *Psychometrika*, 33, 469–506.
Guttman, L. (1977). What is not what in statistics. *The Statistician*, 26, 81–107.
Guttman, L. (1982). What is not what in theory construction. In *Multidimensional data representations: when or why.* (Ed. I. Borg) pp. 47–64. Academic Press, New York. P 47–64, Mathesis Press, Ann Arbor.
Guttman, L. (1985). Multiple structuple analysis (MSA-I) for the classification of Cetacea: whales, porpoises and dolphins. In *Data analysis in real life environment*, (ed. J.F. Marcotorchino, J.M. Proth, and J. Jansen). North Holland, Amsterdam.
Hammond, S.M. (1985). *The measurement and implications of adolescent estrangement.* Paper presented at the Annual Conference of the Psychological Society of Ireland.
Hammond, S.M. (1988a). The meaning and measurement of adolescent estrangement. Unpublished PhD thesis, University of Surrey.
Hammond, S.M. (1988b). *CORRES 1.0: a programme for the correspondence analysis of contingency tables on IBM compatible micros.* Department of Psychology, University of Surrey.

Hammond, S. M. and O'Rourke, M. M. (1987). *Project on young persons' represen-tations of drugs and drug abuse. Preliminary analyses of data from Possil Park.* Report for Scottish Home and Health, drug stopping programme. Southern General Hospital, Glasgow.

Harre, R. (1984). Some reflections on the concept of 'Social representation'. *Social Research*, **51**, 927–38.

Hassan, A. (1986). Social attributions for female circumcision. Unpublished MSc dissertation, University of Surrey.

Heidegger, M. (1969). *Identity and difference*, (trans. J. Stambaugh). Harper Row, London.

Hill, M. O. (1976). Correspondence analysis: a neglected multivariate method. *Applied Statistics*, **23**, 340–54.

Holley, J. W. (1966). *Studies related to Q-R factoring.* Simonsons, Göteborg.

Jaccard, P. (1908). Nouvelles recherches sur la distribution florale. *Bulletin de la Société Vaudoise. Science Naturelle,* **44**, 223–70.

Jansen, S. and Vegelius, J. (1981). Measures of association. *Oecologia*, **49**, 371–6.

Jaspars, J. and Fraser, C. (1984). Attitudes and social representations. In *Social representations*, (ed. R. Farr and S. Moscovici). Cambridge University Press.

Kuhn, T. S. (ed.) (1970). *The structure of scientific revolutions*, (2nd edn). University of Chicago Press.

Lebart, L., Morineau, A., and Warwick, K. M. (1984). *Multivariate descriptive statistical analysis: correspondence analysis and related techniques for large data matrices.* Wiley, New York.

Lingoes, J. C. (1968). The multivariate analysis of qualitative data. *Multivariate Behavioural Research*, **3**, 61–94.

Lukacs, G. (1971). *History and class consciousness*, (trans. R. Livingstone) Merlin Press, London.

McCloskey, H. and Schaar, J. (1965). Psychological dimensions of anomy. *American Sociological Review*, **30**, 14–40.

Moscovici, S. (1973). Foreword to C. Herzlich. In *Health and illness: a social psychological perspective*, (ed. C. Herzlich). Academic Press, London.

Moscovici, S. (1984*a*). The phenomenon of social representations. In *Social repre-sentations*, (ed. R. Farr and S. Moscovici). Cambridge University Press.

Moscovici, S. (1984*b*). The myth of the lonely paradigm: a rejoinder. *Social Research*, **51**, 939–63.

Nishisato, S. (1981). *Analysis of categorical data: dual scaling and its applications.* Toronto University Press.

Potter, J. and Litton, I. (1985). Some problems underlying the theory of social representatios. *British Journal of Social Psychology*, **24**, 81–90.

Ray, J. J. (1972). A new reliability maximisation procedure for Likert scales. *Australian Psychologist*, **7**, 40–6.

Shye, S. (1978). *Theory construction and data analysis in the behavioural sciences.* Jossey-Bass, London.

Simmel, G. (1968). *The conflict of modern culture and other essays*, (trans. K. P. Etzkorn). Teachers College Press, New York.

Sokal, R. R. and Sneath, P. H. (1963). *Principles of numeric taxonomy.* Freeman, San Fransisco.

Sommer, R. and Sommer, B. (1978). Advertising in health journals. *Journal of Orthomolecular Psychiatry*, **7**, 275–81.

Sperber, D. (1985). Anthropology and psychology: towards an epidemiology of representations. *Man*, **20**, 73–89.

Srole, L. (1956). Social integration and certain corollaries: an exploratory study. *American Sociological Review*, **21**, 709–16.

Stephenson, W. (1953). *The study of behaviour: Q-technique and its methodology*. University of Chicago Press.

Tonnies, F. (1974). *Community and society*, (trans. C. P. Loomis). American Book Company, New York.

Vegelius, J. (1978). On the utility of the E-correlation coefficient concept in psychological research. *Educational and Psychological Measurement*, **38**, 605–11.

11 The Lattice of Polemic Social Representations: A comparison of the social representations of occupations in favelas, public housing, and middle-class neighbourhoods of Brazil

David V. Canter and Circe Monteiro

Naming and Classifying

Moscovici (1983, p. 15) emphasizes that a major function of social representations is

to facilitate communication among members of a community by providing them with a code for naming and classifying the various aspects of their world and their individual and group history.

In the process of classification, meaning is assigned to some aspects of the world and other aspects are rendered invisible. The processes of anchoring, whereby aspects of the world are integrated into familiar categorization schemes, and objectification, whereby 'the iconic quality of an imprecise idea' (Moscovici 1984, p. 38) is discovered, are both processes related to the harnessing of linguistic mechanisms in order to create systems of codification. It is these systems that provide individuals with a stable enough social and cultural milieu in which to act.

However, although language has a salient role in representation processes, many studies mistakenly rely totally on fulsome verbal accounts to reveal representations. This leads to a confusion of the analysis of representations with discourse and related linguistic analyses. Yet, Moscovici (1985, p. 92) reflects a century of psychological thinking, going back at least to William James and Sigmund Freud, when he writes:

all that is image or concept does not pass entirely into language. On the contrary the latter can trigger the images and representations shared by the group.

So, for example, when Potter and Litton (1985) propose encompassing the study of social representations within the examination of linguistic repertoires, they are ignoring the warning convincingly presented by Herzlich (1973, p. 397) that when social representations are derived from 'reasoning transmitted during conversation' they are distorted, carrying 'the sign of analysis after material recompilation.'

Therefore, in order to develop an understanding of the 'code for naming and classifying' that is at the heart of social representations, it is important to develop methodologies that will complement the intensively-verbal procedures by allowing people to reflect their ways of anchoring and objectifying aspects of their world without the need for detailed verbal accounts.

The methodological enrichment of social-representation research by the use of verbally-limited procedures also makes possible the comparison of groups in society who may express themselves using very different canons of semantics and syntax. Linguistically-intensive procedures are likely to reveal, for example, much more coherent representations amongst professional, middle-class respondents who are comfortable with the rules of educated discourse than those who live in shanty towns and may be more at home with metaphor and concrete descriptions. In order to compare these populations, a methodology is necessary that gives both groups the opportunities to express the richness of their social representations in a comparable way, therefore limiting the reliance on verbal statements.

Comparison of social groups via their individual membership

The development of a methodology that allows comparisons to be made between different social groups is of great importance. It facilitates the direct examination of a central hypothesis of social-representation theory without spurious distortion produced by the methodology. To quote Moscovici yet again (1984, p. 51):

dominating and dominated classes do not have a similar representation of the world they share, but see it with different eyes, judge it according to specific criteria and each does so according to their own categories.

Yet, this proposed difference in representations must remain a hypothesis requiring empirical test for every set of 'classes' in every culture. Indeed, the ambiguity of the terms 'class' and 'culture' reveals why even the less ambitious task, of describing the difference between social groups so that comparisons can be drawn, is such an important item for the research agenda.

Social representations are like the physicists' gluons that hold physical matter together. But, unlike the reality that physicists explore, social reality must be assumed to be heterogeneous, different types of reality nesting within each other. In slightly less metaphorical terms, the dwellers in a Brazilian favela (shanty town) may be expected to see the world they share with the prosperous middle classes with different eyes, but by virtue of the fact that they *do* share a world with other classes there must be some overlap in their social representations of common experiences. Brazilian citizens, wherever they live, are likely to draw upon representations of Brazil that distinguish them from, say, citizens of Britain.

This is an important theoretical issue that emerges from a close consideration of the methodological problem of studying social representations without imposing a heavy verbal load on them. If it is proposed that people share a world and so must have a common representation system so that they can communicate, but it is also postulated that people within that shared world who have differing relationships to it will have differing representations, then the only resolution of the potential logical conflict of these two propositions is that there will be a lattice of overlapping social representations existing within any culture. Any individual will be hypothesized to have some representations in common with all members of his culture, and some will be specific to the sub-community of which he is a part. This hypothesis of a network of interrelating social representations has a number of important theoretical corollaries. These derive from the recognition that it is precisely the similarities and differences between communities within a culture in their social representations that provides the matrix out of which societies evolve and change. It is the interplay of social representations that have enough in common to allow communication, but are also different enough to require accommodation or assimilation, that creates the dynamics of society.

One more example of a specific hypothesis that derives from the lattice principle is that the closer together any two sub-communities, the more of their system of social representations they will share. This is a development of the theory of environmental role first proposed and most recently elaborated by Canter (1977, 1990). By drawing on the elaboration of environmental role, this hypothesis can be refined by arguing that the closeness of any two systems of social representations will reflect those aspects of the world that the two sub-communities share. If both communities, for example, are actively involved in the same political system but live in very different areas, then it would be predicted that their social representations of politics will be more similar than their social representations of the residential environment.

An important point of clarification here is that it is inherent in the logic of social-representation theory that there will never exist a monolithic coherent representation that characterizes a community, unless that community itself is monolithic and coherent (which few are). The distinctness and clarity of a social representation will be a function of the people used to express the representation and the methods used to explore their expressions. It therefore follows, as Potter and Litton (1985) have pointed out, that methodologies which rely on the calculation of central tendencies, such as the arithmetic mean, give a spurious precision to a phenomena that must be seen as inherently imprecise—except for societies in which there is no dynamic or change. Methodologies are required that allow us to identify the core of a social representation within a particular subgroup, but also allow for the recognition of the representation's boundaries where it merges into the social representations of other subgroups whose world is distinct, yet aspects of which are shared.

This idea of a lattice of representations is inherent in recent writings of the master. In arguing that there are different ways in which representations can become social, Moscovici (1988) draws attention to different ways in which they can be shared and, as a consequence, different classes of social representation. With the gift for neologism that we expect from our continental colleagues, he refers to those representations that are shared by all members of a highly structured group as 'hegemonic', being wide spread, uniform, and (in some senses) coercive.

These all-embracing representations can be contrasted with 'emancipated' ones Moscovici, 1988, p. 221 that are 'the outgrowth of the circulation of knowledge and ideas belonging to subgroups that are in more or less close contact.'

These representations enjoy a certain autonomy with reference to interacting segments of society. They are also distinct from the third class of 'polemical' representations, which are generated in the course of social conflict. Society as a whole does not share them. Indeed they are 'determined by the antagonistic relations between its members and intended to be mutually exclusive' (Moscovici 1984).

Like all elegant classification schemes, this threefold system is of most value as a heuristic device to draw attention to what George Kelly might have called the 'range of convenience' of a representation. Whereas the convenience of a personal construct will range over a limited set of elements, Moscovici points out that social representations will have currency over a limited set of people in society. Some dominant constructs, like 'life-death', will be applicable to many elements, while others, like 'parametric-non-parametric', will be much more circumscribed. The challenge of social-representation theory is to see if the range of people who share any particular representations can be identified. If they can, the subsidiary methodological problem is to establish ways of distinguishing between the all-pervasive, hegemonic representations, the emancipated ones, and if possible those that play a polemic role.

One of the valuable paradoxes that emerges from the proposal of different roles for social representations is that, although they are seen as social phenomena, they have to be studied through the expressions of individuals. It is, in effect, the range of individuals that share a representation which indicates the role, or type of representation, that is present. Representations are fundamentally psychological in that individuals draw upon them and contribute to them, as well as being essentially social. It is precisely this social-psychological nexus in which they exist that gives them their power as conceptual tools. This nexus, however, also provides a methodological challenge in requiring us to use procedures that allow individuals to be studied while still considering any implications of their group membership.

When social psychologists in the past have attempted to face the combined challenge of using procedures that are not heavily verbal and treat individuals in their group context, they have tended to bias their research to handle one challenge at the expense of the other. The present study illustrates one approach to meeting both these methodological challenges together.

The context chosen for this study in Brazil is also of special interest, being a third-world country, for which it is exceptionally important to resolve differences between different classes as a basis for a productive evolution of the country.

Representing society

The example chosen to illustrate the proposed approach was built around the different conceptualizations revealed by people who lived in different areas of Brazil. One group of respondents lived in favelas, one in public housing, and one in middle-class housing. There are many ways in which samples may be drawn in order to reflect different communities within a broader society, but selection on the basis of residential location is particulary appropriate for a country, like Brazil, in which it is important to know if these different locations reflect different world views or whether there is enough sharing of representations to facilitate movement from one to the other. The practical value of such a study was a direct aim of the larger work from which the present study is drawn (Montiero 1989).

The larger study explored many aspects of the place experiences of Brazilians, focusing on those living in shanty towns, with the express purpose of establishing what forms of future planning developments would be acceptable to those currently living in the squalor of the favelas. Many previous attempts had failed, in that the people for whom they were designed were not the groups who eventually ended up living in them. The processes by which the designs failed are certainly not understood, but one strong hypothesis is that the people who live in favelas share social representations of society that distinguish them both from people who live in the middle-class community who plan and manage the society and, more importantly, from those who do take advantage of any public housing that might be available.

A fundamental question, then, is how various people, selected from different groups in Brazil, see their society and what forms of consensus exist within or between these groups. The study to be reported focuses on one particular aspect of society, the occupations that are distributed across it. The aim is to see how these occupations are categorized in relation to a number of salient features that reflect the operation of social processes. Of course, such a process relies on the use of verbal labels and the consequent understanding of the terms used, but this is minimized both by the extensive pilot work (described in Montiero 1989) which ensured that the terminology was familiar to all respondents, and by the reliance on the sorting procedure to be described. This procedure enables respondents to indicate that categorization schemes by the direct assignment of entities to groups without the need for any verbalization of the reasons for that assignment.

The multiple sorting procedure (MSP)

The MSP is a process which makes use of people's classifications in order to explore their conceptual system. The advantages of such a method were acknowledged a long time ago. Brunner *et al.* (1956) stated that it is possible to examine the nature of people's concepts by looking at how they assign categories to various elements. This was also the process behind Kelly's (1955) repertory grid and Tajfel's (1978) social-categorization process. Sorting techniques have been used in several studies in various ways and with regard to various issues, including personal meanings (Szalay and Deese 1978), inter-group behaviour (Tajfel and Israel 1972), and social identity (Tajfel 1978).

Sorting procedures typically have been used as a content-free procedure, applied just to look at cognitive structure, the number of groupings, or whether a particular construct is recognized. It was Kelly (1955) who emphasized the importance of content as part of his personal-construct theory.

A recent approach presented by Canter *et al.* (1985) and Canter and Comber (1985) extends the value of the sorting procedure by using it to explore the content of many different areas of cognitive structure. The applicability of the method has also been increased by the development of methods of analysis which allow the examination of the content domain, generated by the sortings, to be integrated into the consideration of the structure revealed.

These developments in analysis procedures are important because the earlier restrictions on the use of sorting procedures were derived from problems with methods of analysis, most of which were inappropriate to the categorical data generated.

Multiple-sorting procedures provide several advantages, especially regarding the quality of data gathered. The sorting procedure demands very little of the respondent, basically an opinion (indicated through the categorization of elements) according to perceived qualities and characteristics revealed through actions performed, without necessarily any need for verbalization of the reasons for those actions. The sortings are developed in a very relaxed way, with few limitations and no restrictions made on the classification process (Canter *et al*. 1985, p. 14):

The more freedom the interviewee can be given in performing this task the more likely that the interviewer will learn something of the interviewee's construct system rather than just clarifying his own.

It is worth noting that the act of classifying or sorting is easily comprehended by respondents, proving that it is indeed a simple mechanism which people frequently use in their daily life. As Canter *et al*. (1985, p. 3) explain,

this involves working directly with individuals in their own terms, respecting their ability to formulate ways of thinking about the world and their experience of it.

It limits verbal demands because when people start classifying events or objects they use the images, symbols, values, and concepts that are in their minds. They verbalize after completing the sortings, at that time explaining the concepts and categories that they used and their reasons for doing so. Frequently, people communicate their ideas and make statements about the objects being sorted, providing a rich source of background information.
    Canter *et al*. (1985) warn that

an important distinction must be made between the underlying categorisation process and the 'ordinary' explanations that people give for their actions.

People's explanations aid the understanding of the categorical organization of their conceptual process.
    The multiple-sorting procedure consists in asking the respondents to classify the same elements several times according to different categories, in order to understand their ideas about them. It is possible to have great variation in the types of elements sorted, such as illustrations, photographs (Groat 1982; Ward and Russel 1981), labels (Canter and Comber 1985; Oakley 1980), and activities (Grainger 1980). It has been utilized largely in environmental research, because it is particularly appropriate to the use of visual material.
    The multiple-sorting procedure may therefore constitute a reliable way of exploring people's social representations empirically. The approach taken by Moscovici and his followers is that of analysing what people say in general conversation and social interactions, and comparing that content with what is transmitted by the media (newspapers and television). This shows whether people's concepts and representations of any event or object are essentially social. The multiple-sorting procedure permits the identification of the

content on which people are operating, in order to see whether it is socially shared. Thus we consider this procedure a means of access to the processes underlying social representations.

To sum up, this investigation explores socially-shared sets of categorizations by using a procedure that looks at individual categorizations and combines them in order to assess the existence of social representations.

Data collection

Twenty-five flat, unisex, aluminium manikins 8 × 4 cm were made; each was labelled to identify an occupation. The occupations had been derived from pilot research in which free generation of occupations was allowed. From a classification of the occupations freely elicited, the subset was selected to ensure that all types of occupation were represented and that the labels were understood. After an introduction which included a clarification of the academic, non-political nature of the study and questions establishing their identification of 'a wealthy neighbourhood', 'a public-housing estate', and 'a very poor neighbourhood, a favela', and their own neighbourhood, the respondents were given the following instructions:

We have here 25 manikins representing people; they have labels indicating their occupation. You probably know people having some of these occupations; they could be your friends or neighbours or people you deal with. So you should have a general idea of them, but if you don't, I would suggest that you think of things you have heard or read about these kinds of people.

They were then asked to complete the first sort with the following instructions:

According to your *experience* and knowledge about people and using the four neighbourhoods we have listed, I will ask you to indicate *where* you think these people live. Which ones live in a neighbourhood like the wealthy one, or like the public-housing estate, or perhaps in your neighbourhood? I would like you to make different groups, allocating the inhabitants to each neighbourhood.

Respondents were told that they could have as many groups as they wished and allocate as many people as they wanted to a group. Only when the number of groups exceeded seven were they asked about the possibility of limiting or merging some groups. After each sorting, the investigator took note of the sort content and the numbers of the manikins allocated to each group. After each sorting, all the manikins were mixed up again and presented in random order to the respondent.

The results to be presented were derived also from a further three sortings dealing with the following two areas.

Social class

In the case of confusion about the meaning of 'social class', questions were asked in order to make respondents think about the concepts that they had in mind.

If you hear, for example, that middle class people have benefited from an increase of the minimum salary, to what sort of people do you think this is referring?

Considering society as a whole, to what class do you think you belong?

Social mobility

Before starting this sorting, it was stressed to the respondents that they should take into account their perception of their own situation at that time and life prospects for the near future, dealing with aspirations, dreams, and wishes.

Now, I would like to ask you what you think about your son's and daughter's prospects in life. I would like you to put in a group the professions or activities presented by these manikins that you think your son or daughter would probably achieve; and those which they possibly could do, but find it difficult to afford. Could you put them in order, ending with those you think will be impossible for your children to do?

The partial order of social representations

Preliminary analysis revealed that the original 25 occupations contained considerable redundancy in terms of the salient categories to be reported on here. For example, maid, cook, and servant were all treated identically, as were plantation owner and doctor. So, although there is some significance in these similarities which is relevant to understanding the society, from the methodological viewpoint of the present chapter it was decided that nine occupations covered appropriately the range of results. Two sets of analyses were carried out on two different sets of occupations to ensure replicability of the results, but for the current illustration only one will be presented. This dealt with the following occupations:

(1) politician
(2) engineer
(3) me
(4) dentist
(5) shop-clerk
(6) policeman
(7) hairdresser

(8) street trader

(9) odd-job man.

Three groups each of 25 people, (one group living in a favela, one in public housing, and one in a middle-class area of the city), provided the results on which the subsequent analysis as performed.

Deriving testable hypotheses

It is appropriate to restate the research questions in terms of the tasks that respondents were required to perform. There are a number of related issues, but essentially we want to compare people on the basis of their assignment of occupations to categories. For example, if everyone agrees that politicians live in a middle-class neighbourhood then this goes a little way towards supporting the hypothesis that representations of politicians (and middle-class neighbourhoods) are broadly social and indeed may be considered 'hegemonic'.

'Emancipated' representations of politicians would reveal differences between subgroups of people of a rather complex kind. Any group which shared that social representation would be expected to assign components of it to the same category, for example the street-trader to the favela. However, if the occupation 'street-trader' is not part of a socially-shared representation for a subgroup then different people, considering the occupation to mean rather different things, would assign the occupation to a variety of residential areas.

These considerations reveal that 'polemical' representations are not really at the extreme of autonomy, but rather lie between the structure of hegemonic and emancipated representations. For the polemical activities to feed social controversy, it is essential that they have a coherence within subgroups but a distinction between them. Members of one subgroup should assign street-traders, for instance, to the same city area as each other, but to a different city area to the other sub-groups with whom they share a controversy.

If more than one sub-group is involved in the study, there are further subsidiary hypotheses that can be considered. For example, two groups could share a controversy with a third group not being party to that at all. Or, there could be some hypothesized ordered relationship between the sub groups. In the present case, for example, there is a question as to whether the essentially private-enterprise culture that characterizes most favelas puts them closer to the middle-class than to the public-housing residents, or whether public housing is indeed the step from the favela to the middle class that it is intended to be.

Three distinct, testable structures of similarities between people within subgroups and between subgroups, therefore form hypotheses from the general framework of different types of social representation. It is worth emphasizing that these are hypotheses about how people compare with each other in their utilization of concepts associated with representational systems. These systems include the relationships between all the occupations, studied here, in relation to each of the category schemes being explored. So, the hypotheses are most appropriately directed to the overall similarities and differencs between respondents across all their judgements. For simplicity of exposition, in what follows, the judgements will be presented separately for each sorting scheme. Other research, in more focused domains, has analysed all sortings together, allowing respondents to generate their own categories entirely (Wilson and Canter 1990; Crassa 1990).

It is a little disingenuous to present this approach as one of hypothesis testing because, although there are a variety of possible outcomes which can be predetermined in a good hypothetico-deductive tradition, there is also an important sense in which the approach being illustrated is ecological. It aims to give an account of what subgroups occur within a society (perhaps as species within a genus) when that society is examined from the perspective of the assignment of occupations to categories. Social representations are being used to help to identify subgroups at the same time as those subgroups are being used to reveal the underlying structure of representations. This interactive form of research is inevitable when a system of interrelationships is being explored.

The data matrix

The category schemes employed in the current study have an obvious value dimension to them, from wealthy to poor, from ideal to less than ideal, and so on. A form of analysis that takes this into account is therefore quite appropriate. For instance, people living in a favela may have in common the view that anyone who has any regular occupation is likely to be middle class. So, if we assign the number 2 to the middle-class category and the number 1 to a lower-class category, then the nine occupations might each, for example, be given the category 2. We can therefore represent a respondent who put all occupations in one middle-class category as a profile that can be represented as a row of nine 2s,

$$2\,2\,2\,2\,2\,2\,2\,2\,2$$

By contrast, a person who thought that all the occupations were not middle class would be represented by

$$1\,1\,1\,1\,1\,1\,1\,1\,1$$

A simple comparison of these two respondents would reveal, of course, that they had different, indeed opposing, views of occupations. A person who assigned the occupations to a combination of categories, represented by, say,

$$1\,1\,1\,1\,1\,2\,2\,2\,2$$

could be seen to be using the underlying value order half-way between the other two individuals.

It might, therefore, be assumed that a simple addition of the category values would lead to a mechanism for seeing whether individuals were part of the same social-representation subgroup. A clear break in the scores, on this basis, could be taken for evidence that social representations have a discrete existence within each subgroup. However, such simple mathematics denies some very obvious differences in the meaning that the scores have. Consider again our middle respondent, who assigns some occupations to the middle class and some not:

$$1\,1\,1\,1\,1\,2\,2\,2\,2$$

He will share a total score with a person who makes assignments that might be represented as the quite different profile

$$2\,2\,2\,2\,1\,1\,1\,1\,1$$

Yet, these two individuals have only one assignment in common; on all other eight occupations they completely disagree.

Therefore, if we are to compare individuals, we need a process that will take account of both the quantitative ordering that underlies the categorization and the qualitative ordering that can exist within this. We wish to represent each individual on the basis of all his category assignments so that overall comparisons can be made within and between groups.

Partial order scalogram analysis by the use of coordinates (POSAC), developed by Shye (1985) as a form of non-metric multiple scaling procedure, provides one form of analysis that meets the requirements of the present study. Using the idea of a 'trait' that has a number of facets to it (in the example above, occupational class status reflected in different occupations), he writes that the objective of POSAC (p. 46) is:

> to rank individuals according to their possession of the trait, to distinguish among individuals by their tendencies to stress certain aspects of the trait, and otherwise to structure the investigated population of individuals.

In the present case, POSAC provides a representation of all individuals according to their 'tendency to stress certain aspects of' the categorization of occupations. In doing so, it allows ready identification of each individual who has a unique profile of scores and therefore exploration of whether different subgroups share a common tendency to 'stress certain aspects'.

The way in which the computing algorithm developed by Shye (1985) facilitates the comparison of individuals is to represent each unique profile as a point in a two-dimensional space. The algorithm operates to find the best two-dimensional fit between the positions in the space and the similarity between the profiles, taking into account the overall ordering of the profiles in the space. By convention, the profile that sums to the highest value is put in the top right-hand corner of a rectangular two-dimensional space. The bottom left-hand corner is reserved for the profile that has the lowest total value. The consequence of this is that the top-left to bottom-right diagonal accounts for the qualitative variations amongst the profiles.

It is also a consequence of the computing procedure that each of the facets which contribute to the profile, in the present case the categorization of each of the nine occupations, can be represented as a coding for each respondent on the two-dimensional representation. If the categorization of an occupation has a clear and consistent use, in comparison with the other occupations, then the coding will reveal a region of the plot associated with each element of that categorization.

The spatial representation derived from POSAC therefore provides a direct visual test of the hypotheses considered above. It makes no assumptions about the weightings of the occupations, nor about the relative differences between the categories used. Furthermore, it does not assume that the individuals are drawn from different groups between which comparisons are then made. Each individual is represented by a point. If groups exist, then the point representing individuals in those groups will form a region. The consequence of this is that each of the three hypothesized types of social representation would reveal their existence in a different type of spatial distribution. Hegemonic representations should reveal a strongly-qualitative diagonal with no differences between subgroups. Emancipated representations will reveal regions for some subgroups but not for others. Polemic representations will be revealed by distinct regions for each subgroup; the more closely these regions lie along the quantitative diagonal, the more likely they are to reflect strong conflicts between the subgroups.

This rather novel approach is more fully comprehensible by consideration of the detailed results. These will be presented separately for each of the four sortings described earlier. In order to turn the open sortings into ordered categories, the accounts of the respondents were considered together with other statistical analyses described in Montiero (1989). A composite ordered set of categories was then produced by means of content analysis, and all responses assigned to one of these ordered categories. This is not an ideal approach, and future research may benefit from the sort of extensive pilot work that was not possible given the practical constraints of collecting data in favelas. Such pilot work could then be used to generate standard categories for all respondents.

Results

Occupation and neighbourhood

The data matrix was created by assigning the value of 1 to the category of 'wealthy neighbourhood', 2 to 'public housing', and 3 to 'poor neighbourhood'. The respondent's 'own neighbourhood' was recorded into the category that was their actual neighbourhood, discussions with the respondents having revealed the appropriateness of doing this.

The coding scheme used means that a person who thinks that all the occupations are likely to live in a poor neighbourhood will be found in the top right-hand corner of the two-dimensional POSAC diagram. The person who thinks they will all be found in a wealthy neighbourhood will be found in the bottom left-hand corner of the diagram. Furthermore if a number of people agree exactly on the categorization of occupations to neighbourhood they will only be represented by one point.

Figure 11.1 shows the POSAC diagram. This is a spatial distribution of points where each individual is plotted as a point. In analysing the configuration, the first step is to recognize each point as a respondent and to use their serial number to identify their place of origin. This figure shows the favela dwellers represented by black triangles, the public-housing dwellers by empty squares, and the middle-class dwellers by black circles. The axis from bottom-left to top-right, known as the joint direction, represents the substantive criteria used by the respondents to classify the manikins, in this case wealthiness of neighbourhood.

The similarity of view of middle-class respondents is immediately apparent, both because there were only 11 distinct profiles amongst the 25 respondents and because all those profiles exist in a limited contiguous region of the space. For the middle-class respondents, at least, the relationship between occupation and wealth of residential area is part of their social representation. The distinctness of this group, however, also indicates that this aspect of the representational system is not hegemonic. Further consideration of the configuration allows development of this finding.

The points representing respondents living in favelas cover a wide region of the plot, but none of them is within a contiguous region defined by the location of all the middle-class respondents. Lines have been drawn by eye on the configuration to indicate the main regions identifiable. These lines draw attention to the fact that the favela dwellers, in the main, are in the farthest region from the middle-class dwellers; the public-housing dwellers fall in between. Close consideration of these regions, though, indicate that the public-housing dwellers and the middle-class dwellers have conceptions that, while being similar, are quite distinct. It is the favela dwellers that contain individuals who share representations with those in the public housing.

Two important points follow from this distribution in representational space. One is that, broadly, the three groups have distinct, but related,

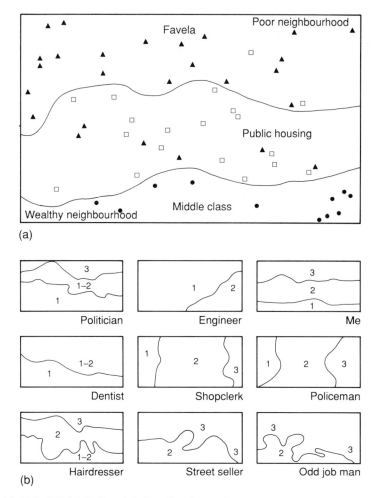

Fig. 11.1(a) POSAC Spatial distribution of respondents based upon their categorization of occupations to neighbourhood

Fig. 11.1(b) Item diagrams for Fig. 11.1(a). 1, wealthy neighbourhood; 2, public housing estate; 3, poor neighbourhood. ●, MDC; □, PHE; ▲, FAV

representations. In the sense discussed above, this is an indication of a polemic system of representations. The polemic is fiercest between the favela and the middle class, with the public-housing group in the middle. The second point is that, in terms of wealth of neighbourhood, the favela group contains the most people who share concepts with those in public housing. It is these 'errant' individuals from whom it would be predicted future public-housing residents might be drawn.

Further clarification of the detailed basis of the regions can be gleaned

by considering each of the occupations separately, examining how it contributes to the overall configuration. For simplicity, the nine regional diagrams
have been placed below the general plot, in Fig. 11.1(b) thereby allowing
direct comparison with the overall configuration on which they are a
perspective.

The first point to notice about these nine occupations is that each of them
does have a reasonably-distinct partitioning of the configuration. So, all
of them appear to contribute in some coherent way to the total plot. Some,
such as the shop-clerk and the policeman, partition the space in a very similar
way, indicating that they contribute to the overall system of representations
in parallel ways, conceptually as well as literally. By contrast, the occupation
of dentist is orthogonal, indicating that the judgements about the residences
of dentists divides the respondents quite independently of the judgement of
shop-clerk or policeman.

These individual partitions for each occupation can also be compared with
the overall partitions for the respondent groups. This reveals that both sets
of partition lines are broadly parallel for the following occupations:

> politician, me, dentist, hairdresser, street-trader, odd-job man.

This may well suggest that wealth of neighbourhood is a basis for distinguishing between social representations, in so far as the individual relates
him/herself to the extremes of the occupational continuum. More detailed
consideration of each occupation also helps to clarify this point.

Each group of respondents stated that the politician lives in 'their'
neighbourhood. Middle-class people consider that the politician lives in a
wealthy neighbourhood, public-housing inhabitants say that he lives on a
public-housing estate, and favela dwellers affirm that politicians also live in
poor places. There are, in fact, all sorts of politicians, from 'vereadores'
(local councillors) up to 'senadores' (senators). It is interesting to note that,
in this sort, the respondents use their experience, and real knowledge about
politicians. Later sorts reveal that all the groups were quite unaminous in
stating that the politician is an upper-class person.

The engineer was seen as a wealthy-neighbourhood dweller by all groups
except by some middle-class respondents, who do not have a unitary vision
of the profession and think that there are also engineers living in 'conjuntos
habitacionais' (public-housing schemes).

The dentist was seen by the middle class as a resident of a wealthy neighbourhood and by the other groups as living in a public-housing estate. There
is a remarkable distinction among dentists, because their status is not determined by the profession but by the kind of clients that they have. Middle-
class dentists are very expensive, and enjoy great prestige; dentists treating
other classes of clients struggle to get an average income.

As noted, the shop-clerk and policeman presented lateral partitionings
of assessments. There are respondents from each of the three groups who

assign these occupations to each of the three neighbourhoods. This reveals different ideas about the supposed neighbourhood of these two occupations.

The hairdresser has a similar configuration to the politician, with each group representing their own experience of people having that occupation. Middle-class hairdressers are quite luxurious and expensive, and it is a sign of social status to be among the clients of such a hairdresser, whereas poor people know the small and perhaps even house-based beauty parlour affordable by all.

These results show that when dealing with a concrete issue, each group had a tendency to interpret the elements according to their experiences, bringing the categories on to familiar ground. So, the distinctions that are apparent here between groups, while reflecting consensus within those groups, are possibly based upon the different realities of which they are a part. Yet, they have the qualities characterised by Moscovici as polemic. They are distinct to subgroups, although they relate to some overall system of shared concepts. In what sense, then, are they polemic? Perhaps this is a property of all social representations in any complex society. This is a significant issue to which we shall return after considering the other sortings.

Occupation and social class

The data matrix for examining the social-class sorting was derived by assigning values from 1 for 'upper class' to 6 for 'extreme lower class', based on the category assignments of the respondents. The POSAC configuration that results from this data matrix is given in Fig. 11.2.

The first aspect of this configuration of points to notice is that it is 'lateral', representing qualitative differences in people's responses. As noted earlier, points that vary along this top-left to bottom-right diagonal do not differ in the value of the assessments (high social class versus lower social class), but in the *kind* of assessments. What makes a person found at a middle-left position different from one at the middle-right, is that they do not agree on the profile of their assessments. The first person could, for example, state that the four first manikins belong to the upper-class and the remaining ones are lower-class, while the second person might assign the same manikins to the opposite categories. So, the general trend apparent in Fig. 11.2 is that there is no broad difference between respondents in the levels of assignment of social class to the occupations. People do not differ greatly on whether they think all occupations are higher or lower class. The differences are in which occupations are assigned to which class.

The second aspect to be noted in the diagram is that, as for the first sort of residential area, there are distinctive groupings of points; the respondents from the middle-class neighbourhood of Boa Viagem are in the lower-right corner, and those from the favela of Cabo Gato are in the upper-left position. The public-housing respondents are located in the middle, between the other two groups. They also include respondents who

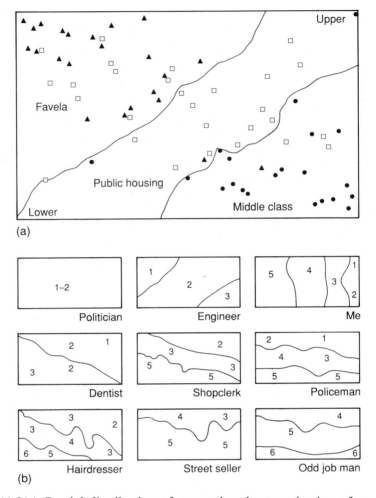

(a)

(b)

Fig. 11.2(a) Spatial distribution of respondents' categorization of occupations to social class

Fig. 11.2(b) Item diagrams for Fig. 11.2(a). 1, upper class; 2, upper middle class; 3, middle class; 4, lower-middle class; 5, lower class; 6, extreme lower class. ●, MDC; □ PHE; ▲, FAV

answered in a similar way to the middle class and to the favela dwellers. The general outcome is the existence of three regions across the lateral axis.

Each of the three groups of respondents, then, has a particular way of interpreting the manikins' social class, although the distinctions, especially for favela and public housing, are not as clear cut as for the first sorting discussed. Yet, here again the general trend is repeated for the favela and middle class groups to be most distinct.

The general social-class assignment of each occupation can be seen from the individual occupation partitionings of the space, in Fig. 11.2a. The first two (politician and engineer) and the fourth (dentist) represent people of a higher status, being assigned to categories 1, 2, or 3. The third element in the profiles represents self (me), covering the five categories excluding 'extreme lower class', as does the sixth (policemen). The shop-clerk and hair-dresser cover the lower end of the range, although having a higher status than the eighth (street-trader) and the ninth (odd-job man), manikins which represent well-known low-status occupations.

Within the general ordering of the occupations, however, it is apparent that the different groups of respondents have a tendency to assign occupations to different points on the range, and so it is this that gives the respondents their overall differences.

Consider, for example, the class status of the policemen. There is a tendency for the favela group to think of this occupation as higher status and the middle-class group to think of this occupation as lower status. This is not a one-to-one relationship between respondent group and occupational assignment. Indeed, only the occupation of engineer has that direct parallel: middle-class respondents considered that the engineer belongs to a middle-class group, the public-housing dwellers saw the engineer as upper-middle class, and the favela dwellers regarded him as upper class. So, the parallel indicates a reverse order from the social class of the respondents.

The partitioning of manikins representing the respondents themselves gives an interesting idea of how this population understood their position in the social structure. The four partitionings demonstrated that each group had a realistic idea of their own class position. The middle-class respondents considered themselves as upper-middle and middle-class people, the public-housing estate respondents regarded their position as middle or lower-middle class, and the majority of favela inhabitants stated that they were poor people and as such belonged to a lower class. This shows that each group was conscious of its own place in the social system. They have hegemonic representations in some senses. However, what is interesting is that there is a difference in emphasis between all three groups; they are similar, but at the same time qualitatively different. A polemic undercurrent appears to be present beneath the hegemonic facade.

This interplay of general agreement with distinct subgroup differences is also clear from the assignment by middle-class people of lower status to the manikins in their own class, and the assignment by lower-class people of higher status to the manikins with lower occupations; the last five elements were evaluated by middle-class respondents as belonging to the lowest classes, while the favela dwellers regarded their position as higher. For example, middle-class respondents considered the shop-clerk, policeman, and street-trader as belonging to the lower class, but the favelados regarded them as middle, upper-middle, and lower-middle class respectively. The former regarded the odd-job man as belonging to particularly low social class, a miserably-poor person, but the favela dwellers regarded him as a lower-middle or lower-class person.

While regarding themselves as lower-class people, the favela inhabitants considered some people, who actually could be classified in their own class, as better off. For example, the shop-clerk and hairdresser were both considered to have middle-class status.

To sum up, the middle-class respondents see their class as being higher than middle class and regard the poor as being extremely lower class, while poor people, by contrast, give a very high status to middle-class people, but also higher status to classes close to their own. Social representations of social class, then, reveal a more complex lattice than the neighbourhood concepts. Its meaning is distorted by distinct, but not entirely antagonistic, processes although there is a general trend to consensus. This serves to illustrate further that representations are unlikely to have a monolithic simplicity to them, although their capability for distinguishing between subgroups, who none the less share a common culture, is not in doubt.

In this framework, it is the polemic representations — or more accurately those polemic aspects of the hegemonic representations — that contribute to the distinctness of communities. What emerges here is that there are anchors of social representation, such as the class position of occupations that pass between communities. In the transition, some of their meaning is distorted, but not enough to produce the break in communication that would characterize emancipated representations.

Social mobility

Social mobility deals with the respondents' sense of their children's prospects for social mobility, expressed through their classification of nine occupations represented by the manikins. The fact that these occupations may be ranked in order according to their social prestige, and that the investigation was carried out with groups from very different backgrounds, suggests that each group will agree internally with the occupations to which its children can aspire. Here, then, the basis for strongly-hegemonic representations seems possible.

Figure 11.3 presents the POSAC diagram, arranging all the respondents according to their assessment of future social mobility. It shows the respondents distributed along the lateral direction, forming three very distinctive regions as before: the middle-class dwellers are concentrated at the lower-right corner and the favela inhabitants at the upper-left, while public-housing dwellers are situated between both groups.

The joint direction, in this case, concerns the respondents' assessments of their children's chances of taking up the occupations presented by the manikins. The criteria of evaluation range from 'easy to be' up to 'impossible' or 'they will be better than this'. The point at the lower-left corner of the

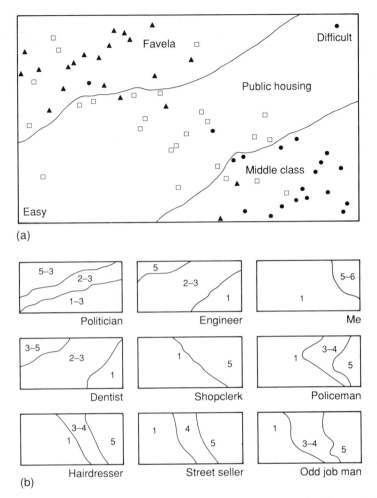

Fig. 11.3(a) Spatial distribution of respondents' categorization of future social mobility to occupation

Fig. 11.3(b) Item diagram for Fig. 11.3(a). 1, easy to be; 2, difficult but with achievement; 3, difficult; 4, will be better than; 5, impossible. ●, MDC; □, PHE; ▲, FAV

diagram represents the 'easy' condition, and that at the upper-right the 'impossible'.

The lateral distribution means that these people did not differ in their expected amount of social mobility, but in the qualitative aspects of such mobility. Regarding the nine manikins that form each profile, it is possible to examine the respondents' different social aspirations. The diagram for each occupation, in Fig. 11.3, shows how they were assessed by all the respondents; the manikins' evaluation regions could then be compared with the main diagram which identifies the respective respondents.

The three manikins representing the prestigious occupations of politician, engineer, and dentist present distributions along the lateral axis, showing a substantive difference in the respondents' judgements. Most favela dwellers consider it 'impossible' for them to achieve such occupations. Public-housing dwellers have a tendency to foresee better conditions for their children than the favela dwellers, and stated the difficulty but not the impossibility of their succeeding in these higher-status occupations.

Middle-class respondents, by contrast, see these occupations as being within a natural range of choice of their class and regarded them as very easy to achieve. The manikin representing the respondent's own occupation has a similar evaluation by all three groups. They stated that it would be very easy for their children to be like them. There were some statements affirming that 'they will be better than me', produced by people from all three groups of respondents.

The direction of the partitioning regions for the remaining manikins are somewhat indeterminate. The regions, in other words, are difficult to identify clearly. Estimates of the correlation of each variable with each of the axes give some guide to the direction of the partitioning, and from this some trends can be found.

The shop-clerk, policeman, hairdresser, street-trader, and odd-job man all presented a slightly laterally-orientated distribution. Even so, the difference between the groups is considerable; favela and public-housing dwellers considered these occupations easy to achieve, while the middle class made clear the impossibility of future social descent and the impossibility of having their children in such occupations. Public-housing dwellers recognized the difficulty of achieving certain occupations, but also made clear their belief that it is possible to overcome these difficulties and even social impediments. They were also the group that most used the criterion 'my children will be better than me', rather than showing determination to remain within the lower class from which they originated.

Results show the existence of an upward sense of social mobility in all three groups. Favela dwellers showed a very realistic view about their conditions in society. They, knew how difficult, and even impossible, it is for poor people to maintain a child in school — especially after the secondary level. They foresaw upward social mobility for their children, but saw this as constrained within limits. The achievement of skilled and semi-skilled occupations was, in their view, an easy and perhaps 'natural' upward mobility.

This result contradicts Pearlman's (1976) findings, with regard to favela inhabitants' perception of class barriers, that (p. 177);

fully half of the population feels their son and the son of a businessman have the same chance to succeed in life.

According to the present results, a minority of the favela and public-housing dwellers share this view. The POSA diagram shows only two favela respondents and three from the public-housing estate who produced similar profiles to the middle class. They, perhaps, share the notion of equal opportunities for their children, but there is no doubt about the existence of group consensus about their children's real chances in the present society. Pearlman stated that,

it is the heartfelt aspiration of many of the favelados to emulate and someday become — perhaps through their children — the middle class.

She perhaps failed to identify these people's notion of middle class. The analysis of content of the social-class sort shows how different was their conception of class from the middle-class one.

Public-housing dwellers presented high expectations of upward social mobility, despite recognizing the difficulties. They also show a consistent degree of consensus in their judgements. Finally, the middle-class respondents showed a high degree of consensus regarding their expectations. Their profiles were quite dichotomous (1 or 5), also reflecting the absence of manikins presenting higher occupations to which they could aspire. Regarding social aspirations, the results show a high degree of consensus within the groups; their representations were more commonly shared than those concerning the manikins' social class.

Conclusion—polemic as glue

Little evidence has been found, in the present examination of aspects of social representations of occupations, for those autonomous representations that are unique to a particular subgroup that Moscovici dubbed as emancipated. This might be expected for an all-pervasive issue like occupations and their status, but the question is thereby raised as to what sorts of representations really will be autonomous and how they can exist. They will need to operate within closed communities and to address issues that have no relevance beyond those communities. Notions like the meaning of the Eucharist to Orthodox Christian groups, or of musical technique to music-lovers, come to mind as possibilities here. But, in what sense are these, then, representations rather than technical descriptions?

The all-pervasive, hegemonic representation of occupations is also difficult to defend from the present data. There is some general agreement but there are, none the less, distinct group differences underlying this agreement. The group differences found do themselves indicate an ordered set of relationships between the aspects of social representations. Contrary to some expressed opinions, those living in public housing would appear in general to be transitional between the favela and middle-class housing in their conceptions of occupations. The divisions in Brazilian society appear to be revealed as having fundamental reflections in processes of social representation. The reasons for the difficulties in designing for favela dwellers, without incorporating them in the design process directly, is also highlighted by these results.

The distinctions in representations across a general pattern of agreement suggests that, for the present context at least, most social representations may most closely fit what Moscovici called polemic, but in English this term carries the implications of conflict and belligerence. Yet, our analyses here suggest that many representations, if not all, may derive their social quality from the fact that they reflect interactions between groups. The question may be raised in a pluralist society of what the dynamics of social interaction can be if social representations are totally shared throughout a society. What can people have to say to each other? Perhaps there is a fourth type of representation that covers most social representation, dynamic.

The discussion above has focused on theoretical issues and this, surely, is the test of the value of any methodology. How does it enrich our theoretical understanding? By harnessing the precision of partial-order scalogram analysis to the open-ended sorting procedures it has been possible to turn the general descriptions of social-representation theory into focused, testable, hypotheses. The way is, therefore, opened for detailed explorations of social representations and the enhancement of our understanding of their central role in social processes.

References

Brunner, J.S., Goodnow, J.J., and Austin, G.A. (1956). *A study of thinking.* Wiley, New York.

Canter, D. (1977). *Psychology of place.* Architectural Press, London.

Canter, D. (1990). Understanding, assessing and acting in places: is an integrative framework possible? In *Environmental cognition and action: an integrative multidisciplinary approach*, (ed. T. Garling and G. Evans), pp. 98–123. Oxford University Press, New York.

Canter, D. and Comber, M. (1985). *A multivariate approach to multiple sorting in sequence analysis.* Surrey Conferences on Sociological Theory and Method, II, pp. 23–34. Gower, Aldershot.

Canter, D., Brown, J., and Groat, L. (1985). Multiple sorting procedure for studying conceptual systems. In *Research interview – uses and approaches*, (ed. D. Canter, M. Brenner, and J. Brown), pp. 79–113. Wiley, London.

Crassa, M. (1990). Conceptualising the threat of cancer. Unpublished PhD thesis, University of Surrey.

Grainger, B. (1980). A study of concepts in the building design process. Unpublished MSc thesis, University of Surrey.

Groat, L. (1982). Meaning in post-modern architecture: an examination using the multiple sorting task. *Journal of Environmental Psychology*, **2** (3), 3–22.

Herzlich, C. (1973). *Health and illness: a social psychology analysis.* Academic Press, London.

Kelly, G. (1955). *The psychology of personal constructs.* Norton, New York.

Monteiro, C. M. G. (1989). The experience of place. A comparative study of a favela, a public housing estate and a middle class neighbourhood in Recife — Brazil. Unpublished PhD thesis, University of Surrey.

Moscovici), S. (1983). *On some aspects of social representations.* Presented at the Symposium on Representations, American Psychological Association. Anheim, California.

Moscovici, S. (1984). The phenomenon of social representation. In *Social representations,* (ed. R. Farr and S. Moscovici, pp. 12-37. Cambridge University Press.

Moscovici, S. (1985). Comment on Potter and Litton. *British Journal of Social Psychology,* **24,** 91-2.

Moscovici, S. (1988). Notes towards a description of social representations. *European Journal of Social Psychology,* **18,** 211-50.

Oakley, R. (1980). Profiles and perspectives of hostel residents. Unpublished MSc dissertation, University of Surrey.

Pearlman, J. (1976). *The myth of marginality — urban poverty and politics in Rio de Janeiro.* University of California Press, Berkeley, California.

Potter, J. and Litton, I. (1985). Some problems underlying the theory of social representations. *British Journal of Social Psychology,* **24,** 81-90.

Shye, S. (1985). *Multiple scaling — the theory and application of partial order scalogram analysis.* North Holland, Amsterdam.

Szalay, L. B. and Deese, J. (1978). *Subjective meaning in culture: an assessment through word association.* Erlbaum, Hillside, N.J.

Tajfel, H. C. and Israel, J. (1972). *The context of social psychology — a critical assessment.* Academic Press, London.

Tajfel, H. C. (1978). The structure of our views about society. *Introduction to social psychology.* Penguin, Harmondsworth.

Ward, L. M. and Russel, J. A. (1981). Cognitive set and the perception of place. *Environment and Behaviour,* **13** (5), 610-32.

Wilson, M. A and Canter, D. V. (1990). The development of central concepts during professional education: an example of a multivariate model of the concept of architectural style. *Applied Psychology: An International Review,* **39** (4), 431-55.

12 Finding social representations in attribute checklists: how will we know when we have found one?

Chris Fife-Schaw

Introduction

In this chapter, I will outline a methodological approach to the study of representations that may open up new possibilities for the elaboration of the concept of social representation. The principal motivation behind this is to encourage researchers towards greater precision in their operationalizations of 'social representation'. Once achieved, investigators should be encouraged to set up criteria for determining when a social representation truly exists and, if it exists, where is boundaries lie.

The method that will be described involves creating attribute checklists in which respondents are asked to say whether a particular object (or set of objects) possess a given set of attributes. The primary aim is to determine whether shared representations of the object exist in the population under study. The intention is to discuss methodological procedures in some detail and to point to the possibilities that are offered by the approach. Of necessity, this will mean that a good deal of the discussion will be at an abstract level and, in the hope of clarifying matters, I will use an example of a study into teenagers' representation of new technology to illustrate the methodology.

Classically, before one begins to deal with methods at all, one is expected to define one's terms and central to this exercise is what it is meant by social representation. Social representations are conceptualized here as being potentially complex and interlinked belief systems that are shared to varying degrees by numbers of individuals. Where there is consensus about an object (be it social or physical), the social representation is that part of individuals' personal representations of the object which is shared *and* can be thought of as having origins in social exchange. It is not necessarily that part of an individual's representation of an object which is the result of direct or 'first-hand' experience of the object.

It is also recognized that all representations of the external world can be influenced or structured by previous experience and that even in the case of everyday objects our experiences of them may have been structured by socially-transmitted knowledge (see Thorndyke 1984 for a survey of related notions in cognitive psychology). However, different classes of object are more likely to be experienced 'first-hand' than others (for example stones versus mothers versus politicians), so different objects will have varyingly complex 'social' representations — if they have them at all.

In certain domains, one might call these complex belief systems ideologies but in others, particularly where the object concerned is not usually considered as especially political, the term social representation seems more appropriate. The essential sharedness of these beliefs is fundamental, but we should be clear that a social representation is more than simply a consensus about an object based on one or two beliefs — it is a consensus about the attributes, evaluations, and consequences of an object in its many manifestations. Social representations as reflected in social structures are transmitted socially and, indeed, are the basis for much of our social interaction (Moscovici 1981).

From the viewpoint of the empirical study of social representations, it is important that we should be able to describe the content of the representations as systematically as possible. We also need to move towards identifying the boundaries of a representation. While it is undoubtedly important to know what the content of a representation is, it is equally important to know what is *not* contained within it. This is an area that has received relatively little attention to date.

Even more fundamentally, some criteria are needed to determine whether or not a social representation exists in relation to a particular phenomenon at all. Researchers, caught up in their enthusiasm for a topic, run the risk of discussing a representation at great length when it may not be a 'real' phenomenon at all. This particular issue runs into a whole range of philosophical issues about definitions and epistemology, but researchers owe it to themselves to set up criteria for determining when they have found a representation. The intention of the current method is to progress in this direction to some degree.

More than merely describing representations, we need to consider how we might at least confirm some of the basic notions that surround the concept of social representation. In particular, a lot has been made of the function that social representations serve for groups (for example Jaspars and Fraser 1984), yet explicit tests that different groups hold different representations are few and often based on traditional attitudinal studies.

This is problematic, since attitudinal theories and methodologies are usually concerned with identifying sources of variation rather than sources of consensus. Only extreme care will prevent the researcher from concluding that accounting for variance is equivalent to finding different group representations. If groups have been defined on *a priori* grounds then, given the usually small amounts of variance that can be accounted for in such studies, statistical significance will not establish conclusively that the groups' members share different representations — there may be considerable overlap in group representations.

A much more satisfactory approach is to attempt to use the very representations themselves to define one's groups, rather than have the groups define the representations. This is essentially a clustering task. Do the those groups of individuals who share the same representation coincide with the 'natural' social groupings that you had expected to share these representations? If the groups of agreeing individuals do not reflect the 'natural' social groupings you had expected to find, then you have evidence that the situation is not what you had initially thought it to be.

To take an imaginary example, we might ask two groups of people about their representations of industrial pollution. One group is selected from an environmental campaign group and another from a society of industrial manufacturers, under the assumption that these groups would hold different representations of pollution — it causes, cures, and financial implications. We elicit representations from the groups and then cluster individuals on the basis of the similarity of their representations. If we find two large clusters of individuals and the members of each cluster are coincident with the members of the two groups, then we would be happy to conclude that each group shares a representation and that the two representations differ.

There is a possibility, however, that such an analysis would not reveal a clear picture like this. The members of the two clustered groups might not coincide with the *a priori* groupings. This would suggest, perhaps, that some industrialists share a representation of pollution that has more in common with the environmentalists than with other industrialists. We would now want to know more about these particular industrialists — for example, what industries they represent, where they live, and, indeed, whether they are members of an environmental group in their spare time!

Another possibility would be that three clusters of individuals were suggested by the analysis. In this case, perhaps, what the researcher had missed might have been a split within the environmentalist group, which may have had an extreme radical wing as well as a more middle-of-the-road core. Yet another possibility is that the two clusters of individuals are so diffuse and weakly linked together that one might wish to question whether there is much consensus out there at all. These kinds of subtleties could easily be missed if the traditional 'variance accounted for' approach had been taken. While such an approach would not preclude reaching these conclusions, the clustering approach is somewhat more parsimonious and has a certain elegance.

If, as I am about to do, one wants to tread this particular path then one has to resort to asking individuals about how they represent the world. This is problematic in some respects. It could be argued that the very act of asking people how they represent the world introduces additional cognitive activity that would distort the elicited representation. The task's demands and/or perceived needs to manage the impressions given to others (compare Lalljee *et al*. 1984) could act to seriously undermine the aims of the study. The problem with such a view is that it makes it very difficult to envisage how our understanding of the relationships between individuals and social representation is ever to be furthered.

These issues are not trivial and may number among the reasons why many of the major works in the social-representation field to date have been based on seeking representations in data that already existed (in media discourses, cultural artefacts, and so on). It is debatable as to whether these forms of data are free from bias and artefact either; ultimately, providing that cautionary measures are taken, I see no reason not to proceed with asking people directly about their representations.

From the earlier discussion of definitions, it becomes clear that one way to study social representations is to see if groups of people share beliefs about the consequences, features, and attributes of a target object and its various manifestations. Perhaps the most straightforward way to do this that permits the study of large numbers of people is to present the object(s) and ask whether or not it (they) possesses given attributes.

While this is straightforward enough to translate into a pen and paper format (or an interview schedule), it is important that the methodology is sensitive to a number of possibilities that could undermine it. For instance, within the population you choose to study, more than one unique representation of the object(s) may exist. Simplistic attempts to aggregate responses may artefactually lead one to the conclusion that a single consensual representation has been found.

Another possibility is that certain members of a sample may not have the good access to the representation(s) that other members of the sample have. It is desirable, then, that the method is capable of assessing the varying degrees to which individuals hold a representation of the target and, as a result, offer the potential of indexing the degree to which any representation is truly consensual.

As a corollary, if one aims to index how much of a representation each sample member possesses, then it becomes possible to identify features of those individuals who have good access to the representation in relation to those who do not. Such a facility would be highly desirable in the exploration of the notion of social representations and their function for groups.

While a method might reveal that a single representation of an object exists, most theorists in this field would allow there to be subtle differences of emphasis in people's *presentation* of the representation. So, while we might come to believe that there is basically one socially-acquired representation of an object, and that there is high consensus about the object's attributes, single individuals may overemphasize certain attributes and neglect others (compare Potter and Litton 1985$a + b$). It is an empirical question as to whether what is emphasized and what is neglected can be related to other known features of the individual (for example special interest group membership).

This is encompassed by Moscovici's (1988) conceptualization of social representations and it is expected that different people will have differential access to social representations. This differential access is itself thought to be a function of a number of features of the individual, primarily their membership of various social groups and categories (for example Jaspars and Fraser 1984). Indeed, there has even been some debate as to whether there is a circularity here in that groups can be defined by the fact of sharing a social representation (see Potter and Litton 1985a; Moscovici 1985) — a definitional issue that surely needs attention.

The researcher in the field will not have any *a priori* evidence that any sample chosen is truly homogeneous with respect to the representations held of the target. A sample may appear to have been drawn from a single 'natural' grouping but this is not in itself evidence that they will all hold the same 'version' of the representation — this is the empirical point at issue.

A final consideration for the time being is that it should be apparent that when generating attributes to test for linkage with an object (the representation) some attention is paid to the range of attributes included. It would be a mistake to select only those attributes which one already expected to be central to a sample's representation of the object. The folly of this is that it (i) increases the likelihood of finding a false consensus and (ii) may restrict one's understanding of what the sample's representations of the object are — many additional and potentially-crucial attributes might be linked to the object, but these would remain unidentified.

As a result of (i) above, attributes that are not thought, on any *a priori* basis, to be linked to the object need to be included. Naturally, such attributes should not be trivially irrelevant nor inappropriate for the object under scrutiny (such as 'bring joy to mothers' as a potential attribute of political parties). Some element of 'real-world' knowledge is required on the part of the researcher. This, ironically, requires the researcher to have some other means of access to the representation of the object, though discussion and/or piloting with likely members of the groups under study is the preferred route to solving this particular problem.

Dealing with the issue of ignoring fundamental attributes, two points need to be made. First, the use of an attribute checklist should not be the first point of entry into the study of a social representation: some form of freely-elicited representation of the target object needs to be sought, through careful pilot work with interviews or naturalistic observations of the likely respondent group. Indeed, it should be clear that what follows is not suggested as being all that one might do empirically within a study.

The second point is the real-world limitation on the number of judgements one may reasonably ask informants to make. This usually implies a limit to the range of attributes that one can ask about, and some loss of quality is inevitable. However, this can be offset to a degree by employing a judgemental process to reduce the number of attributes by fitting them into categories of similar 'classes' of attribute. This is, of course, easier to state than to do.

The example and the method

What follows is a suggested procedure for creating and analysing attribute checklists which will be illustrated by describing a study of teenagers' representations of new technology. It is worth pausing briefly to give some background to this particular research, which was conducted as part of a two-year programme of research into young people's attitudes to technology at work funded by the Leverhulme Trust. General details of the studies are contained in Fife-Schaw *et al*. (1987) and Matthews *et al*. (1989).

This project involved a number of surveys of 13–18-year-old teenagers drawing respondents from both school and the work place. The research was concerned primarily with identifying factors that influenced teenagers' motivations to train for technological work in a period of the rapid growth of what were known as the 'new technologies'.

A problem that became apparent fairly early on in the project was that it was not possible to find a satisfactory definition of the term 'new technology'. At first it seemed obvious that at any historical moment new technologies are being developed and that technologies would be 'new' for only a short period of time. This notion is essentially true, yet it did not help in the quest to know exactly what it was that should be studied. Discussions with teenage groups made it clear that, as a group, the term 'new technology' had some currency; certain technologies were definitely 'new' and others not. It became evident, however, that it was the products of technologies that were considered when we mentioned 'new technology', rather the core technologies themselves.

Attempts to obtain lists of new technologies from open-ended questioning led to further problems. There was a consensus that computers and the applications of robotics to manufacturing processes were new, but there were considerable individual differences in the numbers and range of technologies that were elicited. This gave rise to questions about whether those who had offered only one or two technologies believed that these, and only these, were 'new', or whether they had merely failed to recall other 'new' technologies.

It seems unlikely that individuals are fully conscious of the representations that they hold. When asked 'What sorts of things do you think of as new technologies?', it is doubtful that interviewees perceive the task as being to tightly define the content and extent of their representation of 'new technology'. In addition to problems with task demands, retrieval difficulties may intervene, leaving it unclear what should be made of open-ended responses such as these.

This led to the first checklist exercise, in which we presented 17 manifestations of technologies and asked respondents to indicate whether or not each fell into the category 'new technology'. The technologies included in the list deliberately ranged from the 'new' computers to technologies that we knew were generally considered as old (bricklaying, radar). We also added a few trick and ambiguous technologies, just to test the notion that awareness might be a factor in determining what was considered new. These included such things as turbocharging engines (actually introduced around 1910) and brain surgery (conducted in various forms since time immemorial).

Analysis of these responses proved quite illuminating. Far from providing a clear cut-off date for 'newness', a mixture of factors seemed to be at work. First, those technologies that were chronologically more recent and hence expected to be judged 'new' were not considered as such when they were manifested in everyday objects. Microwave ovens, video recorders, and compact-disc players were less likely to be seen as new when compared with micro-computers, X-ray scanners, and satellite communication links. So, despite some of the latter objects being manifestations of older technologies, familiarity with (and possibly understandings of), certain objects seemed to influence judgements.

The second observation was that manifestations of nuclear technologies were generally agreed to be new, yet the core technology dates from the 1930s. It may be that the time of introduction is less important than, or is overridden by, emotional and political responses to technologies although, of course, the nuclear technologies have not ceased to develop since the 1930s. The other ambiguous items produced little consensus, though there was some suggestion that those who reported greater interest in technological matters made more chronologically-based responses.

Having completed both face-to-face discussions and a preliminary checklist, it was still unclear how teenagers represented new technology or what implications they felt new technology had. Clearly, more was involved in the term than was anticipated. This led to the construction of a more complicated checklist where a number questions about teenagers' representations of new technology could be addressed.

An initial requirement was to know to what degree there was consensus within the sample (in this case, fifth-form school pupils) about: (i) what was considered new and (ii) what was implied by (or associated with) judgements of newness. Could some form of shared representation of technology be found that would allow statements to be made about what was considered to be new technology and what consequences and attributes such technologies had? A related question, though this was not articulated at the time and perhaps should have been, was the issue of whether new technology was really salient to the sample group and whether or not there truly was a social representation of this target.

As had been suggested earlier, there was a question as to whether there were systematic differences in the representations of those who were motivated and interested by technology and those who were not. In essence, were there actually two (or possibly more) social representations of new technology evinced by individuals with measureably-differing backgrounds. Could representations be linked to individual group memberships, interests, concerns, or backgrounds in some way?

This latter question is particularly interesting since, if such links could be demonstrated and interpreted sensibly, this would constitute empirical support for the social nature of these representations and, potentially, for the processes involved in generating them.

Generating a checklist

The various steps in the procedure will be discussed as they relate to the technology example, but are intended to be generalizable principles applicable to any domain or object where creating a task that involves linking the object (or its manifestations) with attributes is appropriate and realistic.

The first steps in the construction of the checklist have only been discussed briefly, so it is worth reiterating them in more detail. The task is essentially to identify (i) salient and non-salient (but appropriate) manifestations of the target object and (ii) salient and potentially non-salient attributes that each of the manifestations of the object might possess. In certain cases, it may not be possible or appropriate to sub-divide a target object into manifestations – this will have to be a judgement made by the researcher based on understandings of the object gained through contact with the target population.

Identifying manifestations and attributes can be done in a number of ways and it is probably best to adopt as many different approaches as is feasible. In the case of the technology example, newspaper and magazine representations of new technology were surveyed and clear statements linking technologies or related products to attributes were sought. This provided some basic attribute–object links which were presented to teenagers (15–18 years old) in face-to-face interviews.

Both open-ended and structured questions were presented in interviews with responses tape-recorded for later analysis. As an additional input into this exercise, the first checklist exercise described above was carried out on a large survey of school-age teenagers' responses to various technologies in relation to their career choices and socioeconomic backgrounds. The results of this exercise have been outlined above.

In addition to these approaches, other sources of representations of the target object could have been tapped. Representations of the target in literature, cinema, and theatre as well as the broadcast media could be surveyed. Group discussions could be held, and monitoring the negotiation of object-attribute links between members would be particularly illuminating if they could be set up in naturalistic settings.

Having collected what could be a very large listing of potential attributes and manifestations of the target object, some form of reduction into broad categories and subsets was required. This exercise is loaded with potential for the introduction of artefacts from the researcher's own representations of what is important in the domain. Unfortunately, it is also inappropriate to do the categorization exercise using samples drawn from the target populations, as this will artefactually increase the likelihood that consensus will be found later unless extreme care is taken.

These problems are not insurmountable, though. In the case of choosing the subset of manifestations, a general guide should be to draw a sample of the most frequently-mentioned manifestations and a sample of those manifestations that are mentioned infrequently. A quasi-random sampling procedure is easily implemented once these manifestations have been identified. Consideration needs to be given to exactly how many manifestations can be reasonably included before overloading the respondents. Figure 12.1 shows the checklist finally presented to the sample and as can be seen each additional technological manifestation increases the number of judgements required by nine.

As far as the attributes are concerned, clear repetitions of themes may be grouped together with only the very broadness of the themes themselves being a problem for the researcher. When it comes to making selections of attributes, the very fact of having the object elaborated into its manifestations makes the choice somewhat easier.

One aim outlined earlier was to include attributes for which there was no *a priori* reason to expect a linkage with the object in its totality. It is likely that, within the sources from which the attributes were generated, there will be examples of attributes which are never apparently linked with certain manifestations of the target object. In the technology example, nobody ever suggested that pocket calculators or word processors were harmful to society, yet the attribute 'harmful to society' is clearly an attribute that could, potentially, be linked to other manifestations of technology.

Fig. 12.1 also lists the attributes used in this exercise. The reader's attention is drawn to the attribute 'never heard of', which is one attribute that should be considered in all such checklist since responses to it are so fundamental to understanding the implications of the other attributes. As will

Technology	(1) Something that you use yourself	(2) Something that is useful to society	(3) Something that you have never heard of	(4) Something that you feel is uncontrollable	(5) Something that you like	(6) Something that is new	(7) Something that makes you feel worried or anxious	(8) Something that you understand	(9) Something that you think is harmful to society
Fibre-optic cables									
Robot welders									
Microcomputers									
Solar-heating panels									
Monoclonal antibodies									
Compact discs									
Nuclear missiles									
Biodegradable plastic bottles									
Surgical lasers									
Microwave ovens									
Ultrasound scanners									
Word processors									
Laser weapons									
Video-cassette recorders									
Communications satellites									
Cash dispensers									
Facsimile-transfer machines									
Nuclear-power stations									
Pocket calculators									

Fig. 12.1. The technology attitude checklist

become apparent, our conclusions about the meanings of newness judgements were informed by the inclusion of this attribute.

The final stage in the generation of the checklists is to conduct some
piloting of the measure. The aims of this should be limited to establishing
whether instructions and the task are understood, and establishing whether
the task is likely to be too demanding of respondent time and effort. The
traditional piloting issues of whether the items were understood fully and
recognized are problematic in the context of this exercise, and researchers
need to exercise caution before eliminating manifestations or attributes. The
fact that nobody linked an attribute with a manifestation is valuable data in
its own right and crucial to a fuller understanding of social representations.

Analysis

Broadly, there are three stages to the analysis of the checklist. First is
the determination of the number and homogeneity of naturally-occurring
clusters of individuals, based on the similarity of their judgements about
the target manifestations. Secondly, having determined that one or a number
of clusters exist it is desirable to establish exactly what it is that is similar
about the judgements being made by members of each cluster. Essentially,
the representations shared by cluster members need to be mapped out.

The nature of the third stage is dependent on the numbers of representation revealed in the first stage. If more than one is revealed, then the
task is to see if additional features of the sample members (for example
other items on the questionnaire, known group memberships) discriminate
between members of the clusters. If this can be done satisfactorily, and
sensible accounts of why these variables might explain the differing representations can be made, then our understanding of the origins of these
representations may be advanced.

If only one representation appears to exist, then the task is to decide
whether there is any reasonable justification for further searches for
differing nuances in the representations of the targets. I will return to this
point later, as it raises a number of interesting questions about the way
social representations have been considered.

Before delving into the details of analysis, it is worth describing the sample
and questionnaire that is being used for the illustration. Three hundred
and one 15–16-year-old (fifth-year) school pupils at a single state-sector
comprehensive in the rural West Country of England were approached
through the school authorities, and asked to participate in the study. Com-
pletion of the questionnaire was not compulsory, though the school had
been urged to include the whole year group if at all possible. In the end,
some 95 per cent of the year group cooperated in the study (Matthews
et al. 1989).

The questionnaire contained the checklist shown in Fig. 12.1 along with requests for basic demographic information. In addition, a scale (Breakwell *et al*. 1986) measuring generalized motivation to train for technological work was included, as were two simple Likert-type items measuring (i) how far the respondents felt that technology (in general) was beneficial to society and (ii) how far they thought that technology would make their working lives better in the future.

Clustering individuals

The basic principle behind the approach here is the search for agreement among individuals. Unlike traditional attitude research, the aim is not to account for variation but for *lack* of variation. Hence, the appropriate mode of analysis is one that groups or clusters individuals together on the basis of how similar their ratings of the objects are.

The following discussion will necessarily assume some basic understanding of the principles behind cluster analysis, and readers are urged to refer to Everitt (1974) for detailed elaborations of logic and algorithms underlying the many popular clustering techniques. Readers unfamiliar with this form of analysis will not be totallay ignored, as attempts will be made to keep matters as simple as possible.

Additional to the above considerations is the unfortunate fact of life that differing computer implementations of cluster analysis packages offer different facilities, and some of those discussed here may not be available on particular systems. We have conducted all the cluster analyses reported here from within the SPSS-X environment (SPSS Inc., 1988).

Cluster analysis, of any data set, needs some form of matrix of the similarities or dissimilarities between all pairs of individuals as basic input. Most popular packages will calculate these matrices, but care needs to be taken in determining which particular metric to choose (association, distance, correlation coefficient, and so on).

As with all statistical analyses, a requirement is that the level of measurement is matched with the appropriate choice of metric. In the technology example, where all judgements are binary (applies/does not apply) judgements, product-moment correlations are inappropriate. Had respondents been allowed to indicate the *degree* to which each manifestation possessed each attribute, then such parametric correlations might have been applicable.

With binary data, association coefficients needed to be calculated, but the decision about which metric to use does not stop here. Association coefficients vary in the degree to which they weight joint absences. Basically, the researcher must decide whether to consider the occasions when two individuals fail to tick one of the boxes as being equally important as occasions where the two individuals both tick a box: can you be certain that failure to tick a box implies that an object *does not* possess the attribute?

This decision will be informed partly by knowledge of the domain under study and partly by the researcher's confidence that respondents were paying attention to the task. If in doubt, two parallel analyses should be run and strong conclusions only drawn when both analyses point to the same position (see Hammond, Chapter 10 of this volume). Providing space for explicit negation of a link (a 'no' as well as a 'yes' box, say) gets over this problem, but at the expense of simplicity and speed for the respondent — not a problem with a short list but a potential consideration with a larger one.

As cluster analysis does not employ statistical inference, there are no simple and clear-cut criteria to indicate when the 'best' solution has been found. Rule-of-thumb criteria are often employed and may seem unduly mysterious and arbitrary to the uninitiated. As demonstrated later, one of the most satisfactory routes to determining the number and nature of the clusters in your data is to adopt a parallel analysis approach such that a number of different criteria are employed in several-analyses until one is satisfied that the various solutions are leading to the same conclusion.

How will one know how many representations of the target exist? Some explanation of the basics of clustering may clarify the situation. Agglomerative types of cluster analysis start by grouping, or clustering, the two most similar individuals together and then searching for the next most similar pairs of individuals, putting them together in a cluster, and so on. These analyses go on linking individuals together in this way until everybody has been considered.

At each stage in the analysis, individuals already clustered together are treated as one single case (a cluster) and compared again with other individuals and/or existing clusters of individuals. This is done by recalculating the similarities (or distances) between all the individuals not yet in a cluster, and all the clusters. This is achieved by making some assessment of each cluster's 'average' similarity (or highest, lowest, and so on, depending on the chosen method) with other individuals or clusters.

There will be anything from one to $n - 1$ (where n = the number of individuals) potential clusters, depending on the stage at which the process is stopped. In the case of the search for social representations, we are more usually concerned with assessing the level of agreement within relatively large clusters (< 5, say, with substantial numbers of individuals in each) than with numerous small ones. If we find that there is little absolute agreement between individuals in large clusters, then this may constitute evidence for there not being large-scale consensual representations of the target within the sample. The sample members have idiosyncratic representations of the object — something which it is particularly valuable to know.

Assessing the homogeneity of clusters

The homogeneity of individuals' ratings within each cluster can be assessed in a number of ways, and all rely on being able to provide information on the cluster membership of each individual. In an ideal world, all possible methods should be employed in order to ensure that one is confident in one's conclusions.

Cohen's kappa is a measure of agreement usually employed to assess agreement between a number of judges. As this is essentially what we want to do here, kappas can be calculated for each cluster and, as kappa has a known distribution, Z-scores can be calculated and probabilistic statements made about the particular level of kappa found. There is an argument that inferential statistics are inappropriate at this stage in the life of the concept of social representations (see Hammond, Chapter 10 of this volume) and researchers would need to make a value judgement as to whether they wished to pursue probability levels in this manner. Regardless of whether probabilities are sought, kappa still gives an indication of relative homogeneity, which is of value.

Kappa needs to be applied with caution. It assumes that joint absences of ticks are as important as joint presences (that is, all the data carry equal meaning). If, when deciding on a similarity/dissimilarity metric you decided that you were unsure of the meaning of joint absences, then kappa would be inappropriate. A number of alternative coefficients are available, of which the Jaccard coefficient is, perhaps, the best known.

A second method for deciding on the number and homogeneity of clusters is to establish the average distance between members of each cluster and the cluster centre and the standard deviation of these averages. As probabilitic statements about the likelihood of finding such an average cannot as yet be made (though it is theoretically possible), other rubrics need to be employed.

One such is to compare average member–cluster-centre distances with the distances between cluster centroids (or centres). If the average member–cluster-centre distance is greater than the distance between cluster centres, then there is evidence that either (i) the clusters are not well differentiated (they may actually be better considered as one cluster), or (ii) one or both clusters is primarily accounting for idiosyncratic 'outlying' individuals. In both cases one would wish to investigate a solution with fewer clusters.

Figure 12.2 is a presentation of various possibilities which should clarify the above. In all three parts of the figure the clusters (of which only two are shown) and their members are presented in two dimensions for clarity. In reality, multidimensional space is required to represent the true spatial relationships between individuals. Similarity is represented as distance here, so greater similarity is presented as a smaller distance.

In Fig. 12.2(a), the cluster centres are well separated and the inter-cluster distance is certainly greater than either cluster's average member–cluster-centre distance. There are clearly two groupings of individuals who represent the target object differently in some potentially systematic and measurable way. Certainly one would not wish to combine these clusters together.

In Fig. 12.2(b), the cluster centres are quite close together relative to their

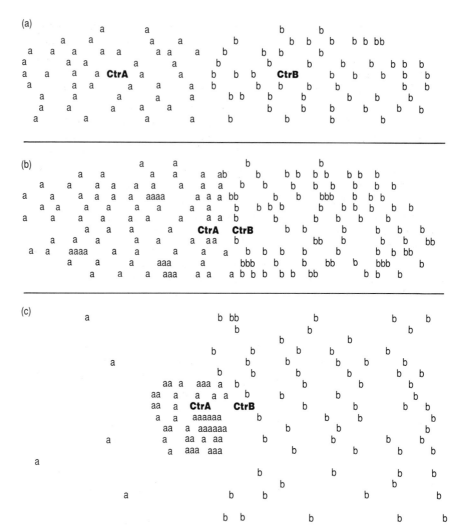

Fig. 12.2. Two-dimensional examples of three idealized cluster sloutions: a = member of cluster A, b = member of cluster B, **Ctr A** = centre of cluster A, and **Ctr B** = centre of cluster B.

members, which are spread quite diffusely about the space. The average member–cluster-centre distance is greater than distance between cluster centres. Here, the clustering algorithm is separating the individuals, but it is clear that it has had to force a solution from the data as there is little homogeneity in the judgements of members of each cluster. One would opt to explore a solution with fewer clusters, remaining aware that the present solution is suggesting that a representation, if one exists at all, is shared to only a limited degree.

In Fig. 12.2(c), one cluster is quite tightly packed, with only the odd outlier to spoil the picture (there are always some outliers). The second cluster, however, is quite diffuse and its average member-to-centre distance exceeds the inter-cluster centre distance. This suggests that there *is* actually a core of individuals who closely agree with one another about the attributes of the target object, but there is probably that only one such cluster (or one less in the case of solutions with more than two clusters). These 'core' individuals share a representation of the target, and those who are not in this core have idiosyncratic representations of the target and/or share only part of the representation.

The cases given in the Fig. 12.2 are prototypical and all shades in between are possible. Approaching the interpretation with a close eye on the relationship between member–centre and inter-cluster-centre distances can considerably enhance the understanding of the data.

The third method of assessing the homogeneity of clusters is to take an overview of how many individuals continue to remain clustered together in solutions with varying numbers of clusters. Assuming that we are interested primarily in looking at widely-shared representations of the target(s), it is appropriate to start from a two-cluster solution and work towards the inclusion of more clusters, rather than starting with solutions with many clusters and working up, so to speak, to two.

All that needs to be done here is to trace the cluster memberships of individuals over a range of, say, two- to five-cluster solutions. This is easily achieved through cross-tabulation procedures. What is sought here is evidence of sizeable (that is, more than 10 per cent of the sample) groups of individuals in single cells of the cross-tabulations. Such sizeable groups of individuals must be relatively homogeneous (with regard to the ratings), since increasing the numbers of clusters progressively decreases the overall likelihood of any two individuals remaining in the same cluster.

Each cell will progressively lose members as the numbers of clusters considered increases but, if homogeneous clusters do truly exist, they will survive together longer in this process than will other groups. In the case where there is truly a single representation of the target, one cell will remain relatively large while the others quickly decay. If there are two representations, two cells will continue to hold the same individuals throughout. Naturally, if there were three representations, then this would not be apparent until the three-cluster solution was considered.

This process is less satisfactory than the kappa or average-distance approach, since one could easily miss these patterns in the data. However, it is best employed as a confirmation of conclusions drawn from these other two methods, and its value lies in that it is not based directly on the similarities between individuals.

The technology example

Having discussed the principles, it is time to demonstrate these in the data set. Two-, three-, and four-cluster solutions all produced evidence that inter-member average distances were considerably greather than between cluster-centre distances. In the case of the two-cluster solution, the between cluster distance was 1.26 yet the average inter-member distances were 5.10 (s.d. = 1.10) and 5.45 (s.d. = 1.30) for each cluster, respectively. Note that each cluster is almost equally diffuse, suggesting that only one representation probably exists and that it is probably shared to only a limited degree.

Cross-tabulating cluster memberships of consecutive cluster solutions confirmed this. One group of individuals remained clustered together between two and five clusters (at sizes of 87, 62, 58, and 45), but this group was decaying rapidly, as did all other groupings, which decayed at a greater rate still. Again this pointed to one diffuse representation of the technological attributes. There was no high level of agreement between respondents and, as we will discuss later on, there is some doubt as to whether a social representation of new technology has been revealed at all in the present data set.

Assessing cluster solutions based on kappa was not carried out using the full sample, as we had more respondents than our microcomputer implementation could deal with.

Representing shared representations

At this stage, it is assumed that the researcher is satisfied that he or she has identified one or more groups of individuals who are attributing similar things to the object and its manifestations. In the technology example, there is some doubt that even one representation exists, but we will persevere with the example for illustrative purposes. How, then, should the content of these representations be investigated?

There are quite a number of methods available for investigating checklist data, and only a small number of them will be discussed here. First and most straightforward is to obtain frequency counts of ticks in each cell. Unless you have detected a cluster of individuals who are in perfect agreement about the objects (which is highly unlikely), few cells of the table will be completely empty or completely full. Therefore, expressing cell frequencies as percentages of the numbers of persons identified with a cluster is likely to be more informative than mere raw scores.

Naturally, cells with very high or very low percentages indicate attribute-object linkages over which there is considerable agreement — these are the linkages that are important to this group's representation of the target. Cells which contain around 50 per cent of ticks indicate little consensus about the particular attribute–object link. So, one technique that can be used to understand a representation is simply to rank-order the attribute–object links in terms of their percentage deviation from 50 per cent (subtract 50 per cent from the raw percentages), remembering that negative figures indicate a consensus that an attribute *is not* linked to an object.

This procedure is quite direct and informative, although it becomes cumbersome when many judgements are involved. An alternative that is appropriate when two or more clusters are present, is to examine univariate F-ratios by treating cluster membership as an independent variable. The F-ratios highlight those judgements that are treated quite differently by the cluster groupings, which makes it easy to see where basic differences in representations lie.

Using this approach requires some caution, and the statistical probabilities associated with the F-ratios should not be interpreted at face value. Depending on the level of measurement used, the parametric assumptions required for calculating F-ratios may not be met (the seriousness of this, however, is hard to ascertain). More serious, though, is the fact that a large number of tests will have been conducted and a number of 'significant' F-ratios may occur by chance. None the less, the magnitudes of the F-ratios are good indicators of the principal differences between the judgements of the two groups.

What would be preferable in this exercise is some method of visually displaying the relationships between the objects (manifestations) and the attributes. A number of metric and non-metric scaling packages exist to deal with this problem, and they solve it with varying degrees of adequacy. The analysis which seems to best deal with our requirements here is generically referred to as correspondence analysis (Benzecri 1971; Greenacre 1984; Hammond's Chapter 10 in this volume).

Correspondence analysis is based on a principal-components analysis of, in the technology case, object manifestations (as they are larger in number than the attributes). The analysis operates on the raw numbers of ticks in each cell, although various data transformations are possible if a case can be made for using them.

This analysis permits the manifestations to be plotted in their component space(s) *and* the attributes to be similarly presented in space(s). Attributes that lie close together on the plots were treated similarly, objects close together were treated similarly, and attributes that are close to objects 'tend towards the objects' in the jargon of such analyses (Greenacre 1984).

To give a clearer idea of what this analysis offers, a correspondence plot is presented for the technology data. As the reader will recall, the cluster analyses indicated that there was only one, relatively diffuse representation of the new technologies. Figure 12.3 is of the two-dimensional plot based on loadings in the space defined by the first two components.

This plot provides a clear understanding of the teenagers' representation of the various technologies. The space defined by the first two components accounts for 85.71 per cent of the variance in object ratings, suggesting that this simple two-dimensional presentation of the data is not obscuring other, major, distinctions between attributes or objects. Notice how the attributes are distributed in the space with usability, usefulness, likeableness, and understandability grouped together. There is a grouping of (manifestations of) technologies that are intuitively correctly linked with these attributes. Again, on an intuitive basis those manifestations that we would

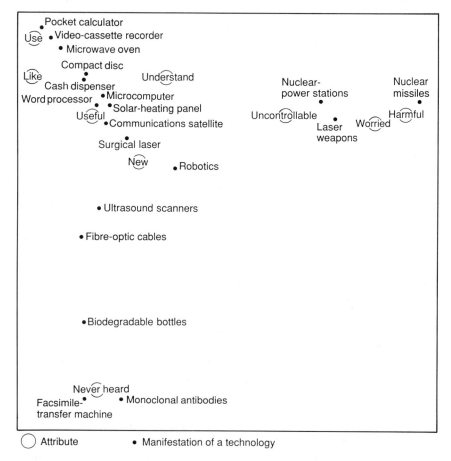

Fig. 12.3. Correspondence analysis plot of the representation of technologies and their attributes

predict to be seen as harmful, anxiety-provoking, and uncontrollable are so represented.

It is interesting to pause here to consider that researchers should recognize that *their* understandings of an analysis output will be influenced by their representation of the target. The reader, for instance, will have to share some element of this representation of new technology in order to recognize the links that I have labelled as 'intuitively correct'. Hence, in domains that are unfamiliar to the researcher, some linkages may appear nonsensical but should not be dismissed on these grounds alone. Hopefully, careful attention to parallel methods and analyses will insure the researcher against such an error.

Another interesting feature of the technology representation is the role of the attribute 'never heard of'. Those technologies that were included in the checklist on the grounds that they were not commonly referred to are indeed those which respondents had never heard of, and they are neither seen as harmful and uncontrollable nor used and liked.

Note that 'new' as an attribute lies between the like, understand, use, and useful to society group of attributes, and the uncontrollable, harmful, and anxiety-provoking attributes. 'New' perhaps is slightly more related to the former grouping than the latter though, indeed, its meaning is still unclear and its use certainly not uniform across respondents. A failure to include more 'obviously' old technologies may account for this in some degree.

Though this group of fifth-form pupils cluster in only a relatively loose fashion, the representation itself is not so diffuse. In the case of single clusters, one could sub-divide the sample into those who are nearer to the cluster centre and those who are relatively far from it, and then look at the representations that these two groups have of the target. Those nearer the centre ought to have the 'real' social representation as they are the individuals who share the greatest part of their representation of the target with others. However, more distal individuals' ratings do *not* differ from those lying near the cluster centre in any systematic way (there would have been two clusters if this had been the case) and so, taken across individuals, the representations remain essentially the same for both groups. There is no advantage in making the dichotomy in this case, and indeed this further suggests that the representation is weak.

Correspondence analysis is not without its limitations. A shortcoming is that the spatial relationship between attributes and objects is indeterminate. It is not appropriate to measure distances between attributes and objects from the plots to provide an indication of the strength of association between and attribute and object (which would be desirable): this is only possible in the case of objects and attributes considered separately. The plots are intended as heuristics, but as long as some caution is exercised they remain very informative.

Where more than one cluster is identified, plots can be produced for each cluster and then the main sources of difference between clusters can be located. Earlier reference was made to the examination of univariate F-ratios which, in the two-cluster case, will give an indication of which judgements were treated differently by the groups. Correspondence plots of the two (or more) representations will give an overview of how the groups represent the *relationships* between attributes and objects. Obviously, minor spacial shifts in object locations should not be overemphasized and attention should be paid to more global structural differences.

In the absence of obvious global differences in representations, then there is an indication that the distinctions between groups are based on a small number of judgements about which there was major disagreement. If these cannot be identified from the F-ratios, then it would be wise to recheck the decisions made about the numbers of clusters present — there may be fewer than was thought.

Linking representations to individuals' backgrounds

In the new technology example it had been expected, on the basis of the early work, that they would be more than one representation of new technology. There was reason to believe that interest in, and motivation to train for, technology might influence the nature of the representations that individuals held. Had two representations been identified, it would have been appropriate to attempt to link cluster membership to levels of interest and motivation through techniques such as discriminant function analysis. However, two representations were not found and thus the example data are of no help here.

Two possibilities exist, in principle, for the further analysis of checklist data. Both have important implications for the development of the concept of social representation. The first of these is to pursue the analyses described in the previous paragraph.

Assuming that it has been possible to identify two or more representations of the target, then it is important to identify those known features of the individual that could account for why they have access to one representation rather than another. The search for these factors can be aided by the use of techniques like discriminant function analysis, in which cluster membership could be treated as an erstwhile dependent variable.

If the variables than turn out to predict the representation held are group memberships, social categories, or concerned with aspects of social identity (see Breakwell, Chapter 9 of this volume), then it will be realistic to set up specific hypotheses about the social nature of individuals' representations. It may then be possible to go on to investigate the processes by which these particular social factors influence (or possibly, are caused by) representations of the target.

For example, belonging to an anti-abortion campaigning group may be associated with holding a particular, unique representation of research techniques involving human material. Since abortion and such research are not linked by any necessary logic, one could hypothesize some social transmission of this representation related to this particular group membership.

The second possibility for the analysis of the representations is appropriate when one has identified large and possibly diffuse clusters. Here, we might wish to ask what it is about those individuals who lie relatively close to the centre of the cluster that makes them different from those who are distant from it. The implication is that those who lie near to the cluster centre have 'more' or 'better' acceptance of the representation of the target than others. Clearly, if this centrality could be linked to other features of the individual such as group memberships, then one could hypothesize about how acceptance is facilitated.

Linking centrality to other aspects of the respondents is, at present, computationally cumbersome in the single-cluster case. Hammond (Chapter 10 of this volume) illustrates how assessing group homogeneity may assist with this problem, and centrality measures are offered by smallest space analyses (SSAs) based on inter-individual similarities or differences.

Centrality assessment is achievable, however, in the multi-cluster case where member–cluster centre distances can be saved for individuals by clustering packages. These distances can be correlated or associated with other known features of the respondents. The beauty of this technique lies in the fact that the nature and importance of the background features is determined empirically, rather than on the basis of *a priori* judgements of the researcher. The researcher is not expected to know which groupings of individuals are expected to lie near to the cluster centre in advance.

The success of discriminant analyses and the sorts of procedures described above will be dependent on a number of factors. Principally, the analyses can operate only on features (variables) that are already known about the individuals. If a key variable has not been measured, then it cannot appear as a major predictor of which representation is held.

This may appear to be a trivial point, but it is central to the interpretation of these analyses where prediction of cluster membership or centrality turns out to be poor — is the solution poor because there really is no systematic explanation for cluster memberships, or was a fundamental variable missing from the analysis? Indeed, even if the prediction of cluster membership is good, there is still the possibility that the important discriminating variables are extracted because they correlate highly with variables not actually measured in the research. For example, it would be inadvisable to conclude that academic achievement was a good predictor of which representation is held, in the absence of knowledge about social class or levels of parental education, which are known to be associated with academic performance.

Despite the above, the potential to link representations with features of the respondent via a simple pen-and-paper technique offers great scope for empirical investigation with the concept of social representation.

Conclusions

This chapter has explained in some detail the generation and use of check-list methods for the explorations of social representations. No claim is being made that checklists can stand alone in this endeavour; multimethod approaches will always be preferable.

Many of the decisions made during the process of using a checklist rely heavily on the ability of the researcher to draw on parallel sources of infor-mation about the target domain, and to make informed readings of analysis output. This is surely an advantage if it means that the researcher both knows more about the domain and knows their data better.

Social representations are thought to be more than merely object–attribute linkages, though these are an important feature of them. The checklist can only be about object–attribute linkages, and there is a potential trap in believing that this is all that is at issue in the field. The current method essentially deals with assessing the *content* of a representation, though I would argue that *processes* will only be revealed empirically if content can be mapped adequately.

The real value of having this method in the representation researcher's armoury lies in the ability to locate naturally-occurring shared representa-tions and to permit the linking of these with other, potentially social aspects of respondents' histories. The process is driven by the data and permits the possibility of concluding that a social representation does not exist, as well as describing one if it is found — surely an important advance. Instead of taking *a priori* groupings of individuals and seeing if they share represen-tations, it finds representations first and then indicates how well groups' memberships account for these representations. Such an approach may help us to avoid the potential pitfall of finding representations because we looked too hard for them.

Indeed, in the technology example, it has been shown that, after the aggregation that goes on in the correspondence analysis, a sensible set of relationships between technologies and attributes exists, although it is far from clear that many of these school pupils share the totality of this repre-sentation. Only one cluster was found, and it was so diffuse as to suggest that there is little global consensus — there are some shared elements but not many. Hence, it is difficult to conclude that a social representation of new technology has been revealed at all; one may not exist, in fact.

This is an important thing to be able to say. There is little utility in discuss-ing the nature of social representations of an object unless one can establish that there is something really 'out there' to study. It is fundamental that we start to ask such questions as 'To what degree is a particular represen-tation really shared?' or 'What is it about a person that allows them access to a particular social representation?', or, indeed, a number of similar questions that would rely on asking individuals how they *personally* represent a particular target. Clustering individuals on the basis of their representations and then mapping these seems to offer a fruitful way forward — if we can answer these questions, then perhaps we can start to firm up the theory of social representation.

Acknowledgement

I would like to thank Glynis Breakwell, Judith Matthews, and John Devereux, who assisted with the generation of the new technology data.

References

Benzecri, J.P. (1973). *L'analyse des données*, (Vol. 2). Dunod, Paris.
Breakwell, G.M., Fife-Schaw, C.R., and Devereux, J. (1986). *Social beliefs about new technology*. Paper presented at the European Association for Experimental Social Psychology, Lisbon.
Everitt, B.S. (1974). *Cluster analysis*. Heinemann, London.
Fife-Schaw, C.R., Breakwell, G.M., Lee, T.R., and Spencer, J. (1987). Attitudes towards new technology in relation to scientific orientation at school: a preliminary study of undergraduates. *British Journal of Educational Psychology*, **57**, 114-21.
Greenacre, M.J. (1984). *Theory and applications of correspondence analysis*. Academic Press, London.
Jaspars, J. and Fraser, C. (1984). Attitudes and social representations. In *Social representations*, (ed. R. Farr and S. Moscovici). Cambridge University Press.
Lalljee, M., Brown, L.B., and Ginsberg, G.P. (1984). Attitudes: disposition, behaviour or evaluation? *British Journal of Social Psychology*, **23**, 233-44.
Matthews, J., Breakwell, G.M., and Fife-Schaw, C.R. (1989). Young people's attitudes to new technology in Devon: an element in regional growth potential. *Geoforum*, **20**(1), 27-35.
Moscovici, S. (1981). On social representation. In *Social cognition: perspectives on everyday understanding*, (ed. J. Forgas). Academic Press, London.
Moscovici, S. (1985). Comment on Potter and Litton. *British Journal of Social Psychology*, **24**, 91-2.
Moscovici, S. (1988). Notes towards a description of social representations. *European Journal of Social Psychology*, **18**, 211-50.
Potter, J. and Litton, I. (1985*a*). Some problems underlying the theory of social representations. *British Journal of Social Psychology*, **24**, 81-90.
Potter, J. and Litton, I. (1985*b*). Representing representation: a reply to Moscovici, Semin and Hewstone. *British Journal of Social Psychology*, **24**, 99-100.
SPSS Inc. (1988). *SPSS-X User's Guide* (3rd edn.). SPSS Inc, Chicago.
Thorndyke, P.W. (1984). Applications of schema theory in cognitive research. In *Tutorials in learning and memory*, (ed. J.R. Anderson and S.M. Kosslyn). W.H. Freeman and Co, San Francisco.

13 Multidimensional scaling as a technique for the exploration and description of a social representation

S. Caroline Purkhardt and Janet E. Stockdale

Introduction

The theory of social representations (Farr and Moscovici 1984; Moscovici 1973; 1982; Moscovici and Hewstone 1983) is a relatively recent development which has attracted increasing interest among European social psychologists. It provides a new framework which has stimulated research into the nature and content of people's beliefs and common-sense knowledge. The major thrust behind this interest has come from the field studies (Herzlich 1973; Jodelet 1984; Moscovici 1961) and, to a lesser extent, the laboratory studies (Abric 1984; Codol 1984; Flament 1984) conducted in France. These studies and subsequent research have employed a diversity of methodological techniques ranging from participant observation (Jodelet 1983) and content analysis (Chombart de Lauwe 1984; Jodelet and Moscovici 1975) to experimental and laboratory methods (Duveen and Lloyd 1986, 1987; Lloyd and Smith 1985; Emler and Dickenson 1985). In this chapter, our aim is to demonstrate the potential value of one methodology, multidimensional scaling (MDS), in the investigation of social representations.

MDS analyses are not usually applied or interpreted within the framework of social representations. However, by examining the application of MDS in other contexts and its relationship with the theory of social-representations, it is argued that MDS is a suitable technique for exploring and describing a social representation. This is illustrated by a detailed example in which the social representation of mental disorders within a student population was examined. Methodological problems and theoretical limitations arising from the use of MDS in social-representations research are discussed. Finally, a major theme throughout this chapter is the need to adopt a multimethod approach and to employ complementary methods of research.

Multidimensional scaling (MDS)

MDS (Davison 1983; Kruskal and Wish 1978; Schiftmann, Reynolds and Young 1981) provides a geometric or spatial representation of relations among stimulus objects, which allows meaningful interpretation of distances among stimulus objects and their interrelationships. In this way, MDS is able to explore the respondents' social representations and their structuring of their social environment. It also presents the data in a form that is useful for further analysis and easily assimilated by the researcher or other interested parties. MDS enables the researcher to uncover underlying dimensions which describe the relations among a representative set of social objects pertaining to the social representation of interest. Some MDS programmes assume that the identified dimensions are common to all individuals. Three-way models have the added advantage of examining individual differences. It is therefore possible both to identify the dimensions underlying the relations among social objects within a representation, and also to measure the importance of each dimension for each respondent. In this way, groups of respondents who share similar representational structures may also be identified.

The principles underlying MDS are congruent with the theoretical principles of social representations, in that knowledge is shared. They also assume that people think about complex stimuli by referring to a number of psychologically-relevant attributes or dimensions of those stimuli. These dimensions are brought together in a mental map in which the stimuli are represented at different locations. The single attribute of similarity along which stimuli are judged is thus assumed to be complex, and the task of MDS is to identify the number and meaning of its component characteristics. The judgemental model implicit in metric MDS models makes three further assumptions. First, it is assumed that the individual conceptualizes the stimuli as though they are points in space. Secondly, the perceived dis-similarities among the stimuli are assumed to be psychological distances that are related to the distances among the points that represent them. Thirdly, the dimensions of the space are assumed to be the relevant psychological dimensions along which the stimuli are judged and compared (Nygren and Jones 1977).

Applications of MDS

Within social pscyhology, there has been an increasing interest in the content and structure of individuals' perceptions and conceptions about themselves and others, of interpersonal relationships, social episodes, social situations, and other social objects. It has also been increasingly recognized that consensus and stability in conceptions of these domains are essential for effective adjustment and coordination in social action. This has led to an examination of the communalities and differences in perception and organization of social objects. Researchers have found MDS methods to be useful for investigating these representations and their communalities. MDS has most frequently been employed to provide a description of the representation being investigated, which includes identification of the content of a representation and the exploration of its structural relationships. The following two examples illustrate how MDS can provide a descriptive model of people's representations and how these models go beyond information gained by opinion polling and survey techniques.

Stockdale (1985) investigated people's perceptions of leisure and the meanings attached to leisure activities. MDS and cluster analysis were employed to identify the domain and examine the representations of leisure, while multiple regression was used to interpret the dimensions of the representation. The results of these analyses were then compared with a content analysis of leisure meanings and considered in relation to additional questionnaire data about leisure-related behaviour. An MDS analysis of 17 activities, used to represent the leisure domain, suggested that this domain could be represented in three dimensions. However, a cluster analysis confirmed that the domain comprised two subsets of activities. One subset contained sporting or social activities and the other contained primarily home-based activities. Further MDS analyses indicated that these two sets of activities were characterized by different attributes. The distinction between these two domains and the way in which they are characterized by the MDS dimensions partially corresponded with the representations of leisure to emerge from the open-ended questions. Thus, the MDS results were able to clarify the content and structuring of representations of leisure. Furthermore, by employing SINDSCAL (Schiffmann et al. 1981), the importance or salience of these leisure characteristics were found to vary among groups of individuals, reflecting a combination of personal qualities and social circumstances.

Di Giacomo (1980) analysed the social representations that a student population held about itself, their potential partners, and the proposed strategies of the National Committee during a protest movement. Nine words relating to the student population and the protest movement were selected as stimuli for a free-association task. A two-way, non-metric MDS was carried out on similarities between the resulting dictionaries. Although the student population agreed with the aim of the movements, they did not support the National Committee. It had not been clear from the opinion survey why this should be the case, but by employing MDS to explore the relevant social representations it was found that the representations of the student population itself and their social representation of the National Committee were incompatible. Hence, the committee was represented as an out-group and did not receive support from the student population. Both these studies demonstrate the usefulness of MDS in exploring social representations or consensual 'theories'. Given the broader context in which the studies were carried out, the MDS analyses clarify how the relevant social representations organize reality, direct activity, and adapt to social change.

Further studies illustrate how MDS has been used, not only to explore the content and structure of a representation, but also to assess the communalities and divergencies between different groups' representations, and to provide a predictive model of behaviour. Nygren and Jones (1977) determined the dimensions of political perception of presidential candidates as well as individual differences in the salience of these dimensions and related these dimensions to voting preferences. Thus, MDS was used to discover the content and structure of a representation, to examine variations in the representation corresponding to distinct groups, and also as a model for predicting personal preferences.

In addition, MDS has been employed to study transformations and changes in the structure of representations over time. Although MDS provides a static model, by carrying out a longitudinal or comparative study it is possible to discover any structural transformations that occur within a representation. This is illustrated by a number of studies focusing on interpersonal relationships in therapy groups, academic departments, and organizations. One of the most comprehensive studies of this type was carried out by Jones and Young (1972). MDS was used to explore a research group's structuring of their social environment. This revealed three dimensions underlying interpersonal perceptions within the group. The salience of these dimensions was found to vary according to role-defined group membership and also predicted sociometric measures of interpersonal communication and behaviour. Transformations in the group's representations were examined by carrying out a longitudinal study. The MDS analysis, using parameters for stimuli, judges (both of which were members of the research unit), and occasions, showed that the transformations were associated with duration of group membership.

In a similar study in a British psychology department, Forgas (1976) used INDSCAL to relate perceived social structure to group membership and social episodes. As in the Jones and Young (1972) study, the integration of different aspects of the social environments within a single study and the use of MDS is of both theoretical and methodological interest. In other studies, Forgas has also demonstrated how MDS can facilitate the classification of representations (Forgas 1976), as well as how results from MDS analyses can be used in the design and interpretion of experimental studies (Forgas 1985).

From the studies described, it can be seen that MDS is a suitable technique for exploring the structure of representations concerning diverse phenomena. Individual and group differences in the salience of these dimensions can be analysed and related to demographic and other relevant information. Results from an MDS analysis also provide a base from which to predict behavioural preferences and sociometric choices, and the outcome of social movements. Furthermore, although MDS is essentially a static model, it is possible to explore transformations in the structure of relationships and the salience of underlying dimensions within a representation.

Theory and method

Moscovici states that the 'study of social representations requires that we revert to methods of observation' for the purpose of providing a 'careful description of social representations, of their structure and their evolution in various fields' which will then 'enable us to understand them'. A 'valid explanation can only be derived from a comparative study of such descriptions' (1984, pp. 67–8). These statements would suggest that the primary aim of any research project must be to provide a description of the structure and content of the social representation and its historical evolution. In Moscovici's view, rather than relying on an experimental methodology, which is suitable only for studying simple phenomena that can be taken out of context, we should be using observational methods which provide comprehensive descriptions of social representations. Although MDS might not be categorized as an observational method, this is largely a reflection of the artificial distinction between quantitative and qualitative methods of research. Observational studies are frequently associated with qualitative methods, and although MDS may be regarded as a quantitative method, it similarly provides a model or description of a representation. It allows the quantification and interpretation of social representations which are naturally circulating in society without manipulating or constraining respondents' judgements. MDS is therefore able to provide a description of the structure and content of a social representation as well as demarcate differences between social groups and trace transformations occurring over time.

Any method of research which is used for investigating social representations must be consistent with the assumptions and underlying principles of the theory. It will be argued that MDS is such a method and, in conjunction with associated techniques, provides a quantitative means for studying social representations. The application of MDS will be discussed in relation to the nature of social reality and social representations; the nature and identification of groups; the dynamics of social representations and the process of anchoring; and, finally, the relationship between social representations, social perception, and social interaction.

The theory of social representations is concerned primarily with the complexity of our social environment and the social construction of reality.

Although MDS does not directly model the processes involved, its assumptions are consistent with these premises. First, social stimuli, whether persons, objects, or events, usually have a number of different attributes which are determined by their position in a system of relationships with other social objects. These relations constitute the meanings of the social objects. The quantification involved in MDS does not imply necessarily that the richness and diversity of people's representations must be lost. MDS allows a social representation to emerge from simple and relatively unconstrained tasks, mirroring the actual complexity of the social environment. Secondly, within the theory of social representations, the individual is seen as an active perceiver, constructing the social reality in which he or she thinks, acts, and communicates. Thus, subject and object, the perceiver and the perceived, are not reified into separate entities but are characterized by a dynamic interdependence. It is, therefore, necessary to explore the environment of thought and the structure of social reality in which people live.

Previously, much research in social psychology concerned with the discovery of attributes of social objects has relied on data-reduction techniques such as factor analysis. Such studies have only employed unidimensional ratings on scales suggested by a theory, interviews, or the investigator's interests. Moreover, the emergent factors are interpreted by the investigator without recourse to the respondents. The categories may therefore be constrained by the investigator's preconceptions and respondents' inability to describe the salient attributes, and contaminated by artefacts resulting from aggregation of data across respondents. In contrast to these more traditional quantitative techniques, MDS is consistent with the theoretical premises in that it elicits respondents' representations of a phenomenon without imposing artificial constraints on their responses. The judgement task used for MDS does not specify the attributes or dimensions on which the social objects are judged. This minimizes the likelihood of experimenter contamination and the danger that the emergent dimensions reflect the researcher's choices of attributes rather than the respondent's representational structure. This means that even if people are unaware of the basis on which they make their judgements, the MDS solution will reflect those attributes.

The theory also emphasizes the interdependence of the form and content of knowledge. In the past, social psychology has relied heavily on the information-processing paradigm. However, this paradigm not only fails to deal with the complexities of our social environment, but also focuses exclusively on the form of representations and the processes of change. In contrast, social-representations theory focuses on the symbolic nature of our social reality. The form of representations and the social-psychological processes by which they are generated and maintained cannot be separated from their content. Social representations have a specific content which differs from one domain to another, and from one society or sub-culture to another. Meaningful investigations of social-information processing cannot be carried out until the structure of representations within a given domain and a given social context has been delineated by previous empirical research. It is precisely the content and structure of relationships which MDS is designed to explore. In conjunction with associated techniques, it is one of the most suitable quantitative methods for the study of social representations. Other methods employed with some success are survey techniques and opinion polling. These elicit opinions and attitudes, in contrast to MDS, which elicits the evaluative criteria underlying a social representation. Thus, two divergent opinions may be based on the same criteria due to differential information and experience. Conversely, the same opinion may refer to different evaluative criteria. In order to reach an understanding of social interaction and group cohesion, it is necessary to explore the social representations that underlie opinions and attitudes.

The studies previously described showed how MDS provides a descriptive model of a variety of representations. Any domain of social objects and the structure of relations existing among them can be explored by using the objects as the stimuli, with resulting dimensions of the representation indicating the salient attributes by which the objects are differentiated and associated. Furthermore, the system of relationships reflects the meaning of each individual object and indicates the nature of peoples' relationship to that object. Associated techniques can be used to facilitate the interpretation of the dimensions. MDS can also be applied to more complex social phenomena, such as social identity and interpersonal relationships. This would involve representations of self and others within an intact group, where distances between self and others are assumed to reflect important information about interpersonal relationships. Representations of social episodes and social situations can also be explored in a similar manner.

Another aspect of the theory to which MDS can be usefully applied is the nature of groups. Social representations provide a consensual environment of thought in which members communicate and interact, and also serve to consolidate the group and provide an identity for the group members. This being the case, it is important to determine the degree to which representations are shared and the nature of consensus. MDS is well suited to dealing with this problem. Comparative studies on previously-identified groups will reveal any differences in the number and identity of dimensions, and hence the content and structure of their representations. MDS also provides an indication of the degree of consensus within a group by the goodness-of-fit measure between the group stimulus space and respondents' judgements. More significantly, perhaps, MDS can facilitate the identification of groups. By including subject parameters, the three-way MDS algorithms offer the opportunity to analyse individual differences in the representation of the group space. Using this information, it is possible to identify different groups of respondents having different salience patterns within the representational structure. This facility enables the investigator to explore the communalities and divergences in representations and their relationship to other group characteristics. For example, groups identified in this way can then be related to patterns of sociometric choices and social interaction. Such multimethodological studies would demonstrate the relationship between the structure of representations, social identity, and patterns of communication and social interaction. MDS thus reflects the social nature of representations with respect to the consensual nature of knowledge. More importantly, it provides a means by which the degree and nature of consensus can be explored. This is important, as it is only with respect to the consensual nature of knowledge that social representations can provide an environment of thought which fulfils their group functions and maintains their conventional nature.

Another important aspect of the theory is the dynamic nature of social representations: they are continually evolving and transforming in relation to the social interactions and social environment by which they are generated and which, in turn, they support. By repeating an MDS analysis on different occasions, changes in both the relationships among the social objects and the salience of the dimensions can be discovered. These transformations may reflect changes in the social interactions and structuring of the group. Alternatively, they may be due to confrontations with new objects and events or a person (or group of people) with a different representation of the phenomenon concerned.

Furthermore, although MDS provides a descriptive structural model of a social representation, the results from an MDS analysis can give some insight into the processes involved in the generation of social representations. This is consistent with the thesis that content and process cannot be distinguished. First, MDS may provide some insight into the process of anchoring, by which new objects enter into a social representation. Unfamiliar objects are classified by comparing them to prototypes. MDS can be used to determine the dimensions underlying the structure of relations among prototypical instances. These will then constitute the criteria by which the unfamiliar object is perceived, evaluated, and conceptualized. Secondly, it has already been seen that results from MDS analyses provide descriptions of the social representations which shape our perceptions and understanding. People construct their social realities through the processes of social interaction and communication. The emergent social representations constitute the social environment in which we communicate and interact, and which determines our perceptions and conceptions and directs our actions. This being the case, a knowledge of the structure and content of the emergent social representations should provide important insights into the social and cognitive processes involved, even though the processes themselves are not being directly modelled. MDS results may thus provide a basis from which to form hypotheses and make predictions concerning sociometric choices, interpersonal communication and social interaction. They may also be intergrated with studies of the actual processes involved in the generation of social representations and of their functions in social life.

In conclusion, MDS can directly contribute to an understanding of social representations: its assumptions are consistent with the premises of the theory; it offers a way of exploring their content and structure; the results from MDS analyses may suggest novel interpretations of complementary studies; and it can also suggest further research.

Complementary research methods

Social representations have been investigated using a range of methodological techniques. In our view, MDS is among those techniques which have the potential to make a significant contribution to a thorough exploration and understanding of this phenomenon. However, we would also argue that the various methods which can be employed should not be seen as mutually exclusive, but rather as complementary approaches to the study of social representations.

The most obvious distinction between the majority of observational methods used in the field studies and MDS is that while the former are largely qualitative, the latter is a quantitative method of research. However, as Fielding and Fielding (1986) argue, these approaches can be interrelated to illuminate substantive problems and research issues. Qualitative methods are often characterized as 'soft, subjective, and speculative' whereas quantitative methods are 'hard, objective, and rigorous'. However, qualitative methods involve a detailed and comprehensive collection of data followed by the accurate analysis of the phenomena within a theoretical context. On the opposite side of the coin, quantitative methods rely on the researcher's judgements in the selection of procedures with regard to the assumptions underlying the analytic techniques and the selective presentation and interpretation of results. A combination of qualitative and quantitative approaches offers the opportunity to counter criticisms on both sides and also to include, rather than ignore, the research process itself. Both forms of research involve issues of design, data collection, and analysis and it is dysfunctional to consider these methods as dichotomous. Furthermore, a set of methods is not inherently linked to a particular paradigm, and the characteristics of a specific research problem and setting are equally as important as the paradigm itself in selecting and combining methods of research.

A further consideration which supports the case for multimethod research is that any single method of research used to describe or represent complex social phenomena encompasses associated limitations, fallibilities, weaknesses, and biases. This points to the advantages of multimethod research designs in two respects. First, the use of multiple data sources and complementary methods offers the opportunity to validate findings through the process of triangulation in which results are systematically compared (Fielding and Fielding 1986). Secondly, certain information can be gained only by specific techniques; methods are, in some respects, particular to specific research problems. This being the case, qualitative and quantitative techniques can be modified in order to form a set of interlocking methods which guide and direct complementary research, as well as facilitate interpretation of results. In this way, it is possible to increase awareness of, and overcome, the problems and limitations associated with any one particular method or data source. Also, the integration of results from a variety of data sources and methods provides a more comprehensive picture of the field, while simultaneously substantiating any practical or theoretical claims.

The majority of field studies concerned directly with the exploration of social representations have employed a variety of complementary methods in order to observe and describe the features of a particular social representation. In the detailed example that follows, MDS was used in conjunction with two complementary techniques, cluster analysis and content analysis, to investigate the content and structure of the social representation of mental illness. Regression analysis was also employed as a property-fitting technique to facilitate the interpretation of the dimensions which emerge in the MDS solution. (This procedure is described more fully in the example itself.)

Cluster analysis is often used in conjunction with MDS. Like MDS, it is a technique which provides a descriptive model of social objects based on measures of similarity. However, it gives a basic description of the objects in terms of their groupings rather than their dimensional structure. In this study, a hierarchical agglomerative technique was used. Starting with each stimulus object being treated as a single member cluster, the stimuli are grouped or clustered at increasing levels of inclusion. The number of groups which best describe the data set may be assessed from the variations in inclusion levels. A large difference between adjacent inclusion levels indicates the level at which groupings should be determined. In this way, the natural groupings of stimulus objects may be established.

Although MDS and cluster analysis may be considered to be in competition with each other, they are more frequently considered to be complementary methods for analysing similarity data. MDS provides an *n*-dimensional spatial representation for proximities which appear to extract information about large dissimilarities between stimulus objects, such that the general configuration and dimensions of the representation are meaningful, whereas the local features may not be meaningful and may vary. Cluster analysis, on the other hand, is categorical and appears to extract meaning from the small dissimilarities forming meaningful groupings or clusters of stimulus objects at lower inclusion levels, whereas larger clusters do not seem meaningful (Kruskal 1977). Also, the two techniques are different in that cluster analysis is designed to uncover any categorical structure in the data while MDS assumes a dimensional data structure. The application of both techniques enables a decision to be made as to which representation is more appropriate, and permits the identification of dimensions within categorical groupings.

Content analysis is a method which allows valid inferences to be made from qualitative data consisting of written or verbal material. One major difficulty of content analysis is that the richness of detail inherent in text precludes analysis without some form of data reduction. Weber (1985) emphasizes the use of both qualitative and quantitative operations depending on the requirements of the particular study. Also, much attention has recently been given to the reliability and validity of content analysis (Krippendorf 1980; Weber 1985). In the brief history of social-representations research, content analysis has been a popular method for the exploration of social representations elicited during interviews or present in the media. It is important that any newly-proposed methodology should be compared to that which has been the generally-accepted method of research. Dimensions of the social representations of mental illness which emerge from the MDS analysis should be convergent with the salient attributes emerging from the content analysis. All three methods, as used in this study, are directly concerned with exploring the content and structure of a social representation.

The social representation of mental disorders

MDS and cluster analysis were employed to identify the domain and explore the structure of the social representation of mental disorders within a sample of students. Associated techniques also allowed the dimensions of the social representation to be determined. The MDS analysis will be presented in some detail, and then a brief comparison of the MDS results with those from the cluster analysis will be given. These are then compared to a content analysis of written descriptions of the individual mental disorders. In order to give a comprehensive presentation of the MDS, the procedure is divided into three sections: the stimulus selection; the construction of the spatial representation; and the interpretation of the dimensions.

Stimulus selection

Stimulus selection forms a vital part of the procedure because the range of stimuli presented affect the conceptual dimensions which emerge within the spatial representation. The stimulus set should be representative of the domain and avoid extreme contrasts or categorizations that override more subtle distinctions among the various stimuli. Furthermore, the stimuli should be reasonably familiar to most subjects.

The initial stimulus set (Table 13.1a) was acquired from lists of mental problems given by 25 subjects and the diagnostic system (DSM II). The initial stimulus set was piloted using MDS analysis. It is sufficient at this stage to know that this resulted in a three-dimensional representation of the stimulus domain (Fig. 13.1).

Looking at the first and second dimensions, it can be seen that the stimulus set contains a categorization on the first dimension with senile dementia, autism, and asthma being isolated from the remainder of the stimulus

Table 13.1 Multidimensional scaling task

(a) Initial stimulus set	(b) Final stimulus set
Schizophrenia	Schizophrenia
Depression	Depression
Agoraphobia	Agoraphobia
Obsessive–compulsive Behaviour	Obsessive–compulsive Behaviour
Alcoholism	Alcholism
Paranoia	Paranoia
Hysteria	Hysteria
Psychopathy	Psychopathy
Senile dementia	Kleptomania
Anxiety	Anxiety
Autism	Multiple Personality
Asthma	Paedophilia

(c) Unidimensional scale

Often makes the news	Seldom makes the news
Has a psychological cause	Does not have a psychological cause
Has an environmental cause	Does not have an environmental cause
Has a genetic cause	Does not have a genetic cause
Affects thinking/reasoning	Does not affect thinking/reasoning
Produces emotional problems	Does not produce emotional problems
Produces behavioural problems	Does not produce behavioural problems
Is extremely disabling	Is not extremely disabling
Is a common mental disorder	Is an uncommon mental disorder
Sufferer is aware of illness	sufferer is unaware of illness
Sufferer is dangerous to self/others	Sufferer is not dangerous to self/others
Effective treatment exists	Effective treatment does not exist
Treatable in the community	Treatable only in special environment
I know something about this	I know nothing about this
Lay-people can cope with sufferers	Lay-people cannot cope with sufferers

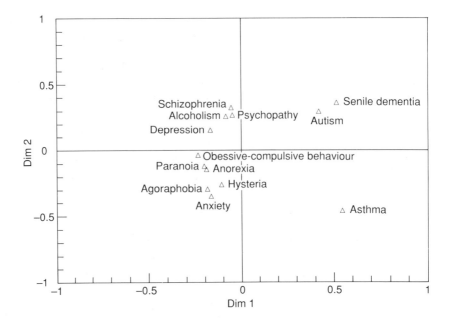

Fig. 13.1. Three-dimensional SINDSCAL plot

objects. Rather than being represented on a continuous dimension, the stimulus set forms two distinct groups. The extreme contrast between these groups overrides more subtle differences in the main body of the stimulus set. It is essential that such a categorization is avoided, as it indicates that there are two domains or social representations present in the stimulus set. These may differ in terms of the number and identity of their underlying dimensions, and therefore must be dealt with separately. In this way, MDS can be used to facilitate identification of the content of a given social representation.

A cluster analysis could have been carried out, but this was considered unnecessary as the categorization is clear from the MDS solution. The three alien stimuli were replaced with three new disorders, kleptomania, paedophilia, and multiple personality. This was piloted a second time using MDS, which provided a fairly even distribution of the stimulus items in the spatial representation. The final stimulus set is shown in Table 13.1b.

MDS analysis: the spatial representation

Having selected the stimulus set, the MDS analysis can be carried out. The first stage is to determine the spatial representation of the structure of relations among the stimuli. The data for this procedure consists of a matrix of proximities which are measures of similarity or dissimilarity, depending on whether the highest scores correspond to pairs which are most or least alike. A distinction can be made between direct and derived similarity measures, where the former consist of direct judgements of similarity between stimulus pairs and the latter are derived from correlational data or covariances, for example from a multiple free-sort of the stimuli or a free-association task. Direct judgements of similarity are least open to experimenter contamination and are most likely to contain the relevant structure. In this case, direct judgements of similarity were made for all pairwise combinations of the 13 stimuli. Subjects responded on a nine-point scale with poles very similar and very dissimilar. The SINDSCAL programme was then run using the data from the similarity judgements. The stimuli are represented by random points on a spatial map. The coordinates of these points are then adjusted using an iterative procedure. Those stimulus objects which are considered to be similar to each other are represented by points close together, whereas those stimulus objects which are considered to be dissimilar are represented by points further apart in the spatial map.

The optimum number of dimensions can be determined on the grounds of statistical goodness-of-fit. For SINDSCAL, goodness-of-fit between distances in the solution space and the corresponding similarities data is expressed in terms of variance accounted for (VAF). As the solution improves, it accounts for more variance in the similarities matrix. A marked reduction or elbow in the VAF with increasing dimensionality gives some indication of the optimum number of dimensions. It is also necessary to ensure that a stable, global solution is reached, as opposed to a local minimum. Using these statistical criteria, two dimensions provided the most suitable spatial representation of the similarities matrix (Fig. 13.2). This accounted for 44 per cent of the variance in the similarities matrix. The first dimension accounts for 32 per cent of the variance and the second dimension accounts for a further 12 per cent. As can be seen, the two-dimensional solution gives an even distribution of the stimuli throughout the stimulus space. On the first dimension, psychopathy, multiple personality, and schizophrenia lie towards the positive pole and anorexia, agoraphobia, depression, and anxiety towards the negative pole. On the second dimension, there are schizophrenia, paranoia, and hysteria towards the positive pole and paedophilia and kleptomania at the opposite pole.

MDS analysis: interpretation of dimensions

Having obtained the MDS solution, we now have the problem of interpreting the dimensions. The interpretability of the solution is also an important consideration in determining the number of dimensions that provides the most suitable description of the similarities matrix. Usually, a solution with

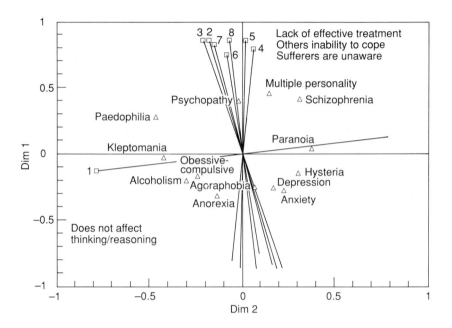

Fig. 13.2. Two-dimensional SINDSCAL plot

two or three dimensions is selected, as these can be more easily interpreted and visualized, although four or more dimensions are sometimes necessary. The dimensions can be identified by examining the spatial configuration in the light of what is already known about the stimulus objects. However, the interpretation of the dimensions can be assisted by employing multiple linear regression on quantitative data from unidimensional rating scales. If the coordinates of the dimensions correspond to locations along the stimulus attributes, then it would be expected that a high correlation would be obtained by regressing an independent measure of the attribute on to the stimulus coordinates. This involves obtaining judgements or ratings of the stimuli on a number of unidimensional scales. In an ideal world, it would be possible to use a large number of scales covering a wide range of potentially salient dimensions. However, the fact that each stimulus is rated on all the unidimensional scales means that the total number of judgements required rapidly increases as the number of stimuli and scales increases. For this reason, it is necessary to limit the number of unidimensional scales employed. The 15 scales used in the study are listed in Table 13.1c. These reflect both constructs which emerged from conversations with the sample population, and theoretical conceptions of mental disorders. Subjects are asked to judge each stimulus on the series of seven-point scales, presented in random order. These judgements provide independent measures on the attributes of the stimulus set.

The mean ratings are calculated from the unidimensional judgements data. The dimensions from the MDS solution are then used as predictors of the scales. The multiple correlation obtained by regressing the independent measures on to the MDS stimulus coordinates indicates the importance of the attributes when making the similarity judgements. Multiple linear regression is employed to locate a vector corresponding to each unidimensional scale in the stimulus space of the MDS solution. In this way, it can be seen if the spatial configuration can predict the scale ratings.

The multiple correlation indexes the goodness-of-fit to the solution. If the resultant vectors have a high multiple correlation with the solution dimensions and a high simple correlation or regression weight on only one of the dimensions, then the attribute measured by that unidimensional scale should provide a satisfactory interpretation of that dimension. These vectors should lie close to the dimensions when plotted on the MDS solution. For example, if we take the unidimensional rating scale 'effective treatment does or does not exist', it has a multiple correlation of 0.863 with the MDS solution. The regression weightings are taken from the standardized beta weights which are used as direction cosines or coordinates for plotting the vector. In this case, beta on dimension I is 0.862 and on dimension II is 0.011 . This gives a vector that lies very close to the first dimension. Six other rating scales were found to have multiple correlations above 0.756 with a high regression weight on the first dimension. These vectors were found to be highly correlated and a number of rational combinations were made. The unidimensional rating scales are combined with equal weighting, and the mean ratings on these composite scales are used as the dependent variables for the multiple regression analysis. Dimension I can thus be identified from the rating scales as effectiveness of treatment/others' ability to cope/sufferers' awareness of their illness.

Does this analysis provide an adequate interpretation of the stimulus space on the first dimension? If we look at the solution, psychopathy, multiple personality, and schizophrenia all lie towards the positive pole of dimension I. This would imply that these mental disorders are perceived as lacking effective treatment, that sufferers are not aware of their illness, and that lay-people cannot cope with sufferers. At the negative pole of dimension I, the stimulus objects include anorexia, agoraphobia, depression, and anxiety. These are considered to have the opposite attributes: that is, they can be effectively treated, sufferers are aware of their illness, and lay-people can cope with sufferers. The second dimension presents more of a problem. Only one of the unidimensional rating scales had a relatively high regression weight on this dimension. This was the degree to which thinking and reasoning were affected by the mental disorder. However, the vector for this scale lies at a considerable distance from the MDS dimension. By examining the MDS solution and the positions of the stimulus objects on the second dimension, a number of other interpretations are possible. These include the sufferer's ability to lead a normal life, the lay-person's ability to identify the sufferer as mentally disturbed, and the generality or specificity of the mental disorder's effects on the sufferer. These attributes were tested by obtaining subjects' ratings of the stimulus objects on the unidimensional scales and using multiple regression (as above). However, this failed to produce vectors lying close to the second MDS dimension. Thus, the interpretation of this dimension still remains problematic, the best option being the degree to which thinking and reasoning are affected by the mental disorder. This would imply that kleptomania and paedophilia are not considered to affect thinking and reasoning whereas schizophrenia, paranoia, and hysteria do affect thinking and reasoning.

At this point, it would have been possible to explore individual differences in the salience of the two dimensions. For example, if the subject group had included those who were familiar and those who were unfamiliar with mentally-disturbed people, it is possible that the two dimensions would have different saliences for the two groups. However, this facility was not used in this study as there was no information, either demographic or otherwise, on which such an analysis could be based.

Thus, in this example it was found that mental disorders are spatially represented in two continuous dimensions. The attributes which are most important in people's social representation of mental disorders are those relating to the first dimension. These are concerned with the effectiveness and means of treatment, the sufferers' awareness of then illness and lay-people's ability to cope with sufferers. Also important in the social representation of mental disorders is the degree to which the mental disorder affects thinking and reasoning.

Cluster analysis

A cluster analysis was carried out on three sets of data: the similarity judgements, the stimuli coordinates, and a similarities matrix compiled from a free-sort task of the stimulus set. The dendrogram here (Fig. 13.3) shows the cluster analysis of the free sort. From the inclusion levels, one can distinguish four clusters. If these are superimposed on to the MDS solution, it is clear that there is not a categorization on either of the dimensions. However, it is possible to explore the clusters that are present in terms of the MDS solution. For example, the cluster containing paranoia, hysteria, anxiety, and depression can be characterized as disorders which affect the sufferer's ability to think and reason but for which effective treatment does exist. The other data sets gave similar results. These results show that the techniques of cluster analysis and MDS are convergent and can be integrated effectively for the exploration of social representations. Their validity is supported by the convergence of results using both different techniques and different data sets. Together, they facilitated the identification of the content of the social representation. Furthermore, they allow the structure of relations among the stimulus objects to be identified as either categorical or dimensional.

Content analysis

Subjects were asked to write a brief description of seven mental disorders from the stimulus set. These lie at the poles of the first MDS dimension. A coding frame was designed solely on the basis of the written material, using words or phrases with symbolic meaning as the units of analysis. The coding frame was used to analyse the frequency of descriptions and attributes given by the same group of subjects. Without going into too much detail, it can be seen that the content analysis of the written descriptions presents a social representation of mental disorders divergent to that given by the MDS. The major categories that emerge from the content analysis are disorder labels, affective symptoms, thought and perception symptoms, consequences of the disorder, behavioural symptoms, causes, states, descriptive terms, disabilities, treatment, and characteristics of the sufferers. Table 13.2 shows the frequency and percentage of the total number of meaningful units that were given for each category.

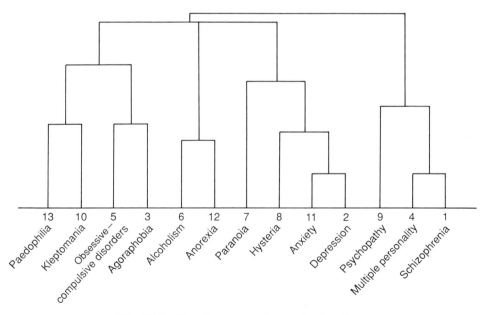

Fig. 13.3. Dendrogram of sorted stimuli

Table 13.2   Content analysis: frequencies and percentage for the major categories

Category	Frequency	Percentage
Categorization	76	21.0
Affective symptoms	48	13.3
Thought/perception/symptoms	40	11.0
Consequences	35	9.7
Behavioural symptoms	32	8.8
Causes	30	8.3
States	30	8.3
Descriptors	23	6.4
Disabilities	21	5.8
Treatment	14	3.8
Character	13	3.6

It can be seen that these results do not converge with the MDS results. The attributes which identify the first dimension of the MDS do not emerge from the content analysis as salient aspects of the social representation. References to treatment are rarely made, either in terms of its effectiveness or styles of treatment available. Nor are there references to others' ability to cope with sufferers. Also, by examining the descriptions of each of the mental disorders, there is no clear distinction to be found between those mental disorders at the positive pole (schizophrenia, multiple personality, and psychopathy) and those at the negative pole of the first dimension (anorexia, depression, anxiety, and agoraphobia). Furthermore, in the written descriptions there were numerous references to observable symptoms, with almost half the total coded responses being disorders in affect, thought, perception, and behaviour. However, symptoms were only of secondary importance in the MDS solution and were restricted to disorders in thinking and reasoning.

Implications

There are a number of possible explanations for the divergent results from the MDS and the content analysis. First, it is possible that multidimensional scaling is not a suitable method for exploring social representations as the results fail to converge with the content analysis. However, the arguments which have been put forward and the previous examples of MDS research given in this chapter suggest that a simple dismissal of MDS is neither warranted nor profitable. Another possibility is that actual results from the MDS are inaccurate. However, this seems unlikely, as the results from the cluster analysis are convergent with the MDS. A third possibility is that the content analysis is invalid. However, great care was taken in the design and application of the coding frame which provides at least some degree of formal analysis. A different explanation of the divergence between results from the MDS and content analysis is that these methods elicit responses which emphasize different elements of the social representation. This has both theoretical and practical implications.

First, the divergence of results may be associated with the nature of the task involved. It is apparent that different attributes of the social representation are salient for the two procedures. The MDS is concerned primarily with relations among stimuli, whereas mental disorders were considered individually and implicitly in relation to normality for the content analysis. It is possible that, by asking respondents to compare and contrast the different mental disorders, or to give a description of mental disorders in general, the salient attributes to emerge from the content analysis and the MDS would not have diverged. These practical considerations, highlighted by the use of multiple methods on a single object of study, raise important theoretical issues. At present there is little theoretical guidance for the selection of social representations which can be studied. Put simply, at what level does a social representation exist and where are its boundaries? In the French research, there has been a tendency to assume a global level, for example 'mental illness', but it is equally feasible to have a social representation of a cluster of mental disorders, or even a single mental disorder such as schizophrenia.

This raises the further question of the relationship between social representations and categories. Moscovici (1984) suggests that in the process of anchoring the unfamiliar object is compared and readjusted to fit the paradigm of a suitable category. This suggests that we have a social representation of a category. The attributes of this representation can be explored in two ways. In the first place, contrasting category A with categories X, Y, and Z will elicit the attributes which distinguish category A from the other categories. (These we may call the comparative attributes.) In the second place, attributes which distinguish individual members or groups of members within category A can be explored. (These might be termed the internal attributes.) Both the comparative and internal attributes of category A should be considered to be aspects of the social representation. The combination of MDS techniques and cluster analysis are well suited to the empirical investigation of this issue. However, this does not altogether overcome the theoretical problem of determining the boundaries of social representations. We suggest that, rather than conceptualizing social representations as discrete entities, it is necessary to consider a system of overlapping hierarchies. The researcher, then, is responsible for selecting the level of social representations to be studied, either on theoretical or empirical grounds which need to be made explicit. As yet, there has been little theoretical or practical work done to determine the levels and boundaries of social representations and the relationships which exist between them.

Secondly, the social context in which the research is carried out may influence the salience of attributes for the respondents. In this study the tasks were performed individually by students in a test-like situation within an academic institution. It may well be that the social significance of a target object and the salience of the attributes may vary with the social situation in which it is illicited. If this is the case, in accordance with McGuire's contextualist approach (1983), it would be necessary to describe when the social representation is likely to be socially significant.

A related issue concerns the different forms of analysis involved in MDS and content analysis. MDS extracts underlying dimensions from the structure of relations among objects in the social representation, whereas the content analysis relies on frequencies of mentions in order to determine the salient attributes. This raises the methodological issue of how to determine the salient aspects of a social representation.

What these points attempt to indicate is that divergence between social representations elicited using different methods of research and in different social contexts are just as informative as convergent results. The divergencies may well provide insight into the social function of the dimensions of representations in relation to the nature of the task and the social situation. As Breakwell (1987) points out, we progress as much through negation and conflict as through convergence and consensus. This applies equally well to comparative studies between groups and historical eras as to comparing different methods of research. Furthermore, such an approach is able to include the research process itself in the exploration of social representations.

Problems and limitations

In the previous sections it has been shown that MDS can be usefully applied to the theory of social representations. However, it is essential that this is accompanied by an understanding of the problems and limitations associated with MDS. These considerations are important, as all too frequently the use of sophisticated statistical techniques has provided a false sense of security; this can lead to a lack of theoretical development and ultimately to the stagnation of research. The issues addressed in this section focus on the problems associated with MDS itself and the limitations of its application. The problems are largely methodological considerations, for example, issues concerning the sampling of social representations and the selection of respondents who possess them. The limitations are primarily theoretical, relating to some of the social and dynamic aspects of the theory.

Methodological problems

MDS is a computerized statistical technique and, as such, will process any proximity matrix which is entered as the data. This being the case, it is vital that the domain of the social representation is selected by the investigator with care. It has already been shown that, with the aid of cluster analysis, it is possible to distinguish between categorical and dimensional structures. It has also been emphasized that the selection of stimulus objects is a vital part of the procedure. It is essential that the social objects which are investigated are socially significant, to ensure that the emergent structure of relationships actually models a social representation, rather than creating a spurious representation. This can be achieved either by pilot work, for example an analysis of interviews or group discussions, or on the basis of theoretical concerns. Thus, the selection of the social representation and the boundaries of its domain are important facets of MDS which should not be overlooked.

A similar potential problem with MDS is the selection of respondents. A random sample of respondents would not be suitable, as this would ignore the cultural specificity of social representations. However, the selection of a specific group as respondents limits the possibility of exploring the relationship between the social representation and the social identity and interactions of that group. We would suggest that representative samples of socially-significant groupings should be used. Again, this can be determined on practical or theoretical grounds. For example, aggregate groups with the same social status but from different social contexts, or structural groups with different social status who directly interact and communicate with each other, could constitute the respondent pool. This would give the opportunity to explore the degree and nature of consensus and its relation to the individual's specific set of social interactions and communications.

Theoretical limitations

Although it has been argued throughout this chapter that MDS is a suitable technique for exploring social representations, it should be realized that its application is limited to certain aspects of the theory. It should also be realized that it is not exclusively applicable to this theory, as is true of most methods which have been used to study social representations. The limitations are most clearly indicated by considering the social nature of representations: they are social in that they are conventional and consensual, being shared by a community or group of people. It has been shown that MDS can be usefully applied to explore the nature and degree of this consensus. However, social representations are also social in a number of other respects which are not directly addressed by MDS.

First, MDS explores the products of social construction and has little to say concerning the active nature of social construction itself. Thus, although MDS provides important information concerning the content and structure of social representations, it is not able to provide a thorough understanding of the active processes of communication and social interaction by which they are generated. Secondly, social representations are social in function. Although three-way MDS analyses facilitate the identification of groups and the corresponding salient dimensions of the representation, they are not able to explore further the function of social representations in maintaining group cohesion. This is also true when considering social identity. MDS may identify the salient dimensions of interpersonal interactions and social identity, but in itself does not provide an analysis of how the representations constrain and direct actions. Thirdly, the symbolic nature of meaning and language and the social significance of objects and events in our social environment is not directly addressed by MDS. It is for this reason that the selection of social representations and relevant stimulus objects must be done with care. It is only if this is taken into consideration that the cultural and conventional aspects of social representations are reflected in the results. Finally, although MDS can be used in longtitudinal studies to trace transformations in the content and structure of representations, it can only provide a static model which gives a limited view of issues relating to the dynamics of social representations. Comparative MDS analyses may be used to explore discontinuities across society and across time, but in and of themselves these analyses do not address the continuity of social interactions which give rise to their transformation.

In general, then, the application of MDS within the theory of social representations is to some degree limited with respect to the active and dynamic nature of social representations and also with respect to their cultural dimension. However, it should be remembered that these limitations also apply to other methods which have been frequently used to investigate social representations. This is particularly true of content analysis, which has been the preferred method of research.

Complementary methods of research revisited

The problems and limitations associated with MDS highlight the necessity of employing complementary methods in the investigation of social representations. This applies not only to MDS, but also to most methods of investigation. It is therefore worth taking another look at the issue of multi-method research.

The use of complementary methods has already been discussed in respect to the methodological problems associated with MDS. These problems can be largely overcome by employing such methods as interviewing, free-association, content analysis, and cluster analysis. The theoretical limitations present more of a problem and require more substantial solutions. The limitations are concerned primarily with the social construction and social function of representations. By combining results from MDS analyses with those from qualitative observation methods, it would be possible to examine the relationship between the content and structure of social representations and the processes of social construction from which they emerge, and by which the social functions are sustained. Methods would include those that have already been used to study social representations, such as participant observation, ethnomethodology, interviewing, and content analysis. MDS analyses could be used to clarify and verify results from these studies, and may also serve as a guide to the design and focus of qualitative studies and interpretation of their results. Such a multimethod approach is advantageous over an ideological adherence to a predetermined line of methodological enquiry.

A comprehensive investigation of social representations would thus not only describe the content, structure, and evolution of social representations, but also the social dynamics by which they evolve and function as well as describing their relationship with groups and social identity. This requires a programme of research which integrates a number of complementary methods. With this in mind, it would be dysfunctional to ignore the quantitative and statistical methods which are available to us. Social-representations theory is, in part, a reaction against reductionism, oversimplification, and an individualistic social psychology. With the focus on the social, cultural, and historical factors there has been a simultaneous reaction against the notion of measurement and consequently the use of statistical analysis. However, with the development of complex mathematical models, there has been a relaxation of constraints on the psychological issues addressed and the design limitations imposed by the statistical analyses. once it is accepted that the distinction between quantitative and qualitative methods is an artifical one, both can be seen to provide an effective means for exploring social representations. We are not suggesting that mathematical representations can fully express the symbolic meaning of our social reality but, just as quantification is an important component of content analysis, they can provide a useful guide to the complexities of our social reality. Such approaches can be effectively combined with the more 'traditional' methods in the investigation of social representations.

In our view, the empirical analysis of the phenomenon of social representations requires a multimethod approach in order to provide an understanding of the interrelationships between the different aspects of the theory. This involves the adoption and integration of methods which explore the content and structure of representations, their generation and evolution, their function in relation to the continuity and stability of our social environment, the formation of groups, and social identity and socialization, as well as the processes involved in communication and social interaction.

References

Abric, J.C. (1984). A theoretical and experimental approach to the study of social representations in a situation of interaction. In *Social representations*, (ed. R.M. Farr and S. Moscovici), pp. 169–84. Cambridge University Press.

Breakwell, G. (1987). Widespread beliefs: some methodological problems. Unpublished paper presented at ESRC—Empirical Approaches to Social Representations Workshop, Surrey University.

Chombart de Lauwe, M.-J. (1984). Changes in the representation of the child in the course of social transmission. In *Social representations*, (ed. R.M. Farr and S. Moscovici), pp. 185–210. Cambridge University Press.

Codol, J.P. (1984). On the system of representations in an artificial social situation. In *Social representations*, (ed. R.M. Farr and S. Moscovici), pp. 239–54. Cambridge University Press.

Davison, M.L. (1983). Introduction to multidimensional scaling and its applications. *Applied Psychological Measurement*, 7, 373–9.

Di Giacomo, J.P. (1980). Intergroup alliances and rejections within a protest movement. *European Journal of Social Psychology*, 10, 329–44.

Duveen, G. and Lloyd, B. (1986). The significance of social identities. *British Journal of Social Psychology*, 25, 219–30.

Duveen, G. and Lloyd, B. (1987). On gender as a social representation. Unpublished paper presented at Annual BPS Conference, University of Sussex.

Emler, N. and Dickenson, J. (1985). Children's representation of economic inequalities: the effects of social class. *British Journal of Developmental Psychology*, 3, 191–8.

Farr, R.M. and Moscovici, S. (1984). *Social representations*. Cambridge University Press.

Fielding, N.G. and Fielding, J.L. (1986). *Linking data: the articulation of qualitative and quantitative methods in Social Research*. Sage, London.

Flament, C. (1984). From the bias of structural balance to the representation of the group. In *Social representations*, (ed. R.M. Farr and S. Moscovici), pp. 269–85. Cambridge University Press.

Forgas, J.P. (1976). The perception of social episodes: categorical and dimensional representations in two different social milieus. *Journal of Personality and Social Psychology*, 33, 199–209.

Forgas, J.P. (1985). Person prototypes and cultural salience: the role of cognitive and cultural factors in impression formation. *British Journal of Social Psychology*, 24, 3–17.

Herzlich, C. (1973). *Health and illness: a social psychological analysis*. Academic Press, London.

Jodelet, D. (1983). Civils et bredins: representation de la maladie mentale et rapport en la folie en milieu rural. Unpublished PhD thesis, EHESS, Paris.

Jodelet, D. (1984). The representations of the body and its transformations. In *Social representations*, (ed. R.M. Farr and S. Moscovici), pp. 211–38. Cambridge University Press.

Jodelet, D. and Moscovici, S. (1975). *La représentation sociale du corps*. Laboratoire de psychologie sociale, Ecole des Hautes Etudes en Sciences Sociales, Paris.

Jones, L. E. and Young, F. W. (1972). Structure of a social environment: longitudinal individual differences scaling of an intact group. *Journal of Personality and Social Psychology*, **24**, 108–21.

Krippendorf, K. (1980). *Content analysis: an introduction to its methodology*. Sage, London.

Kruskal, J. (1977). The relationship between multidimensional scaling and clustering. In *Classification and clustering*, (ed. Van Ryzin), pp. 17–44. Academic Press, New York.

Kruskal, J. B. and Wish, M. (1978). *Multidimensional scaling: quantitative applications in the social sciences*. Sage, London.

Lloyd, B. and Smith, C. (1985). The social representation of gender and young children's play. *British Journal of Developmental Psychology*, **3**, 65–73.

McGuire, W. (1983). A contextualist theory of knowledge: its implications for innovations and reform in psychological research. In *Advances in experimental social psychology*, **16** (ed. L. Berkowitz). Academic Press, New York.

Moscovici, S. (1961). *La psychoanalyse, son image et son public*. Presses Universitaires de France, Paris.

Moscovici, S. (1973). Foreword to C. Herzlich, *Health and illness: a social psychological analysis*. Academic Press, London.

Moscovici, S. (1982). The coming era of social representations. In *Cognitive analysis of social behaviour*, (ed. J. P. Codol and T. P. Leyens), pp. 115–50. Martinus Nijhoff, The Hague.

Moscovici, S. (1984). The phenomenon of social representations. In *Social representation*, (ed. R. M. Farr and S. Moscovici), pp. 3–72. Cambridge University Press.

Moscovici, S. and Hewstone, M. (1983). Social representations and social explanations: from the 'naive' to the 'amateur' scientist. In *Attribution theory: social and functional extensions*, (ed. M. Hewstone), pp. 98–125. Blackwell, Oxford.

Nygren, T. E. and Jones, L. E. (1977). Individual differences in perception and preferences for political candidates. *Journal of Experimental Social Psychology*, **13**, 182–97.

Schiffmann, S. S., Reynolds, M. L., and Young, F. W. (1981). *Introduction to multidimensional scaling. Theory, methods and application*. Academic Press, London.

Stockdale, J. (1985). *What is Leisure? An empirical analysis of the concept of leisure and the role of leisure in peoples' lives*. The Sports Council and ESRC.

Weber, R. P. (1985). *Basic content analysis*. Sage, London.

14 The meaning of work for young people: the role of parents in the transmission of a social representation

Lucia Mannetti and Giancarlo Tanucci

In this chapter, we shall present some results of our current research programme on the social representation of work among young Italians still at school. The topic of our study — work — has been addressed directly or indirectly by at least two traditions of psychological research, first in the context of vocational choice and guidance (see, for example, Abramson *et al*. 1979; Holland 1973; Super 1957) and more recently in studies on the development of economic concepts (for example Berti and Bombi 1988; Jahoda 1979; Stacey 1978, 1982). The perspective of our research, however, is different from both of these traditions.

To address the domain of work within the framework of social representations implies a view of the individual's relationship with work as socially and historically bound, depending upon the ways in which the meaning of work is 'constructed' and 'reconstructed' in any given socio-cultural context. There have already been some studies of work within the social representation perspective (for example, De Polo and Sarchielli 1983; Ripon 1984), but even when these studies have focused on the transformations of this representation (such as addressing changes due to periods of professional training or occurring unemployment), they have never considered the development of the representation during childhood and adolescence.

On the other hand, most of the studies addressing the development of economic concepts during childhood (for example, Berti and Bombi 1988; Jahoda 1979; Stacey 1978, 1982), have been concerned with assessing whether or not there exists a developmental sequence in this domain comparable to the sequence described by Piaget with reference to physical reality. In order to pursue this aim, these researchers have focused on discovering when and how children acquire the adult comprehension of the economical concepts. On the contrary, our principal aim has been to describe the transformation of meanings given to work without, obviously, taking any particular 'correct' meaning as a reference point. Therefore, we have focused on the content rather than on the formal structure of children's knowledge assuming a perspective which is very much like that proposed by Emler (1987) with reference to socio-moral development.

It might even be said that our interest in work was — and is — a secondary one, the primary one being that of addressing empirically the issue of how broad-meaning frameworks are 'reconstructed' by young people. In this perspective, we focused our attention on the role played by parents in the transmission of representation of work.

In the relatively short tradition of empirical research on social representation, quite different views have already emerged about the methodological procedures to be used in addressing central aspects of the representation itself. One of the major points of disagreement appears to have been that of assessing the extent to which a representation is shared within a given group.

The relationship between groups and representations, which is central to the theory of social representations (Moscovici 1983), has been addressed in some empirical studies (Di Giacomo 1980; Hewstone et al. 1982). These studies, though, have been criticized for adopting analytical procedures, which take the intra-group consensus for granted (Potter and Litton 1985). One of the reasons for writing this chapter on research that is still on-going was that we thought it might be of some interest to present the application of an analytical procedure which, in our view, permits the direct assessment of the degree of consensus. What we actually did was to adopt exploratory statistical techniques rather than confirmatory ones, like analysis of variance. The importance of exploratory techniques has come to be acknowledegded within the social sciences as researchers have begun to focus on describing complex patterns of multivariate relationships, rather than on testing univariate relationships. We thought that, in a sense, the paradigm shift proposed by Moscovici (1983, 1984) and his strong criticism of the tradition of social-cognition research, should be 'complemented' by the adoption of a research methodology which could manage the large number of variables, required by the new perspective without imposing, from the beginning, a distinction between so-called independent and dependent variables. This was what we aimed to do by using analysis of correspondences (Lebart et al. 1984) and cluster analysis in the different phases of our research. We shall say more on the way in which we applied these techniques and on the rationale for choosing them in the following description of our research.

In order to study the role of parents in the transmission of representation of work, we planned a developmental study using cross-sectional samples of children aged 10–18 years together with their parents. One crucial issue in this kind of research is that of the choice of instruments. In the recent tradition of research on social representations, there has been the tendency to prefer less obtrusive methods such as open-ended questions in semi-structured interviews. As this method would have been too time-consuming when applied to a large number of subjects, and might have made it very difficult (if not impossible) to get at the parents, we decided to undertake a preliminary investigation using open-ended questions, which provided the basis for the development of a structured questionnaire which could be used in the main study.

We constructed the questionnaire in both of the cases on the assumption that a representation is a complex system of interrelated elements which need to be addressed by means of several questions referring to the central object in more or less direct ways. In this paper we shall describe the results concerning those questions most directly related to work, in both the pilot study and the main investigation.

The pilot study: open-ended questions and the analysis of correspondences as suitable tools to investigate the structure of a representation

The population of the pilot study consisted of 300 pupils aged 13–15 years in their last compulsory year of schooling (the compulsory schooling lasts eight years, and children are expected to complete it when they are 13, but some of them do the same class twice).

Among the questions that pupils were asked to answer were the following: (i) 'What comes into your mind when thinking of work?'; (ii) 'Why do you think people need to work?'; and (iii) 'Which features do you think your future work should have?'. For each of the above questions, subjects were allowed to give as many answers as they wished. Each answer was then content-analysed by means of a category system, constructed in order to code all the spontaneous answers given by the respondents. Thus, for each subject we obtained a profile consisting of different categories which were used or not used when answering a given question; obviously each subject could (and did) use more than one meaning category.

The ordinary analytic procedure applied to this kind of data has been, so far, the analysis of frequencies and percentages in order to describe the representation, assuming that the categories with a 'high' frequency (the limit is usually not specified) are the shared ones. In our view, this procedure is, at least potentially, a misleading one. In fact, when looking at frequency distributions, we are not taking into account how the subjects actually used these categories (the actual co-occurrence of these categories within the individuals' talk). Thus, the above-mentioned procedure is one of those which take for granted the very degree of consensus which is to be empirically assessed.

Let us take a glance at these percentages in our pilot study (see Table 14.1).

Table 14.1 Answers categories: percentages of use

Question 1: *'What comes into your mind when thinking of work?'*	
Work done to earn money for life	28.6
Work done to earn money for one's family	14.9
Work as stressful and tiresome activity	12.1
Work as a moral duty/serious activity	15.9
Work as interesting and likeable	11.4
Work done for social-utility reasons	10.8
Question 2: *'Why do you think people need to work?'*	
In order to earn money for basic needs	54.9
In order to earn money for one's own family	28.6
In order to be useful to society	11.1
In order to get a high social status, as well as a lot of money	10.2
Question 3: *'What kind of work would you like to do in the future?'*	
A kind of work one is keen on	62.2
A kind of work which is socially useful	11.1
Question 4: *'Which features do you think your future should have?'*	
It should not be tiresome	16.2
It should give success and a lot of money	19.7
It should be interesting and appealing	40.6

Without going into any detailed comment about them, it is easy to see that, among others things, these percentages suggest the existence of a somewhat ambivalent representation of work among young people. In fact, among the answers to the question about work in general, the most frequent categories are those which relate work to money, while among the answers to the questions concerning subjects' future work, the most frequent categories are those describing the desidered work as something which should be interesting — something they should be keen on. As we shall see, this conclusion would not be justified. In fact, these results provide a good example of quite a common category of biased inferences in social psychology. Such a conclusion would attribute to an intra-individual psychological process what is really the result or expression of a social phenomenon, namely the existence of subgroups of subjects who share partially different views of work, each of which is quite coherent, as we shall see in the following analysis.

In order to get a description of the structure of the representation in terms of its principal-meaning dimensions, taking into account whether and how subjects differ in their use of these dimensions, we adopted correspondence analysis.

Given that this technique is not yet well-known within the English-speaking research community, we shall say something about it, referring more interested readers to the exhaustive presentations by Lebart *et al.* (1984) and Greenacre (1984), and to Lebart and Morineau (1982) for the SPAD package used to perform the analysis. Correspondence analysis can be seen as very similar to principal-component analysis, since both the techniques are, in fact, forms of principal-axis analysis and aim to represent a rectangular data matrix in terms of reduced number of dimensions. Principal-component analysis and correspondence analysis differ in terms of the type of data to be analysed: the first is used when data are measured on a continuous or interval scale, while correspondence analysis is used with categorical or nominal data. Correspondence analysis, though, is not just a special case of principal-component analysis as it 'can be viewed as finding the best *simultaneous representation* of two data sets that comprise the rows and the columns of a data matrix' (Lebart *et al.* 1984, p. 30 — italics in original). The interpretation of results is again very similar to the interpretation of principal-component analysis, and is usually helped by graphs representing the configuration of points in projection planes formed by the first principal axes, taken two at time. The interpretation of the axes is actually based on two series of coefficients, namely absolute contributions, indicating the proportion of variance explained by each variable in relation to each principal axis, and squared correlations, indicating the part of the variance of a variable explained by a principal axis.

All the categories of the answers given to the first two questions entered the analysis as 'productive' variables, which means that they contributed to the construction of the principal axes. The answers to the third question as well as subjects' socio-demographic features entered the analysis as 'supplementary' variables, that is being positioned on the plane(s) defined by principal axes only subsequently and, thus, not contributing to the construction of the axes themselves.

The results of our analysis showed the existence of three principal axes explaining about 41 per cent of total variance. On the positive side of the *first principal axis*, the most significant categories are those referring to work both as an activity performed to earn one's living, and as an activity that people need to do for this reason; while on the negative side, the most significant categories were those referring to work as an activity done to get money for one's own family. We interpreted this axis as expressing the distinction between an individualistic view of work and a family-centred one.

On the positive side of the *second principal axis*, the most significant categories were those referring to work as a stressful and tiresome activity, as a moral duty and as an interesting and likeable activity. As one can see, each of these categories refers directly to the intrinsic meaning of work or to the description of the intrinsic features of work. On the negative side of this axis, we found a more instrumental view of work considered again as a way of earning one's living, or of keeping one's own family. So, we interpreted this axis as expressing a distinction between a non-instrumental and an instrumental view. It is, perhaps, worth stressing that while the first axis expresses a distinction between two different instrumental views (individualistic versus familistic), the second one expresses a distinction between an instrumental and a non-instrumental view of work.

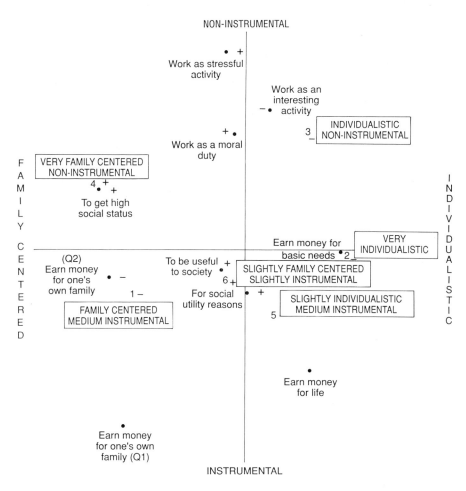

Fig. 14.1. Display with respect to first and second principal axes of the meaning categories and the centroids of the seven groups emerged from cluster analysis (cathegories and groups with a significant position on the third axes are marked by + and −.)

Last, on the positive side of the *third principal axis*, the most significant categories are those referring to work as an activity done for social utility and (less importantly) as a moral duty. On the negative side, the most significant categories are those referring to work as an interesting, likeable activity and as a way to keep one's own family. We considered this axis as expressing a distinction between a socially-orientated and a private view.

The description of the social representation shared by our subjects which results from this analysis can be better appreciated from Fig. 14.1, where we can see all the significant 'productive' categories displayed on the plane defined by the first two principal axes. These categories are marked with a '+' when they have also a significant position on the positive side of the third axis (that is, a socially-orientated view) and with a '−' when they have a significant position on the negative side (that is, a private view).

After this, we performed a cluster analysis of subjects on the basis of their coordinates in the space defined by the principal axes, in order to assess the existence of clusters of subjects within this semantic/representational space. Cluster analysis was used as it is a method which searches for relatively homogeneous groups of subjects. In our study, if the three principal dimensions were homogeneously shared by all subjects, it should not be possible to uncover subgroups with high internal homogeneity. On the contrary, the emergence of subgroups satisfying the appropriate statistical criteria can provide indirect evidence that within the research sample there is no such a thing as a homogeneous view of work but, rather, there are several different views, each of which stresses differently the three principal dimensions. Cluster analysis was performed by SPAD package (Lebart and Morineau 1982) which adopts a two-step procedure: first a partitioning technique (clustering around moving centres) and second an agglomerative technique (hierarchical classification). The choice of the best partition was done relying upon: (i) inspection of the dendrogram; (ii) inspection of the histogram of increasing indices of aggregations; (iii) consideration of the number of iterations needed to stabilize each basic classification; and (iv) consideration of the percentage of variance explained by each partition. On the basis of the above criteria, the best partition appeared to be into seven groups which explained 62 per cent of the total variance. Again on Fig. 14.1, the centroids of the seven groups are displayed on the plane defined by the first two axes. The '+/−' again express the significant position on the third axis ('+' positive side, that is socially-orientated view; '−' negative side, that is, private view).

Looking at their position as well as taking into account the 'productive' categories which characterize each group, that is, the view of work which they share, we labelled the group as following:

(1) very family centred, instrumental, and very private view ($N = 80$);

(2) very individualistic, very instrumental, and very private view ($N = 91$);

(3) individualistic, non-instrumental, and very private view ($N = 27$);

(4) very family-centred, non-instrumental, and very socially-orientated view ($N = 30$);

(5) very non-instrumental view — this group does not have a significant position on the first and the third axes ($N = 30$);

(6) very instrumental and very socially-orientated — this group does not have a significant position on the first axis ($N = 30$);

(7) very socially-orientated view — without any significant characterization due to the first and second principal axes ($N = 27$).

As we said, the answers given to the question about subjects' own future work, as well as subjects' sex and family background, were entered into the analysis as 'supplementary' variables. This, among other things, allowed us to use these variables in order to describe the emerged seven groups. Within the specific subroutine of the SPAD programme (Tamis), category is said to characterize a given group if its percentage within the group is significantly higher than its percentage within the whole research sample.

We shall consider, first, to what extent the answers given about future work resulted to be significantly related to the emerged general views of work. While none of the groups sharing a private view (groups 1, 2, and 3) were characterized by any specific expectation about future work, all of the three socially-orientated groups stressed significantly more than the whole sample one of the following features of future work: a non-tiresome activity (67 per cent versus 46 per cent in the whole sample); an activity which gives success (33 per cent versus 20 per cent); and an interesting and appealing activity (67 per cent versus 41 per cent). These results do surely need to be supported by further evidence in order to provide a meaningful description of the relationship between representation of work and future work intentions among young people. However, the point we would like to make here is that the analytical procedure we adopted did help to go beyond the potentially misleading description given by frequencies and percentages calculated on the whole sample. The reason why the latter procedure is, in our view, wrong is not that it is purely descriptive, but that it is based on an unwarranted assumption about the nature of the observations collected, namely that all subjects within the group can be seen as equivalent expressions of a non-better-qualified social representation. In other words, the 'social' is reached by simply ignoring that the observations actually consisted of individual subjects' different answers.

Before describing the seven groups in terms of subjects' sex and family background (mother's and father's level of education and job), it may be worth saying again that cluster analysis was applied as a tool to indirectly assess the degree of consensus, and/or to detect different representations or views of work within our research sample. The extent to which a given representation or view is shared is not seen, obviously, as implying by itself the existence of a social group of which members are aware, with all the implications of this in terms of interpersonal and inter-group relationships. In our case, 'group' simply means a cluster of subjects using the same representation, and determining whether or not – and to what degree – each of these 'groups' or views' does in fact correspond to different social backgrounds, is a further step.

As far as subjects' sex is concerned, only two significant relationships emerged: males were more represented in the very family centred, non-instrumental, socially-orientated group (73 per cent versus 60 per cent in the whole sample) and females were more represented in the instrumental, very socially-orientated group (61 per cent versus 40 per cent in the whole sample).

As far as family background is concerned, although there were several significant differences on these variables between the actual percentage in each group and the percentage of the whole sample, only two of them were large enough to be worth mentioning here. First, father's job appeared to be associated with the representation of work: the very non-instrumental view was, in fact, more frequent among subjects whose fathers were craftsmen and tradesmen, while the very socially-orientated view was more frequent among subjects whose fathers were teachers and clerks. Second, the socially-orientated view was more frequent among pupils with highly educated mothers.

Despite the lack of strong effects emerging from this phase of analysis, it seems worth saying that we used this procedure not to provide further statistical support to the existence of different social representations within our sample, but to test another aspect of social-representation theory in the context of development of social cognitions, namely the claim that significant variations in children's beliefs are due to the mediation of different family backgrounds. Furthermore, as the different representations emerged in our pilot study do differ in terms of content and not in terms of logical or formal features, the role played by different family backgrounds was not conceived in terms of different rates of intellectual development.

The main study: parents' and children's representations

On the basis of this pilot study we decided to address more directly the issue of the role of parents in the transmission of social representations. If the social representation of work shared by adults at a given time is to be considered as an 'environment' within which children grow up and learn to see this side of the world (Moscovici 1984), what we have to see is whether this environment is to be conceived as an abstract entity—a consensual universe—affecting all children in the same way or, instead, as a complex system of groups of adults who, while sharing the same general meaning dimensions of work, do differ in the way in which they stress each of these dimensions, thus expressing peculiar views of work. In the first case, children would be expected to develop different representations of work at different ages, largely as a function of their cognitive development: at the end of this development, young adults should share a representation of work which is very similar—if not identical—to that of adults. In the second case, different representations of work could be expected to develop among children (from the beginning, and at every age) as a function of the representations shared by relevant adults as well as—if not more—than on their own cognitive development.

In order to test the effects of age as a mediator of developmental factors, against the effects of parents' view of work, we interviewed three groups of 24 pupils aged 10, 13, and 18 along with their parents. The groups were balanced as far as children's sex, parents' job, and parents' level of education were concerned.

Subjects were presented with a list of the 19 meanings or possible definitions of work, which had been drawn from the content analysis of the pilot study, and requested to say how much each of those meanings corresponded to their own general idea of work. The 19 meanings were the following: thing of social utility, human right, way of becoming wealthy, way of expressing one's own creativity, way of being together, social duty, thing which has to be interesting and likeable, thing which is done to earn one's living, way to get satisfaction, way to get self-realization, way to get high social status, thing which is typical of human condition, thing which is done to keep one's family, necessary sacrifice, moral duty, way to become independent, chance to express one's abilities, thing which is difficult to find, and tiresome thing.

Thus, our data can be thought of as 216 profiles expressing the degree to which each subject agreed with the general idea proposed by our list. This list, which contains all of the descriptions or meanings given by the subjects of the pilot study with a frequency equal or higher than 5 per cent, is best conceived as a list of all possible meanings of work available to a population of adolescent Italian speakers. Asking a second sample of subjects to say how much they think each meaning corresponds to their own general idea of work is both a way to assess the validity of this 'vocabulary' of meanings and a way to measure the degree of similarity among the new subjects. The list can, in fact, be seen as a point of reference against which each individual view is compared.

Even though we had different categories of subjects in terms of age, sex, and family role, we did not perform a classical multivariate analyis of variance, again because this would have meant an assumption of within-cell homogeneity, that is of intra-group consensus. We decided to adopt, instead, a two-step analytic procedure: first, to apply cluster analysis in order to uncover natural clusters of subjects with similar profile descriptions; second, to apply discriminant analysis (using cluster membership as the grouping variable and the 19 meanings as predictor variables) in order to see which meanings contributed most to the differences between the clusters (see Dillon and Goldstein 1984, p. 202). This, in our view, is an analytic procedure which allows within-group consensus to emerge without disguising potential diversity. Cluster and discriminant analysis were performed by SPSSX package (Norusis 1985). The 'average linkage within groups' method was used to combine clusters in agglomerative hierarchical clustering. As this method combines clusters so that the average distance between all cases in the resulting cluster is as small as possible, we thought it was the most suitable one to uncover subgroups with relatively homogeneous views or representations. The choice of the best partition was based on both the inspection of icicle plots and the information about the percentage of variance explained by each partition when it was used as grouping variable in discriminant analysis.

Given that the first aim of our study was to analyse the relationship between children's and parents' views of work, we decided first to apply the above outlined procedure to each of the three subgroups of children along with their parents, that is to examine the relationship between children's and parents' views within each age level, and then to apply it to the whole sample of children in order to test the effect of age.

The best partition to emerge from the analysis of 10-years-old children and their parents was a partition into two groups of 31 and 37 subjects each, plus four residual subjects. In this case, as in the following ones, we chose the partition with three groups (even though one was small enough to be ignored) since even at a higher aggregation level the third small group was still distinct, while the two larger ones aggregated into one group. Thus, the residual group seemed to express a very peculiar view which was ignored only because the very reduced number did not allow us to perform any further analysis.

Returning to the results of discriminant analysis, in the group of 10-year-old children the only significant discriminant function explains 74 per cent of total variance (canonical correlation = 0.861).

High values of this function correspond to high agreement between subjects' own general idea of work and the following meanings: thing difficult to be found, tiresome thing, necessary sacrifice, human condition, and thing of social utility. Low values of the function mean high agreement with the following meanings: way of getting satisfaction, thing which has to be interesting and likeable, way of expressing one's own creativity, and something done in order to earn one's living.

From the inspection of the positions of the centroids (group 1 = 1.825, group 2 = −1.525; F between groups (9, 58) = 18.532, p < 0.00001; well classified = 97.1 per cent of Ss), we can say that subjects in the first group view work mostly as an hard duty peculiar to humankind, while subjects in the second one view work generally as an interesting and satisfying activity.

In order to see whether or not the uncovered different views did correspond to groups of subjects characterized by specific socio-demographic features, we looked at the descriptions of the two groups in terms of subjects' family role, level of education, and sex. The percentages of each descriptive category in the two groups were then compared by means of a z test using as population percentage the actual percentage of the research sample.

While the first group appears to be characterized by a relative prevalence of children (45.2 per cent), people with low level of education (61.3 per cent), and females (58.0 per cent), and the second group by a prevalence of parents (mothers 40.5 per cent and fathers 40.5 per cent), people with higher level of education (high school 27 per cent and university 21.6 per cent), and males (56.8 per cent), it is worth saying that the only statistically-significant differences were in the percentages of children and in the percentages of subjects with primary and university level of education (PHo < 0.05, PHo < 0.01, PHo < 0.01).

Even though age and level of education are obviously not independent descriptors, those subjects with primary-school level of education in the first group were not only the 10-year-old children, as can be seen from the percentages, and this means that both age and level of education play a role in the preference for the view of work as an hard duty.

Finally, looking at subjects' family membership, 9 out of 24 children (37 per cent) clustered in the same group as both their parents, with no differences between the groups.

These results appear, at least, to suggest that subjects' generation membership is not the only factor influencing variations in responses.

From the cluster analysis of profiles of 13-year-old children and their parents, two groups emerged with 44 and 27 subjects respectively, plus one residual subject. The only significant discriminant function explains 71 per cent of total variance (canonical correlation = 0.844) and high values of it indicate high agreement with the following meanings: necessary sacrifice, way of getting high social status, thing done in order to keep one's own family. Low values mean high agreement with: way of getting independence, opportunity of expressing one's own abilities, and human right. The position of group centroids (group 1 = −1.214, group 2 = 1.979; F(11, 59) = 13.272, p < 0.00001; well classified = 97.2 per cent of Ss) shows that subjects of group 1 see work as a way of getting independence and expressing one's own abilities, while subjects of group 2 see work as a sacrifice done for one's own family and social status.

There is no significant difference between the two groups in terms of socio-demographic descriptors, even though it can be mentioned that there was a tendency towards a prevalence of children in the second group (44 per cent) and a prevalence of fathers in the first one (41 per cent).

The percentage of children clustered together with both their parents is about 33 per cent, which is slightly lower than among the younger children. In this case, though, children sharing their parents' view are represented in group 1 more than in group 2.

The cluster analysis of the profiles of 18-year-old children and their parents produced two main groups containing 24 and 41 subjects, plus two very small residual groups of 5 and 2 subjects. The following analysis considers only the two main groups. The only significant discriminant function explains about 65 per cent of total variance (canonical correlation = 0.805). High values of the function mean high agreement with the following meanings of work: thing difficult to be found, thing done in order to keep one's own family, and tiresome thing, while low values of the function mean high agreement with the following meanings: way of getting self-realization and thing which has to be interesting and likeable. Thus on the basis of group centroids (group 1 = -1.749, group 2 = 1.023; $F(8, 56) = 12.928$, $p < 0.00001$; well classified = 96.9 per cent of Ss) we can see that subjects in group 1 share a view of work as a means of self-actualization, while subjects in group 2 see work as a tiresome activity done for one's own family.

In this case, too, there is no significant difference in the socio-demographic descriptors between the two groups, even though there is, again, a tendency towards a prevalence of children in the group which sees work as a means of self-actualization (50 per cent of group 1) and a prevalence of mothers in the group which sees work as a tiresome activity (41 per cent in group 2).

The percentage of children sharing the same view as both their parents is about 27 per cent, again lower than in the two groups of younger children. In this case, it is the view of work as tiresome activity done for one's own family which seems to be most influenced by parents' mediation.

In order to assess directly the effect of children's age on their representation of work, the same analytic procedure (cluster analysis followed by discriminant analysis) was applied to the whole sample of 72 children without their parents. The reason for excluding parents from this analysis was simply that here we wanted to assess a purely developmental hypothesis, after having explored the role of parents in the earlier analyses.

If different views of work were mostly related to developmental factors mediated by age, then three natural clusters, characterized by subjects' age, should result from this analysis. Indeed, cluster analysis results show two groups of 52 and 19 subjects each, plus one isolated subject. The discriminant analysis shows a discriminant function explaining 69 per cent of total variance (canonical correlation = 0.831).

High values of this function mean high agreement with the following meanings of work: human right, tiresome thing, way of getting independence, way of expressing one's own creativity, way of becoming wealthy, and way of getting satisfaction, while low values of the function mean high agreement with the following meanings: necessary sacrifice, thing of social utility, and thing done to earn one's living. From the group centroids (group 1 = 2.432, group 2 = 0.889; $F(9, 61) = 15.079$, $p < 0.00001$; well classified = 94.4 per cent) it can be seen that group 1 views work as a sacrifice useful for society and necessary for one's own life, while group 2 sees work as an activity which, even though it is tiresome, does help to get independence and money as well as to express creativity.

A significant difference between the two groups ($PHo < 0.01$) is due to the distribution of the youngest children (10 years old) who were more represented in group 1 (68 per cent) than in group 2 (21 per cent). No significant difference emerged between 13- and 18-year-olds, nor between male and females.

Conclusion

These results do not yet allow us to draw any conclusion about the role of parents' representations in the development of children's representation of work. In fact, these results do not contradict the hypothesis of an influence of parents' view since a proportion ranging from 27 per cent to 37 per cent of children shared the same view of both their parents. In addition, age differences as well as family role give only a partial account for the different views of the clusters of subjects.

At the same time, however, our results do not provide enough evidence to support the claim of a major role for parents' views of work in the representation of this object to the younger generation.

One possible reason for this lack of evidence is found in the restricted variety of views of work which emerged in the main study: both among adults and among children only a few different views of work emerged, so that it was obviously more difficult to detect a correlation between parents' and children's views. As the sample of the main study had been collected in order to provide a larger variety of social categories than in the pilot study (and consisted of subjects aged from 10 to 50), this lack of variety may be due to the way we asked subjects to express their own general idea of work. When requested to list the meanings which contribute most to their own general idea of work, people are likely to use meanings which are easily accessible to them, namely the most salient and/or relevant ones.

On the contrary, when requested to evaluate how much several meanings correspond to their own general idea, people's answers may not depend on the availability of the different meanings. Thus, we think it might be the case that through the closed question, we assessed the comprehension that subjects had of all potential meanings of work in their own cultural and linguistic community, while the open-ended questions used in the pilot study assessed which subset of these meanings was most relevant for the subjects. Thus, by offering subjects different opportunities to answer the same question we may have revealed different aspects or levels of the social representation of work; levels which, among other things, differ in terms of degree of consensus.

These, however, are only tentative explanations which need to be tested by comparing the answers to the questions that we have referred to here to other ones given to open-ended questions, referring to other topics related to work, which were also included in the main study questionnaire. If the lack of variety was really due to the format of the question concerning work, then we should be able to find a larger range of views expressed in the free answers given to the open-ended questions.

In fact, some preliminary results referring to a question about explanations for unemployment (Mannetti and Civitarese 1987) seem to support the claim that the sample of our main study does have different views. The open-ended questions on unemployment were analysed by means of correspondence analysis, using families as subjects and the answers of each member as variables: the results showed that some kinds of parents' views about unemployment, namely the more critical ones, did indeed influence children's views more than other kinds. In other words, children's critical views seem to be related to parents' similar views.

Finally, we would like to make some further comments on the issue of the analytical procedure adopted in our research on social representations and on the reasons for preferring them to more usual methods such as analysis of variance. First, on a general level, we believe that the theoretical framework we adopted is much more in keeping with descriptive statistical procedure than with confirmative ones. As Jahoda (1988) has recently pointed out, it is not yet clear whether social representations should be considered as dependent or independent variables within socio-psychological research. We would like to suggest that thay can assume both roles only if one adopts analytical procedures like those we have used here. Second, as far as analysis of variance is concerned, we think that this procedure has at least two major limits when used to study social representations: (i) it does not allow description of the structure of the representation as it results from the relationships between its different elements and (ii) it looks for significant differences between groups which are defined *a priori* by means of external variables, implicitly assuming that the representation is shared within each of the compared groups. Analysis of variance is, in fact, the ideal method to analyse experimental research designs, where the independent variable is actually manipulated by the experimenter and subjects are assumed to be equivalent aside from the experimental conditions, in other words this means that a high within-group homogeneity is assumed. In our study, and usually in empirical research on social representations, the degree to which a view is shared is the very thing to be assessed. Furthermore, in our view, the degree of similarity between subjects' representations, which have to be conceived as multidimensional entities, has to be used as a basis to construct groups, which, therefore, can be said to actually share a given representation. Thus, to conclude, while we are certainly not claiming that the procedures we adopted are the 'right' or the 'best' ones, we do think that they satisfy, at least, two fundamental needs of empirical research in social-representation domain. These procedures, in fact, allow us both to study the multidimensional structure of a social representation and to assess empirically the degree of intra-group consensus of the same representation.

Acknowledgements

The authors are grateful to Glynis Breakwell, David Canter, and Gerard Duveen for their helpful comments on earlier versions of this chapter. The chapter was written in part while the first author was a Visiting Research Fellow at the University of Sussex, supported by a British Council award.

References

Abramson, T., Tittle, C.K., and Cohen, L. (1979). *Handbook of vocational education evaluation*. Sage, Beverly Hills.

Berti, A.S. and Bombi, A.E. (1988). *The child's construction of economics*, (trans. G. Duveen). Cambridge University Press.

De Polo, M. and Sarchielli, G. (1983). Le rappresentazioni sociali del lavoro. *Giornale Italiano di Psicologia*, **3**, 501-19.

Di Giacomo, J.P. (1980). Intergroup alliances and rejections within a protest movement (analysis of social representations). *European Journal of Social Psychology*, **10**, 329-44.

Dillon, W.R. and Goldstein, M. (1984). *Multivariate analysis: methods and applications*. Wiley, New York.

Emler, N. (1987). Socio-moral development from the perspective of social representations. *Journal for the Theory of Social Behaviour*, **17**, 371-88.

Greenacre, M.J. (1984). *Theory and applications of correspondence analysis*. Academic Press, London.

Hewstone, M., Jaspars, J., and Lalljee, M. (1982). Social representations, social attribution and social identity: the intergroup images of 'public' and 'comprehensive' school boys. *European Journal of Social Psychology*, **12**, 241-71.

Holland, J. L. (1973). *Making vocational choices: a theory of careers*. Prentice Hall, Englewood Cliffs, NJ.

Jahoda, G. (1979). The construction of economic reality by some Glaswegian children. *European Journal of Social Psychology*, 9, 115–27.

Jahoda, G. (1988). Critical notes and reflections on 'social representations'. *European Journal of Social Psychology*, 18, 195–209.

Lebart, L. and Morineau, A. (1982). *SPAD, systeme portable pour l'analyse des données*. CESIA, Paris.

Lebart, L., Morineau, A., and Warwick, K. M. (1984). *Multivariate descriptive statistical analysis: correspondence analysis and related techniques for large matrices*. Wiley, New York.

Mannetti, L. and Civitarese, D. (1987). *La rappresentazione sociale della disoccupazione*. Unpublished manuscript, University of Rome 'La Sapienza'.

Moscovici, S. (1983). The coming era of representations. In *Cognitive analysis of social behaviour*, (ed. J. P. Codol and J. P. Leyen), pp. 115–50. Nijhoff, The Hague.

Moscovici, S. (1984). The phenomenon of social representations. In *Social representations*, (ed. R. Farr and S. Moscovici), pp. 3–69. Cambridge University Press.

Norusis, M. J. (1985). *SPSS-X advanced statistics guide*. McGraw-Hill, New York.

Potter, J. and Litton, I. (1985). Some problems underlying the theory of social representations. *British Journal of Psychology*, 24, 81–90.

Ripon, A. (1984) L'étude des représentations en psychologie du travail: la représentation du travail et de l'emploi. *Psychologie du Travail*, 15–16.

Stacey, B. G. (1978). *Political socialization in Western society*. Edward Arnold, London.

Stacey, B. G. (1982). Economic socialization in pre-adult years. *British Journal of Social Psychology*, 21, 159–73.

Super, D. E. (1957). *The psychology of career*. Harper and Brother, New York.

15 Social representations of mental illness: lay and professional perspectives

Bruna Zani

Introduction

The findings presented in this paper are part of a wider research project on 'the social representations of mental illness', carried out in three Italian cities: Bologna, Rome, and Naples (see Bellelli 1987) in coordination with foreign colleagues working in Belgium, Switzerland, and Spain (Ayesteran 1984; Baldassarre 1984).

This topic has been the subject of considerable discussion and debate in Italy over the past few years, following the profound changes in the fields of psychiatry and health care. Indeed, reforms were passed in 1978 that initiated an extremely important process of change affecting not only the theoretical categories used to interpret mental illness, but also the methods of psychiatric assistance: the juridical concept of 'social dangerousness' of the mentally ill has disappeared; psychiatric hospitals have been closed to new inmates; decentralized services at a local level have been strengthened; and psychiatry's primary function as custodian (curing was only secondary) has become health-orientated, centred around prevention and therapy.

This process has obviously affected the professional roles and skills of mental-health practitioners (psychiatrists, psychologists, and nurses): as the organizational framework changed, so the methods and aims of their daily work changed (see Zani 1987*b*).

Even the community at large has been affected by the problem in one way or another: the introduction into society of patients once treated in psychiatric hospitals, the treatment of mentally-ill patients by local services, and the emphasis laid on the importance of prevention in psychic suffering have all brought the general population, including non-experts, into contact with the problem.

These social changes have meant that a more detailed and systematic understanding of the responses of the social actors involved, both practitioners and non-experts, is called for. Our interest was focused on the analysis of the social representations of mental illness, which not only give order and meaning to individuals' beliefs but also guide their actual behaviour, bringing it into line with that of the social groups to which they belong (see Moscovici 1976).

From a theoretical viewpoint, I was interested in addressing some problematic aspects of the study of social representations, which have received considerable attention in the literature (see, for example, Farr and Moscovici 1984; Farr 1987; Jodelet 1989*a*):

1. the identification of a 'central core' in the representations of a social object (mental illness) so as to outline what is *permanent* in images of and attitudes towards the mentally ill, and what, on the other hand, is *variable* according to social grouping.

2. the analysis of the relation between the ways in which social representations are produced and the function they serve — that is, as behavioural guidelines. Farina and Fisher (1982) have, in fact, already remarked that 'what groups believe to be the nature of mental disorders will influence such matters as who becomes mentally ill and how mental patients are (or could be) treated'.

3. the relevance of the *self* in the subjects' semantic universe concerning the field of physical and mental health, given that, according to Turner's self-categorization model (1987), the conception of self serves as a central reference point from which comparisons with others are made. The self occupies a central position within the set of categories considered as most significant for subjects' experience, but the self is clearly different from all these categories.

The ideas underlying our analysis are as follows:

1. There are numerous social representations of the mentally ill and of mental illness, differing in terms of both content and the more-or-less favourable attitudes they express.

2. The characteristics of these social representations vary as a function of 'social criteria' relating to: the socio-professional position of the social actors who formulate them, to their cultural background, and to their degree of familiarity/contact with the problem in question.

3. The variety of these representations enables us to grasp the differences between social group with regard to the relational and behavioural strategies considered appropriate *vis-à-vis* the mentally ill.

In particular, we feel we may advance the following hypotheses:

1. A basically similar *structure* of the representational field in all the social groups considered (professional and non-expert) was expected: we assumed that the definition of mental illness refers to the dimension of strangeness/difference, in contrast with both a concept of 'normality' and a notion of organic illness.

2. As regards the *self*, it has been hypothesized that the 'oneself' image and the representation of normal person are polarized positively and are used as normative criteria of reference to evaluate the other stimuli.

3. As regards *content*, differences between the social groups may be detected, varying in line with the degree of their proximity and involvement in the issue in question: as far as our study is concerned, we believe that, alongside a professional representation of the mentally ill and of mental illness, elaborated by the health workers (whose work brings them into everyday contact with the mentally ill), there is a lay or non-expert representation, formulated by other social actors — university students, who are not directly involved in this problem.

4. We may expect to find intra-group variations in the model of mental illness and in the formulation of treatment strategies towards the mentally ill, in accordance with social criteria linked, in the case of health workers, to their professional *roles* (psychologists, psychiatrists, and psychiatric nurses), and, in the case of students, to their *educational orientation* and cultural backgrounds (students of medicine, psychology, mathematical sciences, or nursing).

Method

Subjects

The sample includes two group of subjects: university students from different disciplines (medicine, psychology, mathematical sciences, and nursing, making a total of 480 subjects divided into four subgroups of 120 students from each discipline); and social and health workers attached to local consultancy and psychiatric units (a total of 264 subjects, including 89 psychiatrists, 90 psychiatric nurses, and 85 psychologists).

The subjects came from the three cities where the study was carried out (Bologna, Rome, and Naples), a third from each.[1]

Instruments

The instruments used were as follows:

1. A *list of free associations* to some stimulus words, chosen from those that seemed best suited for helping the subjects to describe the semantic universe of mental illness and madness which we believe is constructed by means of comparison with other key elements such as the concept of normality, of (physical) illness, and, on the basis of our hypothesis, of the self. We therefore used five stimulus words: normal person, sick, mentally ill, madman, and yourself, appropriately rotated in order to check the effect of their order of presentation. Subjects were required to respond with up to ten association for each stimulus, in order to obtain a reasonably detailed

'map' of their social representations. The delivery technique is very simple: 'If I say . . . (madman), what do you think of? Tell me ten adjectives that come to your mind thinking of . . . (madman).'

We used the method described by Di Giacomo (1980, 1981): according to this author, this method 'has the advantage (over the semantic differential for instance) of leaving the choice of significant categories to the subject' (Di Giacomo 1980, p. 333). The procedures used for the data elaboration were: the reduction of the diversity of all words associated, according to classical rules of content analysis; the calculation of the similarity between two dictionaries (number of common words) and the transformation of that number into Ellegard's association index; the analysis of the similarity matrix obtained according to Kruskal's multidimensional scaling method (Kruskal 1964) (for more details, see Di Giacomo 1980); and finally, a correspondence analysis of the data matrix of the most frequent words associated to each stimulus was carried out (see Benzécri 1973).

2. A *Semi-structured questionnaire* touching on themes such as the definition of the causes, the course, and the consequences of mental illness; the individuation of the treatment strategies considered most suitable for use with the mentally ill, inferred from items relating to the goals of treatment, to the types of intervention thought to be most effective, and to the places considered most appropriate for the treatment.

This instrument allowed us to examine further specific aspects of the subjects' social representation, identifying certain indicators of both the model of mental illness and the therapeutic strategies. The questionnaire was given after the free-association test.

Results

The representation of normality and 'otherness'

The analysis of the free associations supplied by the subjects was made separately for each of the subsample of the three cities involved. The data for Bologna will be presented here as an example to save time and space (for economy of the presentation). It emerged, nevertheless, that the results were relatively uniform in the other cities (Naples and Rome) (see Bellelli 1987, in press).

As far as the *structure* of the representational field was concerned, the configurations that emerged were similar in the two groups of subjects considered, health workers and students. Let us consider first the group of *students* divided according to the faculty to which they belong: two-dimensional space was given by Kruskal's analysis from the similarity matrix between all the stimulus-words. The stress is 0.157. The resulting configuration (see Fig. 15.1) clearly opposes on the first axis the sphere of *normality*

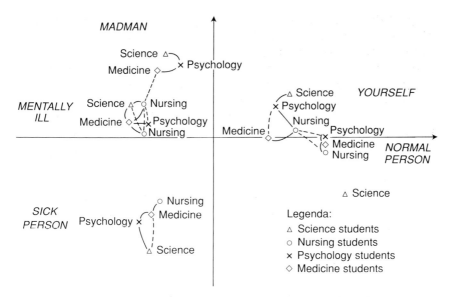

Fig. 15.1. Position of the stimulus-words in the two-dimensional space given by Kruskal's analysis (students' sample)

(normal person or oneself) to that of *abnormality* (sick person, mentally ill person, or madman). The other axis opposes the area of *physical pathology* to that of *mental illness*: a sick person is in fact quite separate from a mentally-ill person and from a madman.

Generally speaking, a significant similarity can be detected between the dictionaries used by the psychology students and the medical students in response to all the stimulus-words (with the exception of their definition of 'yourself'). The doctors-to-be responded with words similar to those employed by student nurses in the case of four of the five stimulus words (the exception was 'madman').

The future nurses and science students were the two most widely differing groups: there was, in fact, no significant similarity between their responses, which indicates a different way of representing this social reality to themselves.

In order to analyse the semantic universe constituted by the dictionaries associated with each stimulus, a correspondence analysis was made. In the resulting configuration, the positions of the stimuli and of the associated words describe a parabolic-shaped curve (see Fig. 15.2), the so-called 'horseshoe effect', known also as *the arch* or *Guttman effect* (Benzécri 1973; Volle 1985). This is one of the 'classic' dispositions of the data in which

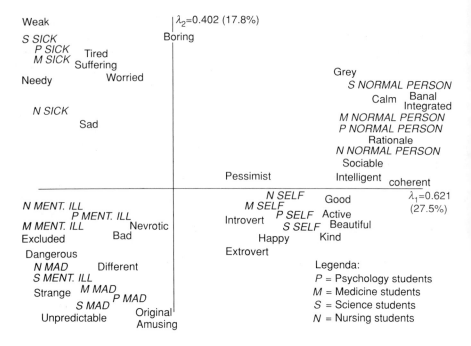

Fig. 15.2. Correspondence analysis (students' sample)

the principal axes reveal a non-linear relationship: it refers generally to a model of a single underlying gradient which simultaneously orders the rows and the columns in this way (Greenacre 1984). In our case this configuration, already described by Kruskal's analysis, is far from trivial: it means that for the subjects involved, the five stimulus-words are clearly considered along a dichotomous dimension (health/illness, normality/deviance) which implies a more basic distinction between identity and otherness, similarity and difference.

The first three factors explain 57 per cent of the whole variance with an eigenvalue respectively of 0.62, 0.40, and 0.27.

The stimulus-word *normal person* expressed by the four subgroups of subjects is responsible for the first factor. *Sick* and at the opposite pole *madman*, expressed by all groups, define the second factor. The third factor is explained by the two stimulus-words *normal person* and *yourself* which for psychology, medicine, and science students are at opposite poles at the axis while student nurses place them both at the same pole.

Let us now analyse the representational field evoked by the terms chosen. The stimulus-word *normal person* elicits such associations as rational, well-balanced, intelligent, sociable, healthy, hardworking, active, and calm—but also banal, grey and integrated. It is opposite to the definition of *yourself*, which brought forth an emphasis on aspects more closely connected to character and to emotions such as introvert–extrovert, optimist–pessimist, sincere, happy, kind, and friendly. It could be said that the banality and greyness of normality were contrasted with the vitality and uniqueness of one's own personality. The term 'normal person' also contrasts with *sick person*, defined as suffering, tired, sad, worried, weak, and needy: thus, the balance and rationality of a 'normal person' (and therefore an efficient person) is seen as being in opposition to a concept of illness, seen as loss of control and suffering.

In its turn, the semantic field associated with the *sick person* is in opposition to that of the *madman*: if the former is connected above all to suffering and the state of need (but is also qualified as being boring and sad), the madman is associated above all with being different, unpredictable, strange, as well as original and amusing.

The term *mentally-ill person* does not fit into this play of opposing areas,

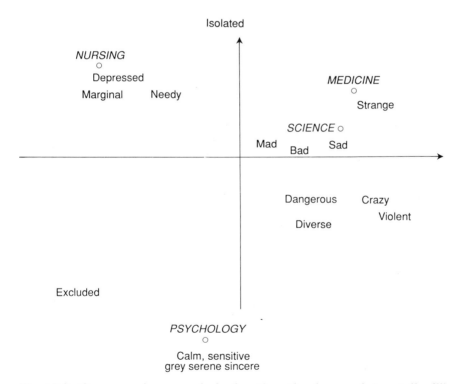

Fig. 15.3. Correspondence analysis for the stimulus-word 'mentally ill' (students' sample)

and we have therefore analysed it separately, with a further correspondence analysis (see Fig. 15.3).

The first factor is due to the definitions given by the nurses which are in contrast to those given by the medicine and science students. The associations proffered by the psychology students which contrast particularly with those of the student nurses are responsible for the second factor. The total variance explained by the two factors is 74 per cent.

Different ways of representing this social object to oneself emerged clearly in the different groups: the medical and science students were still firmly tied to a stereotyped and traditional image of the mentally ill (such as a person who is dangerous, strange, violent, and even sad); the student nurses emphasized more the idea of isolation (excluded, closed in upon himself, depressed, aggressive, and needy); and the psychology students used terms (such as excluded, but also calm, serene, sincere, shy, and sensitive) that were uncommon, or at least new, in descriptions of a mentally-ill person.

Let us now proceed to an analysis of the free associations of the *health workers* according to their role within the mental-health services. The space obtained, using the analysis of Kruskal, presents a positioning of the stimuli, along the two axes, similar to that already shown for the students (a normality/abnormality axis and a second physical pathology/mental illness axis). The stress is 0.202. Generally, there is no similarity between psychologists and nurses (with the exception of their associations to the stimulus word 'sick person'). The dictionaries of the psychiatrists and psychiatric nurses are much more similar: evidently, the fact of working together in local teams has helped to create common symbolic universes for speaking both of normality and of 'otherness' (abnormality).

A correspondence analysis was then performed on the words most frequently associated to the stimuli (see Fig. 15.4). The first three factors explain (on the whole) 56.8 per cent of the total variance, with an eigenvalue of, respectively, 0.68, 0.23, and 0.20. Two stimulus-words are responsible for the first factor, *normal person* and *yourself* for the nurses (absolute contribution 19.7 and 12.9) and *normal person* for psychiatrists and psychologists (absolute contributions 12.4 and 8.7). This factor explains between 39 per cent and 55 per cent of the variability in these dictionaries. The second factor is defined by the opposition between *sick person* and *madman* for all the groups of practitioners. The variability explained is between 17 per cent and 55 per cent. For the third factor, two stimulus-words are responsible: *yourself* for the psychologists and *normal person* for the nurses. The variability is between 30 per cent and 53 per cent.

The analysis revealed that, in general, health workers possess a number of fairly commonly-shared definitions of the term 'sick person' and 'madman'. For the former, the aspects of need, help, suffering, and hospitalization, as well as weakness and boringness, are emphasized, whereas the latter is

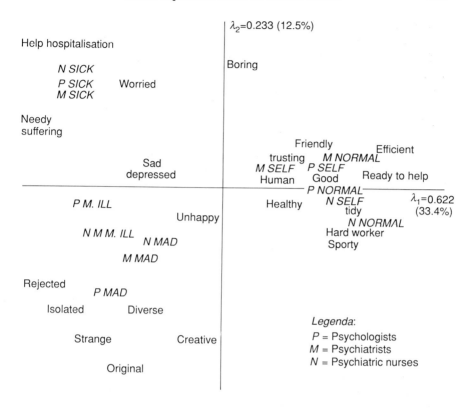

Fig. 15.4. Correspondence analysis (health workers' sample)

connected with isolated and rejected, but also strange and original.

It might be of interest here, however, to point out that the analysis of the fifth factor further modifies the picture: it is striking how the definitions of 'madman' and 'mentally ill' given by the psychologists differ from those of the psychiatrists and nurses. While the former connote the psychically-ill person as original and ready to help as well as anguished and isolated, the other two groups of workers fall back on traditional nosographic termino-logy such as agitated, depressed, delirious, psychotic, and a person who has hallucinations.

However, different ways of defining 'normality' and the characteristics of 'one's own personality' appear; the psychologists in particular tend to differ in the image they have of themselves — connected to terms that refer to moral characteristics (understanding, ready to help, human, and trusting) in contrast to the image of the normal person, as does that of the nurses' definition of themselves (in this case, the references are to characteristics of good behaviour — hard worker, tidy, healthy, and sporty).

Models of mental illness and treatment strategies

From an analysis of some of the items of the questionnaire, it was possible to obtain information useful for the identification of both shared models of mental illness and workable strategies for the treatment of the mentally ill.

At first, we tried to underscore those aspects that highlighted the differences in representations of the two subject groups: a highly significant ($p < 0.00001$) function (accounting for 52.2 per cent of all the variance) emerged from the discriminant analysis carried out on the whole of the sample from the three cities (Bologna, Rome, and Naples), which clearly opposes the students to the workers. (eigenvalue 1.44, canonical correlation 0.768) The former felt that mental illnesses are likely to be progressive in nature (-0.14) and that biological factors (-0.19) may represent an important cause, whereas health workers emphasized the range and variety of symptoms which mental illness may present, and therefore drew attention to both periodic crises (0.13) and acute episodes (0.25).

For the students, the objectives of the treatment are the need to increase the ability of the mentally ill to form relationships with other people and their acceptance by society at large (-0.14). Health workers took the view that the alleviation of symptoms (0.19) and an increase in the ability of mentally-ill people to adapt to the demands made upon them by society were important goals of treatment. Likewise, while it is commonly held that forms of psychotherapy may represent effective treatment, it was again the health workers who underlined the importance of bringing about changes in the social environment (0.15), in the use of drugs (0.28), and in recourse to hospitalization (0.27). Lastly, regarding the places considered appropriate for treatment, students felt that psychiatric hospitals could also be effective (-0.45), whereas health workers demonstrated a strong conviction that the mentally ill should be treated above all in local mental-health centres (0.36) and in their own homes (0.29), in surroundings familiar to them.

We then analysed intra-group differences both for the students and the health workers (see Zani 1987a).

It is worth noting that the *students* have different cultural backgrounds: the subjects declared that they possessed different levels of information regarding problems of mental health and psychiatric care in Italy. There were, in fact, significant differences between the four groups of students: the science students were situated at the lowest level ($\bar{x} = 1.83$) on a four-point scale (4 = very well informed, 1 = not informed at all), and the psychology students at the upper level ($\bar{x} = 2.60$) ($p < 0.00001$).

We shall now make a few comments on data emerging from the discriminant analysis (see Fig. 15.5).[2] The first function (accounting for 46 per cent of all the variance) opposes the psychology students (-1.39) to other groups, in particular to the medical students (0.92) and, to a lesser extent, to the

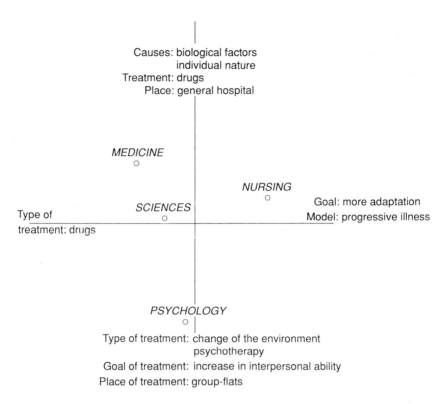

Causes: biological factors
individual nature
Treatment: drugs
Place: general hospital

MEDICINE
○

NURSING
○

Goal: more adaptation
Model: progressive illness

SCIENCES
○

Type of
treatment: drugs

PSYCHOLOGY
○

Type of treatment: change of the environment
psychotherapy
Goal of treatment: increase in interpersonal ability
Place of treatment: group-flats

Fig. 15.5. Discriminant analysis (students' sample)

student nurses (0.44). The psychology students reveal a *psycho-social* conception of mental illness: they believe that the most effective treatment lies in an alteration of social surroundings (−0.31) and in family psychotherapy (−0.11). They also argue that the most appropriates places of treatment are group flats (−0.41) and local mental-health units (−0.27); that the objective of treatment should be to increase the ability of the mentally ill to form relationships (−0.11); and that the principal consequence of mental illness is the isolation into which the mentally ill are forced (−0.27).

In contrast, the other three groups express a *medical–clinical* conception of mental illness, believing that the causes of mental illness are of an individual nature and relate to biological factors; the most effective treatment is to involve drugs; and the most appropriate place for treatment is the general hospital.

The second function (accounting for 31 per cent of all the variance) discriminates within the so-called 'health' group —between student nurses

(1.12) and medical students (−0.71). Student nurses express a conception hinged on the *macro-social* aspect of the problem (mental illness as a progressive condition, the need for the mentally-ill person to adapt to social demands, and the role played by neighbours in sending the mentally ill to mental-health units). The medical students, on the other hand, showed strong support for a *medical conception* of the problem, both regarding the skills necessary to make a diagnosis of mental illness (the doctor should be the one to decide) and also the most suitable treatment for mental illness (drugs).

The third function (accounting for 23 per cent of all the variance) opposes science students (− 1.10) to the other three groups of students, and above all to medical students (−0.58) and psychology students (−0.34). Indeed, the science students' conception of mental illness differs markedly from that of psychology students, being much more inclined towards a medical-biological view (this also emerges, though less strikingly, from comparison with student nurses). Yet, in comparison with the positions of medical students, the conception of science students appears to hinge less on clinical

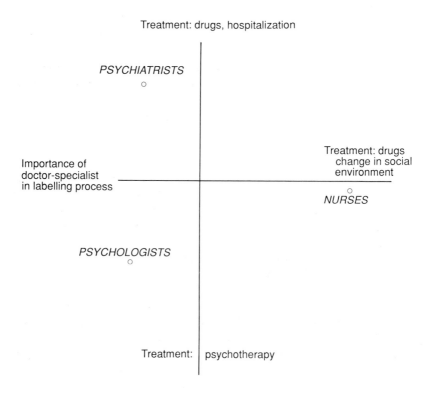

Fig. 15.6. Discriminant analysis (health workers' sample)

aspects.

Within the *professional world*, too, there are different standpoints regarding the model of mental illness and the treatment strategies favoured, varying according to the role played. Discriminant analysis yields a number of interesting differences (see Fig . 15.6).[3]

From the first function (accounting for 63 per cent of all variance) there emerges, on the one hand, a medical and social dimension of mental illness, in which references to biological factors are to be found (causes cited include drug addiction and alcoholism, and pharmacological treatment is favoured) but also aspects of enviromental and social control (goal: to prevent the mentally ill from disturbing others, and treatment involves modification of the social environment). On the other hand, there also emerges a more institutionalized view, centred on professional roles (the importance of the doctor and specialist in the diagnosis of mental illness). The nurses are grouped at the former pole (2.30) and have difficulty squaring medical and sociological concepts of mental illness; at the latter pole there are, above all, the psychologists ((−1.13) who insist on the need to give professionals more responsibility.

The second function (accounting for 37 per cent of all variance) demonstrates a medical and organizational dimension (centred on treatment involving the administration of drugs and hospitalization), in contrast with a social-relational conception (importance of family psychotherapy). This opposes psychiatrists (1.50) to psychologists (−1.91); psychiatric nurses appear to occupy an indifferent position.

Concluding remarks

What is peculiar to the Italian experience as compared to that of other countries is the imposition of radical change in the psychiatric field by a law. The law itself was the result of a good deal of brave and tireless endeavour on the part of a minority of social workers deeply involved in the problem. A few years after the passing of the law, what has changed in the perception of mental illness, and what social representations have been elaborated by health workers and 'non-experts'?

On the face of it, it would appear that the message of the change has got across. The data in the questionnaire show how some of the elements laid down in the reform law are shared by both workers and students: more tolerance towards the mentally ill, greater emphasis on the social environment and dehospitalization as therapeutic instruments, and the affirmation of a psychosocial model of mental illness. Some interesting differences also arose between the groups in the sample on the basis of certain well-defined social criteria: *role* in the case of workers, and the level of *information* and *educational background* in the case of the students.

The complexity of the problem that mental illness poses subjects is, however, especially highlighted by the projective techniques such as the free associations. The data substantially confirm the hypotheses proposed: all the subgroups of the sample present a similar structural configuration of the representational field. This indicates that at a more general cultural and social level, there are a series of shared ways in which basic categories such as normality/abnormality and physical pathology/mental deviance are elaborated and brought into play.

Normality and self are described positively: the self, in particular, constitutes a point of reference for defining other social objects by an evaluation of what is similar and what is different. The abnormality/pathology is described negatively, as 'other than self': here, a distinction is made with the physically ill, seen as weak and needy but not especially distant, and as a threat to one's own integrity, but as being in a situation that potentially could well become one's own – and which therefore requires understanding and empathy. The mentally-ill person, on the other hand, is seen as extremely distant from the self, completely different, with a quite clear indication of his perceived 'otherness', as Jodelet (1984, 1989b) has shown in her classical study.

The use of the multimethod approach to the study of social representations of mental illness has, therefore, proved to be particularly useful for highlighting the different dimensions underlying the representations as well as the criteria that help to organize them.

Acknowledgment

The research reported in this paper was supported by the Italian Ministry of Education.

The article is a revised version of a paper given at the Annual Conference of the British Psychological Society, St Andrews (Scotland), April 1989.

I wish to express my gratitude to Prof. Jean Pierre Di Giacomo, University of Lille (France), for his helpful comments.

Notes

[1] The research was conducted in collaboration with the Universities of Naples (Prof. G. Bellelli, Dr C. Serino, Dr G. Petrillo) and Rome (Dr A.M. De Rosa). The data of the three cities were collected by the respective local research groups.
[2] Discriminant analysis (students' sample):

Function	Eigenvalue	Per cent of variance	Canonical correlation	Significance
1	0.778	45.96	0.661	0.00001
2	0.520	30.74	0.585	0.00001
3	0.394	23.30	0.532	0.002

Percentage of 'grouped' cases correctly classified: 70.72 per cent.

[3] Discriminant analysis (health workers' sample):

Function	Eigenvalue	Per cent of variance	Canonical correlation	Significance
1	2.39	63.03	0.8396	0.00001
2	1.40	36.97	0.7639	0.00001

Percentage of 'grouped' cases correctly classified: 90 per cent.

References

Ayesteran, S. (ed.) (1984). *Psicosociologia de la enfermedad mental, III cursos de verano en San Sebastian*. Imprenta Boa, Bilbao.

Baldassarre, A. (1984). *Approche de la maladie mentale à travers les représentations sociales des professionnels de la santé*. Mémoire de Lycence, Louvain-la-Neuve.

Bellelli, G. (ed.) (1987). *La représentation sociale de la maladie mentale*. Liguori, Naples.

Bellelli, G. (ed.) (in press) *L'altra malattia. Come la società pensa la malattia mentale*. Liguori, Naples.

Benzécri, J.P. (1973). *L'analyse de correspondences*. Dunod, Paris.

Di Giacomo, J.P. (1980). Intergroup alliances and rejections within a protest movement. Analysis of the social representations. *European Journal of Social Psychology*, **10**, 329–44.

Di Giacomo, J.P. (1981). Aspects méthodologiques de l'analyse des représentations sociales. *Cahiers de Psychologie Cognitive*, **1**(4), 397–423.

Farina, A. and Fisher, J.D. (1982). Beliefs about mental disorders. Findings and implications. In *Integrations in clinical and social psychology*, (ed. G. Weary and H. Mirels), pp. 48–71. Oxford University Press, New York.

Farr, R. (1987). Social representations: a French tradition of research. *Journal for the Theory of Social Behaviour*, **17**, 343–69.

Farr, R. and Moscovici, S. (ed.) (1984). *Social representations*, Cambridge University Press.

Greenacre, M. (1984). *Theory and applications of correspondence analysis*. Academic Press, London.

Jodelet, D. (1984). Civil et brédins. Représentations sociales de la maladie mentale et rapport à la folie. Unpublished PhD Thesis, EHESS, Paris.

Jodelet, D. (ed.) (1989a) *Les représentations sociales*. Presses Universitaires de France, Paris.

Jodelet, D. (1989b). *Folies et représentations sociales*. Presses Universitaires de France, Paris.

Kruskal, J.B. (1964). Nonmetric multidimensional scaling, a numerical method. *Psychometrika*, **29**, 115–19.

Moscovici, S. (1976) *La psychanalyse, son image, son public*, (2nd edn). Presses Universitaires de France, Paris.

Turner, J.C. (ed.) (1987). *Rediscovering the social group: a self-categorization theory*. Blackwell, Oxford.

Volle, M. (1985). *L'analyse des données*. Economica, Press.

Zani, B. (1987a). Strategies thérapeutiques et représentations sociales de la maladie mentale. In *La représentation sociale de la maladie mentale*, (ed. G. Bellelli), pp. 107–20. Liguori, Naples.

Zani, B. (1987b) The psychiatric nurse: a social psychological study of a profession facing institutional changes, *Social Behaviour*, **2**, 87–98.

Epilogue: methodological contributions to the theory of social representations

David V. Canter and Glynis M. Breakwell

The development of psychology, like that of any science, consists of the creation of new concepts and new ways of perceiving and describing aspects of human experience. Some of these concepts radically challenge the day-to-day ways of thinking and talking about ourselves and our dealings with each other. The set of concepts relating to the degree of activation of the nervous system, with its proposal that the system can have too much as well as too little stimulation, exemplifies the power of new ways of conceptualizing psychological phenomena.

Other important concepts arise as clarifications and elaborations of ideas in daily use. 'Personality', 'learning', and 'attitudes' are all examples of terms around which a special, detailed understanding has grown within psychology, even though less specific popular usage of these terms survives outside of academic realms.

More recently, psychology has developed by embracing strong, often physically-orientated metaphors. The metaphor of processing information, with many parallels to hydraulic flows, for example, is slowly giving way to no less mechanical, but more complex, metaphors taken from dynamic networks like those identified between organic cells. Such metaphors are attractive because they encompass concepts about the processes which generate variety and change in human actions and experience. Earlier, more directly descriptive concepts, for instance 'memory' or 'perception', could be vehicles for any number of explanatory frameworks, each altering, often covertly, the meaning of the central concepts that they were attempting to explain.

Concepts in science are the building blocks of theories, but the theories do themselves redefine the constituents out of which they are built. To take an early example which was central to a generation of psychological theorizing, those aspects of experience which influence human action without coming into awareness may be regarded as unconscious and hidden from awareness through psychodynamic processes, or as habits that are never assigned to cognitively-describable categories. Whether habits and the unconscious are really overlapping phenomena or quite distinct was difficult to establish, because the theoretical contexts within which they were defined were so different.

Enter measurement and methodology: while philosophers attempted to resolve by debate the confusions and ambiguities of the concepts that helped account for human experience, little progress was achieved in developing a science that could be harnessed directly to an understanding of the details of human experience. No amount of debate on the nature of human individuality could resolve the question of which characteristics of people were most crucial in explaining their ability to cope with a particular job or variations in mental health. It was the attempts to measure human variations in a variety of ways which generated such a rich understanding of the different facets of individuality.

The distinction, then, between theory and methods is always a dubious one in science, but it is especially doubtful in psychology for two reasons. One is the close association between everyday speech and the vocabulary used by psychologists, which means that the process of measuring further defines what is being explored. In this sense an 'operational definition' is not a definition at all but an abrogation of the act of defining at a theoretical level. Definition and measurement are logically integrated. The second is that since the rejection of a naive, pure behaviourism it has been firmly accepted that the phenomena of psychology are fundamentally covert: neither actions nor experience can be directly observed and must be inferred from what people do and say. This inference process needs to be part of the speculations about what is being measured and how the measurement process reveals it; in other words, part of the theory.

This perspective on the interpenetration of theory and method leads to the conclusion that most theories, when looked at closely, are actually specifications (even if rather vague ones) for exploring the phenomena which they describe. Computer modelling has made this aspect of theory building even more overt by demonstrating that most of the concepts that are the building blocks of psychology may be treated as nascent procedures. In specifying the procedures, the concepts are clarified. Of course, in such clarification it is often apparent that many different concepts are nested within what was originally considered as one simple entity. The elaboration of many different types of memory is a striking illustration of this.

Our contention, then, is that theories may be ambiguous about methods but never ignore them. Furthermore, often the richness of a theory stems from the productive ambiguity of its early methodological formulations.

The theory of social representations is emerging from its early stages of productive ambiguity through the development of methods that explore the issues to which the theory draws attention. Our understanding of social representations will change under this onslaught of people who wish to study the phenomena in ways that make sense to them. So, although this book focuses on methods, we see its main contribution in helping to clarify, elaborate, and broaden the coverage of the theory.

The empirical study of social representations has contributed to the enhancement of the theory itself. For, although it is of great importance to explore what the concept of social representations may mean and the various metatheoretical implications that the whole approach may have (as Farr, McKinlay, and Billig have in the present volume and in other publications) some developments of the theory are only possible by setting about the task of recording and analysing social representations. Such empirical studies do considerably more than test hypotheses derived from the theory or add content to prescribed structures; they actively develop an understanding of what the processes are that underlie social representations.

Research methods, then, do more than provide tools for mechanics who know the principles on which they are operating. The development and application of measurement procedures take theories forward in a number of important ways.

The very process of setting about studying proposed phenomena forces a clarification of what those phenomena are. The recent rapid developments in computer modelling, for example, have shown how much is inherent in taken-for-granted processes. But, all empirical research uncovers ambiguities in the concepts being studied. In the present volume, the most notable illustration of this has been the various ways in which researchers have approached the central issue of what it means for a representation to be 'social'. Duveen and Lloyd (Chapter 4), for instance, may be contrasted with Hammond (Chapter 10). The former are concerned to see the social qualities of representations reflected in the social processes that will reveal them. Hammond, by contrast, proposes statistical procedures that will reveal average correlations between people.

There is the important and, as yet, untested question of whether these two different implicit definitions of the 'social' are empirically and conceptually related. Indeed, in drawing our attention to the role of group processes in Chapter 9, Breakwell opens up the possibility of predicting situations in which the two types of social representation, the communal and the correlational, may be less closely related and even autonomous.

The clarification of key concepts that is brought about by setting up empirical processes clearly goes beyond the mere clarification. Elaboration and development of the theory ensues. In the present volume, some interesting examples of the elaboration of social-representation theory come from the application of the multivariate statistical approach. Purkhardt and Stockdale discuss this most directly in Chapter 13, where they explore social representations as consisting of a set of elements that are assigned various attributes. The parallels with earlier studies of meaning, whether

at the cultural linguistics level of Charles Osgood or the individual therapeutic level of George Kelly are obvious, but the focus on consensual structures among the elements, as revealed in all of the last six chapters, provides
a new set of very specific concepts for describing and comparing social
representations.

Some followers of what might be called the social-representation movement may be rather disappointed in the multivariate statistical approach of
the later chapters of this volume. These are the followers who saw the theory
as a radical break with the highly numerate, statistically-complex traditions
of an essentially experimental psychology. However, we think that they
should not be dismayed. To take a notion from George Kelly, by drawing
on other methodologies, the range of convenience of social-representation
theory has been broadened. Many earlier theories within psychology can be
seen to be operating on similar phenomena. The questions to be answered
now relate to the important differences. For example, should we expect
that any dimensions which structure social representations will reflect the
much vaunted evaluation, potency, and activity dimensions of Osgood?
Should personal construct therapists be alerted to the communal construct
systems on which their patients draw?

A second difference of perspective that might have been expected between
the early papers in this volume and those in the second half is that the
early papers with their emphasis on *in situ* qualitative approaches all, in
different and varying ways, draw attention to the inherent complexity and
constant changes that are to be expected of social representations. In
Chapter 6, McKinlay *et al.* highlight how the framework of discourse
analysis reveals the fluid renegotiation of the content of representations;
from the slightly different perspective of rhetoric, Billig, in Chapter 2, also
emphasizes the dynamic vitality and subtle variations between representations that are essential to any thinking society.

Yet, although those using multivariate analysis are searching for identifiable structures in their data, they all also recognize the complexity of the
representations they are exploring. Canter and Monteiro, in Chapter 11,
show quite graphically the overlapping, yet distinct, representations that
characterize sub-cultures in Brazilian society. Even more dynamic is the
study by Uzzell and Blud, in Chapter 5, of how children's representations
change after visiting an exhibition.

The combination of authors, each arguing from the perspective of her
or his own particular methodology, together provide insights about complexities of social representations and the ways in which they can be
explored. The ethnographic, context-embedded studies of Billig, Emler,
and Ohana and other contributors show the important social roles that
the variety and vitality of social representations play. The multivariate
analyses point more directly to the structures that exist and therefore give

a more precise framework for examining what varies and what changes.

Here again, however, the multiplicity of methods reveals the possibility of differences between them that could have important theoretical implications. In particular, as mentioned in our introduction, the different multivariate computing algorithms do make quite different assumptions about the appropriate models for describing social representations. Do people belong to one community of shared representation or another as assumed by the clustering approach, or do they merge into each other, being distinct only on underlying facets, as in the partial-order and multidimensional-scalogram approaches? Should we be considering the orthogonal, latent dimensions that characterize social representations, or their distinct but related facets?

Seen as theoretical questions, rather than debates about statistical niceties, these issues can be explored most fruitfully in relation to the roles ascribed to such complexities by, say, Billig or McKinlay *et al*. If there are rhetorical demands to alter the emphasis of representations in relation to the context in which they have significance, as many contributors to the present volume suggest, then what structures would most readily facilitate such vitality? Moving from one cluster to another is much more distinct than sliding along a dimension. A system of related facets allows the possibility of particular facets being revealed for particular contexts, literally putting a 'face' on things, where the emergence of a new dimension requires more fundamental structural changes.

It seems likely, of course, that social representations of many different structures may serve many different purposes, just as it has been found that the shape of large molecules carries biological implications. The notion of a social representation having a structure that may or may not relate to its particular type of content and to the particular processes in which it plays a part is of some considerable theoretical significance, but it would have been difficult to begin to formulate without the exploration of methodologies. Chapters in the present volume, however, allow us to do more than formulate these questions: they give clear directions for how they can be studied.

Index